Large–Scale Data Streaming, Processing, and Blockchain Security

Hemraj Saini
Jaypee University of Information Technology, India

Geetanjali Rathee
Jaypee University of Information Technology, India

Dinesh Kumar Saini
Sohar University, Oman

A volume in the Advances in
Information Security, Privacy, and
Ethics (AISPE) Book Series

Published in the United States of America by
    IGI Global
    Information Science Reference (an imprint of IGI Global)
    701 E. Chocolate Avenue
    Hershey PA, USA 17033
    Tel: 717-533-8845
    Fax: 717-533-8661
    E-mail: cust@igi-global.com
    Web site: http://www.igi-global.com

Library of Congress Cataloging-in-Publication Data

Names: Saini, Hemraj, 1977- editor. | Rathee, Geetanjali, 1990- editor. |
    Saini, Dinesh Kumar, 1974- editor.
Title: Large-scale data streaming, processing, and blockchain security /
    Hemraj Saini, Geetanjali Rathee, and Dinesh Kumar Saini, editors.
Description: Hershey, PA : Information Science Reference, an imprint of IGI
    Global, [2020] | Includes bibliographical references and index. |
    Summary: "This book explores the latest methodologies, modeling, and
    simulations for coping with the generation and management of large-scale
    data in both scientific and individual applications"-- Provided by
    publisher.
Identifiers: LCCN 2019052981 (print) | LCCN 2019052982 (ebook) | ISBN
    9781799834441 (hardcover) | ISBN 9781799834458 (paperback) | ISBN
    9781799834465 (ebook)
Subjects: LCSH: Data mining. | Streaming technology (Telecommunications) |
    Blockchains (Databases)
Classification: LCC QA76.9.D343 L368 2020 (print) | LCC QA76.9.D343
    (ebook) | DDC 006.3/12--dc23
LC record available at https://lccn.loc.gov/2019052981
LC ebook record available at https://lccn.loc.gov/2019052982

This book is published in the IGI Global book series Advances in Information Security, Privacy, and Ethics (AISPE) (ISSN: 1948-9730; eISSN: 1948-9749)

British Cataloguing in Publication Data
A Cataloguing in Publication record for this book is available from the British Library.

All work contributed to this book is new, previously-unpublished material.
The views expressed in this book are those of the authors, but not necessarily of the publisher.

For electronic access to this publication, please contact: eresources@igi-global.com.

Advances in Information Security, Privacy, and Ethics (AISPE) Book Series

ISSN:1948-9730
EISSN:1948-9749

Editor-in-Chief: *Manish Gupta* State University of New York, USA

MISSION

As digital technologies become more pervasive in everyday life and the Internet is utilized in ever increasing ways by both private and public entities, concern over digital threats becomes more prevalent.

The **Advances in Information Security, Privacy, & Ethics (AISPE) Book Series** provides cutting-edge research on the protection and misuse of information and technology across various industries and settings. Comprised of scholarly research on topics such as identity management, cryptography, system security, authentication, and data protection, this book series is ideal for reference by IT professionals, academicians, and upper-level students.

COVERAGE

- Information Security Standards
- Internet Governance
- IT Risk
- Cyberethics
- Technoethics
- Risk Management
- Electronic Mail Security
- CIA Triad of Information Security
- Privacy Issues of Social Networking
- Data Storage of Minors

IGI Global is currently accepting manuscripts for publication within this series. To submit a proposal for a volume in this series, please contact our Acquisition Editors at Acquisitions@igi-global.com or visit: http://www.igi-global.com/publish/.

Titles in this Series

For a list of additional titles in this series, please visit:
http://www.igi-global.com/book-series/advances-information-security-privacy-ethics/37157

Applied Approach to Privacy and Security for the Internet of Things
Parag Chatterjee (National Technological University, Argentina & University of the Republic, Uruguay) Emmanuel Benoist (Bern University of Applied Sciences, Switzerland) and Asoke Nath (St. Xavier's College, Kolkata, India)
Information Science Reference • © 2020 • 295pp • H/C (ISBN: 9781799824442) • US $235.00

Advanced Localization Algorithms for Wireless Sensor Networks
M. Vasim Babu (Institute of Technology and Sciences, India)
Information Science Reference • © 2020 • 300pp • H/C (ISBN: 9781799837336) • US $195.00

Social, Legal, and Ethical Implications of IoT, Cloud, and Edge Computing Technologies
Gianluca Cornetta (Universidad CEU San Pablo, Spain) Abdellah Touhafi (Vrije Universiteit Brussel, Belgium) and Gabriel-Miro Muntean (Dublin City University, Ireland)
Information Science Reference • © 2020 • 333pp • H/C (ISBN: 9781799838173) • US $215.00

Multidisciplinary Approaches to Ethics in the Digital Era
Meliha Nurdan Taskiran (Istanbul Medipol University, Turkey) and Fatih Pinarbaşi (Istanbul Medipol University, Turkey)
Information Science Reference • © 2020 • 300pp • H/C (ISBN: 9781799841173) • US $195.00

Sensor Network Methodologies for Smart Applications
Salahddine Krit (Ibn Zohr University, Morocco) Valentina Emilia Bălaş (Aurel Vlaicu University of Arad, Romania) Mohamed Elhoseny (Mansoura University, Egypt) Rachid Benlamri (Lakehead University, Canada) and Marius M. Bălaş (Aurel Vlaicu University of Arad, Romania)
Information Science Reference • © 2020 • 279pp • H/C (ISBN: 9781799843818) • US $195.00

For an entire list of titles in this series, please visit:
http://www.igi-global.com/book-series/advances-information-security-privacy-ethics/37157

701 East Chocolate Avenue, Hershey, PA 17033, USA
Tel: 717-533-8845 x100 • Fax: 717-533-8661
E-Mail: cust@igi-global.com • www.igi-global.com

Editorial Advisory Board

Table of Contents

Section 1

Chapter 1
Dinesh Chander, Panipat Institute of Engineering and Technology, India
Hari Singh, Jaypee University of Information Technology, India
Abhinav Kirti Gupta, Jaypee University of Information Technology,
*   India*

Chapter 2
Khyati Ahlawat, University School of Information, Communication and
*   Technology, Guru Gobind Singh Indraprastha University, India*
Anuradha Chug, University School of Information, Communication and
*   Technology, Guru Gobind Singh Indraprastha University, India*
Amit Prakash Singh, University School of Information, Communication
*   and Technology, Guru Gobind Singh Indraprastha University, India*

Chapter 3
Oshin Sharma, PES University, Bangalore, India
Anusha S., School of Engineering and Technology, Jain University,
*   Bangalore, India*

Detailed Table of Contents

Section 1

Chapter 1

> *Dinesh Chander, Panipat Institute of Engineering and Technology, India*
> *Hari Singh, Jaypee University of Information Technology, India*
> *Abhinav Kirti Gupta, Jaypee University of Information Technology, India*

Data processing has become an important field in today's big data-dominated world. The data has been generating at a tremendous pace from different sources. There has been a change in the nature of data from batch-data to streaming-data, and consequently, data processing methodologies have also changed. Traditional SQL is no longer capable of dealing with this big data. This chapter describes the nature of data and various tools, techniques, and technologies to handle this big data. The chapter also describes the need of shifting big data on to cloud and the challenges in big data processing in the cloud, the migration from data processing to data analytics, tools used in data analytics, and the issues and challenges in data processing and analytics. Then the chapter touches an important application area of streaming data, sentiment analysis, and tries to explore it through some test case demonstrations and results.

Expansion of data in the dimensions of volume, variety, or velocity is leading to big data. Learning from this big data is challenging and beyond capacity of conventional machine learning methods and techniques. Generally, big data getting generated from real-time scenarios is imbalance in nature with uneven distribution of classes. This imparts additional complexity in learning from big data since the class that is underrepresented is more influential and its correct classification becomes critical than that of overrepresented class. This chapter addresses the imbalance problem and its solutions in context of big data along with a detailed survey of work done in this area. Subsequently, it also presents an experimental view for solving imbalance classification problem and a comparative analysis between different methodologies afterwards.

## Chapter 3

The emerging trends in fog computing have increased the interests and focus in both industry and academia. Fog computing extends cloud computing facilities like the storage, networking, and computation towards the edge of networks wherein it offloads the cloud data centres and reduces the latency of providing services to the users. This paradigm is like cloud in terms of data, storage, application, and computation services, except with a fundamental difference: it is decentralized. Furthermore, these fog systems can process huge amounts of data locally and can be installed on hardware of different types. These characteristics make fog suitable for time- and location-based applications like internet of things (IoT) devices which can process large amounts of data. In this chapter, the authors present fog data streaming, its architecture, and various applications.

Trust is a firm belief over a person or a thing in distributed environment based on its feedback on review based on its performance by others. Similarly, in cloud, trust models play an important role in solving various open challenges in cloud environment. This chapter showcases all such issues that can be solved by trust management techniques. This work discourses various trust management models and its categorization. The work discourses existing work using trust models from the field of grid computing, cloud computing, and web services because all these domains are sub child of each other. The work provides an abstract view over all trust models and find the suitable one for cloud and its future prospects.

Section 2

Chapter 5

*Randhir Kumar, Department of Information Technology, National
Institute of Technology, Raipur, India*
*Rakesh Tripathi, Department of Information Technology, National
Institute of Technology, Raipur, India*

The future applications of blockchain are expected to serve millions of users. To provide variety of services to the users, using underlying technology has to consider large-scale storage and assessment behind the scene. Most of the current applications of blockchain are working either on simulators or via small blockchain network. However, the storage issue in the real world is unpredictable. To address the issue of large-scale data storage, the authors have introduced the data storage scheme in blockchain (DSSB). The storage model executes behind the blockchain ledger to store large-scale data. In DSSB, they have used hybrid storage model using IPFS and MongoDB(NoSQL) in order to provide efficient storage for large-scale data in blockchain. In this storage model, they have maintained the content-addressed hash of the transactions on blockchain network to ensure provenance. In DSSB, they are storing the original data (large-scale data) into MongoDB and IPFS. The DSSB model not only provides efficient storage of large-scale data but also provides storage size reduction of blockchain ledger.

    Rohit Shukla, Department of Biotechnology and Bioinformatics, Jaypee
        University of Information Technology, India
    Arvind Kumar Yadav, Department of Biotechnology and Bioinformatics,
        Jaypee University of Information Technology, India
    Tiratha Raj Singh, Department of Biotechnology and Bioinformatics and
        Centre for Excellence in Healthcare technologies and Informatics
        (CEHTI), Jaypee University of Information Technology, India

The meaningful data extraction from the biological big data or omics data is a remaining challenge in bioinformatics. The deep learning methods, which can be used for the prediction of hidden information from the biological data, are widely used in the industry and academia. The authors have discussed the similarity and differences in the widely utilized models in deep learning studies. They first discussed the basic structure of various models followed by their applications in biological perspective. They have also discussed the suggestions and limitations of deep learning. They expect that this chapter can serve as significant perspective for continuous development of its theory, algorithm, and application in the established bioinformatics domain.

    Swarup Roy Chowdhury, Sabre Corporation, India
    Suman Saha, Jaypee University of Information Technology, India

We can name many industries that are still based on the same working practices and business models that they have had for a long time – maybe since they started. Despite the wealth of modern technology now available, public infrastructure, a critical component for the well-being of the society, is still an industry based on the paperwork, letters, emails, manual approvals, and a large amount of guess work. It involves a lot of manual effort and is also error prone. It is really very hard for the stakeholders and end users to get an update on the progress of the project, which impacts them directly or indirectly. The authors intend to develop a groundbreaking blockchain platform that can meet the needs of all the different stakeholders involved in creating and providing a better infrastructure. They plan to automate the entire process by using smart contracts to minimize paperwork for the government officials. This will not only eliminate the errors that can happen during manual execution but will also provide a real-time update to all the stakeholders in making the process more transparent.

Chapter 8

Nguyen Ha Huy Cuong, Vietnam-Korea University of Information and
*   Communication Technology, University of Da-Nang, Vietnam*
Gautam Kumar, CMR Engineering College, India
Vijender Kumar Solanki, CMR Institute of Technology (Autonomous),
*   Hyderabad, India*

The usage of information is essential for data-driven capabilities in artificial intelligence. The data-driven AI techniques lead to several security and privacy concerns. Among various digital techniques, digital rights management is required as one of collaboration scheme that ensures the security and privacy of intellectual rights. Though a number of researchers have proposed various security techniques, none of them have proposed an efficient and effective privacy procedure for digital rights. Recently, blockchain technique is considered as one of the major security methods to ensure a transparent communication among individuals. It can be used by various applications such as industries, marketing, transportation systems, etc. The aim of this chapter is to propose an ensured resource allocation algorithm that validates the scheme by comparing various security measures against previous approaches. Further, the proposed phenomenon ensures the transparency on security and privacy due to its integration.

Chapter 9

Hemraj Saini, Jaypee University of Information and Technology, India
Geetanjali Rathee, Jaypee University of Information Technology, India
Dinesh Kumar Saini, Sohar University, Oman

In this chapter, the authors have detailed the need of blockchain technology along with its case studies in different domains. The literature survey is described that describes how blockchain technology is rising. Further, a number of domains where blockchain technology can be applied along with its case studies have been discussed. In addition, the authors have considered the various use cases with their recent issues and how these issues can be resolved using the blockchain technology by proposing some new ideas. A proposed security framework in certain applications using blockchain technology is presented. Finally, the chapter is concluded with future directions.

Chapter 10

Madumidha S., Sri Krishna College of Technology, India
SivaRanjani P., Kongu Engineering College, India
Venmuhilan B., Sri Krishna College of Technology, India

Internet of things(IoT) is the conception of interfacing the devices to the internet to make life more efficient. It comprises the large amount of data in its network where it fails to assure complete security in the network. Blockchain is a distributed ledger where it mainly focuses on the data security. Every block in the blockchain network is connected to its next block, which prevents threats like large data loss. In the area of agri-food supply chain, where IoT plays a very important role, there occurs data integrity issues or data tampering. This can lead to improper supply chain management, timely shortage of goods, food spoilage, etc. So the traceability of agri-food supply chain is necessary to ensure food safety and to increase the trust between all stakeholders and consumers. Many illegal activities can be prevented, and cold chain monitoring can be achieved by bringing in transparency and traceability.

Chapter 11

Geetanjali Rathee, Jaypee University of Information Technology, India
Hemraj Saini, Jaypee University of Information Technology, India

India is the largest democracy in the world, and in spite of that, it faces various challenges on a daily basis that hinder its growth like corruption and human rights violations. One of the ugliest phases of corruption and political mayhem is visible during the election process where no stone is kept unturned in order to gain power. However, it is the common citizen who suffers most in terms of clarity as well as security when it comes to his/her vote. Blockchain can play a very important role in ensuring that the voters registering their votes are legit and the counting of votes is not manipulated in any way. It is also needed in today's times where the world is available to people in their smart phones to also give them the opportunity to register their votes hassle free via their smart phones without having to worry about the system getting hacked. Therefore, in this chapter, the proposed layout will be based on a smart contract, using Ethereum software to create an e-voting app. In this chapter, the authors have proposed a secure e-voting framework through blockchain mechanism.

Foreword

In recent years, there has been an enormous diffusion of large-scale data technologies, usually oriented to data processing, omitting an equally important aspect related to the transformation of data to be ready for this process. In fact, it is increasingly urgent to address the issue of heterogeneity, diversity, and complexity of data, and how to normalize, integrate, and transform the data from many sources into the format required to run large-scale analysis. This edited book addresses the research about large-scale data management with semantic technologies as a unified data access layer and a consistent approach to analytic execution. Semantic technologies have been used to create domain models describing mutually relevant datasets and the relationships between them.

In addition, security of the information is also a primary challenge for the large-scale data which can be ensured by blockchain. This book is intended as an exploration of the broader concepts, features, and functionality of Bitcoin and blockchain technology, and their future possibilities and implications; it does not support, advocate, or offer any advice or prediction as to the industry's viability. The blockchain industry is in an emergent and immature phase and very much still in development with many risks. Right now is the time to learn about the underlying technologies; their potential uses, dangers, and risks; and perhaps more importantly, the concepts and their extensibility. The objective here is to provide a comprehensive overview of the nature, scope, and type of activity that is occurring in the cryptocurrency industry and envision its wide-ranging potential application. The account is necessarily incomplete, prone to technical errors, and could likely soon be out-of-date as different projects described here fail or succeed. Or, the entire Bitcoin and blockchain technology industry as currently conceived could become outmoded or superseded by other models.

The challenges in Large-Scale Data Streaming, Processing, and Blockchain Security are both difficult and interesting. People are working on them with enthusiasm, tenacity, and dedication to develop new methods of analysis and provide new solutions to keep up with the ever-changing threats. In this new age of global interconnectivity and interdependence, it is necessary to provide security practitioners, both professionals and students, with state-of-the art knowledge on the frontiers in information assurance. This book is a good step in that direction.

Rakesh Belwal
Faculty of Business, Sohar University, Oman & Business School, University of Queensland, Australia

Preface

At the highest-level description, this book is about large-scale data mining. However, it focuses on data streaming, processing, and security of very large amounts of data, that is, data is so large and does not fit in traditional category. Further, the identified topics for call for book chapters provide it emphasis over streaming, processing and blockchain security of large-scale data. The principle topics of this book cover Large scale data, Large scale Data streaming, Large scale data streaming models, Large scale data processing models, Large scale data and machine leaning, blockchain Security concerns in large scale data, blockchain Security models for large scale data, Large scale data in cloud or fog, Scheduling of Large scale data processing on clouds or fog, and blockchain Security and privacy in big data clouds or fog. The identified contents of this book will be helpful to a set of companies or organizations those are flooding an enormous amount of data and need frequent mining of required contents. In addition, presently, IoT structures are frequently used in a number of applications and generating large scale data which needs affective processing and streaming with sufficient security and our book will help in this aspect.

The book will provide proper understanding, methodologies, modeling, and simulation to cope up the current requirement of the technological world generating large scale data not only in scientific applications but also in applications affecting individual's day to day life.

This book will aim to provide relevant theoretical frameworks and the latest empirical research findings in the area. It will be written for professionals who want to improve their understanding of the strategic role of Large-Scale Data Streaming, Processing, and Blockchain Security at different levels in the related applications.

The target audience of this book will be composed of professionals and researchers working in the field of Large-Scale Data Streaming, Processing, and Blockchain Security in various domains, e.g. social networking, banking, agriculture, chemistry, data mining, cloud computing, finance, marketing, stocks, BDA, health care etc. Moreover, the book will provide insights and support executives concerned with the management of expertise, knowledge, information, innovative technologies and organizational development in different types of work communities and environments. A short review about the commitments for this book is as underneath-

Chapter 1: Data processing has become an important field in today's big data dominated world. The data has been generating at a tremendous pace from different sources. There has been a change in the nature of data from batch-data to streaming-data, and consequently, data processing methodologies have also changed. Traditional SQL is no more capable of dealing this big data. This book chapter describes the nature of data and various tools, techniques, and technologies to handle this big data. The chapter also describes the need of shifting big data on to cloud and the challenges in big data processing in the cloud, the migration from data processing to data analytics, tools used in data analytics, and the issues and challenges in data processing and analytics. Then the chapter touches an important application area of streaming data: sentiment analysis, and tries to explore it through some test case demonstrations and results.

Chapter 2: Expansion of data in the dimensions of volume, variety or velocity is leading to big data. Learning from this big data is challenging and beyond capacity of conventional machine learning methods and techniques. Generally, big data getting .generated from real time scenarios is imbalance in nature with uneven distribution of classes. This imparts additional complexity in learning from big data since the class that is under-represented is more influential and its correct classification becomes critical than that of over-represented class. This chapter addresses the imbalance problem and its solutions in context of big data along with a detailed survey of work done in this area. Subsequently, it also presents an experimental view for solving imbalance classification problem and a comparative analysis between different methodologies afterwards.

Chapter 3: The emerging trends in fog computing has increased the interests and focus in both industry and academia. Fog computing extends cloud computing facilities like the storage, networking, and computation towards the edge of networks wherein it offloads the cloud data centres and reducing the latency of providing services to the users. This paradigm is like cloud in terms of data, storage, application and computation services, except with a fundamental difference - it is decentralized. Furthermore, these Fog systems can process huge amount of data locally and can be installed on hardware of different types. These characteristics make Fog to be suitable for time and location-based applications like Internet of Things (IoT) devices which can process large amount of data. In this chapter we present fog data streaming, its architecture and various applications.

Chapter 4: Trust is a firm belief over a person or a thing in distributed environment based on its feedback on review based on its performance by others. Similarly, in cloud trust models plays an important role to solve various open challenges in cloud environment. This chapter showcases all such issues that can be solved by trust management techniques. This work discourses various trust management models and its categorization. The work discourses existing work using trust models from the field of grid computing cloud computing and web services because all these domains are sub child of each other. The work main focus it provide abstract view over all trust models and find the suitable one for cloud and its future prospects.

Chapter 5: The future applications of blockchain are expected to serve millions of users. To provide variety of services to the users using underlying technology has to consider large-scale storage and assessment behind the scene. Most of the current applications of blockchain are working either on simulators or via small blockchain network. However, the storage issue in the real world is unpredictable. To address the issue of large-scale data storage, we have introduces the data storage scheme in blockchain (DSSB). Our storage model executes behind the blockchain ledger to store large-scale data. In DSSB, we have used hybrid storage model using IPFS and MongoDB (NoSQL) in order to provide efficient storage for large-scale data in blockchain. In this storage model, we have maintained the content-addressed hash of the transactions on blockchain network to ensure provenance. In DSSB, we are storing the original data (Large-Scale data) into MongoDB and IPFS. The DSSB model not only provides efficient storage of large-scale data but also provide storage size reduction of blockchain ledger.

Chapter 6: The meaningful data extraction from the biological big data or omics data is a remaining challenge in bioinformatics. The deep learning methods, which can be used for the prediction of hidden information from the biological data, are widely used in the industry and academia. We have discussed the similarity and differences in the widely utilized models in deep learning studies. We first discussed the basic structure of various models followed by their applications in biological perspective. We have also discussed the suggestions and limitations of deep learning. We expect that this chapter can serve as significant perspective for continuous development of its theory, algorithm, and application in the established bioinformatics domain.

Chapter 7: We can name many industries that are still based on the same working practices and business models that they had since a long time – maybe the time they started. Despite the wealth of modern technology now available, public infrastructure - a critical component for the well-being of the society, is still an industry based on the paperwork, letters, emails, manual approvals, and a large amount of guess work. It involves a lot of manual effort and is also error prone. It is really very hard for the stakeholders and end users to get an update on the progress of the project which impacts them directly or indirectly. We intend to develop a ground-breaking blockchain platform that can meet the needs of all the different stakeholders involved in creating and providing a better infrastructure. We plan to automate the entire process by using smart contracts to minimize paperwork for the government officials. This will not only eliminate the errors which can happen during manual execution but will also provide real time update to all the stakeholders in making the process more transparent.

Chapter 8: The usage of information is essential for data driven capabilities in Artificial intelligence. The data driven AI techniques leads to several security and privacy concerns. Among various digital techniques, digital rights management is required as one of collaboration scheme that ensures the security and privacy of intellectual rights. Through number of researchers have proposed various security techniques, however, none of them have proposed an efficient and effective privacy procedure for digital rights. Recently, Blockchain technique is considered as one of the major security method to ensure a transparent communication among individuals. It can be used by various applications such as industries, marketing, transportation systems etc. The aim of this chapter is to propose an ensured resource allocation algorithm, that validates the scheme by comparing various security measures against previous approaches. Further, the proposed phenomenon ensures the transparency on security and privacy due to its integration.

Chapter 9: In this chapter, we have detailed the need of Blockchain technology along with its case studies in different domains. The literature survey is described that intricate how Blockchain technology is rising now-a-days. Further, number of domains where Blockchain technology can be applied along with its case studies has been discussed. In addition, we have considered the various use case with their recent issues and how these issues can be resolved using the blockchain technology by proposing some new ideas. A proposed security framework in certain applications using blockchain technology is presented. Finally, the chapter is concluded with future directions.

Chapter 10: Over the last few years, development of technology took a major role in day to day life. Internet of Things (IoT) is the conception of interfacing the devices to the internet to make life more efficient. It comprises the large amount of data in its network were it fails to assure complete security in the network. Blockchain is a distributed ledger and it mainly focuses on the data security. Every block in the blockchain network is connected to its next block which prevents threats like large data loss. In the area of Agri-Food Supply Chain, where IoT plays a very important role, there occur data integrity issues or data tampering. This can lead to improper Supply Chain Management, timely shortage of goods, food spoilage, etc. So the traceability of Agri-Food Supply Chain is necessary to ensure food safety and to increase the trust between all stakeholders and consumers. Many illegal activities can be prevented and cold chain monitoring can be achieved by bringing in transparency and traceability.

Chapter 11: India is the largest democracy in the world and in spite of that faces various challenges on a daily basis which hinder its growth like corruption and human rights violations. One of the ugliest phases of corruption and political mayhem is visible during the election process where no stone is kept unturned in order to gain power. However, it is the common citizen who suffers most in terms of clarity as well as security when it comes to his/her vote. Blockchain can play a very important role in ensuring that the voters registering their votes are legit and the counting of votes is not manipulated in any way. It is also needed in today's times where the world is available to people in their smart phones to also give them the opportunity to register their votes hassle free via their smart phones without having to worry about the system getting hacked. Therefore, in this paper, the proposed layout will be based on a smart contract, using Ethereum software to create an e-voting app. In this paper, we have proposed a secure e-voting framework through blockchain mechanism.

We hope that the quality chapters published in this book will be able to serve the concerned humanity, science and technology at the best.

ACKNOWLEDGMENT

The editors are thankful to the authors and reviewers who contributed to this book with their scientific work and useful comments, respectively.

Hemraj Saini
Jaypee University of Information Technology, India

Geetanjali Rathee
Jaypee University of Information Technology, India

Dinesh Kumar Saini
Sohar University, Oman

Acknowledgment

We take this opportunity to express our gratitude to our Vice Chancellor, Professor Vinod Kumar and Director & Academic Head, Professor Samir Dev Gupta for their continuous motivation and for the support given in allowing using Institutional resources for the topic. We thank our colleagues for their support, and also the students who helped us in organizing the materials. We are also very thankful to the reviewers for providing their valuable input for the chapters.

We would also like to thank the team of IGI Global for the enthusiasm and support extended to us during various stages of the project. Finally, we would like to thank all the valuable contributors for the book.

Hemraj Saini, Geetanjali Rathee, & Dinesh Saini

Introduction

It feels like every distinct day we are hesitant across added use-cases for the blockchain technology. Large number of industries is verdict out that either the blockchain technology is going to take them to the next level, or may end up fetching their major threat. One of the various fields that have exposed a symbiotic association with blockchain is large data (big data) streaming and processing. In this book, we are going to explore the relationship among large data and blockchain technique. Before we go further, let's appreciate what blockchain and large data mean.

The reason why blockchain and large data can have a very abundant relationship is that the blockchain technique can easily and efficiently cover the defects of large data. There are three major motives why this corporation can be productive:

- **Security and Privacy**: Blockchain's biggest benefit is the security that it conveys to the information stored inside it. All the information that is inside the blockchain is non-altered.
- **Transparent**: The transparent networking structure of the blockchain can help further to trace information back to its origin point.
- **Flexibility**: The blockchain can record all types and kinds of information.
- **Decentralization:** All the information that is recorded inside a blockchain is not possessed by one single individual. Therefore, there is no chance of information stolen and alteration even if that individual gets concessioner in any way.

By considering all these features, the conclusion that we can sketch is that whatever information comes out of the blockchain network is worthy. The information is fraud-proof and already been cleaned through it. Now, this brings us to the next question what exactly are the characteristics of blockchain that enables this relationship? Now let us understand how the blockchain mechanism can further provide a better relationship in large data streaming and processing along with transparency and worthy security.

1.1 Interdisciplinary Aspects of Large-Scale Data Streaming, Processing, and Blockchain Security

To understand it in a better way let's look at various cases of large data streaming and processing. If used properly, large data can help in diverse areas of commerce activities.

- **Machine Learning Models:** Along with blockchain technology, machine learning is also considered as other hottest and emergent topic in the world recently. The reason being that it permits devices/machines/sensors to generate working models based on the information that it is fed. We can analyze why accurate large data can be useful in this context.
- **Enhance Customer Experience:** Customers are everything. It is that simple as that for an organization, if companies lose their customers means they are going to die and if a company gains more customers then they will grow. Large data may help to gather/collect customer information from various sources like web visits, social media etc. to help buff their customers acquisition strategy.
- **Fraud Prediction:** Successful companies are not just up against a few isolated intruders. There could be teams of experts who might be trying to take them down. Large data can help these organizations to identify various attacking patterns to help envisage fraud.
- **Predictive Maintenance:** By identifying certain patterns and indicators one can easily forecast the occurrence of defects before it happens. Large data analytics can help organizations save millions of dollars by measuring or analyzing cost-effective maintenance.
- **Improving Company Operations:** One of the biggest use cases of large data lies in improving the operations of a company. Using large data one can measure certain parameters like customer returns, feedback and various factors to recover decision making and be more in tune with the recent market demand.
- **Product Development:** Using large data, it is possible to acquire exactly what the customer desires and predict their requirements beforehand. The model is built by the categorization of key features of current and past products.
- **Improve Innovation:** Large data can help organizations to study the relationship between institutions, humans, and various other individuals to create insights. These imminent can further help organizations to create and innovate strategies and products to gain an edge over their rivalry.

1.2 Content of This Book

This book is on Large-Scale Data Streaming, Processing, and Blockchain Security, dealing with Large-scale data Streaming, Processing, and providing fundaments of achieving security using blockchain. The primary objective is to provide a comprehensive panorama of Big data processing and blockchain. Understanding of the close relationship among the wide range of discipline and components that make up a Large-scale data system and using blockchain is a key design principle towards successful building of secure Large-scale data processing system and their applications.

This book is structured as a reference book, so that it allows fast familiarization with all issues concerned. However, it can be also used in education process as an introductory book for an undergraduate Large-scale data processing and blockchain systems in computer science and related fields. It is important to stress that readers will enjoy the book more and will be helpful to them if they would have solid background on concept in Large-scale data Streaming, Processing, and providing fundaments of achieving security using blockchain.

1.3 Organization of This Book

As mentioned above, this book is an overview and practical view of Large-scale data Streaming, Processing, and providing fundaments of achieving security using blockchain. Figure 1 shows the global view of the most important Large-scale data Streaming, Processing, and blockchain fields. The overall organization attempts to explain the largest dependencies between the components involved in terms of space and time.

We distinguish between:

- Basics
- Large-scale Processing
- Security
- Applications

In this book, we present the basics of Large-scale data Streaming, Processing, and blockchain in the processing and security field as depicted in Figure 1 with overall integration through appropriate synchronization mechanisms.

This book covers four major areas: (1) basic concepts of big data, (2) processing of Large-scale data, (3) blockchain concepts, and (4) synchronization of large-scale streams and various systems and security to achieve the secure and the best end-to-end perceptual quality for the users.

Figure 1. Global presentation of the most important fields, as discussed in the book

Applications	Applications		
	Crypto Currencies	Enterprise Security Systems	Data prediction systems

Security	Types of Securities			
	Data Security	Content Security	....	Transaction Security

Processing Systems	Processing steps			
	Sampling	Filtering	Counting	optimizing

Basics	Possible implications			
	Feature Extraction	Data Mining	Missing Value Imputation	Crypto currencies

1.3.1 Large-Scale Data Streaming

Numbers of organizations are adopting modern data streaming deployment full stack approaches, rather than relying on focusing together open-source technologies. The recent information platform is erect on organization-centric value chains instead of IT-centric coding schemes, wherein the complexity of conventional architecture is preoccupied into a solitary self-service platform that revolves event flow into analytics-ready information.

The idea behind this new technique is to act as the centralized information platform that regulates the manual parts of working with streaming information such as streaming and batch ETL, message ingestion, preparing data for analytics and storage management. A sample overview of the modern streaming architecture is depicted in Figure 2.

Figure 2. Modern streaming architecture

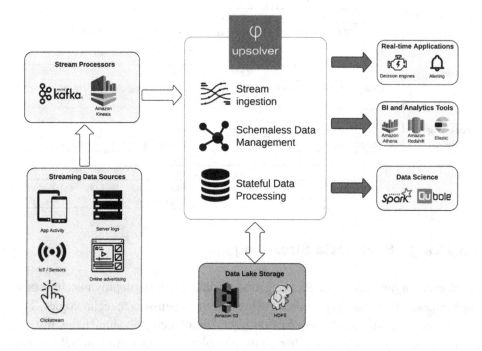

Benefits of using modern large streaming architecture:

- Can eliminate the necessitate for large information engineering projects
- Built in high availability, Performance and fault tolerance
- Can be deployed easily as newer platforms are cloud-based with no upfront investment
- Supportive and flexible for multiple use cases

1.3.2 Large-scale data processing

A. Data collection

The first step in data processing is information gathering where information is pulled from available resources, including data warehouses and data lakes. Further, it is significant that the data resources available are legitimate and well-built so the information gathered (and later used as meaningful information) is of the peak possible quality.

B. Data Preparation

Once the data is gathered, it then comes into data preparation stage. Data preparation is also referred as "pre-processing". It is the phase at which raw data is organized and cleaned up for the following phases of data processing. During the data preparation, raw information is initially diligently checked for any errors and mistakes. The purpose of this step is to delete or remove bad information such as incomplete, redundant, and incorrect data and then begin to generate high-quality information for the best organization intelligence.

C. Data Input

The clean information is then entered into its final destination (perhaps a CRM like data warehouse like Redshift and Salesforce), and translated into a language that it can be easily understand. Data input is the first phase in which raw data starts to take the form of serviceable information.

D. Processing

During this stage, the information inputted to the computer in the previous phase is actually practiced for interpretation. Processing is done using machine/deep learning techniques and algorithms, though the data processing itself may vary vaguely depending on the source of information being processed such as social networks, data lakes, and connected devices etc. and its anticipated use such as medical diagnosis from connected devices, examining advertising patterns, and determining customer needs.

E. Data Output/Interpretation

The interpretation/ output stage is the phase at which information is finally serviceable to non-data scientists. It is readable, translated and often in the form of videos, graphs, plain text, and images, etc. Members of the institution or organization can now start to self-serve the information for their own analytics projects.

F. Data Storage

The final stage of information processing is storage. After all of the information is processed, it is then stored for the future purpose. While some data may be put to use at once, much of it can be served as a purpose later on. In addition, properly stored information is a necessity for observance with protection legislation like GDPR.

Whenever the information is properly stored, it can be easily and quickly accessed by members of the businesses when needed.

1.3.3 Blockchain Security

A blockchain, as the name entails, is a chain of digital "blocks" that hold records of transactions. Each block is gathered to all the blocks after and before it. This makes it hard to interfere with a single data because an intruder would require changing the block having that record as well as those associated to it to delete detection. This alone might not seem like much of deterrence, however, blockchain has some other inherent features that provide further means of security.

The data or information stored on a blockchain is secured through cryptography. Network applicants have their own private keys that are allocated to the transactions they make and act as an individual digital signature. If stored information is altered, the signature will turn out to be invalid and the peer network will know right away that incredible has happened. Early announcement is critical to preventing additional damage.

Unfortunately for those ambitious intruders, blockchains are distributed and decentralized across peer-to-peer networks that are repeatedly kept and updated in sync. Because they aren't enclosed in a central location, therefore, blockchains don't have a central point of failure and cannot be altered from a single device. It would necessitate massive records of computing power to entrance every instance (or at least a 51 percent majority) of a definite blockchain and change them all at the same instance. There has been some argue about whether this defines smaller blockchain networks that could be susceptible to threat, however a verdict hasn't been accomplished. In any case, the bigger your network is, the more tamper-resistant your blockchain will be. At a glance, blockchains have some desirable features that would help to secure your transaction information. Though, there are other requirements and conditions to believe when you desire to use a blockchain for commerce.

1.3.4 Blockchain in Streaming and Processing

Figure 3. Reference architecture for blockchain and middleware

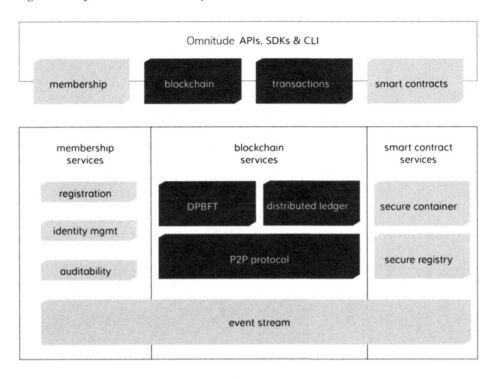

Blockchain is the next big thing for middleware! There is no such question around this. You need to intersect other applications, cloud offerings and micro-services with a blockchain infrastructure to acquire real value out of it. Further, machine learning and visual analytics have to be leveraged to get patterns and insights in non-blockchain and blockchain data. Finally, streaming analytics is worn to apply these patterns and insights to new events in a blockchain communications. There is a variety of applications like compliance issues, fraud detection, supply chain processes, optimization of manufacturing or any kind of circumstances with the Internet of Things (IoT). Reference architecture for blockchain and middleware is depicted in Figure 3.

Section 1

Chapter 1
A Study of Big Data Processing for Sentiments Analysis

Dinesh Chander
Panipat Institute of Engineering and Technology, India

Hari Singh
Jaypee University of Information Technology, India

Abhinav Kirti Gupta
Jaypee University of Information Technology, India

ABSTRACT

Data processing has become an important field in today's big data-dominated world. The data has been generating at a tremendous pace from different sources. There has been a change in the nature of data from batch-data to streaming-data, and consequently, data processing methodologies have also changed. Traditional SQL is no longer capable of dealing with this big data. This chapter describes the nature of data and various tools, techniques, and technologies to handle this big data. The chapter also describes the need of shifting big data on to cloud and the challenges in big data processing in the cloud, the migration from data processing to data analytics, tools used in data analytics, and the issues and challenges in data processing and analytics. Then the chapter touches an important application area of streaming data, sentiment analysis, and tries to explore it through some test case demonstrations and results.

DOI: 10.4018/978-1-7998-3444-1.ch001

DATA PROCESSING

Since last decade, rapid development of Internet enabled services such as social media, Internet of Things, and cloud based services have led to tremendous growth of data termed as big data. This data has become very difficult to be handled and managed for further processing (Jin et al., 2015). It has been estimated that around 2.5 quintillion bytes of new data is generated per day and expected to be more in near future as the number of internet users are growing unprecedentedly. This exponential growth of data has posed many challenges in front of researchers, academia and Industry across the globe. Moreover, the big data is unstructured: it varies in volume, velocity, veracity and variety makes (4Vs) it more challenging to manage and process (Mishra, R. K., & Mishra, R. K., 2018). This sudden explosion of data in terabytes, petabytes and exabytes could not be handled by the traditional database such as SQL led to the emergence of new tools and techniques to process the big data (Storey, V. C., & Song, I. Y., 2017).

Figure 1. Big data chain

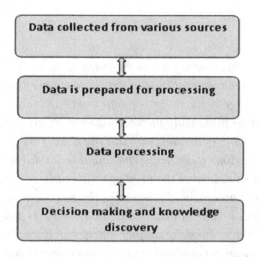

Big data processing and analysis have become very crucial for better decision making, knowledge discovery, business intelligence and actionable insights. The Fig-1 represents the big data chain i.e. from data collection to decision making (Janssen, M., van der Voort, H., & Wahyudi, A., 2017). Big data is collected in raw form from various sources of interest which need to be prepared for processing. Next the quality data sets are prepared for further processing using data cleansing and standardization. After that, data processing takes place which includes transformation, aggregation and pattern generation. Once the data processing is completed, various reports are generated and analyzed for better decision making, knowledge discovery and insight or trends. Analysis of data could be classified as descriptive, diagnostic, predictive and prescriptive (Perwej, Y., 2017).

This book chapter proposes to show various tools, techniques, and technologies of data processing and analytics. Later, the use streaming data for sentiment analysis through executable test cases is presented. Sentiment analysis is performed on run-time tweets with Python using twitter API "tweepy" and obtained results are presented through plots.

A survey on various sentiment analysis methods used by researchers is also presented. This would also help in identifying the best one and possibly may be in predicting a newer one.

FAILURE OF TRADITIONALSQL IN HANDLING BIG DATA

The volume of data is expected to grow 50% per year, and data production by 2020 will be 50 times larger than what it was in 2009. This rapid increase in volume requires powerful tools and techniques to process big data (Yaqoob, I., Hashem, I. A. T., Gani, A., Mokhtar, S., Ahmed, E., Anuar, N. B., & Vasilakos, A. V., 2016). The conventional tools such as SQL are unable to process it due to high volume, velocity and veracity of data. With such a diversification of data, ACID properties (Atomicity, Consistency, Integrity, and Durability) of databases are very difficult to meet using conventional tools; also desired outcome is difficult to produce within a reasonable frame of time period.

Secondly, most of the data are being generated in semi-structured or unstructured format in the form of images, text, audio, video and mails. Traditional tools are mainly designed to deal with structured data only. Therefore, new and advanced technologies have been devised to cope up the processing of big data in batches. In the next section, Hadoop based technologies to handle this increasing amount data has been discussed.

Database Technologies for Big Data Based on Hadoop

Apache Hadoop is one of widely used open source batch processing software for big data. Hadoop serves the basis for software that aim to work on parallel processing on large volume of data (Mishra, A.D., & Singh, Y.B., 2017). Hadoop works in two main phase i.e. storage and computation. Hadoop is assisted by two main components as shown in Figure 2, the first component is Hadoop distributed file system (HDFS) and the second component is MapReduce.

Figure 2. Hadoop component

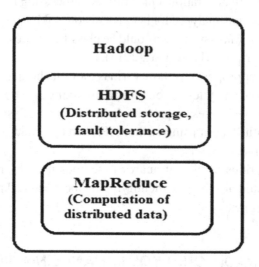

HDFS allows a network of computers to form a cluster for data storage and processing. The MapReduce performs computation on stored data (Huang, W., Wang, H., Zhang, Y., & Zhang, S., 2017). The HDFS follows a master slave model to process data. The main issue with MapReduce is that it is unable to process iterative algorithms up to an optimum level. This section discusses some advanced technologies (Hadoop eco system) which have contributed in improving performance in batch processing of big data.

1. **Apache Spark:** Apache Spark is also a general purpose, distributed open source project that extends the capabilities of MapReduce by supporting processing of multiple data types such as SQL-like queries, streaming, machine learning, graph and data flow processing (Mavridis, I., & Karatza, H., 2017). Spark is considered to be very good for iterative as well as batch processing algorithms which processes data in memory. It reduces usages of disk by keeping data in memory during map and reduce phases. Spark has many higher level specialized library items to process specific kind of data as shown in Figure 3. Many programming tools such as Java, Python, R and Scala can be used for implementation of algorithms.

Figure 3. Spark with specialized library to process the data

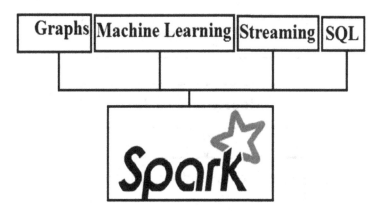

2. **Apache PIG:** Apache Pig is a scripting platform to process and analyze the large volume of data set present in Hadoop cluster (Kaur, R., Chauhan, V., & Mittal, U., 2018). The language used for scripting is known as PIG Latin. PIG runs the programs, convert it into the map reduce tasks, and finally executes the tasks. PIG is best suitable for the programming of the data in semi structured form.

3. **Apache Hive:** Hive is a Haddop eco-system tool which acts as an interface for the data warehouse for MapReduce programming. Hive has its own SQL, known as Hive query language (HQL). HQL is used to query data from the HDFS, generate MapReduce code and finally execute on Hadoop cluster as shown in Figure 4. Hive is not compatible with only HDFS, but also with Spark and other big data frameworks. Hive is fast, extensible and scalable, mainly developed for the OLAP (Mahmood, Z., 2016).

4. **HBase:** HBase is an open source, column-oriented, distributed, and non-relational database management system that runs on top of HDFS. HBase belong to the family of NoSQL database with the capability to handle massive amounts of data from terabytes to petabytes. Tables in Hbase are stored logically in the form of rows and columns. The benefit of such table storage is that they can process a million of rows and columns (Oussous, A., Benjelloun, F. Z., Ait Lahcen, A., & Belfkih, S., 2018). It provides many features at low latency such as, natural language processing, real-time queries, linear and modular scalability, and consistent access to Big Data from various sources. However, HBase has the limitation of not supporting a structured query language like SQL.

Figure 4. Hive code execution

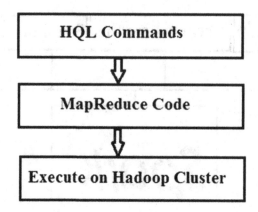

5. **Apache Kafka:** Apache Kafka is an open-source stream-processing software platform written in Scala and Java with an aim to provide low-latency platform for handling real-time data feeds with high throughput. The main components of Kafka architecture are Producer, Consumer, Broker and Topic (Vohra, D., 2016). In Kafka, a message is termed as the smallest unit of data that can flow from a producer to a consumer through a Kafka server (Broker) as shown in Figure 5. The message can persist on the server to be processed at a later time and feeds in topics. A topic, in Kafka, is a stream of messages of a similar category. In comparison to other messaging systems, Kafka has better built-in partitioning, replication, inherent fault-tolerance and throughput which make it one of best suitable platform for large-scale message processing applications.

Figure 5. Message flow in Apache Kafka

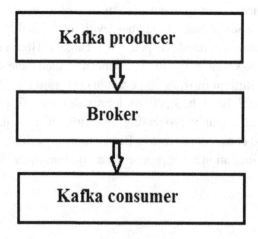

All the above mentioned Hadoop based technologies are a very popular data analytics framework for the distributed batch-data processing to produce patterns, knowledge and actionable insights. However, shortcomings are found in the Hadoop framework in processing and analyzing the streaming data.

NATURE OF DATA PRESENT AT PRESENT

As discussed in previous sections that data are generated from various resources such as social networks, web logs, e-commerce transactions, sensors and emails, could be batch-processed using the Hadoop framework with long period of latency. Data-stream processing and batch processing are considered as two different types of applications (Carbone, P., Katsifodimos, A., Kth, †, Sweden, S., Ewen, S., Markl, V., Haridi, S., & Tzoumas, K., 2015). A batch processing frameworks works on MapReduce component and is generally focus on the size and complexity of tasks than latency period of computation (Vakilinia, S., Zhang, X., & Qiu, D., 2016). There are many research works that improved efficiency of data processing in MapReduce. One such indexing in Hadoop is presented (Mittal, M., Singh, H., Paliwal, K., & Goyal, L. M., 2017). Similarly, MapReduce has been exploited for spatial data processing (Singh, H., & Bawa, S., 2012) and (Singh, H., & Bawa, S., 2016).

Now a day, big data applications are rapidly moving from batch oriented processing to stream oriented processing. The exponential growth of stream data, real-time stream processing becomes a major concern for research community and industry. Processing and analysis of stream data have become necessary in today's world to support a variety of applications such as IOT, medical, transportation, e-commerce, finance, and gaming. The major concern of data stream processing is real-time processing, high throughput, low latency period, and highly scalable to adjust large number of producers. The processing of data streaming heavily relies on immediate

Figure 6. Data streaming pipeline

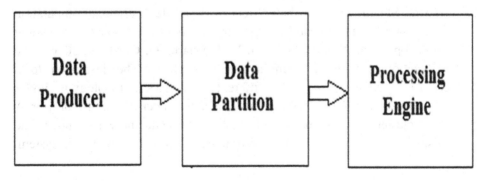

data partitioning of data generated by producers (Marcu, O., Costan, A., Antoniu, G., & P, S., 2018). A typical stream data processing pipeline is shown in Figure 6. Data producer refers all sources that generate continue data streams. Secondly, the data partition phase, acquires the stream for partition and preprocessing, to facilitate the consumption. At last, the processing engine consumes data stream for analysis.

DATA STREAM PROCESSING TOOLS

Unlike batch processing where data is defined by a start and an end in a job and a job finishes after processing that finite data, streaming refers to processing unbounded data coming in real-time continuously on a regular basis. Stream processing is harder to achieve as many characteristics such as fault tolerance, guaranteed delivery, low latency and throughput are the essential QoS parameters to be adhered by the applications. In this section few widely used stream processing tools have been discussed:

1.   **Apache Flink:** Apache Flink is distributed open source framework for stream data processing. It is capable to handle huge amount of data for real time processing with low latency and high fault tolerance (García-gil, D., Ramírez-gallego, S., García, S., & Herrera, F., 2017). It support two main API i.e. data stream and data set for stream and batch processing respectively. Flink supports following four libraries to support stream processing:
     a.   Flink ML: This library is concerned with ML algorithms to deal with supervised and unsupervised learning.
     b.   Gelly: It contains the methods and utilities to support graphical processing and analysis in Flink.
     c.   Flink CEP: This library is helpful in the processing of complex events and to generate the complex event patterns.
     d.   Table API and SQL: It supports the execution of SQL like statements for the relational data stream.
2.   **Apache Storm**: It is distributed, real time, and fault tolerant computation system; written in Java and Clojure to process the large amount of streaming data (Lopez, M. A., Lobato, A. G. P., & Duarte, O. C. M. B., 2016). The working of storm cluster is similar to Hadoop cluster. The clusters on storm can use different topologies for different storm tasks. A topology is similar to a MapRedude Job in Hadoop, but it operates under the control of user. A storm cluster has two types of nodes i.e. master node and worker node. The master node assigns the job to worker node and monitors the whole system.

Whereas, worker nodes process assigned tasks for analysis (Achariya, D., & Kauser, A., 2016).

3. **Apache Spark streaming:** Spark is distributed platform stream processing is written in Java and Sacala. Spark has special libraries called Spark Streaming to support the stream processing with short latency. An Apache Storm topology consumes streams of data; repartition the streams between each stage of the computation for real time processing. It is primarily based on micro-batch processing mode where events are processed together based on specified time intervals. Spark has three main components; the driver program responsible for the proper scheduling the task and creating spark context; cluster mangers are responsible for the resource allocation between applications; task managers responsible for computation and storage. The processing rate of Spark is lower as compared to Strom and Flink due to formation of micro-batch before processing (Hesse, G., & Lorenz, M., 2016).

CLOUD COMPUTING IN DATA PROCESSING

As discussed, 4Vs has posed many challenges in efficient processing of big data. Now, need of the hour is transformation of 4Vs in to 5Vs. Value is big issue for the processing capacity (Yang, C., Yu, M., Hu, F., Jiang, Y., & Li, Y., 2017). Cloud computing has become an amazing computation utility to address issues associated with big data with on demand service, ubiquitous network access, location independent resource pooling, rapid expansion and metered services (Verma, D.C., Mohapatra, A.K., & Usmani, K., 2012).

The rapid development in virtualization has made computation more economical sharable and accessible. Cloud computing eliminate the need of expensive resources such as processor, storage, operating system and memory for the large scale processing and complex computation. Large amount of data from the web and cloud are kept in a fault-tolerant distributed database and processed by a programming model for large volume of dataset with the help of parallel distributed algorithm in a cluster (Hashem, I. A. T., Yaqoob, I., Anuar, N. B., Mokhtar, S., Gani, A., & Ullah Khan, S., 2015).

After processing of a large dataset, data visualization is used to present results in different graphs for decision making. The Figure 7 depicts the use of cloud computing for big data processing and analysis. Data sources in Figure 7 represent main contributor of data such as web, IOT, sensors and cloud. The main components of cloud data processing are: fault tolerant databases to store captured data, programming data model to process the clustered data through parallel computing and the query engine to execute queries.

Figure 7. Cloud computing for big data processing and analysis

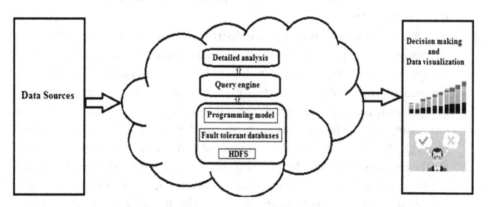

There are many cloud service model that offers the storage and computing facilities for big data, such as Amazon, Google, Microsoft, and Cloudera with different tools and techniques. Therefore, cloud computing technologies are the platform used to process and analyze big data without any major investment on resources such as tools, storage, and processors. But there are certain issues that must be adhered of while dealing with big data processing with a cloud service model.

Challenges in Big Data Processing in the Cloud

Though cloud computing is seen as an emerging technology for users and enterprises to process big data without any major investment. But, it poses few challenging and issues in front of industry, academia, and researchers that need be addressed to make it sustainable technology for big data processing (Stergiou, C., Psannis, K. E., Gupta, B. B., & Ishibashi, Y., 2018).

1.   **Data security:** Data is considered as an asset for the users and the enterprises. In cloud, data located at some third-party data center for the processing. Although, most of the cloud service providers use encryption techniques to ensure the security issues of the user's data, still some security breach makes the users reluctant to use the cloud computing services (Moreno, J., Serrano, M. A., & Fernández-Medina, E., 2016).
2.   **Privacy:** Big data processing in cloud also leads to privacy issues. For example, social media and medical records contains personal information may be misused by the third party or by the attackers raises serious concerns while dealing in cloud computation.

3. **Performance:** Encryption techniques used to secure the data at third party is directly related to the performance issues of the cloud service providers. The consequences of the complex encryption techniques may lead to degraded performance in terms of computation and data decryption. Therefore, a light-weight and secure encryption technique is required for the optimized performance.

4. **QoS:** It is very difficult to meet all the QoS parameters while processing the big data in the cloud. QoS parameters such as throughput, efficiency, time to upload and download the data from the cloud are few essential parameters to achieve.

5. **Reliability:** Data processing with cloud computing also raises the question mark on the reliability and the accessibility of the infrastructure.

6. **Heterogeneity and compatibility:** One of the major challenge need to be adhered of with cloud computing are the heterogeneity and compatibility of the devices, platforms, operating systems, infrastructure and services.

7. **Network bandwidth:** Big data processing is directly affected by the available network bandwidth (Yang, C., Huang, Q., Li, Z., Liu, K., & Hu, F., 2017).

8. **Data integration:** The 5th V (value) of the big data is very critical to achieve through the cross-domain processing and analysis is also a major concern of cloud computing.

All the above mentioned challenges are very critical to achieve while processing the big data through the cloud computing and most of the issues are open for the further research work.

MIGRATION FROM DATA PROCESSING TO DATA ANALYTICS

The data generated from various sources such as social networks, sensor networks, IOT, web logs, e-commerce transactions and email are of no use if they are not processed and analyzed for better decision making, knowledge discovery and meaningful pattern search (Acito, F., & Khatri, V., 2014). Big data analytics refers the quantitative and qualitative techniques and processes used to enhance the decision making capability for business gain.

Data analytics involve applying an algorithmic or mechanical process systematically to derive meaningful patterns and correlations between the data sets. Today's almost every organization has maintained data warehouse to collect data related to their customers, markets and business process for data processing. This data is then stored, categorized, and analyzed to transform the 4Vs into 5th V i.e. value or sense of it to derive meaningful insights from it. In next section various types of data analytics that is used to infer some logical conclusion from the data set will be discussed.

Challenges in Big Data Processing in the Cloud

In the literature various types of data analytics methodology are found to infer meaningful and logical information for the processed data set, few of them are discussed here (Chakraborty, K., & Bhattacharyya, S., 2018) as shown in Figure 8.

1. **Predictive analytics**: It refers the process of prediction of the events in advance based on the use of big data can (Akter, S., & Wamba, S. F., 2016). The quality of the prediction depends on the availability of the robust data set and it's mining. Therefore, predictive analytics helps the organizations to prepare more precise budgets and optimized processes. The preparation of these budgets helps e-commerce firms predict future sales trend, inventory management, and customer behavior from past data. The major concern that must be adhered of with predictive analysis is faster data access and mining methods for structured and unstructured for the improved prediction (Marjani, M., Nasaruddin, F., Gani, A., Karim, A., Hashem, I. A. T., Siddiqa, A., & Yaqoob, I., 2017). Predictive analytics helps in answering to the questions 'What will happen?'

Figure 8. Types of Data Analytics

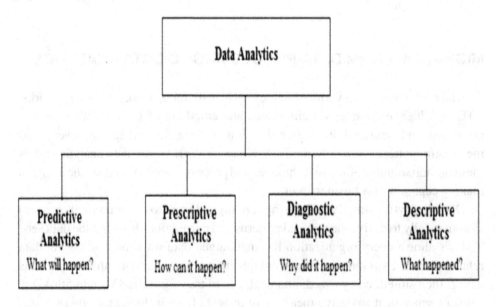

2. **Prescriptive analytics**: touches various aspects of business processes to provide insights on what is required to do in terms of data analytics. Predictive analytics talks about an analysis based on a defined set of rules and recommendations in order to prescribe a certain analytical path for the organization. A firm can deploy prescriptive analytics regardless of the industry vertical based on the same rules and regulations. Prescriptive analytics helps in finding the answers to the question 'How can we make it happen?'

3. **Diagnostic analytics**: is used for the specific purpose, such as discovering or determining why a certain course of action took place in the past. For example, this analytics are very useful to review a certain social media campaign and its outcome based on the number of followers, page views, reviews, fans, and such other metrics to diagnose why a certain thing happened. Diagnostic analytics are used answers to the questions 'Why did an event happen?' (Coraddu, A., Oneto, L., Baldi, F., & Anguita, D., 2017).

4. **Descriptive analytics:** used to explain what is happens in a given situation and uncovering patterns that can add value to an organization (Amirian, P., Loggerenberg, F. van, Lang, T., Thomas, A., Peeling, R., Basiri, A., & Goodman, S. N., 2017). Descriptive analytics basically answers to the question 'What happened to system?'. For example, the credit risks assessment of a customer. It takes into consideration various aspects such as the previous financial performance of the customer, inputs from past financial institutions, and CIBIL report and other online information available on web-based solutions.

Since no organization in this competitive era can survive with business gain without using proper data processing and data analytics, so data analytics is an indispensable part of the data life cycle in an organization. In the next section we discuss few widely used data analytics tools and techniques for better decision making and knowledge discovery.

Tools Used in Data Analytics

Data analytics tools are required in almost every organization to analyze the large, diverse and complex dataset to extract meaningful insights for business gains and to overtake the competitors. There are many platforms available nowadays for the efficient data analytics; few of them are briefly discussed here (Chawda, R. K., & Thakur, G., 2016).

1. **Apache Spark:** Spark is very powerful open source framework used for real-time Data analytics. As discussed in section 2.1, Spark is a component of the

Hadoop ecosystem and used to store, process and analyze the stream at low very low latency.

2. **IBM InfoSphere BigInsights:** InfoSphere is a big data analytics platform developed by IBM. InfoSphere build on the top of Hadoop for the big data analytics through interactive user interface. It is used for analytics of social media data, sensor data, GPS data and textual data. The main components of InfoSphere are BigSQL (SQL interface), Jqal (Declarative query language) and Bigsheets (spreadsheet interface) modules which are used in data analytics.

3. **Cloud based analytics:** There are many cloud based data analytics tools to deal with huge volume of data. Amazon EC2, Microsoft Azure, and Google AppEngine are few popular cloud platforms are used by the organizations to draw meaningful insights. With ample of advantages of cloud based analytics, data security and privacy are major concern for the research community.

4. **Python:** Python is open and free to use data analytics tool with rich set of libraries, package, and dictionary to achieve the outcome in a well organized way (Siddiqui, T., Alkadri, M., & Khan, N. A., 2017). This is one of the most versatile programming languages that are rapidly being deployed for various applications including Machine Learning. Python ecosystem includes packages like Numpy, Pandas, SciPy, Matplotlib and PySide for the efficient data analytics.

5. **SAP HANA:** SAP's Event Stream Processor (ESP) has made the SAP HANA a standalone, in-memory analytics platform used for stream analysis. SAP HANA is a combination of software and hardware, which integrates different components like SAP HANA Database, SAP SLT (System Landscape Transformation) Replication server, SAP HANA Direct Extractor connection and Sybase replication technology. SAP HANA can be deployed on premises or in cloud to provide real-time reporting at very high speed. The main limitation of SAP HANA is difficult maintenance of HANA database.

6. **SAS:** SAS is an advanced analytical tool for accessing, transformation and reporting data through its extensible, flexible and web based interface. The SAS platform comes with many applications such as SAS Text Miner, SAS Model Manager, and SAS Forecast Server for working with huge volumes of data and deriving valuable insights from it.

7. **Tableau:** This is one of the most popular Business Intelligence tools that is deployed for the purpose of business analytics and data visualization in the best presentable way. Tableau is the best tool among its competitor product such as Qlikview and Spotfire. The main advantages of the Tableau are amazing data visualization, excellent mobile support and low-cost solutions to upgrade (Yaqoob, I., Hashem, I. A. T., Gani, A., Mokhtar, S., Ahmed, E., Anuar, N. B.,

& Vasilakos, A. V., 2016). Whereas, the major limitation of Tableau is lack of predictive capabilities.

8. **Splunk:** Splunk is scalable and fault tolerant tool of choice for parsing the machine-generated data and extracting valuable business insights out of it. Splunk used for the real time data analytics tool for generating reports, alerts and data visualization from the stream.

9. **R Programming:** R is created by a group of colleagues at the University of Auckland in New Zeaklan in 1993. R is free and open source software and most widely used analytics tool used by data Scientists. R enables to perform the statistical computation and graphical presentation on dataset for better analysis as compared to other analytics tools (Ozgur, C., Colliau, T., Rogers, G., Hughes, Z., & Myer-Tyson, E. B., 2017).

DATA PROCESSING AND ANALYTICS: ISSUES AND CHALLENGES

This section discusses few important issues that are being faced by the industry in data processing and open for future research.

1. **Understanding of data:** It is very crucial to understand and select the right dataset out of the huge lump of data. It is just like finding the signal in the noise. Right dataset may lead towards the leap and bound business gain, whereas wrong dataset and correlation may lead to drastic loss.

2. **Scalability:** It refers the capability to accommodate the increasing amount of data. Data are generated at very rapid and unpredictable manner, which very difficult to store and process. Traditional databases are not suitable to handle this uneven data generation leads to the popularity of NoSQL (Hashem, I. A. T., Yaqoob, I., Anuar, N. B., Mokhtar, S., Gani, A., & Khan, S.U., 2015). Although, the scalability issue has been addressed by many advance tools and techniques, but still lot many issues are open and need to be further researched.

3. **Data quality:** The heterogeneity of data creates lot many issues during processing and analysis. Therefore, obtain the highest quality data from the various sources is an open challenge for the research community.

4. **Privacy:** Encryption techniques are used to maintain the privacy of the data, but somewhere encryption and decryption of data consume significant amount processing time, which need to be optimized.

5. **Security:** Security threats to data have always been a major issue for the research community. This issue magnified in the case of big data due to volume, velocity, and veracity of the data and need to be talked wisely.

6. **Computation complexity:** The design of energy efficient, high performance computing frameworks with low latency is one of the biggest and open challenge for the Industry and researchers (Jin, X., Wah, B. W., Cheng, X., & Wang, Y., 2015).

7. **Communication between systems:** Most of the computation involved in big data are of distributed in nature and based on parallel computation (Tsai, C. W., Lai, C. F., Chao, H. C., & Vasilakos, A. V., 2015). This kind of the framework needs stringent coordination and communication among the constituent systems for efficient processing, failing which results in high cost and degraded performance.

8. **Data integrity:** Integrity refers that only authorized users can access the data. It is utmost important to prevent the misuse of data and frauds. Data with the third party need a mechanism to ensure the integrity of the data. Therefore, a strong and robust authorization scheme mechanism to maintain the data correctness.

9. **Data transformation:** Data must be pre-processed before the storage in the database and further analysis. Improper transformation leads to wrong knowledge discovery and correlations of the datasets, results in huge business loss.

SENTIMENTS ANALYSIS AND REVIEWS

The opinion mining and sentiment analysis deals with computational treatment of opinion, sentiment, and subjectivity in text. A deep survey on the opinion oriented information seeking system along with challenges faced in the sentiment aware application as compared to the fact-based system is presented (Pang, B., & Lee, L., 2008). The following section presents a survey of various existing techniques of sentiment analysis.

A domain-specific sentiment analysis using contextual feature generation uses clue set (Choi, Y., Kim, Y., & Myaeng, S.-H., 2009). The clue set contains most likely feature words for the word that is to be checked. This method has a four step algorithm for generating the new clue set of sentiment words. Initially, this is consisting of sentence as well as polarity (training) example, then generates corresponding clues. Second step involves the identification of sentiment topics from training (sample) example. Then the sentiment clues which gets identified to sentiment topics are put to its current clue set. This updated classifier is then used for identifying other domains under sentiment clues from the sample data set. Recently, automatic opinion analysis in many domains has become very popular.

In another approach, exploiting new sentiment-based meta-level features for effective sentiment analysis is presented (Canuto, S., Gonçalves, M. A., & Benevenuto,

F., 2016). This method contains large set of pre-classified words/sentence. For a new word that has to be checked the features (which discuss issues for the work) are checked for similarities with the pre classified data set. The one with the most resembling contents matched is considered as the true sentiment word for the given content. Thus the given contents' sentiment is taken as the sentiment of the pre-classified sentence with whom the maximum feature similarities are got.

The measure of sentiment of user towards each political party is checked using sentiment index which takes the log of ratio of total words raised to the power positive and negative added to unity (Sandoval-Almazan, R., & Valle-Cruz, D., 2018).

$$Sentiment\ Index = ln\left[\frac{1 + Total^{Positive}}{1 + Total^{Negative}}\right].$$

The study indicated that the emotions of voters can be found but not their intention to vote. It was found that the political party that won had a bad perception on social media while the one having well was unable to win the Mexican election.

Another approach allowed a multi level representation of three categories: Target, Modifier, and Appraisal group (Bari, M. D., Shroff, S., & Thomas, M., 2013). Target is the expression that the sentiment refers to. Modifier is the expression conveying the sentiment and appraisal group includes the set of targets and modifiers. The meaning of a sentence gets reversed when certain words were present which are k/a modifiers.

In another approach, evaluation of features on sentimental analysis is presented (Shahana, P., & Omman, B., 2015). This involves four step procedures. Firstly data is preprocessed, in it initially all text are converted into lowercase words for simplicity of feature extraction. Then the words ending with apostrophizes are converted back to original form like don't -> do not, any non ASCII character is removed. This is followed by removal of stop words (e.g. aan the) as they do not convey any feature so removal of stop words is preferred. Second setup involves partitioning data into training and test data. For training data after performing stemming (removing suffixes like ing eg.: computing->compute) feature selection is to be performed in which various statistical methods are applied to check whether sentiment of review can be extracted from the count of words in each sample.

Review of sentimental analysis methods using lexicon based approach is presented (Rajput, R., & Solanki, A. K., 2016). This approach includes the calculation for the inclination of sentiments in words by checking their semantic alignment of words in the document .Phrases can also be used. Lexicon-based approach dictionaries can be created automatically as well as manually; with the help of seed words we can expand the list of words. This research was focused mainly on using adjectives as predictors of the semantic alignment of text. It starts with compilation of adjectives and their (SO) Sentiment Orientation into a dictionary and from there patterns are matched for sentimental calculation.

Sentimental analysis of twitter data using text mining and hybrid classification approach is presented (Goyal, S., 2016). This begins with the extraction of tweets which is then pre-processed followed by application of classifier algorithm. It involves five step mechanisms. Firstly a structured data is formed, and then common grammar words like verbs, preposition articles (c/a stop words) are removed. This is followed by the step where words ending with "ing","ize","ed" are reduced to their root word. This is known as steaming. The term frequency – inverse term frequency score is calculated for each term and a 2D matrix is created in which rows represent documents and columns represent the word extracted from document after the above preprocessing which is filled with the TF-IDE score.

Sentimental analysis of Flipkart reviews using Naïve Bayes and Decision Tree algorithm is presented (0Kaur, G., & Singla, A., 2016). Naïve Bayes approach for classifying is based on probabilistic classifying where Bayes Theorem is used and theory of total probability is used. The paper claims it's suitability for large datasets. Just like text mining it starts with tokenization then removal of stop words followed by text transformation. Then features are selected for the parts of document that contribute for positive and negative words. These parts are joined in such a way such that the probability is maximum of the resulting sentence existing in either of the two positive or negative terms.

Sentiment analysis using Neuro-Fuzzy and Hidden Markov Models of text is presented (Rustamov, S., Mustafayev, E., & Clements, M. A., 2013). The data were taken from different files c/a data set which was combined into a one source file called "corpus". Once combined, the text was converted into array of words and further step was to sort this array of collection. Like other works stemming was skipped so that the words like remind and reminded make different sense to the text in consideration. Now a final part of calculation of membership degree of each term is calculated by an analytical formula before being processed by the neural network.

Rating prediction based on social sentiment from textual reviews is presented (Lei, X., Qian, X., & Zhao, G., 2016). Here two type of list is discussed: Word List: Contains both positive polarity and negative polarity words. Topic list: Contains list of topics that will be depicted as the root sentiment. The model involves the following steps: Firstly pre-processing tasks such as stop word removal, noise word removal are performed and then remaining product features are extracted using Latent Dirichlet Allocation (which computes the relationship of reviews and topics with words). The generative process is followed that matches user words to a set of its most probable topic list. Secondly sentiment degree is matched by the SDD(sentiment degree dictionary).From the combined word list(sentiment dictionary) from where a review is matched before the product feature and assigned a score +1.0,-1.0for positive and negative respectively.

Finally the words with prefix words as negative from ND (negation dictionary) are checked and a default value coefficient of +1.0 c/a negation check coefficient is added the sentiment polarity is reversed, and the coefficient is set to −1.0 if the sentiment word is preceded by an odd number of negative prefix words and hence therefore the normalized score is generated.

In another approach, a Hidden Marker Model (HMM) is used that assumes data to be in unobserved states (Jurafsky, D., & Martin, J. H., 2019). According to it, the results are a probabilistic function of the classes to which the classification is to be performed. The data set are pre classified as objective or subjective using Naïve-Bayes model. The Sequence recognition feature includes probabilistic distribution of subjectivity degree. The HMM parameters were calculated from them using specific equations and results stored.

A pattern based approach uses binary to multi-class classification (Bouazizi, M., & Ohtsuki, T., 2016). Binary Classification refers to classifying the work in either of two polarities i.e. positive or negative. The model works on a pattern based approach and had accuracy of 87.5% in binary classification .The author defined seven classes for which tweets were matched namely happy, sad, anger, love, hate, sarcasm and neutral. Emotional scores for words are calculated using Senti-Strength that assigns a score ranging from -1 to -5 and +1 to +5 based on the severity of the sentences. This is followed by getting a total of four parameters

i)   Net score for PW (+ve words)
ii)   Net score for NW(-ve words)

Using it ratio of emotional words is calculated as:

$$\rho(t) = \frac{PW(t) - NW(t)}{PW(t) + NW(t)}$$

In another research work, the most frequent words are to be generated as output in the form of a word cloud and its size will depends upon the extent of the frequency of occurrence of words collected (Bouazizi, M., & Ohtsuki, T., 2015). This implements the sentimental analysis algorithm for searching the most used words in Smartphone industry. The data set is taken from CSV (common separated value) file. The category to which these words used for is also checked. Each frequency is noted for the term. These words are displayed in a clustered manner and its size depends upon the frequency meaning large frequency words are having size that is large in number.

SENTIMENT ANALYSIS: CASE STUDIES

The work presented in this section is implemented on Intel Core i5 processor with 64 bit Windows 10 operating system with Python 3.7. It is highly recommended to use i5 or higher processor. A total of five test cases are presented here; three test cases are taken from the variable search space and two from the continuous search space. The section starts with describing the processing model used, libraries used, processing model's code, results and performance analysis, and lastly ends with a conclusion.

Processing Model

The functioning of the processing models is described in four stages: Input, Processing, Fetch and Store, and Data Visualization as also shown pictorially in Figure 9.

1. **Input:** The tweets are take these can include the live streams also or tweets generated in a particular date.

Figure 9. Processing model

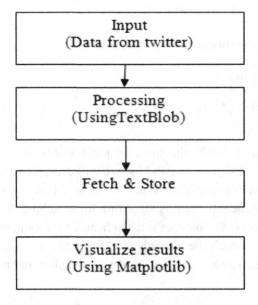

2. **Processing:** The textblob library is an open source library that is maintained in github and includes functions specifically for natural language processing tasks. Through it the characterization is either positive, negative or neutral is performed

3. **Fetch and Store:** On run time when the results are calculated then the need to be stored in file to be viewed at a later stage. Thus those results are stored in csv format and the file name is the search-term itself.

4. **Data Visualization:** The matplotlib is used to extract data from the saved files to show the variation in positive and negative with respect to their creation dates.

Libraries Used

Three main libraries have been used: tweepy, textblob, and matplotlib.

1. **tweepy:** Tweepy is the official Programming interface for dealing with twitter related works. It was utilized for getting tweets. This Programming interface has techniques for doing retweets, refresh status, seek terms, get client data, getting devotees and so forth. The following classes are used.

   a. API: This class has methods to confirm an application to interact with twitter.

   b. OAuthHandler: It takes customer key and buyer mystery as parameters that are novel for every application.

   c. Cursor: This class can play out all the page association related works. This was utilized in getting tweets from a few courses of events.
   The following methods are used.

   d. set_access_token: It takes get to token and access token mystery as parameters and is utilized in verifying that the 4 parameters relate to a substantial application.

   e. Cursor: The programming interface protest was passed as first contention and the term to be sought as second.

   f. items(): This was utilized to process result per page for the tweets.

2. **textblob:** It is that library that has vast methods for the purpose of data processing. The Sentiment class is used that examines techniques that can be utilized in getting conclusion from words or some other dialect handling. The Polarity method distinguishes extremity from a content that is inputted in its bracket.

3. **Matplotlib:** Matplotlib is accounts for the graphical visualization of data for 2D plotting. It uses pyplot class that incorporates capacities to give a pictorial

perception of the inputted information. It was utilized in producing the pie outline. The following methods are used.

a. pie: Produces pie outline for first contention with hues in second contention.
b. legend(): Creates legend that contains depiction identified with shading.
c. title():Assign title to outline for better comprehension of pie chart.
d. axis():sets hub information limit for the sort of diagram being utilized.
e. light_layout(): Naturally change subplot parameters to give cushioning.
f. appear():It shows the pie outline with title, legend as provided.

Processing Model's Code

```
import tweepy

from tweepy import OAuthHandler

from textblob import TextBlob

from matplotlib.pyplot import plt

class twitter_sent(object):

consumer_key = 'XXXXXXXXXXXXXXXXXXXXXXXX'

consumer_secret = 'XXXXXXXXXXXXXXXXXXXXXXXXXXXX'

access_token = 'XXXXXXXXXXXXXXXXXXXXXXXXXXX'

access_token_secret = 'XXXXXXXXXXXXXXXXXXXXXXXX'

try:

# create OAuthHandler object

auth = OAuthHandler(consumer_key, consumer_secret)

# set access token and secret

auth.set_access_token(access_token, access_token_secret)

# create tweepy API object to fetch tweets
```

```
api = tweepy.API(self.auth)

except:

print("Error: Authentication Failed")

pos=[]

neg=[]

dy=[]

def process():

query=input('Enter the search term')

count=int(input('Please provide the number of search terms'))

start_date= input('Please enter the start date')

end_date = input('Please enter the end date')

mth = input('Please enter the month')

tweets = []

try:

# call twitter api to fetch tweets

For d in range(start_date,end_date+1):

dd=str(d)+'-'+str(mth)+'-2019'

d2=str(d+1)+'-'+str(mth)+'-2019'

fetched_tweets = self.api.search(q = query, count = count, from= dd,to=d2)

# parsing tweets one by one
```

```
posc=0

negc=0

for tweet in fetched_tweets:

# empty dictionary to store required params of a tweet

parsed_tweet = {}

# saving text of tweet

parsed_tweet['text'] = tweet.text

# saving sentiment of tweet

analysis = TextBlob(tweet)

# set sentiment

if analysis.sentiment.polarity > 0:

sent='positive'

posc=posc+1

elif analysis.sentiment.polarity == 0:

sent='neutral'

else:

sent= 'negative'

negc=negc+1

pos.append(posc)

neg.append(negc)
```

dy.append(d)

parsed_tweet['sentiment'] = sent

 # appending parsed tweet to tweets list

if tweet.retweet_count > 0:

 # if tweet has retweets, ensure that it is appended only once

if parsed_tweet not in tweets:

tweets.append(parsed_tweet)

else:

tweets.append(parsed_tweet)

 # return parsed tweets

#return tweets

except tweepy.TweepError as e:

 # print error (if any)

print("Error: " + str(e))

for twt in tweets:

print(twt)

def draw():

plt.plot(pos,dy,label='Positive')

plt.plot(neg,dy,label='Negative')

plt.show()

obj=twitter_sent( )

obj.process( )

obj.draw( )

Results and Performance Analysis

This section presents the search set tested on twitter stream, result classification on various test cases, and the conclusion in the end.

Search Set Used

Several test plans are conducted over the following search set on the twitter stream.

1. **New set:** Here both the keyword variable and the number of tweet variable are reset and manually stored.
2. **Same keywords but on different number of tweets:** Keeping the keyword/ hashtag same, user is asked to input a fixed number of tweets upon which the keyword is to be matched after execution the new set.
3. **Different keywords but same number of tweets**: Keeping the number of matching words/hashtags same the value of number of tweets is to be re entered that will be used in getting the sentiments reflected over, after executing either the first or second search set.

Result Classification

Results are classified over variable search set and continuous search set categories.

1. **Variable Search Set:** Values of trending words are matched to the number of tweets and the results are plotted. The ratio of positive, negative and neutral are combined to form the whole set. A pie chart is presented to depict their corresponding shares in respective categories; and is presented in Figure 10, Figure 11, and Figure 12.
    Test Case#1: This shows the result of search set 1. Here the search term and number of search terms both are inputted initially to start the working of the software.
    Test Case#2: This is search set 2, where we keep the search term same <modi>, only the <no of search terms> are changed from 15 to 150.

Figure 10. (Test Case #1)

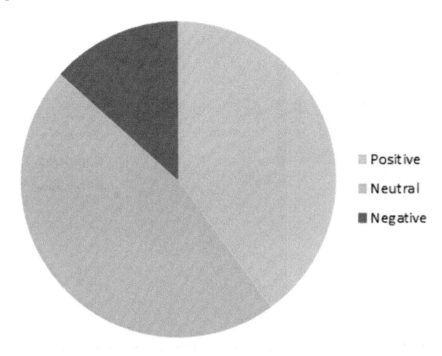

Figure 11. (Test Case #2)

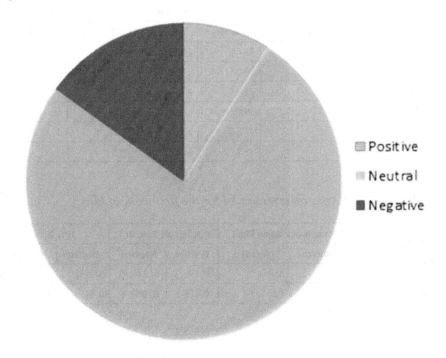

Figure 12. (Test Case #3)

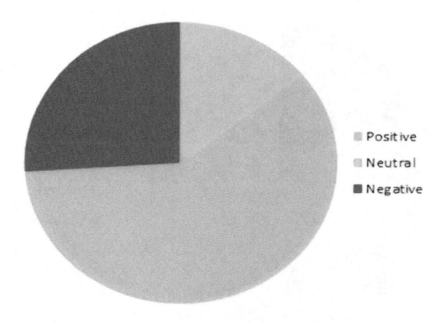

Table 1. Recorded positive and negative sentiments on test case #4 (Cricket) for the first week of May

	Champions League Final		Kings XI Punjab		IPL 2019	
Day	Positive	Negative	Positive	Negative	Positive	Negative
1	0	4.67	28.64	14.13	49	6
2	0	0	30.08	11.50	42	3
3	20	0	32.84	4.07	38	3
4	20	0	39.01	10.28	34	6
6	33.33	0	42.81	8.23	33	2
7	42	11	38.18	18.78	42	3

Table 2. Statistical analysis on test case #4 for the first week of May

Statistical analysis	Champions League Final		Kings XI Punjab		IPL 2019	
	Positive	Negative	Positive	Negative	Positive	Negative
Mean	19.22	2.94	33.79	14.14	38.71	3.71
Standard deviation	14.58	4.35	4.93	10.30	4.54	1.48

Test Case #3: This is search set 3, the search term is kept as #Congress and the number of Search Terms <150> is remained same.

2. **Continuous Search Set:** The following domains are collected from twitter by setting the tweet limit to hundred and the results are plotted for the starting week of May for the domains underlined.

Test Case #4: Cricket: In this category, the results of Champions League Final, Kings XI Punjab, and IPL 2019 are plotted in Figure 13, Figure 14, and Figure 15. The tabular analysis for the same is presented in Table 1 and Table 2.

Figure 13. Variation of tweets in percentage (y-axis) on Champions League Final for the first week of May (x-axis)

Figure 14. Variation of tweets in percentage (y-axis) on Kings XI Punjab for the first week of May (x-axis)

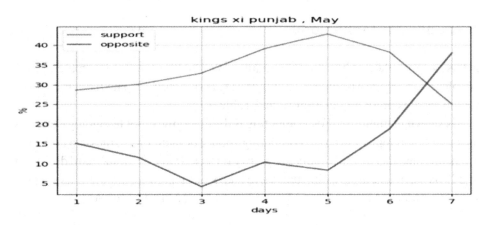

Figure 15. Variation of tweets in percentage (y-axis) on IPL 2019 for the first week of May (x-axis)

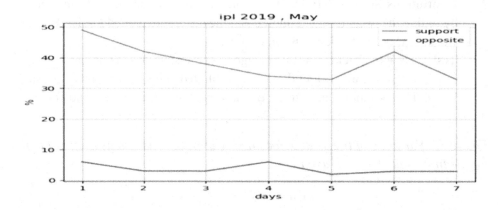

From the Figure 14, it is shown that there has been an increase in tweets for opposition for this team which reached a maximum of 38% from 8.2% in just an interval of two days only, moreover the support reduced from 42% to just 25% that was a decline in around 20% of popularity while parallel the increase in opposition had around 30%.

As per the Figure 15, the overall craze for IPL as reflected from tweets had been in its favor, the tweets in opposition could hardly had an average of less than 4%. On the other hand the maximum supporting tweets were close to 50% on the start of the month while the minimum being at a fraction of 33% in support and 2% for non favorable tweets. As of May7, we conclude that the sentiments (average) for the search term: "IPL 2019" was the highest amongst the 3 terms takes. On the other hand the maximum positive sentiments recorded were for IPL 2019.

Test Case #5: Technology

In this category, the results of Fog Computing, 5G, OnePlus7Pro, and Cryptocurrency are plotted in Figure 16, Figure 17, Figure 18, and Figure 19. The tabular analysis for the same is presented in Table 3 and Table 4.

As shown in Figure 16, Fog computing is the emerging art of technology that has the potential in replacing cloud computing sooner or later. From, the data collected it was revealed that the maximum popularity reflected was 83% a standard deviation of 22% is sufficient in revealing that there had been an high variation for its support since the minima was 3.3% recorded i.e. a very high difference of 80%.

Table 3. Positive and negative sentiments on test case #5 (Technology) for the first week of May

Day	Fog Computing		5G		OnePlus7Pro		Cryptocurrency	
	Positive	Negative	Positive	Negative	Positive	Negative	Positive	Negative
1	3.33	13.33	17	7	15	3	60	4
2	40.90	0	23	15	52	1	34	6
3	37.5	8.33	14	10	55	2	39	5
4	81.81	9.09	10	9	27	7	35	8
6	47.36	4.26	18	10	60	5	35	17
7	17.94	10.25	20	8	36	0	43	16

Table 4. Statistical analysis on test case #5 for the first week of May

Statistical analysis	Fog Computing		5G		OnePlus7Pro		Cryptocurrency	
	Positive	Negative	Positive	Positive	Positive	Negative	Positive	Negative
Mean	37.33	8.39	17.57	9.57	44.28	2.57	40.14	9.85
Standard deviation	22.82	4.23	4.10	2.44	18.54	2.44	8.62	4.99

Figure 16. Variation of tweets in percentage (y-axis) on Fog Computing for the first week of May (x-axis)

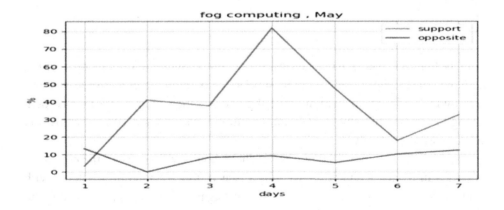

Figure 17. Variation of tweets in percentage (y-axis) on 5G for the first week of May (x-axis)

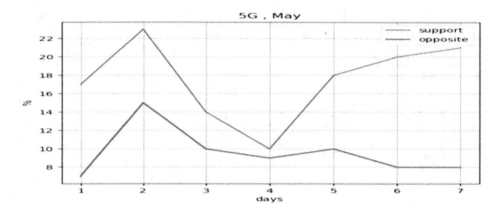

Figure 18. Variation of tweets in percentage (y-axis) on OnePlus7Pro for the first week of May (x-axis)

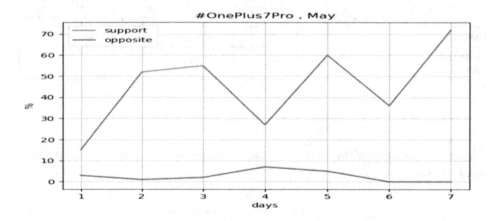

In the Figure 17, on each interval taken, the tweets counted in opposition were not more than the tweets considered in its support. Maximum recorded tweets covered an altitude of 15% in opposition while the one in support were 23% as recorded. Taking the minimum value in account the number was 7% and 10% in opposition and support respectively.

It appears from Figure 18 that this handheld device will be one of the next most successes in device technology. Making place in top 10 trending hashtags with good support of average 45% tweets in support against 2.5% in opposition and the

Figure 19. Variation of tweets in percentage (y-axis) on Cryptocurrency for the first week of May (x-axis)

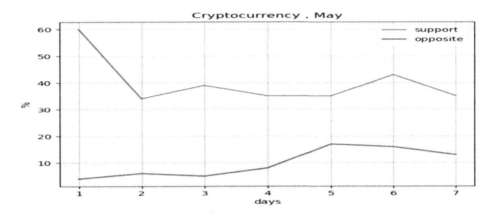

maximum support of 72% when no tweets were recorded in opposition reveals the fact of it's becoming a grand success for technological goods.

The Figure 19 shows that cryptocurrency on each sample interval has a net positive support of 34% while the opposition is just 17% as recorded. Cryptocurrency could help in contributing in saving the global warming scenario also since using this technology could replace the current use of paper-based currency for which to manufacture a lot of damage had been caused to the ecosystem. Thus the support reflected form the platform of colleting tweets is true. From the weekly analysis we conclude that fog computing got the maximum positive tweets on Saturday i.e. May 4 while the average analysis showed that OnePlus&Prohad the most highlighted positive with maximum reaching to 72% on May 7. It is shown that 5G had the minimum standard deviation and the maximum of opposite were close to the average in positive.

CONCLUSION

The section present a different way of analysis for prediction for topics like product launch success, political campaigns etc. In general the opinions were collected through polling each individual from regions to know the status of their taste. This method consumed a lot of human work and was tedious too. In contrast to that if the required work is carried from the largest social network then it could be efficiently done also, we can analyze the trend in the same as collection of tweets from previous posts is still feasible. It has seen that there occurs a vast variation of polarity and sentiments collected over time that helps in governing the mood of global people across different geographical locations. Moreover some words like study showed zero negative ratios.

REFERENCES

Achariya, D., & Kauser, A. (2016). Survey on Big Data Analytics: Challenges, Open Research Issues and Tools. *International Journal of Advanced Computer Science and Applications*, 7(2), 511–518.

Acito, F., & Khatri, V. (2014). Business analytics: Why now and what next? *Business Horizons*, 57(5), 565–570. doi:10.1016/j.bushor.2014.06.001

Akter, S., & Wamba, S. F. (2016). Big data analytics in E-commerce: A systematic review and agenda for future research. *Electronic Markets*, 26(2), 173–194. doi:10.100712525-016-0219-0

Amirian, P., van Loggerenberg, F., Lang, T., Thomas, A., Peeling, R., Basiri, A., & Goodman, S. N. (2017). Using big data analytics to extract disease surveillance information from point of care diagnostic machines. *Pervasive and Mobile Computing*, 42, 470–486. doi:10.1016/j.pmcj.2017.06.013

Bari, M. D., Shroff, S., & Thomas, M. (2013). SentiML: functional annotation for multilingual sentiment analysis. *Proceedings of the 1st International Workshop on Collaborative Annotations in Shared Environment: Metadata, Vocabularies and Techniques in the Digital Humanities*. 10.1145/2517978.2517994

Bouazizi, M., & Ohtsuki, T. (2015). Opinion mining in twitter: how to make use of sarcasm to enhance sentiment analysis. *2015 IEEE/ACM International Conference on Advances in Social Networks Analysis and Mining*, 1594–1597. 10.1145/2808797.2809350

Bouazizi, M., & Ohtsuki, T. (2016). Sentiment analysis: From binary to multi-class classification: A pattern-based approach for multi-class sentiment analysis in Twitter. *2016 IEEE International Conference on Communications, ICC 2016*, 1–6. 10.1109/ICC.2016.7511392

Canuto, S., Gonçalves, M. A., & Benevenuto, F. (2016). Exploiting new sentiment-based meta-level features for effective sentiment analysis. *WSDM 2016 - Proceedings of the 9th ACM International Conference on Web Search and Data Mining*, 53–62. 10.1145/2835776.2835821

Carbone, P., Katsifodimos, A., Sweden, S., Ewen, S., Markl, V., Haridi, S., & Tzoumas, K. (2015). *Apache Flink™: Stream and Batch Processing in a Single Engine*. Academic Press.

Chakraborty, K., & Bhattacharyya, S. (2018). *Comparative Sentiment Analysis on a Set of Movie*. doi:10.1007/978-3-319-74690-6

Chawda, R. K., & Thakur, G. (2016). Big data and advanced analytics tools. *2016 Symposium on Colossal Data Analysis and Networking, CDAN 2016*. 10.1109/CDAN.2016.7570890

Choi, Y., Kim, Y., & Myaeng, S.-H. (2009). Domain-specific sentiment analysis using contextual feature generation. *Proceedings of the 1st International CIKM Workshop on Topic Sentiment Analysis for Mass Opinion*, 37–44. 10.1145/1651461.1651469

Coraddu, A., Oneto, L., Baldi, F., & Anguita, D. (2017). Vessels fuel consumption forecast and trim optimisation: A data analytics perspective. *Ocean Engineering, 130*(September), 351–370. doi:10.1016/j.oceaneng.2016.11.058

Dev Mishra, A., & Beer Singh, Y. (2017). Big data analytics for security and privacy challenges. *Proceeding - IEEE International Conference on Computing, Communication and Automation, ICCCA 2016*, 50–53. 10.1109/CCAA.2016.7813688

García-gil, D., Ramírez-gallego, S., García, S., & Herrera, F. (2017). Open Access A comparison on scalability for batch big data processing on Apache Spark and Apache Flink. *Big Data Analytics*, 1–11. doi:10.118641044-016-0020-2

Goyal, S. (2016). Sentimental analysis of twitter data using text mining and hybrid classification approach. *International Journal of Advance Research Ideas and Innovations in Technology*, 2(5), 1–9.

Hashem, I. A. T., Yaqoob, I., Anuar, N. B., Mokhtar, S., Gani, A., & Ullah Khan, S. (2015). The rise of "big data" on cloud computing: Review and open research issues. *Information Systems*, 47, 98–115. doi:10.1016/j.is.2014.07.006

Hesse, G., & Lorenz, M. (2016). Conceptual survey on data stream processing systems. *Proceedings of the International Conference on Parallel and Distributed Systems - ICPADS*, 797–802. 10.1109/ICPADS.2015.106

Huang, W., Wang, H., Zhang, Y., & Zhang, S. (2017). A novel cluster computing technique based on signal clustering and analytic hierarchy model using hadoop. *Cluster Computing*, 1–8. doi:10.100710586-017-1205-9

Janssen, M., van der Voort, H., & Wahyudi, A. (2017). Factors influencing big data decision-making quality. *Journal of Business Research, 70*, 338–345. doi:10.1016/j.jbusres.2016.08.007

Jin, X., Wah, B. W., Cheng, X., & Wang, Y. (2015). Significance and Challenges of Big Data Research. *Big Data Research, 2*(2), 59–64. doi:10.1016/j.bdr.2015.01.006

Jurafsky, D., & Martin, J. H. (2019). Part-of-Speech Tagging. Speech and Language Processing.

Kaur, G., & Singla, A. (2016). Sentiment analysis of flipkart reviews using naive bayes and decision tree algorithm. *International Journal of Advanced Research in Computer Engineering & Technology, 5*(1), 148–153.

Kaur, R., Chauhan, V., & Mittal, U. (2018). Metamorphosis of data (small to big) and the comparative study of techniques (HADOOP, HIVE and PIG) to handle big data. *International Journal of Engineering & Technology, 7*(2.27), 1. doi:10.14419/ijet.v7i2.27.11206

Lei, X., Qian, X., & Zhao, G. (2016). Rating Prediction Based on Social Sentiment from Textual Reviews. *IEEE Transactions on Multimedia, 18*(9), 1910–1921. doi:10.1109/TMM.2016.2575738

Lopez, M. A., Lobato, A. G. P., & Duarte, O. C. M. B. (2016). A performance comparison of open-source stream processing platforms. *2016 IEEE Global Communications Conference, GLOBECOM 2016 - Proceedings*. 10.1109/GLOCOM.2016.7841533

Mahmood, Z. (2016). Data science and big data computing: Frameworks and methodologies. *Data Science and Big Data Computing: Frameworks and Methodologies*. doi:10.1007/978-3-319-31861-5

Marcu, O., Costan, A., Antoniu, G., & P, S. (2018). *KerA: Scalable Data Ingestion for Stream Processing*. doi:10.1109/ICDCS.2018.00152

Marjani, M., Nasaruddin, F., Gani, A., Karim, A., Hashem, I. A. T., Siddiqa, A., & Yaqoob, I. (2017). Big IoT Data Analytics: Architecture, Opportunities, and Open Research Challenges. *IEEE Access: Practical Innovations, Open Solutions, 5*(c), 5247–5261. doi:10.1109/ACCESS.2017.2689040

Mavridis, I., & Karatza, H. (2017). Performance evaluation of cloud-based log file analysis with Apache Hadoop and Apache Spark. *Journal of Systems and Software, 125*, 133–151. doi:10.1016/j.jss.2016.11.037

Mishra, R. K., & Mishra, R. K. (2018). The Era of Big Data, Hadoop, and Other Big Data Processing Frameworks. *PySpark Recipes*, 1–14. doi:10.1007/978-1-4842-3141-8_1

Mittal, M., Singh, H., Paliwal, K., & Goyal, L. M. (2017). Efficient Random Data Accessing in MapReduce. *International Conference on Infocom Technologies and Unmanned Systems (Trends and Future Directions)*, 552–556.

Moreno, J., Serrano, M. A., & Fernández-Medina, E. (2016). Main issues in Big Data security. *Future Internet*, *8*(3), 44. Advance online publication. doi:10.3390/fi8030044

Oussous, A., Benjelloun, F. Z., Ait Lahcen, A., & Belfkih, S. (2018). Big Data technologies: A survey. *Journal of King Saud University - Computer and Information Sciences, 30*(4), 431–448. doi:10.1016/j.jksuci.2017.06.001

Ozgur, C., Colliau, T., Rogers, G., Hughes, Z., & Myer-Tyson, E. B. (2017). MatLab vs. Python vs. R. *Journal of Data Science: JDS, 15*(3), 355–372.

Pang, B., & Lee, L. (2008). Opinion mining and sentiment analysis. In *Foundations and trends in information retrieval* (Vol. 2, pp. 1–2). Issues.

Perwej, Y. (2017). An Experiential Study of the Big Data. *Science and Education, 4*(1), 14–25. doi:10.12691/iteces-4-1-3

Rajput, R., & Solanki, A. K. (2016). Review of sentimental analysis methods using lexicon based approach. *International Journal of Computer Science and Mobile Computing, 5*(2), 159–166.

Rustamov, S., Mustafayev, E., & Clements, M. A. (2013). Sentiment analysis using Neuro-Fuzzy and hidden markov models of text. *Proceedings of IEEE Southeastcon*.

Sandoval-Almazan, R., & Valle-Cruz, D. (2018). Facebook impact and sentiment analysis on political campaigns. *ACM International Conference Proceeding Series*. 10.1145/3209281.3209328

Shahana, P., & Omman, B. (2015). Evaluation of features on sentimental analysis. *Procedia Computer Science, 46*, 1585–1592. doi:10.1016/j.procs.2015.02.088

Siddiqui, T., Alkadri, M., & Khan, N. A. (2017). Review of Programming Languages and Tools for Big Data Analytics. *International Journal of Advanced Research in Computer Science, 8*(5), 1112–1118.

Singh, H., & Bawa, S. (2012). Evolution of Grid-GIS Systems. *International Journal of Computer Science and Telecommunications, 3*(3), 36–40.

Singh, H., & Bawa, S. (2016). Spatial Data Analysis with ArcGIS and MapReduce. *Proceedings of International Conference on Conference Computing, Communication and Automation*. 10.1109/CCAA.2016.7813687

Stergiou, C., Psannis, K. E., Gupta, B. B., & Ishibashi, Y. (2018). Security, privacy & efficiency of sustainable Cloud Computing for Big Data & IoT. *Sustainable Computing: Informatics and Systems*, *19*, 174–184. doi:10.1016/j.suscom.2018.06.003

Storey, V. C., & Song, I. Y. (2017). Big data technologies and Management: What conceptual modeling can do. *Data & Knowledge Engineering*, *108*(February), 50–67. doi:10.1016/j.datak.2017.01.001

Tsai, C. W., Lai, C. F., Chao, H. C., & Vasilakos, A. V. (2015). Big data analytics: A survey. *Journal of Big Data*, *2*(1), 1–32. doi:10.118640537-015-0030-3 PMID:26191487

Vakilinia, S., Zhang, X., & Qiu, D. (2016). Analysis and optimization of big-data stream processing. *2016 IEEE Global Communications Conference, GLOBECOM 2016 - Proceedings*, 9–14. 10.1109/GLOCOM.2016.7841598

Verma, D., Mohapatra, A., & Usmani, K. (2012). Light Weight Encryption Technique for Group Communication in Cloud Computing Environment. *International Journal of Computers and Applications*, *49*(8), 35–41. doi:10.5120/7649-0743

Vohra, D. (2016). Practical Hadoop Ecosystem. *Practical Hadoop Ecosystem*, 339–347. doi:10.1007/978-1-4842-2199-0

Yang, C., Huang, Q., Li, Z., Liu, K., & Hu, F. (2017). Big Data and cloud computing: Innovation opportunities and challenges. *International Journal of Digital Earth*, *10*(1), 13–53. doi:10.1080/17538947.2016.1239771

Yang, C., Yu, M., Hu, F., Jiang, Y., & Li, Y. (2017). Utilizing Cloud Computing to address big geospatial data challenges. *Computers, Environment and Urban Systems*, *61*, 120–128. doi:10.1016/j.compenvurbsys.2016.10.010

Yaqoob, I., Hashem, I. A. T., Gani, A., Mokhtar, S., Ahmed, E., Anuar, N. B., & Vasilakos, A. V. (2016). Big data: From beginning to future. *International Journal of Information Management*, *36*(6), 1231–1247. doi:10.1016/j.ijinfomgt.2016.07.009

Chapter 2

An Insight on the Class Imbalance Problem and Its Solutions in Big Data

Khyati Ahlawat
University School of Information, Communication and Technology, Guru Gobind Singh Indraprastha University, India

Anuradha Chug
iD https://orcid.org/0000-0002-3139-4490
University School of Information, Communication and Technology, Guru Gobind Singh Indraprastha University, India

Amit Prakash Singh
iD https://orcid.org/0000-0002-8675-6903
University School of Information, Communication and Technology, Guru Gobind Singh Indraprastha University, India

ABSTRACT

Expansion of data in the dimensions of volume, variety, or velocity is leading to big data. Learning from this big data is challenging and beyond capacity of conventional machine learning methods and techniques. Generally, big data getting generated from real-time scenarios is imbalance in nature with uneven distribution of classes. This imparts additional complexity in learning from big data since the class that is underrepresented is more influential and its correct classification becomes critical than that of overrepresented class. This chapter addresses the imbalance problem and its solutions in context of big data along with a detailed survey of work done in this area. Subsequently, it also presents an experimental view for solving imbalance classification problem and a comparative analysis between different methodologies afterwards.

DOI: 10.4018/978-1-7998-3444-1.ch002

INTRODUCTION

Large scale data, commonly known as Big data is the data that is having any of the several V's characteristics associated with it like Volume, Velocity, Variety, etc. These characteristics of big data makes it unsuitable for processing under traditional methodologies and tools. The challenges that such large scale data poses on conventional systems are to be addressed properly in order to extract knowledge from big data (Wu, et al., 2014). The contemporary approaches of machine learning and artificial intelligence are also applied to gain an insight on trends hidden in big data (Al-Jarrah, et al., 2015).

Generally, big data (Tsai, et al., 2015) that is generated from surveillance, application of sensors in any environment, etc. has a special property. The data of such an origin is produced on very large scale out of which very less data is of main concern for processing or prediction. Data mining is the process of extracting important information form data available ignoring the noise and redundant information (Han, Kamber, Pei, 2012). Extracting important information from such data becomes a critical task and hinder the process of mining. (Hu, et al., 2014) Moreover, such data has un-even distribution of class instances which characterize it as imbalanced big data and this problem is commonly known as imbalance classification problem or class imbalance problem. Data that belongs to above specified concept deals with bias in number of instances of classes involved (Galar, et al., 2012). One class which is of main concern from prediction point of view is generally present in very small amount of tuples or instances and is termed as minority class. Other one, which is of least concern is present in abundant and is termed as majority class. This problem also persists in multi class data where two or three classes are identified as minority classes and rest are majority classes that are found in abundance (Krawczyk, 2016).

The main challenge posed by imbalanced class problem is the biasing nature of machine learning algorithms. Generally, classifiers show a biasness towards majority class instances and minority class instances are ignored. Accuracy metric that shows the effectiveness of any classifier also fails in such a scenario because even if all majority class instances are classified correctly and no minority class instance is predicted correct, the classifier will still show a good accuracy number. However, the classifier was failed to classify important class instances correctly. To solve this problem and to make traditional classifiers work well on imbalanced data, certain techniques and different performance metrics are available.

This chapter gives an overview of class imbalance problem and its solutions along with related work done in this field. An experimental analysis and comparison is also presented in this chapter on available solutions for class imbalance problem in big data. This chapter will prove as a baseline study to work further in the area of big data analytics and class imbalance problem.

BACKGROUND

This section gives an overview about the problem that lies in the scope of this chapter and its probable solutions available. The section also incorporates a baseline study of some considerate work done in the field of problem domain including all types of solutions in the form of literature survey.

As briefly discussed in the introduction section, the problem of imbalance classification in any dataset exists where there is an occurrence of uneven class distribution. This problem can persist in binary classification as well as multi class classification. The importance to understand this problem lies in the fact that the class which is present in minority is of main concern. So, its correct classification becomes more important than classification of majority class instances. Solutions available to handle this problem lie in two categories:

1. Data Level Solutions
2. Algorithmic Solutions

Data Level solutions are also known as pre-processing techniques because they pre-process the dataset and make it balanced in nature so that conventional classifiers can be easily applied over them. These pre-processing techniques may include over sampling, under sampling or a combination of both. Over sampling approach improves the dataset by increasing the instances of minority class by replicating the similar samples or by re-constituting new samples from original ones. On the other hand, under sampling approach removes extra samples of majority class to make the dataset more balanced. A hybrid approach will incorporate both techniques in parallel manner so as to attain the benefit of both the approaches.

Algorithmic solutions do not cause any change in the dataset. Instead of this they change the conventional classifiers in such a way that their functioning address imbalanced occurrence of class instances. This can be done via cost sensitive approach, ensemble techniques or any other hybrid solution. Cost sensitive approach introduce a cost matrix or a weight matrix to the classifier such that every wrong classification of minority class sample incurs a high cost as compared to wrong classification of minority class sample. In this way, classifiers tend to decrease overall cost of the system thus making the solution feasible for imbalanced data. Ensemble techniques are known for grouping two or more classifiers in a pre-defined manner such that they overall improve the efficiency of model. These techniques may include bagging, boosting, stacking, etc. Apart from this, hybrid approaches based on different classifiers and other optimization techniques also proves to be useful in solving this problem.

In the scope of this chapter, a literature survey based on data level as well as algorithmic approaches is presented as Table 1.

Table 1. Literature Survey

S No	Dataset Used	Pre-processing Techniques used	Measurement Techniques	Hadoop Component Used	Classifiers Used	Reference No
1	7 datasets from UCI	None	Accuracy	Map Reduce	Fuzzy Random Forest	(Bechini, et al., 2016)
2	KDD, Poker, RLCP	None	AUC	Map Reduce	Chi-FRBCS-BigDataCS	(López, et al., 2015)
3	RLCP, KDD, PokerHand, Covertype, FARS, Census KDD	None	Accuracy, Run Time	Map Reduce	CHI-FRBCS	(Río, et al., 2015)
4	11 datasets from UCI	None	G Mean, AUC	Map Reduce	SVM	(Wang, Matwin, 2014)
5	PDB Repository CM Datasets	Oversampling, Feature Selection	TPR, TNR	Map Reduce, Mahout	Random Forest	(Triguero, et al., 2015)
6	Korean TrafficData	Oversampling	Accuracy	Map Reduce	Logistic Regression	(Park, Ha, 2014)
7	Poker Hand Dataset	Clustering based approach	Accuracy, AUC, Duration	Map Reduce	SVM, Decision Tree, k-NN	(Ahlawat, Chug, Singh, 2019)
8	Poker Hand Dataset	k-means	Accuracy, FN Rate, duration	Map Reduce	SVM	(Ahlawat, Chug, Singh, 2019)
9	6 datasets from UCI	Noise filteration	Accuracy, MCC, Recall, F-Measure	None	Cost sensitive SVM	(Wang, Yang, 2018)
10	KEEL datasets	k-means, Discretization approach	AUC	None	Fuzzy decision tree	(Sardari, Eftekhari, Afsari, 2017)
11	KEEL datasets	Feature vector selection	F-Measure, G-Mean	None	SVM	(Liu, Zio, 2019)
12	Real world credit datasets	Bagging	TP, TN Accuracy	None	SVM, Deep Belief Networks	(Yu, et al., 2018)

The above table describes some latest research work done in the field of imbalance classification both in terms of normal data and big data. The table is divided into two parts, one for data level solutions and other for algorithmic ones. S. No 1-4 specifies some purely algorithmic solutions while S. No 5-12 specifies a combination of data level and algorithmic solutions. As we can infer from this table that researchers have focussed more on data level solutions rather than algorithmic ones in the case of dealing with big data. Also, in data level solutions, oversampling and clustering approaches have been mostly used and in algorithmic solutions, SVM technique is used frequently. On the statistical parameters side, accuracy has been used but along with some other parameters that do not get affected by imbalance nature of dataset like AUC, G-Mean, F-Measure, etc.

In the next section, an experimental overview to demonstrate the impact of both types of solutions on the imbalance classification problem in case of large scale data is given.

EXPERIMENTAL OVERVIEW

In view of above described problem, this section consists of an experimental framework based on two possible solutions to the class imbalance problem on large scale data often termed as big data. This section will describe the datasets used in this experiment along with the machine learning classifiers used to test the impact of solutions available to solve the problem. This section also specifies the statistical parameters, other than accuracy that are used to assess the performance of the classifiers dealing with imbalanced big data.

As described in previous section, there are two types of solutions available for class imbalance problem, data level solutions and algorithmic solutions. The major aim of the experiment in this chapter is to understand and compare the impact of both types of techniques on the imbalance class problem in case of big data. The efficiency of one technique over another in big data scenario helps in gaining insights of both approaches thus improving their usage in building hybrid solutions to deal with the problem in big data.

In this experiment, two popular techniques, SMOTE from data level solutions and Cost Sensitive approach from algorithmic approaches have been used to study the impact of these solutions on class imbalance problem. SMOTE is a popular synthetic minority oversampling technique that deals with oversampling minority instances by synthetically generating them based on nearest neighbouring approach from existing samples of minority class. On the other hand, cost sensitive learning is based on imposing an extra cost to every misclassification of a minority class sample. While SMOTE balance the dataset first and then classifiers are applied on it, in later approach, cost sensitive version of classifiers is used directly on the imbalanced datasets. The two classifiers used in this experiment are SVM and k-Nearest Neighbour.

In the current experiment, the dataset that has been used is PokerHand Dataset, originally from UCI Repository consisting of over 1 million instances of multiple classes. The same has been redefined and made imbalanced by bifurcating it into

Table 2. Summary of Imbalanced Datasets

S No	Datasets	Class(maj;min)	#Majority	#Minority	IR	Skewness
1	Poker_0-2	(0;2)	51338	4914	10.44	2.93
2	Poker_0-3	(0;3)	51412	2121	24.23	4.73
3	Poker_0-4	(0;4)	51373	394	130.38	11.17
4	Poker_0-5	(0;5)	51389	186	276.28	15.10
5	Poker_0-6	(0;6)	51377	139	369.33	18.32
6	Poker_0-7	(0;7)	51370	23	2233.47	46.24
7	Poker_1-2	(1;2)	43333	4859	8.91	2.65
8	Poker_1-3	(1;3)	43314	2159	20.06	4.28
9	Poker_1-4	(1;4)	43307	400	108.26	10.37
10	Poker_1-5	(1;5)	43308	206	210.23	15.45
11	Poker_1-6	(1;6)	43312	143	302.88	16.33
12	Poker_1-7	(1;7)	43306	23	1882.86	43.37

majority and minority classes with the help of Apache Hive platform that works internally on the concept of Map-Reduce. Following table 2 gives a short description of datasets considered for study.

Above table 2 demonstrates all 12 imbalanced big datasets used for study. Moreover, every dataset is differently skewed from other, e.g. Dataset Poker_0-7 and Poker_1-7 are most skewed datasets and Poker_0-2 and Poker_1-2 are least imbalanced ones. This way, the study holds compliance over all range of imbalanced ratios.

To study the impact of solutions on imbalanced datasets, accuracy cannot be considered as best method to assess the performance of a classifier. This is due to the biasing nature of accuracy parameter towards only correct classification of any type of samples be it majority or minority. Since, in the current study, imbalanced datasets are taken into consideration, therefore, correct classification of minority samples holds much more value than correct classification of other class samples. To solve this purpose, a better version of accuracy which is termed as Balanced Accuracy is being used in this study. Balanced Accuracy is based upon correct classification of minority as well as majority samples in following manner:

$$Balanced\ Acuuracy = (TPR + TNR) / 2 \tag{1}$$

Where TPR and TNR are as follows:

$$TPR = (TP) / P \qquad\qquad (2)$$

$$TNR = (TN) / N \qquad\qquad (3)$$

Here, TPR is True Positive Rate which is the ratio of True Positive and Total Positive samples and TNR is True Negative Rate which is the ratio of True Negative and Total Negative Samples. This version of balanced accuracy shows an improved assessment for classifiers in imbalance classification scenario.

RESULTS AND ANALYSIS

This section analyse the performance of two classifiers for both types of solutions to deal with imbalanced big data sets. The big datasets are pre-processed using standard balancing algorithm SMOTE in first technique and then classifier SVM and k-NN are applied on them. And in second case, cost sensitive version of SVM and k-NN algorithms are applied without pre-processing datasets. Following table 3 describes the results in terms of balanced accuracy for both classifiers and both types of solutions.

As per above table, SMOTE+SVM and SMOTE+k-NN symbolizes data level solutions and CS-SVM and CS-k-NN are cost sensitive versions of SVM and k-NN respectively. It is clearly visible that data level solutions are providing better results than algorithmic approaches in 8 out of 12 datasets. Following are the comparison graphs for same.

As per graphs ploted, it is clearly visible that in most of the datasets, data level solutions are performing better than algorithmic level solutions. A probable reason for that is in case of big data or large scale data, pre-processing of data becomes a crucial phase in extracting important information from it. Since, data size is so large that it becomes cumbersome to treat complete data at once on large scale and apply classifiers on it. Also, in large scale data, all data that is generated is not of use for mining purpose. Therefore, it becomes more efficient to process data to eliminate redundancy and noise first and then classify it.

Table 3. Balanced Accuracy values for both solutions

S No	Dataset	SMOTE + SVM	SMOTE + k-NN	CS- SVM	CS-k-NN
1	Poker_0-2	0.63	**0.67**	0.62	0.49
2	Poker_0-3	0.7	**0.72**	0.66	0
3	Poker_0-4	**0.89**	0.67	0.88	0
4	Poker_0-5	**0.91**	0.85	**0.91**	0.53
5	Poker_0-6	0.68	0.58	**0.7**	0
6	Poker_0-7	0.66	0.38	**0.73**	0
7	Poker_1-2	0.56	**0.8**	0.52	0.49
8	Poker_1-3	**0.61**	0.59	0.59	0
9	Poker_1-4	**0.82**	0.67	0.8	0
10	Poker_1-5	0.91	0.538	**0.94**	0.59
11	Poker_1-6	0.64	0.57	**0.69**	0
12	Poker_1-7	**0.65**	0.46	0.56	0

Figure 1. Comparison of SMOTE SVM and CS-SVM

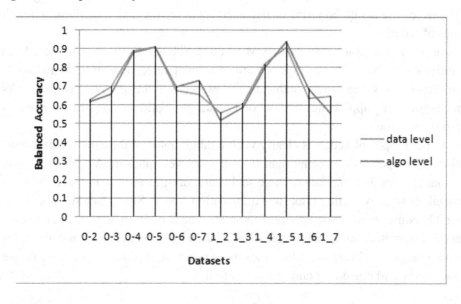

CONCLUSION AND FUTURE SCOPE

In this chapter, a thorough study on class imbalance problem and its solutions are discussed. A brief literature survey is also presented to know about recent work done in this field. Analysis on applicability and effectiveness on both types of solutions, data level and algorithmic level, for large scale data is also presented based on experiment performed on big data. It can be concluded that data level solutions are performing better than algorithmic solutions when it comes to large scale data. This indicates that performing analysis of big data using sampling approaches and its variants is more desirable in terms of performance of overall model is considered.

For future work, better advancements in both type of solutions can be done in order to gain scalability of existing solutions for large scale data. Moreover, optimization techniques along with machine learning classifiers can be applied to obtain an effective model.

Figure 2. Comparison of SMOTE k-NN and CS-k-NN

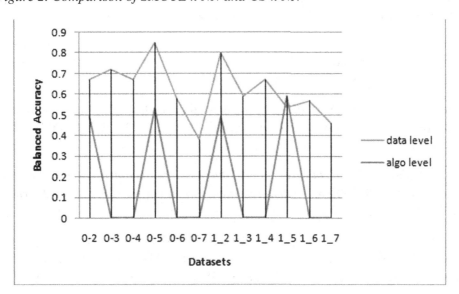

REFERENCES

Ahlawat, K., Chug, A., & Singh, A. P. (2019). Benchmarking framework for class imbalance problem using novel sampling approach for big data. *International Journal of System Assurance Engineering and Management. Springer, 10*(4), 824–835. doi:10.100713198-019-00817-6

Ahlawat, K., Chug, A., & Singh, A. P. (2019). Empirical Evaluation of Map Reduce Based Hybrid Approach for Problem of Imbalanced Classification in Big Data. *International Journal of Grid and High Performance Computing, 11*(3), 23–45. doi:10.4018/IJGHPC.2019070102

Al-Jarrah, O. Y., Yoo, P. D., Muhaidat, S., Karagiannidis, G. K., & Taha, K. (2015). Efficient Machine Learning for Big Data: A Review. *Big Data Research*, 2(3), 87–93. doi:10.1016/j.bdr.2015.04.001

Bechini, A., Matteis, A. D. D., Marcelloni, F., & Segatori, A. (2016). Spreading Fuzzy Random Forests with MapReduce. *International Conference on Systems, Man, and Cybernetics*, 2641-2646.

Galar, M., Fernandez, A., Barrenechea, E., Bustince, H., & Herrera, F. (2012). A Review on Ensembles for the Class Imbalance Problem: Bagging-, Boosting-, and Hybrid-Based Approaches. *IEEE Transactions on Systems, Man and Cybernetics. Part C, Applications and Reviews*, 42(4), 463–484. doi:10.1109/TSMCC.2011.2161285

Han, J., Kamber, M., & Pei, J. (2012). Classification: Basic Concepts. In Data Mining Concepts and Techniques (3rd ed., pp. 327-383). Waltham: MK.

Hu, H., Wen, Y., Chua, T., & Li, X. (2014). Toward Scalable Systems for Big Data Analytics: A Technology Tutorial. *IEEE Access: Practical Innovations, Open Solutions*, 2, 652–687. doi:10.1109/ACCESS.2014.2332453

Krawczyk, B. (2016). Learning from imbalanced data: Open challenges and future directions. *Progress in Artificial Intelligence*, 5(4), 221–232. doi:10.100713748-016-0094-0

Liu, J., & Zio, E. (2019). *Integration of feature vector selection and support vector machine for classification of imbalanced data. Applied soft Computing Journal*. doi:10.1016/j.asoc.2018.11.045

López, V., Río, S. D., Benítez, J. M., & Herrera, F. (2015). Cost-sensitive linguistic fuzzy rule based classification systems under the MapReduce framework for imbalanced big data. *Fuzzy Sets and Systems*, 258, 5–38. doi:10.1016/j.fss.2014.01.015

Park, S.-H., & Ha, Y.-G. (2014). Large Imbalance Data Classification Based on MapReduce for Traffic Accident Prediction. *Eighth International Conference on Innovative Mobile and Internet Services in Ubiquitous Computing*, 45-49. 10.1109/IMIS.2014.6

Río, S. D., López, V., Benítez, J. M., & Herrera, F. (2015). *A MapReduce Approach to Address Big Data Classification Problems Based on the Fusion of Linguistic Fuzzy Rules. International Journal of Computational Intelligence Systems*. doi:10.1080/18756891.2015.1017377

Sardari, S., Eftekhari, M., & Afsari, F. (2017). *Hesitant fuzzy decision tree approach for highly imbalanced data classification. In Applied Soft Computing.* Springer. doi:10.1016/j.asoc.2017.08.052

Triguero, I., Río, S. D., López, V., Bacardit, J., Benítez, J. M., & Herrera, F. (2015). ROSEFW-RF: The winner algorithm for the ECBDL'14 big data competition: An extremely imbalanced big data bioinformatics problem. *Knowledge-Based Systems, 87*, 69–79. doi:10.1016/j.knosys.2015.05.027

Tsai, C. W., Lai, C. F., Chao, H. C., & Vasilakos, A. V. (2015). *Big data analytics: a survey. Journal of Big Data.* doi:10.118640537-015-0030-3

Wang, X., & Matwin, S. (2014). A Distributed Instance-weighted SVM Algorithm on Large-scale Imbalanced Datasets. *International Conference on Big Data*, 45-51. 10.1109/BigData.2014.7004467

Wang, Y., & Yang, L. (2018). *A robust loss function for classification with imbalance datasets. Neurocomputing.* doi:10.1016/j.neucom.2018.11.024

Wu, X., Zhu, X., Wu, G. Q., & Ding, W. (2014). Data Mining with Big Data. *IEEE Transactions on Knowledge and Data Engineering, 26*(1), 97–107. doi:10.1109/TKDE.2013.109

Yu, L., Zhou, R., Tang, L., & Chen, R. (2018). *A DBN-based resampling SVM ensemble learning paradigm for credit classification with imbalanced data. Applied Soft Computing.* doi:10.1016/j.asoc.2018.04.049

Chapter 3
Large–Scale Data Streaming in Fog Computing and Its Applications

Oshin Sharma
PES University, Bangalore, India

Anusha S.
School of Engineering and Technology, Jain University, Bangalore, India

ABSTRACT

The emerging trends in fog computing have increased the interests and focus in both industry and academia. Fog computing extends cloud computing facilities like the storage, networking, and computation towards the edge of networks wherein it offloads the cloud data centres and reduces the latency of providing services to the users. This paradigm is like cloud in terms of data, storage, application, and computation services, except with a fundamental difference: it is decentralized. Furthermore, these fog systems can process huge amounts of data locally and can be installed on hardware of different types. These characteristics make fog suitable for time- and location-based applications like internet of things (IoT) devices which can process large amounts of data. In this chapter, the authors present fog data streaming, its architecture, and various applications.

DOI: 10.4018/978-1-7998-3444-1.ch003

INTRODUCTION

Fog computing is a distributed architecture where the data is processed and stored in a place between the data source and the cloud. This reduces the overhead in data communication, and thus improves the Cloud computing performance by minimizing the need to process large amount of data and to store them.

This paradigm of fog computing has become a necessity as there is a stupendous increase in the IoT devices, an increased generation of data with respect to speed and volume. Functionality of IoT device is often data centric where the devices need infrastructure to process the data. However, those processes that need immediate action or decisions must have a high functionality which could lead to issues relating to reliability issues and scalability problems. This happens while using a traditional client-server architecture, wherein the data is requested by the client and is processed by the server. In a traditional client server architecture, a server becomes overloaded with data handling from many IoT devices. Fog computing aims to provide a distributed solution which is not centralized but also scalable, by creating a new hierarchically dispersed and a local platform located between the end-user devices and the Cloud system.

This platform is capable to filter, aggregate, process, analyse and transmit the data, which reduces the time and interaction between the devices. Cloud computing provides many benefits such as highly availability and efficient computing resources. But they are not suitable for abeyance, portable wears and for applications for which position sensitive devices, such as IoT, Smart Grids, Wearable device computing, Software-Defined-Networks and Connected Vehicles. Latency depends on the Internet speed, resource contention of guest virtual machines (VM) and this could increase with distance. Also, these applications will generate large amount of varying data in a high speed and the time by which this large data is analysed by the cloud, the time sensitive IOT devices may not be able to do a reactive action because of latency for example, the IoT devices in medical equipment where the delay of action on the data would be life-critical. To avoid this, Fog was developed which brings the cloud closer to the user end devices. Thus, It would be helpful for many unsolved challenges such as processing of huge amount of data, trafðc congestion, and communication expenses.

Even though this amalgamation of cloud and IOT devices seems to be advantageous, cloud is not able to address many issues in IOT. It is due to the centralization of resources which results in a huge separation of the cloud and devices at user end which increases the average network latency and jitter. Because of this delay, users are not able to access accurate data from the delay-sensitive applications like smart trafðc lights. This gave to the rise of a new paradigm coined as "Fog Computing" by Cisco which has a prime objective is to support location aware, delay sensitive and mobility supported applications (Buyya et al. 2016). Fog computing provides numerous cloud services to the network edge. It brings out the advantage for both edge and cloud resources, as shown in Figure 1. This technology processes the IoT data locally by using edge/fog devices which are near the users to carry considerable storage, control, communication, management and configuration. This approach has an advantage of being near to the edge devices to the sensors and to provide on-demand scalability of resources in cloud (Buyya et al. 2016).

EXISTING LITERATURE

There are many research articles on Fog computing which are published and having applications like smart grid, healthcare, smart city and industrial automation (Lin et al. 2018). The model for fog computing was developed by Sarkar and Misra (Sarkar et al. 2016). wherein a relative performance of cloud computing is analysed with respect to the amount of energy used and latency in service. In the next paper by (Varghese et al. 2017) the viability of Fog computing is analysed and a comparison was done with cloud where the analysis showed that the Fog reduces the average time for response by 20% for each user and the data traffic has got reduced by 90% in the place linking cloud and the edge devices.

Figure 1. Fog computing: Distributed data processing

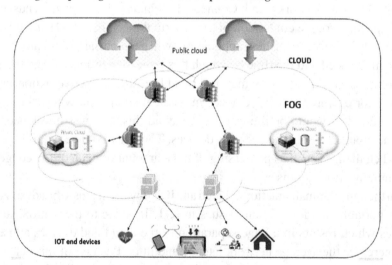

The analysis of suitability of fog is done by (Sarkar et al. 2016) by classifying the carbon di-oxide emissions, consumption of power, delay in service, cost and performance analysis for a domain with many end-devices which needs services with lesser response time. The result was that the delay was reduced by 50% while using Fog when compared with using cloud.

(Dantu et al. 2017) has mentioned the adaptable and reliable use of fog nodes on Android phones and has analysed the probability of smart phones using the fog environment. Depending on this feasibility, (Simmhan et al. 2017) have researched the applications of fog paradigm in drones, urban surveillance and power grid and have made a comparison of various features of cloud, edge and fog on physical access of resources, its characteristics and the support for mobility.

(Perera et al. 2017) has done a survey on the use cases in applications in smart cities and has found the common features of Fog in identifying the IOT objects dynamically, manging those devices and their configurations.

(Roman et al. 2018) has identified the security threats in network infrastructure, virtualization infrastructure, edge data centre and end user devices. Also, many security challenges have been reviewed and the mechanisms to resolve these challenges in the existing system. A comprehensive analysis has been made on fog paradigm, its privacy and security issues are discussed: (i) cloud - fog computing evolution; (ii) Fog based IoT applications categorized based on various role of fog nodes; (iii) security and privacy issues of fog computing, the existing solutions and mechanisms; The security threats have been analysed, its challenges and the mechanisms is presented to explore the potential synergies and the ways of research of all the edge paradigms, like, mobile edge computing, fog computing and mobile cloud computing. (Roman et al. 2018)

FOG DATA STREAMING ARCHITECTURE

This new paradigm is an augmentation for the existing technology i.e. cloud that provides computation, and network services to the end-user devices and the traditional cloud servers. Fog is not a substitution of the cloud technology but a complement of it, by providing a remote data storage and processing.

The fog enhances the cloud infrastructure to the IoT devices' proximity, also called as fog nodes. The deployment of fog nodes is heterogeneous at the edge of network with the proximity to the end-devices. These fog nodes can be positioned anywhere in a network connection: on top of a power pole, on a factory floor, across a railway tracks and many more places. A fog node can be any device with storage, computation and network connectivity. Few examples of fog nodes can be routers, embedded servers, switches, industrial controllers and video surveillance cameras.

According to the estimates of International Data Corporation, the amount of data which are analysed by the devices close to IoT devices is nearing 40 percent. The reason is that analysing IoT data near to the place where it is generated reduces latency. It also discharges gigabytes of traffic from core network and while keeping the critical data inside the network.

Examples of Fog Applications include door locking mechanism, applying brakes on a train, changing equipment settings, video camera zooming, automated valve opening based on the pressure value readings, bar chart creation based on dynamic values and so on. The possibilities are unlimited. Fog applications are rapidly finding its applications in manufacturing, mining, oil and gas, utilities, transportation, and public sector.

Fog systems usually use a sense-process-activate and a stream-process programming model. Sensors outflow this data to IoT networks and applications running on various fog devices, process that information and are translated into actions driving the actuators.

The Figure 2 represents a Fog architecture where the lower layer has the end devices— like sensors to collect the data and actuators through which a reactive response can be done so that application functionality can be enhanced. These devices make use of the next above layer - the network, for communication with the edge devices like gateways. Then it is communicated with the cloud services. The management layer has the infrastructure and does enforces QoS analysis. Lastly, the applications use fog-computing programming model to provide services to users (Buyya et al. 2016).

Fog Computing can be considered in the situations if: ● the data is generated at an extreme edge: railways. vehicles, factory floors, ships, roadways and so on. ● There are millions of devices generating data which are spread across a large geographical area. ● There is a necessary to analyse data and act on them in less than a second.

How Does Fog Work? At the network edge, the developers either write or port IoT applications for fog nodes. Nodes closer to the network edge get the data from IoT devices. Then the fog IoT application directs these data to a place for analysis as in Table 1. The following observations can be made:

A.   The critical data is analysed on a fog node that is nearer to the devices that is generating the data.
B.   The data which can wait for seconds to minutes for response is passed through a collecting node to be analysed and to act.
C.   Those data which are less critical are sent directly to the cloud for big data analytics and for storing them for a long term.

Figure 2. Fog Data Streaming Architecture

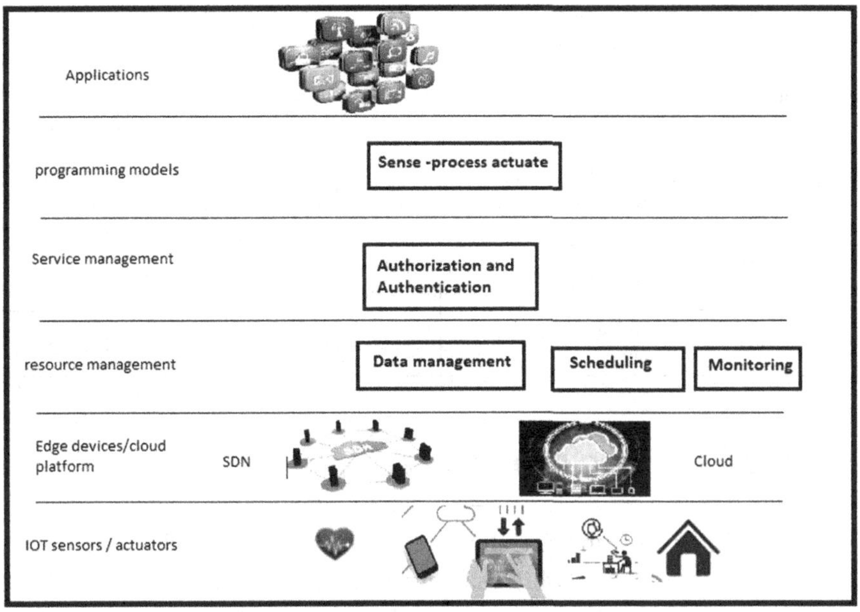

Working inside a Fog/Cloud fog node:

Receive feeds from various IoT things in real time by using any protocol ● Run applications with millisecond response time, which are IoT-enabled for analysis and real-time control ● Providing a temporary storage for about 1 to 2 hours ● Periodic summaries of data are sent to the cloud.

Working at the cloud:

Receive and aggregate the data collections from different fog nodes. ● Analyse data from various IoT devices and from other sources for gaining a business insight. ● Based on these, the cloud can send new rules for that application to the fog nodes

Table 1. Fog computing: An extension of Cloud

	Fog Nodes in IoT Device proximity	Fog Collector Nodes	Cloud platform
Time to respond	Milli-second to less than a second	Seconds to minutes	Minutes, days, weeks
Examples	M2M communication Haptics2, including telemedicine and training	Visualization analytics	Big data applications Graphical displays
Duration of data storage	Temporary	Short duration: Hours or days, or few weeks	Months or years
Range of coverage	Local storage (within a city)	Larger coverage	World-wide coverage

CHALLENGES IN FOG DATA STREAMING

Fog computing follows distributed architecture of computational nodes which involves several challenges such as: network challenges, structural challenges, Management challenges, computing challenges, security challenges and many others. Here, we have discussed few among them:

Architectural challenges: Distributed architecture of fog computing makes it more complex in terms of redundancy and network connectivity. As, the same data needs to be replicated among the network in various location or edge devices. Moreover, there is a need of network middleware to maintain the pool of resources among edge devices and to allocate the resources among computational workloads. The selection of appropriate nodes based on their configuration and deployment position is also tedious task. The heterogenous nature of devices provides diversity in computing system which is a main challenge for any fog application.

Computational challenges: Fog computing goes through several computing challenges such as: (A) In fog environment, several fog edge or end devices communicates with different cloud servers. Sometimes, they perform certain computations and respond to the users within a specific period. However, some computations need to be sending to cloud servers and they takes less computational cost for execution, but more time as compared to edge devices. Thus, to offload the computations to cloud servers instead of edge devices and to find the trade-off between computational cost and response time is a challenging task in fog computing while designing any application. (B) Deployment of different application scenario needs different configuration of resources but, edge devices my not always provides all the resources for the deployment. Thus, a need of common pool of resources has generated to distribute the resources among other devices. Design of common pool using different technologies is also very challenging task in fog environment. (c) Distributed architecture of fog computing provides inconsistencies in the computations. Thus, while developing fog computing applications these inconsistencies should be confirmable by application developers.

Management issues: The design of an appropriate management of architecture to handle user's services is one of the main challenges. As, in fog computing these services are separated into different micro level services and they are forwarded to cloud & edge device (Ghosh S. K et al. 2018). Thus, there is a need of service orchestration system to provide the services to users using less response time. In fog computing environment, different fog and cloud nodes are available for the hosting of several services. SOA -Service oriented architecture is used to divide the user's problems in to micro level services which is a challenging task in itself (Georgantas N et al. 2011). SOA does it with three main components: Producer, Consumer, registry and beneficial for health-related applications. Several micro services such as: temperature, blood pressure, heart beat, cholesterol monitoring and many others can be done on edge devices and instead of offloading all these sensor data to cloud servers only the output of micro services are offloaded into cloud. Thus, it will reduce the processing overhead, amount of data transfer in cloud and response time simultaneously.

APPLICATIONS OF LARGE-SCALE DATA STREAMING IN FOG ENVIRONMENT

Fog computing overcomes the problems of latency, bandwidth, reliability and can accomplish the requirements of different application areas such as: Smart transportation, Smart cities, Health care, computer vision and many more. This study will depict the details discussion on following two different applications areas along with their limitations.

1. **Smart Cities:** the objective of fog computing is to shift the computations to the edge of network to make the processing faster. Instead of shifting complete application logic to cloud server, this concept of fog computing is very much suitable for smart cities by dealing with the problem of network congestion. Smart cities deal with various smart services such as: smart vehicles, smart traffic lights, smart roads, smart billboards, smart street lights, smart waste management, smart farming and many more. Commencing with all these smart services, researchers have provided various frameworks using fog computing with low cost of storage and communication. For example, smart waste management is a combination of several processes such as monitoring

of waste materials, waste collection, processing of data and then concerned transportation. Thus, in this scenario fog computing is helpful due to its feature of connecting the computations to the edge of network rather than uploading it to cloud server. Similarly, for vehicle tracking fog computing is using multi-target tracking systems rather than single tracking systems. Another example related to smart cities is smart farming, for which fog computing has provided low cost communication by removing unnecessary sensing of data before sending it to edge devices (Peddemors A et al. May 2009). Smart cities are the inclusion of smart agriculture system, smart transportation system, smart road safety, smart energy management system and many others.

(a) *Smart Agriculture:* With the adoption of new era of technology i.e. Internet of Things (IoT), the communication of things to things has penetrated everywhere. Smart farming is also one its example and it has become more technology driven these days. Moreover, with the help of smart gadgets farmers are capable to predict and control the process of growing crops in an efficient way. Tons of data is collected from different sensors such as temperature sensor (RTD- Resistance Temperature Detector) and Thermocouples, Soil moisture sensor (it will work will the smart irrigation system which will automatically turn on the system whenever there is a need of water) and forwarded to fog nodes for further processing. Phenonet and openIoT (Hamida A. B et al. 2011) are two real projects based on smart agriculture. Researchers of Phenonet Project tested a network of smart sensors to monitor the climatic conditions as well as growths of plants. They used different techniques and sensing devices such as: sensor stations in the fields to monitor plants, air balloons to sense the ground area from the sky, phenomobiles (vehicles) to capture all the related data of growing plants. Thus, in their scenario fog computing plays an important role as phenomobiles and air balloons are acting as a gateway device and collecting all the necessary data to perform the data aggregation techniques. Later, all the processed data is forwarded to cloud platform which will provide sensing as a service with the help of Bio scientists, Agriculture Scientists, Microbiologist and many others

(b) *Smart Transportation*: Smart transportation system is an application of Vehicular Ad-hoc Networks (VANETs) which uses the concept of fog computing these days. In the era of cloud computing, Vehicular networks-maintained traffic efficiency, safety trends and public convenience (Wang D et al. 2018). Moreover, smart vehicles need to control the speed depending upon real time infrastructure of roads, people and traffic on road. Cloud computing is not always a good solution for such application whereas, fog computing plays a significant role due to its local decision-making abilities, real time load balancing and geo-distribution. But then again, the use of fog computing for VANET is a challenging task due to latency sensitive and high mobility of applications such as dynamic nature of smart vehicles. Recently, the concept of vehicular Fog Computing (VFC) presented in (Chen S et al. 2016). made the use of near-use edge devices to provide better utilization of communication and computation resources. It also used the resources of both parked and moving vehicles.

Figure 3. Real time Road safety Scenario

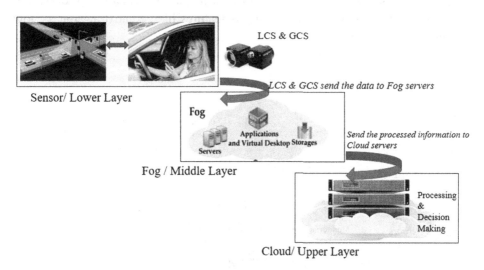

(c) ***Road Safety:*** It comes under intelligent transportation system and proposed by S. Roy et.al to sense the driving rules follows by drivers in day to day life. This system works on three different layers: upper, middle and lower layer. Lower layer will make the use of camera sensors to check out the vehicle number and detect the location of vehicles using the handheld devices used by drivers while driving. All this information would be collected and forwarded to fog servers. Later, fog servers in middle layer will process the data and confirms that whether vehicle is disobeying the traffic rules or not. If it is, fog server will send the vehicle information (i.e. identifier number) to the cloud server to take further actions. Lastly, the upper layer takes the necessary action according to traffic rules. Figure 3 demonstrates the road safety scenario using fog computing.

2. **Health Care:** This industry is facing many challenges either due to aging population or chronic diseases. Moreover, many countries are also facing shortage of staff nurse in their hospitals to provide high quality care to patients. Consequently, this industry has adopted the advancement of IoT (Internet of Things) to provide a remote tele care for patients by increasing the efficiency and quality of health care by reducing its cost. This paradigm is very useful for patient's early diagnosis, current and long-term fitness monitoring. To capture the current location and status of patients and provide the more accurate picture of patient using different sensors. Besides this, it has few limitations such as delay during emergency conditions, complex architecture, latency and response time. Fog computing has played an important role to overcome all these limitations due to its various features like: context awareness, low latency, localized nature.

Figure 4. Real time Health-care scenario

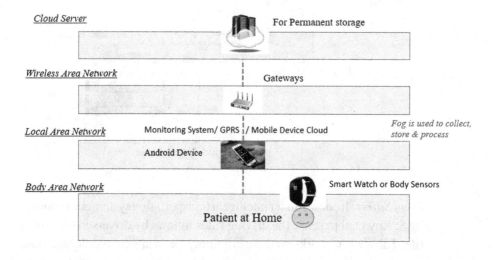

One major challenge in healthcare informatics is sensor-to -cloud data communication which is not feasible in some cases. Hospitals administration do not allow to store patient's data outside the hospital because of patient's safety and data centre's failure. Thus, fog computing is a solution and provide distributed architecture to healthcare informatics which means all the application specific logic resides very close to them in various infrastructural components such as: routers, gateways, actuators and access points. Figure 4 shows the deployment scenario for Health-care applications which is involving different users, devices and connectivity.

But this scenario also differs on different situation like: home Deployment scenario, hospital deployment scenario, Hospital's Transport deployment scenario.

Home treatment: During this scenario patient's internet access would be used to provide connectivity along with android phones of user. These android devices will act as a hub between cloud and sensor devices (Palma A. D et al. 2017). and collect data from several sensing nodes and process it before sending it to permanent storage. The objective of adding fog computing in LAN level is to increase the battery life of body sensors, reduce network traffic and latency. For example, in (Debabrata S et al. 2015) have depicted the home deployment scenario to generate the alarm about fire and gas leakage.

Hospitals Deployment Scenario: It includes smart wearable sensors like t-shirts, arm-band, smart-belt and many more attached with some sensors to monitor patient's location within hospital and to monitor his/her physiological data. Two important nodes play an important role here: Wireless Transmission Board (WTB) and Data Acquisition and processing Board (DAPB). DAPB collects the data from sensor, process it and send it to WTB which will further combine all the data and forwarded it to monitoring systems located at LAN layer. These monitoring systems will identify the location of patient's and his/her problem for which alarm has raised. Inside hospitals the system of deployment is complex, all the devices are maintained by hospital administration and as, they are proprietary only professionals can use them.

Hospital's Transport Deployment Scenario: It is a complex deployment scenario used in remote healthcare. It deals with the collection of data from patient wearing wearable sensors during emergency and how to share this data with several on-site devices (either in hospital or in ambulance). Thus, the complexity lies during the distribution of data among different fog nodes.

RESEARCH ISSUES & FUTURE DIRECTIONS

Fog computing paradigms provides major challenges for researchers and practitioners.

Computational offloading: application and computational offloading is the backbone of cloud computing by transferring heavy computational tasks to cloud servers. Although the cloud servers have infinite computational capabilities, but this centralized model causes more delays on service response and moreover, it is not energy efficient. Thus, new extension of this model i.e. fog computing extends the computing resources to network edge (Hamida A. B et al. 2011) so that fog nodes can execute the computations for cloud servers. By doing this, service response can be reduced, and cloud servers can remain free from heavy computational tasks. Although, this offloading process is not always efficient with respect to delay, bandwidth and energy consumption and requires a lot of exercise to predict the parameters that affects the performance of computational offloading (Georgantas N et al. 2011).

Resource Management: efficient resource allocation is a big research issue in fog computing because it does not have enough storage and computing resources. Already, so many models exist in literature that deals with efficient management of resources (Ghosh S. K et al. 2018). Fog nodes present inside this computing system must be very quick and flexible to respond various issues like resource shortages or transient failures. The failure of these fog nodes affects the whole system and resources would not be available. Thus, we need to manage those resources so that it ensures the availability of resources by avoiding the downtime.

Energy Consumption: fog computing comprises with large number of fog nodes and thus the computations are really distributed in this environment and makes it less energy efficient than cloud environment. Hence, the minimization of energy consumption is very important challenge in fog computing. Existing literature depicts that fog computing can provide slighter increase in energy consumption by significantly cut down the communication latency. However, there are many ways to improve the energy efficiency with in sensor devices by using fog computing. One of them is to offload the energy intensive computations from battery driven nodes. Second is the use of Nano datacentres instead of cloud data centres decreases the energy consumption in the network.

Security: in general, fog computing provides more secure architecture than cloud computing (Hamida A. B et al. 2011) because data is locally stored in fog nodes and makes it difficult for hackers to access user's data. Even though hackers may attack to interrupt the fog computing architecture in several ways such as: forgery, tampering, spam, jamming, Denial-of-services, Collusion and many more. Along with this, privacy of data is also very important research issue and includes four different aspects: data privacy, identity privacy, location privacy and usage privacy. As, because of insufficient security protections IoT devices are vulnerable to be hacked or stolen and acting like weapons for hackers.

CONCLUSION

Fog computing is an emerging paradigm which extends the storage, networking, and computing facilities of cloud computing towards the edge of the networks thereby offloading the cloud data centres and minimizing the service latency to the end users. There are several IoT applications, and cloud environment alone cannot provide real time responses for the location aware real time applications. Thus, we need wireless devices, several nodes and their widespread geographical distribution. We need computation and storage near to the end devices to make these applications more efficient. Therefore, the concept of fog computing & its benefits we have discussed in this survey. In this paper we have depicted the evolution of fog computing to cloud computing and its architecture. We have provided the details of fog computing architecture and its benefits for two different application areas such as: smart cities and healthcare. Fog computing provides several issues for future research directions and security, resource management are two among them which needs to be resolved for the efficiency of fog environment.

REFERENCES

Aazam, M., & Huh, E.-N. (2015). Dynamic resource provisioning through Fog micro datacenter. In *Pervasive Computing and Communication Workshops (PerCom Workshops), 2015 IEEE International Conference on*. IEEE.

Commonwealth Scientific and Industrial Research Organisation (CSIRO), Australia. (2011). *Phenonet: Distributed Sensor Network for Phenomics supported by High Resolution Plant Phenomics Centre*. CSIRO ICT Centre, and CSIRO Sensor and Sensor Networks TCP.

Dantu, K., Ko, S. Y., & Ziarek, L. (2017, April). RAINA: Reliability and adaptability in android for fog computing. *IEEE Communications Magazine*, *55*(4), 41–45. doi:10.1109/MCOM.2017.1600901

Dastjerdi & Buyya (Ed.). (2016). *Fog Computing: Helping the Internet of Things Realize its Potential*. IEEE Computer Society.

Fog Computing and the Internet of Things: Extend the Cloud to Where the Things Are. (2015). Cisco White Paper.

Hou, X., Li, Y., Chen, M., Wu, D., Jin, D., & Chen, S. (2016, June). Vehicular fog computing: A viewpoint of vehicles as the infrastructures. *IEEE Transaction.*, *65*(6), 3860–3873. doi:10.1109/TVT.2016.2532863

Issarny, V., Georgantas, N., Hachem, S., Zarras, A., Vassiliadist, P., Autili, M., Gerosa, M. A., & Hamida, A. B. (2011). Service-oriented middleware for the future internet: State of the art and research directions. *Springer Journal of Internet Services and Applications*, *2*(1), 23–45. doi:10.100713174-011-0021-3

Jalali, F., Hinton, K., Ayre, R., Alpcan, T., & Tucker, R. S. (2016, May). Fog computing may help to save energy in cloud computing. *IEEE Journal on Selected Areas in Communications*, *34*(5), 1728–1739. doi:10.1109/JSAC.2016.2545559

Kraemer, F. A., Braten, A. E., Tamkittikhun, N., & Palma, A. D. (2017). Fog Computing in Healthcare- A Review and Discussion. *IEEE Access: Practical Innovations, Open Solutions*, 5, 9206–9222. doi:10.1109/ACCESS.2017.2704100

Mukherjee, M., Lie, S., & Wang, D. (2018). Survey of Fog Computing: Fundamental, Network Applications and Research Challenges. *IEEE Communication, Survey & Tutorials.*

Nath, Gupta, Chakraborty, & Ghosh. (2018). *A Survey of Fog Computing and Communication: Current Researches and Future Directions, Networking and Internet Architecture*. Academic Press.

Ni, J., & Lin, X. (2018). Securing Fog Computing for Internet of Things Applications: Challenges and Solutions. *IEEE Communications Surveys and Tutorials*, 20(1), 601–628. doi:10.1109/COMST.2017.2762345

Ni, J., Zhang, K., Lin, X., & Shen, X. (2018). Securing Fog Computing for Internet of Things Applications: Challenges and Solutions. *IEEE Communications Surveys and Tutorials*, 20(1), 601–628. doi:10.1109/COMST.2017.2762345

OpenIoT Consortium. (2012). *Open Source Solution for the Internet of Things into the Cloud*. Author.

Perera, C., Zaslavsky, A., Christen, P., & Georgakopoulos, D. (2017, April). Sensing as a service model for smart cities supported by Internet of things. *Transactions on Emerging Telecommunications Technologies*, 25(1), 81–93. doi:10.1002/ett.2704

Roman, R., Lopez, J., & Manbo, M. (2018, January). Mobile edge computing, Fog et al.: A survey and analysis of security threats and challenges. *Future Generation Computer Systems*, 78, 680–698. doi:10.1016/j.future.2016.11.009

Sandeep, R., Rajesh, B., & Debabrata, S. (2015). A Fog Based DSS Model for Driving Rule Violation Monitoring Framework on Internet of Things. *International Journal of Advance Science & Technology*, 82, 23–32. doi:10.14257/ijast.2015.82.03

Sarkar, S., Chatterjee, S., & Misra, S. (2018, January). Assessment of the suitability of fog computing in the context of Internet of Things. *IEEE Trans. Cloud Comput.*, 6(1), 46–59. doi:10.1109/TCC.2015.2485206

Sarkar, S., & Misra, S. (2016). Theoretical modelling of fog computing: A green computing paradigm to support IoT applications. *IET Netw.*, 5(2), 23–29. doi:10.1049/iet-net.2015.0034

Sarkar, S., & Misra, S. (2016). Theoretical modelling of fog computing: A green computing paradigm to support IoT applications. *IET Netw.*, *5*(2), 23–29. doi:10.1049/iet-net.2015.0034

Teixeira, Hachem, Issarny, & Georgantas. (2011). Service oriented middleware for the internet of things: a perspective. In *Proceedings of the 2011 Springer European Conference on a Service- Based Internet.* Springer.

Varghese, B., Wang, N., Nikolopoulos, D. S., & Buyya, R. (2017). *Feasibility of fog computing.* Available: https://arxiv.org/pdf/1701.05451.pdf

Varshney, P., & Simmhan, Y. (2017). *Demystifying fog computing: Characterizing architectures, applications and abstractions.* Available: https://arxiv.org/pdf/1702.06331.pdf

Wac, Bargh, Beijnum, Bults, Pawar, & Peddemors. (2009). Power- and delay-awareness of health telemonitoring services: The mobihealth system case study. *IEEE J. Sel. Areas Commun.*, *27*(4), 525-536.

Chapter 4
Trust and Reliability Management in Large-Scale Cloud Computing Environments

Punit Gupta
iD https://orcid.org/0000-0001-7606-3014
Manipal University Jaipur, India

ABSTRACT

Trust is a firm belief over a person or a thing in distributed environment based on its feedback on review based on its performance by others. Similarly, in cloud, trust models play an important role in solving various open challenges in cloud environment. This chapter showcases all such issues that can be solved by trust management techniques. This work discourses various trust management models and its categorization. The work discourses existing work using trust models from the field of grid computing, cloud computing, and web services because all these domains are sub child of each other. The work provides an abstract view over all trust models and find the suitable one for cloud and its future prospects.

INTRODUCTION

This chapter discourses the various trust models for performance improvement in the cloud environment. Cloud is the best example of a distributed system where different vendors/services provide collaboration to provide services to the client. The service providers may be located at different geographical locations, which

DOI: 10.4018/978-1-7998-3444-1.ch004

also mean that all the service providers do not provide the same quality of service to users in terms of computing and security. In such scenarios where the user pays for the services provided the controller has to select the service provider based on the requirement and cost that the user has been charged for. Trust models resolve the problem of judging any service provider by its past performance and help in selecting the correct service provider for the client to complete the task within the SLA (Service Level Agreement) between user and service provider. The trust model ensures that all the requests are completed and the user gets the best quality of service. Trust means a firm belief, confidence, and reliance in something that can deliver an expected behavior with high reliability. This belief allows you to rely on something in the future for more tasks (Khan, 2010; Gambetta, 2000; Perez,2009; Bret, 2009). Cloud computing supports various types of models like public, private, and hybrid models. A public and hybrid model public and hybrid model has to face the problem of trust. As given in figure 1 we have assumed that private cloud stores important and sensitive data in soft Com but the other public cloud provides the capability to compute and process the data. Now the issue of trust becomes a problem because all the service providers are at different locations like 1) Boston server which provides a temporary storage 2) China server is providing processing service 3) Rome server provides filers and other processing. The issue is that the secured data will be stored on servers with low reliability and which cannot be trusted, in this case, trust model solves the problem by evaluating the servers and provides you the reliability of the server which helps to decide where to process the data and temporarily saved. Private cloud does not deal with such issues because all the servers are owned by single service providers may be at different locations or cities.

Trust model in cloud majorly deals with two issues:

1. Security Challenges.
   a. Control of Data
   b. Control of process
   c. Security profile
2. Scheduling and load balancing.
   a. Certification
   b. capabilities

Figure 2 shows various issues that are addressed by trust models in cloud computing some of them are listed above.

Figure 1. cloud computing- sample example (Khan, 2010)

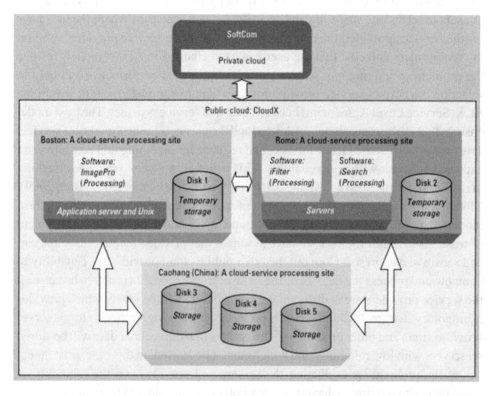

Figure 2. Issues addressed by trust models

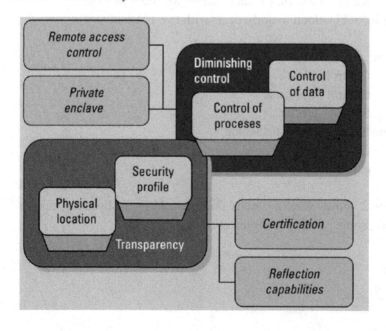

Security Challenges

Cloud being a distributed environment and collaborative framework where many service providers come together to serve the client, which raises security challenges with each of the service providers. To manage these security challenges cloud controller and trust model play an important role. Some of the security challenges are as follows:

- Outsourcing Data and Applications

If we process our private data on the cloud the first security breach is while transferring the data and second issue is how reliable is the cloud datacenter application which is used for processing the data since the data is residing at a remote location and with unknown service provider no one can ensure the security of the data.

Extensibility and Shared Responsibility

It is the shared responsibility of both cloud controller and service providers to ensure the data integrity and security, which refines the reliability of the system because cloud controller is the face to the client where the data is never processed by controller it is handled by third-party vendor which becomes a share reliability of with service provider to ensure security.

- Service-Level Agreements

This is one of the most important components of cloud computing, where the cloud is not meant for simply storage of data cloud, is designed to process the data in an efficient manner on remotely located resources on a pay-per-use manner. So the cloud ensures the client with service level agreement about the minimum and maximum service time, waiting time and many more such processing parameters before taking the task for execution. So it becomes the task for the cloud controller to assign the task to a VM/ resources which can complete the task without violating the SLA even the server is overloaded. In such cases the insure the reliability of a server under average load and overloaded condition. The trust model is considered as the most effective mechanism to ensure the SLA.

- Authentication and Identity Management

A most obvious part of the working in a distributed environment is to identify an agent/service provider remotely and assuming that the system is the correct system.

In such cases, you use various security mechanisms to resolve the issue but in the real-world rather than completely relying on security mechanisms one should also take into consideration the past of the system which can only be evaluated using trust mechanism.

- Privacy and Data Protection

As discoursed in figure 1 when we transfer data over a channel to cloud or datacenter data protection is an issue that has been reported in many literatures and case studies reporting leakage and privacy violation while transfer or as storage level.

The trust model proposed in various literature is used to resolve the issues for better SLA, access control, computing or scheduling lever, data protection and load balancing algorithms. Next section discourses about the methods to evaluate trust and various performance parameters used to evaluate trust for better performance at last section 4 discourses various existing works from the field of trust.

Role of Trust in Multilayered Cloud

The multi-layered cloud refers to cloud layered architecture where each layer is placed over each other to serve as a stack and each layer is proved with a set of functionalities at SaaS, PaaS and IaaS layer. The functionalities at each layer are connected to each other for working but do not have any information about the performance of functionalities in each layer. This lack of information creates a gap between various layers of cloud architecture as a section in figure 4. On the other hand, figure 3 shown below shows an example of multi-cloud architecture which shows one cloud controller named Inter cloud resource manager that is connected to 4 different cloud provider to render services is such environment without trust model the cloud services cannot provide quality of service and can never ensure SLA. The figure shows 4 trust service providers also this may solve the problem of individual cloud provider but as a whole their need to have a global trust model.

The global trust model connects all the trust service providers to make better decisions if one of the clouds gets exhausted or overloaded.

Figure 4 is a combination of cloud layered architecture and trust model which connects and serves all the functionalities in the cloud and allows them to make better decisions. Various components of layer architecture are:

SLA monitor agent: This functionality is responsible to record any SLA violation in the system at the application level or request level if any of the service providers are not able to fulfill the SLA of the task is considered to be failed.

VM monitor: VM monitor is responsible to monitor the functioning of virtual machines for SLA violation and any fault or any failure at VM lever or storage failure.

Figure 3. Multi cloud framework

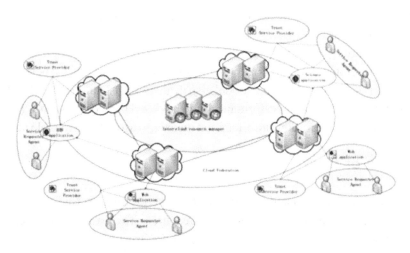

Figure 4. Trust model and multi-layered cloud architecture (Fan et.al, 2014)

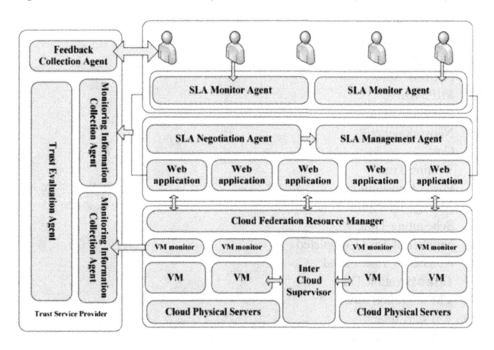

Web application: These are the application which generates a request for IaaS lever for a task to be executed.

Resource manager: This is the most important functioning unit of the system which is responsible to allocate resources in term of storage, bandwidth, MIPS, RAM and processor to VM

Trust evaluation Manager: This is the unit that keeps an eye over all the units in cloud layered architecture. This is responsible to record the working and performance of the system as a whole. The trust model also evaluates trust value for each VM and datacenter based on the past performance which is used by access control, resource allocation, resource migration and allocation mechanism to select a reliable resource.

Evaluation of Trust

Trust in the cloud is evaluated as a multi-objective problem to find the reliability of the resource based on the performance resource. The trust model uses many performance parameters if the model is used for trust evaluation for resource managers rather than security.

Parameters affecting trust value:

1. Make span
2. Storage utilization
3. Storage SLA
4. Network SLA
5. MIPS SLA
6. Processor SLA
7. Network delay
8. Cost
9. Waiting Time
10. Power Consumption
11. Average Execution Time
12. Scheduling Time
13. Number of Task Completed
14. Number of Task Failed
15. Task Migration Time
16. VM migration time
17. VM start time
18. VM utilization model
19. Number of tasks Migrated
20. Number of Tasks Meeting Deadline
21. Average Load over Datacenter/Host
22. Number of Hot Spot
23. Number of Over Loaded Datacenter/Hosts

24.   Average Task Execution Time
25.   Number of Under Loaded Servers

If we discuss the trust model for security and privacy in cloud computing architecture. In that case, the performance affecting the trust values are:

1.   Length of security Key
2.   Encryption algorithm
3.   Time taken to decrypt and encrypt the algorithm
4.   Access protocol
5.   Data encryption techniques
6.   Relative reliability between datacenters.

These are various parameters affecting the trust-based security mechanism for highly reliable services.

Trust Management and Performance improvement

For the cloud, various trust models are been proposed like using a direct trust, Indirect trust model, relative trust model, reputation-based trust model, collaborative key-based trust model, and many more.

Trust models are being proposed for all types of distributed environments like grid computing, computer networks, wireless networks, e-commerce, etc. All have a similarity that resources are distinctly located and to study the performance of the resource trust models are used. In general, reputation-based trust model and relative trust models and their variants are most popular among all types of distributed environments even in cloud computing.

Existing Trust Based Solutions in Cloud

(Muchahari et.al. 2012) proposed a dynamic trust model for the cloud. This work overcomes feedback based trust models which are considered to be inaccurate and malicious in many cases. The proposed trust model has taken into consideration the Cloud Service Registry and Discovery into consideration where registration refers to adding new resources to cloud and discovery refers to finding the best resource for the cloud environment. The trust model is defined upon two things previous trust value and credibility of the resource where the credibility of the resource is the average feedback or trust for a resource by other resources.

The system considers when a new resource is added then a default trust value will be assigned then after trust value is updated based on performance and credibility. Trust value is updated as an average of previous trust and credibility of the resource.

$$T_{cons}(P_i) = \frac{\sum_{j=1, j\neq i}^{n} fb(P_i, C_j)}{n} \tag{1}$$

Where fb(P,C) is the feedback value of provider pi assigned by Cj and n is the total number of such contributors. Figures 5 and 6 demonstrate the same process of registering and discovery of the best resource of a service provider for the task.

Figure 5. Proposed trust model (Muchahari et.al. 2012)

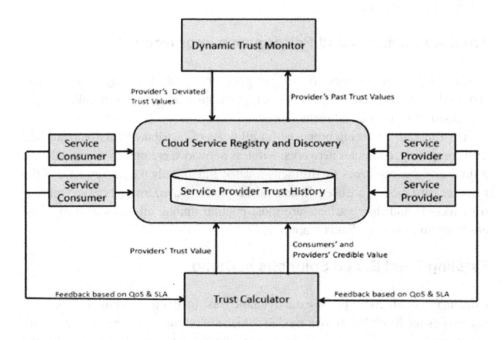

The Trust Model for Cloud Service Registry and Discovery

Figure 6. Service registry model (Muchahari et.al. 2012)

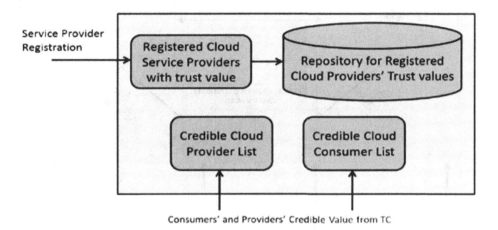

Cloud Service Registry and Discovery Architecture

(Talal H et.al., 2011) have proposed a credibility based trust model for cloud computing. Where they have discussed the drawback of the centralized trust model which is prone or DoS attack and gets malicious feedbacks. To overcome this a credibility based trust framework is proposed. The model is divided into three parts: A Credibility Model: this module is responsible to differentiate between credible feedback and malicious feedback from an attacker. Reputation model: this model is responsible for evaluating your reputation and other reputation in your view at each resource i.e. reputation determination model is replicated at each service provider. To decentralized trust evaluation helps to overcome the drawback of a centralized approach. Distributed Trust Feedback Assessment and Storage:

This module is responsible to store the feedback after an equal interval of time at replicated models s and when we need to find the trust value the average of trust value of a service provider from all replicated models is taken and the average is taken. Figure 7 shows the working of the proposed model where the trust service layer manages the trust value in replicated form and all the services interact with the trust model for finding the trust value for a service.

M. Alhamad et.al. (Alhamad, 2010) proposed an SLA based trust model to overcome exiting models which only takes into consideration the performance of the resources. The proposed model is divided into SLA agent: This module is

Figure 7. distributed trust model architecture (Talal H et.al., 2011)

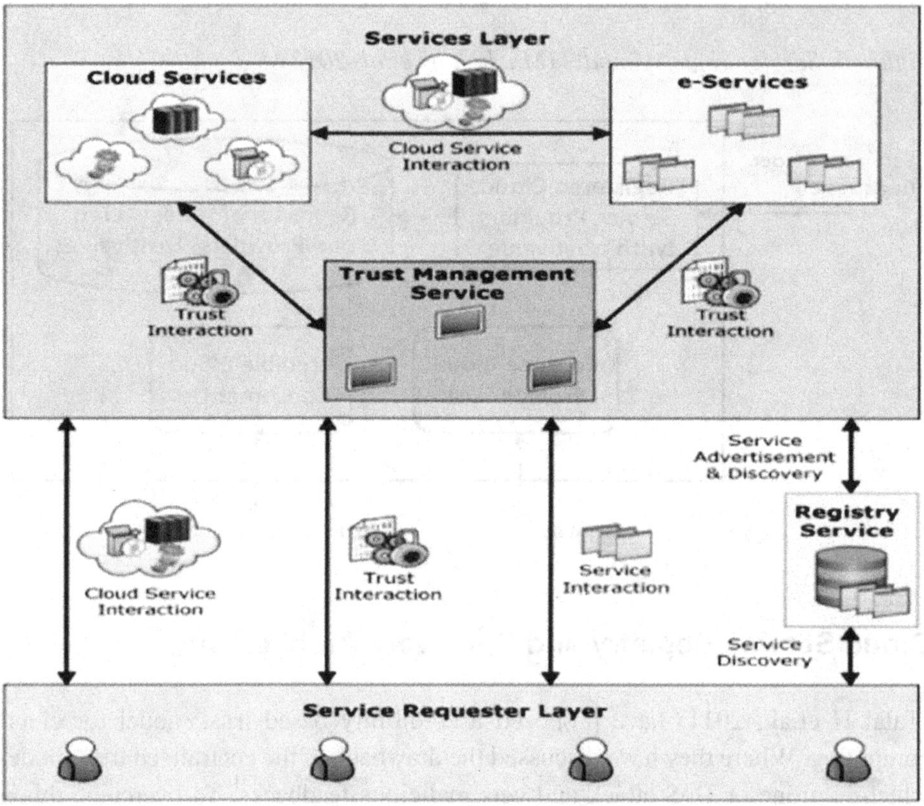

responsible to set up an agreement for SLA between the partners. The agent has to perform the following functionalities:

- Monitoring SLA
- Monitor activities of a customer
- Negotiations between cloud providers

Cloud Consumer Model: This module is responsible for trust management between the cloud service providers and all users. The model also takes into consideration the trust value of user based on its activity to prioritize the users. This also evaluates the trust value of service providers based on their SLA performance in a cloud environment.

Figure 8 demonstrates the functioning of the proposed model and shows the workflow of how the trust value is evaluated based on input from the SLA manager

Figure 8. Propose SLA based trust model (Mohammed et.al., 2010)

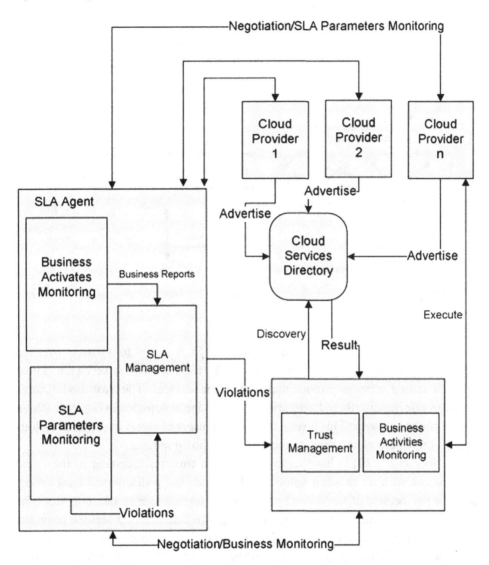

and negotiation manager. Where the trust value is further used by cloud service discovery for the selection of suitable service providers based on its past performance.

(T. Noor et.al., 2011) proposed a credibility based model for cloud web services where the complete architecture is divided into 3 players. Cloud service provider layer: This layer consists of all cloud providers like AWS, IBM, google cloud, etc to provide various services to users. Trust manager layer: this layer is the backbone of this architecture where the trust management layer is responsible to evaluate each

Figure 9. Trust layer in cloud architecture

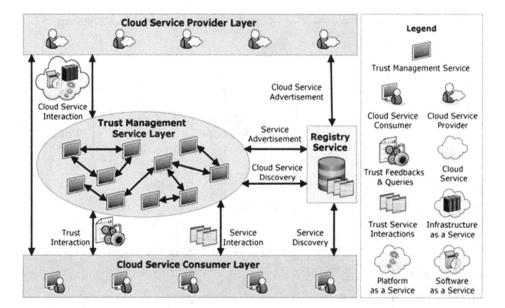

service provider, their services performance and SLA served to the users over the period. Trust management service interact with the registration service to know about all exiting services provide and about their services. The trust model stores the trust value in a distributed network of trust storage as depicted in Figure 9. Cloud service consumer layer: This layer consists of all users of cloud which uses various applications of cloud to complete their tasks as shown in figure 9.

(T. Noor et.at., 2013) have done a survey on trust management in the cloud environment with its existing solutions. The work has a discoursed trust model from the perspective of the service provider and service user or the requester. The service user takes the help of the trust manager to find the best service provider, on the other hand, the service provider interacts with the trust model for the trust evaluation and the trust model evaluates the trust value for each service provider for further usage as shown in figure 10 & figure 11.

According to US Berkley security and trust between the user and service provider is among the top 10 obstacles in the cloud that the industry is facing (Anthony, 2010). This article has proposed a comprehensive trust layered architecture as shown in figure 12. The trust model is distributed into 3 basic layers which are as follows. Trust feedback sharing layer: This layer constitutes of consumers and provider which provide feedback to the trust layer and each other about the performance of another service provider This module is responsible to store all such reviews and provide it to next layer for evaluation. Trust assessment layer: This layer is responsible for

Figure 10. Trust manager and cloud user

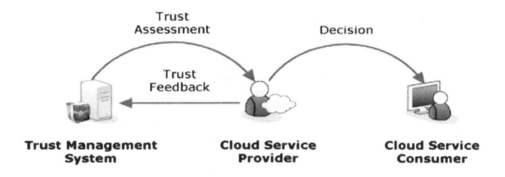

Figure 11. trust model and service provider

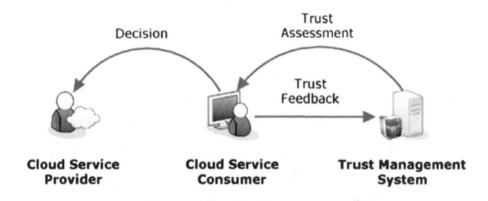

core computing of the trust management layer in cloud architecture. This layer is responsible for trust initialization, trust evaluation, and assessment based on the feedback and updates the trust value based on the performance of the system and service provider. The evaluated trust is given to the next layer for distribution to several functional modules for decision making. Trust result distribution: this is similar to the first layer only rather than collecting feedback this layer is responsible for the delivery of trust value to various parties that generate queries for trust assessment. The users of this trust value are cloud service consumers, users, cloud controller, load balancing algorithm, resource allocation algorithm, and providers.

Comparison With Various Reported Literature

Cloud being a distributed architecture uses trust model architecture to solve various issues in the cloud environment. Various trust management techniques and models

Figure 12. Trust layered architecture

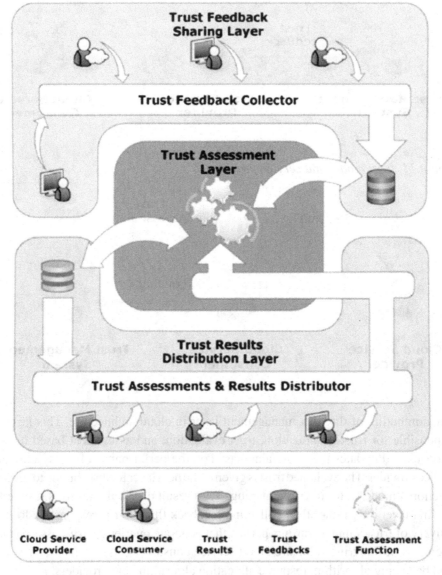

are being proposed in the past to improve the performance of the cloud. These existing trust models aim to improve security, quality of service, and various other performance parameters. The existing models can be categorized into the following categories like:

- Trust policy (Fan et.al., 2004)
- Recommendation based trust
- Reputation-based trust (Papalilo et.al, 2007)
- Trust prediction models

Trust Policy

Policy-based trust models refer to most traditional rule-based trust model which already exist in grid computing, distributed computing, and wireless network. These models are generally threshold and rules-based driven models for SLA checking and performance parameter checking based models.

Some of the existing models are:

Cloud Environments (Yao,2010; Alhamad, 2010), Grid: (Song,2005; Song, 2006; Vimercati, 2012), Web applications (Vimercati, 2012), the service-oriented environment (Skogsrud, 2007, Skogsrud,2009),SLA based trust (Xiong,2003), feedback credibility (Xiong,2003; Xiong, 2004; Srivatsa, 2006; Noor, 2011a; Noor, 2011b; Malik, 2009a; Malik, 2009b; Habib, 2011).Figure 13 shows a pictorial view of the policy-based trust model.

Figure 13. Pictorial view of the policy-based trust model

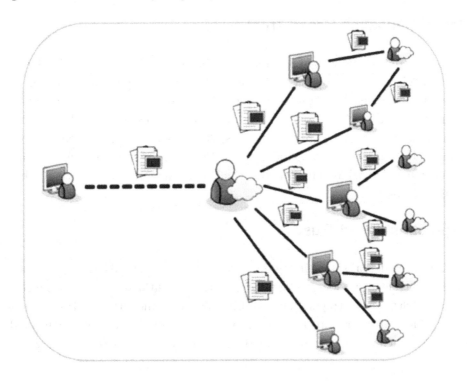

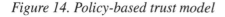

Figure 14. Policy-based trust model

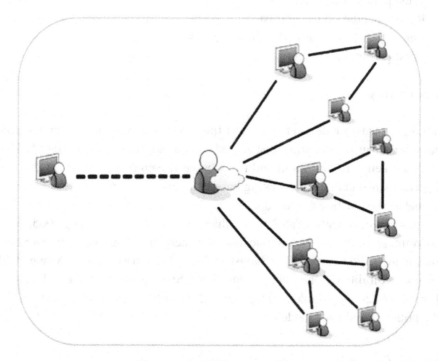

Recommendation Based Trust

In this form of trust model based on the recommendation of other service providers. Such models are more popular in a cloud environment only the difference in the function of recommending the trust may depend on many other values and performance parameters as dictated in section 2. Some of the work in this area are: Cloud (Habib, 2011; Krautheim,2010), Grid (Domingues, 2007), Service-oriented environment (Park et.al., 2005; skopik et.al, 2009) Figure 15 shows a pictorial representation of the recommendation based trust model which makes a more clear overview of how the model works.

Reputation-based Trust

These trust models as shown in Figure 15 and Figure 16 are used because feedbacks from various cloud providers and service providers may influence in a single direction to avoid such a situation reputation feature is added to the model to avoid the decision been influenced by a group of service providers. Existing work from various fields is as follows. Cloud environment: (Noor, 2011; Krautheim, 2010; Manuel, 2009),

Figure 15. Recommendation based trust model

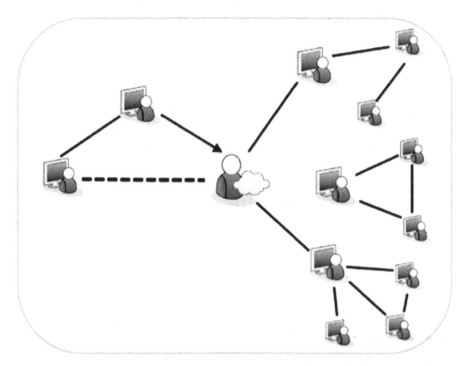

Figure 16. Reputation-based trust models

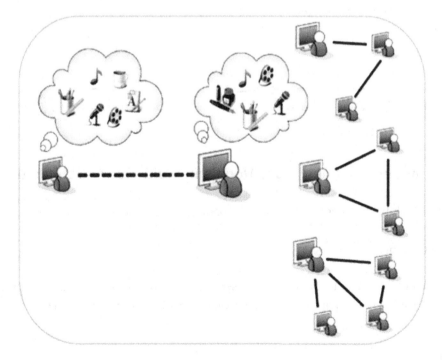

Grid (Farag et.al., 2002a; Farag et.al., 2002b; Srivatsa, 2006; Lin, 2004) Figure 15 shows a pictorial representation of Reputation-based trust model

Trust Prediction Models

These models are new to cloud computing environment which help the trust model to predict the future trust value based on the past learning and performance which helps the trust model to make better decisions in term of the prospect of the cloud environment as depicted in Figure 17 and 18. Some of the work from this field is as follows:

T. Noor proposed as predictive trust model for cloud environment based on the learning of trust model (Noor et.al, 2011)

Figure 17. Predictive trust models

Figure 18. Notations used in the trust model

Parameters Affecting Trust Models in Multi-cloud Architecture:

In feedback based trust model following parameters are there:

- Credibility

Credibility refers to the quality of service. the service provider has provided to the customer. The parameter depends on the feedback of the consumer or user.

- Privacy

This parameter mostly refers to the level of security in terms of encryption the service provider provides and the level of sensitive information providers can deal with.

- Personalization

This refers to the level of customizable feature cloud provider has served to the user to make it more comfortable in term of design or task and environment customization

- Integration

Here it refers to the level of integration a service provider gives with other applications without affecting other parameters. The parameters also show how well the provider is integrated with various trust models since it is multi-cloud architecture so the provider has to interact with multiple trust models at the same time.

- Perception:

This is a hypothetical view where it refers to the perception of users and another service provider toward the cloud provider.

- Technique

This is a multi-dimensional view where the technique to evaluate the trust is referred to, which can be a static, dynamic or learning-based algorithm.

- Adaptability

This refers to the capability of the trust model to adapt to the performance of various cloud providers. Some trust models work on a weight-based system where they may be favorable to certain service providers.

- Scalability

This refers to the behavior of a dynamic cloud environment to scale up and down based on the load on the server. This parameter refers to the ability of the trust model to changes in the system which may grow or reduce in terms of resources and various other aspects at run time.

For rule-based trust following parameters are there:

- Response time
- Redundancy
- Accuracy
- Security

Many other parameters affecting trust discourse in section 2of this chapter. These parameters help the model to be more dynamic and evaluate the cloud provider based on all its performance parameters

SUMMARY

This chapter gives a brief overview of the importance of the trust model in any distributed architecture and how trust models can deal with various challenges and issues in a cloud environment. The chapter gives a categorization of trust models and existing work done from the field of trust in the cloud, grid computing, and web services. The work presents all essential knowledge and parameters required to design a trust model. The chapter focuses on disclosing all possible direction trust models can improve the performance of cloud in cloud architecture starting from the infrastructure layer to the application layer.

REFERENCES

Alhamad, M., Dillon, T., & Chang, E. (2010). Sla-based trust model for cloud computing. *2010 13th international conference on network-based information systems*, 321-324. 10.1109/NBiS.2010.67

Azzedin, F., & Maheswaran, M. (2002). Integrating trust into grid resource management systems. *2002 Proceedings International Conference on Parallel Processing*, 47-54. 10.1109/ICPP.2002.1040858

Azzedin, F., & Maheswaran, M. (2002). Towards trust-aware resource management in grid computing systems. *2002 2nd IEEE/ACM International symposium on Cluster Computing and the Grid (CCGRID'02)*, 452-452.

Castelfranchi, C. (2004). Trust mediation in knowledge management and sharing. In *2004 International Conference on Trust Management*. Springer. 10.1007/978-3-540-24747-0_23

Fan, W., & Perros, H. (2014). A novel trust management framework for multi-cloud environments based on trust service providers. *Knowledge-Based Systems*, *70*, 392–406. doi:10.1016/j.knosys.2014.07.018

Gambetta, D. (1988). Can We Trust Trust? In Trust: Making and Breaking Cooperative Relations. Basil Blackwell.

Grandison, T., & Sloman, M. (2002). Trust management formal techniques and system. *2002 Proceeding of Second IFIP Conference*, 1-10.

Habib, S. M., Ries, S., & Muhlhauser, M. (2011). Towards a trust management system for cloud computing. *2011 IEEE 10th International Conference on Trust, Security and Privacy in Computing and Communications*, 933-939. 10.1109/TrustCom.2011.129

Halvard, S., Benatallah, B., Casati, F., & Toumani, F. (2007). Managing impacts of security protocol changes in service-oriented applications. *2007 Proceedings of the 29th international conference on Software Engineering*, 468-477.

Joseph, A. D., Katz, R., Konwinski, A., Gunho, L., Patterson, D., & Rabkin, A. (2006). A view of cloud computing. *Communications of the ACM*, *53*, 4.

Khan, K. M., Malluhi, Q. (2010). Establishing trust in cloud computing. *IT Professional, 12*(5), 20-27.

Li, W., & Ping, L. (2009). Trust model to enhance security and interoperability of cloud environment. *2009 IEEE International Conference on Cloud Computing*, 69-79. 10.1007/978-3-642-10665-1_7

Li, W., Ping, L., & Pan, X., (2010). Use trust management module to achieve effective security mechanisms in cloud environment. *2010 International Conference on Electronics and Information Engineering*, *1*, 1-14. 10.1109/ICEIE.2010.5559829

Ll, W-J., Wang, X. D., Fu, Y. G., & Fu, Z. X. (2005). Study on several trust models in grid environment. Fuzhou DaxueXuebao (ZiranKexue Ban). *Journal of Fuzhou University*, *34*(2), 189–193.

Michael, B. (2009). In clouds shall we trust? *IEEE Security and Privacy*, *7*(5), 3–3. doi:10.1109/MSP.2009.124

Muchahari, K. M., & Sinha, S. K. (2012). A new trust management architecture for cloud computing environment. *2012 International Symposium on Cloud and Services Computing, 1*, 136-140. 10.1109/ISCOS.2012.30

Noor, T. H., & Quan, Z. S. (2010). Credibility-based trust management for services in cloud environments. *International Conference on Service-Oriented Computing*, 328-343.

Noor, T. H., & Quan, Z. S. (2011). Trust as a service: A framework for trust management in cloud environments. *International Conference on Web Information Systems Engineering*, 314-321. 10.1007/978-3-642-24434-6_27

Noor, T. H., Sheng, Q. Z., Zeadally, S., & Yu, J. (2012). Trust management of services in cloud environments: Obstacles and solutions. *ACM Computing Surveys, 46*(1), 1–12. doi:10.1145/2522968.2522980

Papalilo, E., & Freisleben, B. (2007). Managing behaviour trust in grids using statistical methods of quality assurance. *2007 Third International Symposium on Information Assurance and Security, 1*, 319-324. 10.1109/IAS.2007.51

Perez, S. (2009). In Cloud We Trust? *ReadWriteWeb*. ww.readwriteweb.com/enterprise/2009/01/incloud-we-trust.php

Selvi, S. T., Balakrishnan, P., Kumar, R., & Rajendar, K. (2007). Trust based grid scheduling algorithm for commercial grids. *2007 International Conference on Computational Intelligence and Multimedia Applications (ICCIMA 2007), 1*, 545-551. 10.1109/ICCIMA.2007.281

Skogsrud, H., Motahari-Nezhad, H. R., Benatallah, B., & Casati, F. (2009). Modeling trust negotiation for web services. *Computer, 42*(2), 54–61. doi:10.1109/MC.2009.56

Song, S., Hwang, K., & Kwok, Y-K. (2005). Trusted grid computing with security binding and trust integration. *Journal of Grid Computing, 1*(2), 53-73.

Song, S., Hwang, K., Zhou, R., & Kwok, Y.-K. (2005). Trusted P2P transactions with fuzzy reputation aggregation. *IEEE Internet Computing, 9*(6), 24–34. doi:10.1109/MIC.2005.136

Vimercati, S. D. C., Foresti, S., Jajodia, S., Paraboschi, S., Psaila, G., & Samarati, P. (2012). Integrating trust management and access control in data-intensive web applications. *ACM Transactions on the Web, 6*(2), 2, 6–12. doi:10.1145/2180861.2180863

Yang, Z., Yin, C., & Liu, Y. (2011). A cost-based resource scheduling paradigm in cloud computing. *2011 12th International Conference on Parallel and Distributed Computing, Applications and Technologies*, 417-422.

Yao, J., Chen, S., Wang, C., Levy, D., & Zic, J. (2010). Accountability as a service for the cloud. *2010 IEEE International Conference on Services Computing*, 81-88. 10.1109/SCC.2010.83

Section 2

Chapter 5

Large–Scale Data Storage Scheme in Blockchain Ledger Using IPFS and NoSQL

Randhir Kumar

ⓘ https://orcid.org/0000-0001-9375-2970

Department of Information Technology, National Institute of Technology, Raipur, India

Rakesh Tripathi

Department of Information Technology, National Institute of Technology, Raipur, India

ABSTRACT

The future applications of blockchain are expected to serve millions of users. To provide variety of services to the users, using underlying technology has to consider large-scale storage and assessment behind the scene. Most of the current applications of blockchain are working either on simulators or via small blockchain network. However, the storage issue in the real world is unpredictable. To address the issue of large-scale data storage, the authors have introduced the data storage scheme in blockchain (DSSB). The storage model executes behind the blockchain ledger to store large-scale data. In DSSB, they have used hybrid storage model using IPFS and MongoDB(NoSQL) in order to provide efficient storage for large-scale data in blockchain. In this storage model, they have maintained the content-addressed hash of the transactions on blockchain network to ensure provenance. In DSSB, they are storing the original data (large-scale data) into MongoDB and IPFS. The DSSB model not only provides efficient storage of large-scale data but also provides storage size reduction of blockchain ledger.

DOI: 10.4018/978-1-7998-3444-1.ch005

INTRODUCTION

According to the estimations, in 2020 there will be more than 20 million connected devices and all these devices will generate a large volume of data. The increasing volume of data will demand a requirement of data storage and management. The connected devices combine with different applications to share the data. The process of sharing data inherently requires the immutability and long term retention (the provenance of data) (Al-Mamun et al., 2018). The applications may be healthcare, supply chain management, and identity management (Liu et al., 2019). To consider the healthcare problem, there is a need for patient medical treatment records for a long duration of time to provide better curability to the specific diseases. Today, most of the records are stored in vulnerable centralized storage (including cloud) that can be easily manipulated or compromised for personal benefit.

The long term retention of data demands for a technology where provenance can be maintained easily. The requirements highlight the use of blockchain owing to its feature of provenance, immutability, privacy, security, and availability (Wang, 2018). The blockchain address the existing issue of centralized storage where data can be compromised. The blockchain works with the distributed ledger technique (DLT) to store the data. The DLT ensures tempered-proof storage of data owing to the integrity (previous hash) of a chain. The blockchain stores data in a block known as a transaction in DLT and the structure of block consists of a previous hash of subsequent blocks. These hashes provide tempered-proof storage because if one block gets change then others will be tempered automatically. The provenance of the records is maintained by using the timestamp feature of the blockchain technology. The privacy in the blockchain DLT is maintained by a hash of the transactions. However, the large scale of data storage limits the expansion of the blockchain network. This storage limits demands for the distributed storage of files in the blockchain network.

The requirements of large scale data storage highlight the Interplanetary file system (IPFS) that provides distributed storage structure in a peer-to-peer network (Khqj et al., 2018). The IPFS maintains a distributed hash table (DHT) that ensures the mapping of the content in the hash table by their content-addressed hash. The IPFS fulfills the dream of large scale data storage in the blockchain DLT. The dream of large scale data storage is fulfilled by the content-addressed hash which takes 46 bytes of storage irrespective of the original files of the data (Benet, n.d.). However, the IPFS does not provide query-based storage and that limits the beauty of the distributed storage. The need for query-based blockchain storage highlights the use of NoSQL based implementation. The NoSQL based implementation guarantees the persistent storage of each transaction of the DLT. This also provides the facility where once can make a query to search the specific records of the DLT. The NoSQL is suitable in the implementation of the blockchain technology as it can store data in JavaScript object notation (JSON) (Gattermayer & Tvrdik, 2017). In this chapter, we have used a hybrid storage scheme where IPFS is combined with NoSQL (MongoDB) so if the changes are made in the hash of the files in MongoDB the changes will reflect in DLT storage of blockchain and the suitability of content can be easily verified.

BACKGROUND

To maintain the large scale data like video, audio files there must be a need for off-chain storage (Arslan & Goker, n.d.; Wang, 2019) to mitigate the scalability issue in the blockchain technology. The distributed ledger required the least storage space, discussed in (Arslan & Goker, n.d.) Compression and decompression scheme. However, the audio and video compression and decompression scheme suffer from loss of data. Similarly, the healthcare data storage on a large scale with privacy and better security the blockchain-based application has been proposed (Colloquium & Zrt, 2017; Xu et al., 2019). The growing size of data storage in blockchain limiting development to improve the storage the authors have proposed in (Dai, 2018) network coded distributed storage (NC-DS) to reduce the storage room of blockchain network. The NC-DS reduces the storage size with the transaction division in small pieces. However, this approach limits the NC-DS due to correction and inconsistency problems.

The integration of blockchain and IoT is facing a problem of scalability due to the large scale data generation by IoT devices. To address the issue of data storage with blockchain and IoT, the distributed hash table (DHT) based storage has been proposed (Li et al., 2018). The IoT nodes data will be stored in the DHT storage and pointer or address of the data will be stored in the blockchain ledger. The DHT nodes are accountable to store and share data from/to authenticated IoT devices. However, the DHT does not support query (user can access the data by writing a query) based operation. Similarly, the integration of mobile edge computing with a vehicular network is facing a problem of data storage in blockchain-based structure (Zhang & Chen, 2019) (Yang et al., 2019; Lu et al., 2019). To address the large-scale data storage the authors (Kang et al., 2019) have used mobile edge cloud computing to assist the gap of storage in a blockchain network. However, cloud storage suffers from audibility.

The decentralized cloud-based storage is proposed in (Selvanathan, 2018) to store the data in DHT based storage. The authorized peers or node can access the records from the decentralized cloud. The collaboration of decentralized cloud and blockchain is much more efficient in storage, privacy, security, and availability of the data. However, the decentralized cloud storage again suffers from the query-based transaction access owing to the DHT based storage. The authors (Zheng et al., 2018) have addressed the issue of large storage data in blockchain technology by proposing the integration of cloud and blockchain technology. The encryption techniques have been proposed to store the data into the cloud-based off-chain storage and the meta-data is stored in the blockchain network. The underlying technique can improve the storage scheme in blockchain-based applications. However, the limitation of the underlying scheme is that one should not trust easily on the cloud federation by putting the private and sensitive information (like healthcare dataset of a patient) at risk of data breaches and sharing the concern of security to unauthorized hand.

The integration of blockchain and cloud is proposed in (Ali et al., 2020) for secure data provenance by using smart contracts. Blockchain integration with cloud computing emerges as comprehensive security for IoT devices (Wang, 2019). The actual IoT data is stored into the cloud storage and the meta-data (cryptographic-hash) is stored into the blockchain network (Liu et al., 2019). The underlying scheme provides scalability for IoT deployments. The smart contracts are maintained by the underlying scheme is to validate the information and provide data provenance. However, the smart contracts are vulnerable in most of the situation due to automatic executions and modification is required every time according to the actual environment of the blockchain network and IoT devices (Dika & Nowostawski, 2018).

To manage the large scale data on blockchain network "Mystiko" is proposed by (Bandara et al., 2018) which is built on the top of the Apache Cassandra database. The "Mystiko" supports various features like throughput, availability, and scalability in the blockchain network. Cassandra is a distributed storage model that supports big data storage; however, working with "Mystiko" there is a need for highly equipped nodes in a blockchain network.

The authors (Liu et al., 2018) have introduced TrustChain for the large data storage in blockchain structure. The TrustChain separates the data layer from the consensus layer in the blockchain network. The generated data by each peer of the network is stored into the traditional database and the TrustChain keeps the hash of data that ensures the verification, integrity, and correctness of data. The underlying model acts as a control channel to record the overall transactions of the IoT devices. The approach of TrustChain removes the redundancy form the storage and improves the transaction processing speed. However, the approach needs a suitable consensus algorithm to share information among the peers of the network. The authors have (Li, & Sforzin, n.d.), introduced "satellite-chain" to mitigate the issue of large storage data into the blockchain network. The satellite-chain is maintained for the parallel execution of the transactions by the peers in the network. The underlying process removes the computation overhead of the main chain. To proper execution of the "satellite-chain" regulator has to refine the policy every time to maintain the integrity in a network. However, the off-chain storage approach is not discussed.

The authors (Gao et al., 2018) have reported various challenges in the blockchain technology like scalability issues and discussed how the issue can be addressed using an integration of different techniques such as IoT, Big Data, Cloud and Edge Computing. The authors have introduced TrustChain to provide data storage and also used a parallel distributed structure that isolates the data layer from the control layer (Liu et al., 2018). The data generated by each node in the data layer will be stored into the local traditional database and the TrustChain will maintain the reference of the data that ensures the correctness and integrity of the data. The data reference is stored as an identifier of the data into the TrustChain. The TrustChain is acting here, as a control layer and records all over the state of the IoT devices. However, the redundancy has not been maintained by the TrustChain which limits the efficiency of the chain and entire IoT structure.

The authors (Ismail et al., 2019)have reported the performance of the blockchain with large-scale deployment at UAE University (UAEU) concerning an increasing number of nodes, block, and block size. The authors have reported that the bandwidth and execution time degrades concerning several validations. In the case of public blockchain almost 2/3rd of the total nodes involved in the validations of the transactions. The block size increment in the blockchain performs better on-chain storage but at the same time it degrades the propagation time and that can be an issue of security. In authors (Maiyya et al., 2018) have comprised two different layers that are application layer and storage layer. The application layer involves the public keys and private signature of the identities which is generated by the private keys. The transaction submission from one client to another client must be signed and sent to the storage-layer (on-chain). The storage layer consists of two different processes that are mining and validation by nodes. The signed transactions are stored into the blocks and each block gets chained with their subsequent blocks using a previous hash. However, the authors have reported the issue of scalability due to the large storage of data into the storage layer of blockchain. The authors (Dorri et al., n.d.) have reported various issues in the integration of blockchain and VANET due to the large-scale storage of data. In this article, speedy-chain is maintained for the smart city infrastructure. The permissioned blockchain is adapted to transmit the data to the Roadside Unit (RSU) which ensures trust-based communication. The proposed model reduces the latency during transferring data and storing it to each RSU in a separate block. However, the large-size data limits the growth of the speedy-chain. The authors in (Wu, n.d.) applied a data masking approach for the privacy of data for secure electronic healthcare record (EHR) using IPFS based storage. The authors have used data masking instead of encryption. However, the data masking time increases as the volume of data increases.

The authors in (Stoykov et al., n.d.) extend Visualizations of Interactive, Blockchain, Extended Simulations (VIBES) which extends Bitcoin-Simulator with significant improvements. Firstly, VIBES supports a visual interface for the tracing of transaction growth in the network. Secondly, VIBES improves performance by using the best guess on the block creation time. The authors have proposed a BlockLite simulator to address the issue of scalability. The blocklist can be scale-out up to 20000 nodes with a fixed and small set of data storage into the chain. The BlockLite is completely decentralized which built trust among the nodes in the network. The BlockLite is efficient in usability owing to the easy-to-use interface. However, the BlockLite does not support a large volume of data storage into the blockchain network.

In (Abe, 2018) the authors have reduced the complexity of node storage using lower degree self blockchain replication with DHT based storage. Each blocks stores in a specific node and the hash of the block into the chain. The proposed model also improves the block validation process. The miner keeps a record of each block validation with its full state. The DHT based storage provides the hash of the stored transactions.

The aim of the authors in (Sel et al., n.d.; Nygaard, n.d.) to divide the network into shards (a subset of nodes). The number of shards improves the performance of the network. The shards based data storage also improves the security of the complete state of the blockchain. However, shard based storage sometimes does not work efficiently due to inter-shard communication. The authors have (Bartoletti et al., 2017) proposed a framework to support data analytics on both Bitcoin and Ethereum which are two most famous cryptocurrencies. The authors have integrated the blockchain data into the other sources and organize them into the database like SQL or NoSQL. The database is maintained to store large size of data. The SQL supports query-based structure so that, the peers of the network can access the specific transactions from the blockchain.

The authors have (Bragagnolo et al., 2019; Wang et al., n.d.) reported that blockchain is emerging as fraud detection in the distributed network. However, the growing size of the data in volume has become challenged for the blockchain networks. The size of blockchain ledger has become 300GB which is reported in the year 2018 (Bartoletti et al., 2017; Kim, 2018). To maintain the growing size of the data, authors have introduced the integration of the blockchain network with Big Data. The process of offloading the data into the Big Data storage improves the scalability of the complete blockchain structure.

The authors have (Dang et al., 2019) introduced the sharding approach to maintaining the scalability into the blockchain network. To get better efficiency in the shard based operation, the Byzantine consensus has been enhanced. To secure the transaction into the network distributed transaction protocol has been used. The authors have reported that the overall storage of the chain must be offloaded in the shard in such that the integrity of the transaction gets maintained. Also, the authors have raised the issue of inter-shard communication maintenance because inter-shard communication affects multiple shards at a time.

The authors (Bhuiyan et al., 2018) have introduced the blockchain-based emergency medical services where patient details are stored into the distributed ledger. The model is proposed for real-time patient monitoring by a responsible health provider (doctor or hospital). The model removed the hurdle of various vulnerability issues of the existing centralized model. The authors have divided the model into three different parts that are healthcare providers, emergency facilities, and patient details. The inquiry of the data on the blockchain has been maintained by the role-based access control. Thus, the introduced model ensures privacy and security in the healthcare network. The model is capable to manage the individual patient records. The medical data of the individual patient can be shared among various parties like a hospital, insurance company, and clinical research. The authors have stored the patient detailed in the database with the encrypted format to ensure the privacy of the patient information and at the same time, the identifier of the patient data is maintained into the blockchain network.

The authors have proposed a blockchain-based sharing model for personal health records using cloud storage and machine learning (Bhuiyan et al., 2018). The model ensures security and privacy into the network where a patient can share their medical information including various benefits. However, the model does not provide the integrity and correctness of the medical records returned from the cloud servers. The model is not efficient in terms of fine-grained access control with cloud-based storage. The cloud storage of medical records may risk of privacy of the patient's critical information. The model can be improved with the encrypted storage of the medical data of patients into cloud storage. However, to verify the encrypted record of patients every time consumes time and energy both.

The authors of (Hanley, 2018) present a centralized off-chain storage model to keep medical data records of patients. The model is designed such that the medical professionals (doctor) can access the patient data from anywhere. The blockchain is providing the beauty of the model with the storage of the identifier of each patient record. The identifier based storage provides query operation on the model to access the records of an individual patient from the blockchain network. The off-chain storage model stores the data in unencrypted format to apply machine learning algorithms, and various data mining algorithms in terms of many benefits to the medical industry. The authors have used permissioned blockchain (access control to the user- who will access what content from the blockchain network) technique to implement the model that ensures privacy in the system. Any interruption in the blockchain network can be easily identified by looking at the history of the chain. The permission revoke takes place when any peer of the network is performing an illegal operation.

The authors in (Cheney, 2011) have proposed PDC (patient data contract) which is world state architecture where each registered user data will be stored. However, blockchain will store only the encrypted URL data such as names, usernames, and emails. To access the data of a patient with other entities the permission contract (PC) was created and notification will be sent to the patient for accepting and rejecting the permission of entities. Once the notification is accepted then the entity can see the information of the patient. Otherwise, the PC (permission contract) will be discarded automatically. This process takes more time in verification for sharing the HIE information. The authors in (Hua et al., 2018) have introduced the data sharing between the participant using Personal identification number (PIN) and medical identification no (MIN) which is provided by the hospital. To share the information between two parties such as patient and doctor both identification should be verified by the contract. This paper is using hyper ledger fabric solo which works using centralized storage and private blockchain technique. The objective was to share the information with valid parties. This approach is not suitable for security, integrity, and transparency of information. However, the model is not appropriate to store the large scale of patient records. The model is not scalable due to the large scale data storage.

MOTIVATION

The work in this chapter is motivated by the following observations from the literature. The existing blockchain model suffers from scalability issues due to large file size storage into the blockchain. To address the problem of large-scale data management, we have proposed the DSSB model which can store only the hash of the file into the distributed ledger rather than original files. The DSSB mitigates the scalability issue of the blockchain network owing to the feature of content-addressed hash. The original files are mapped into the DHT (distributed hash table) with their content-addressed hash in IPFS that ensures size reduction of a distributed ledger.

LIMITATIONS IN EXISTING VANET SYSTEM

1. Single point of failure (Centralized storage model)
2. The mutability of record (Uploaded transactions might be modified by the third-party entity)
3. Third-party dependency for access and storage (Transactions might be compromised)

4.   Does not provide provenance (audibility) of record(History of transactions in DSSB)

Figure 1. DSSB Model for large-scale data sharing in Centralized Environment

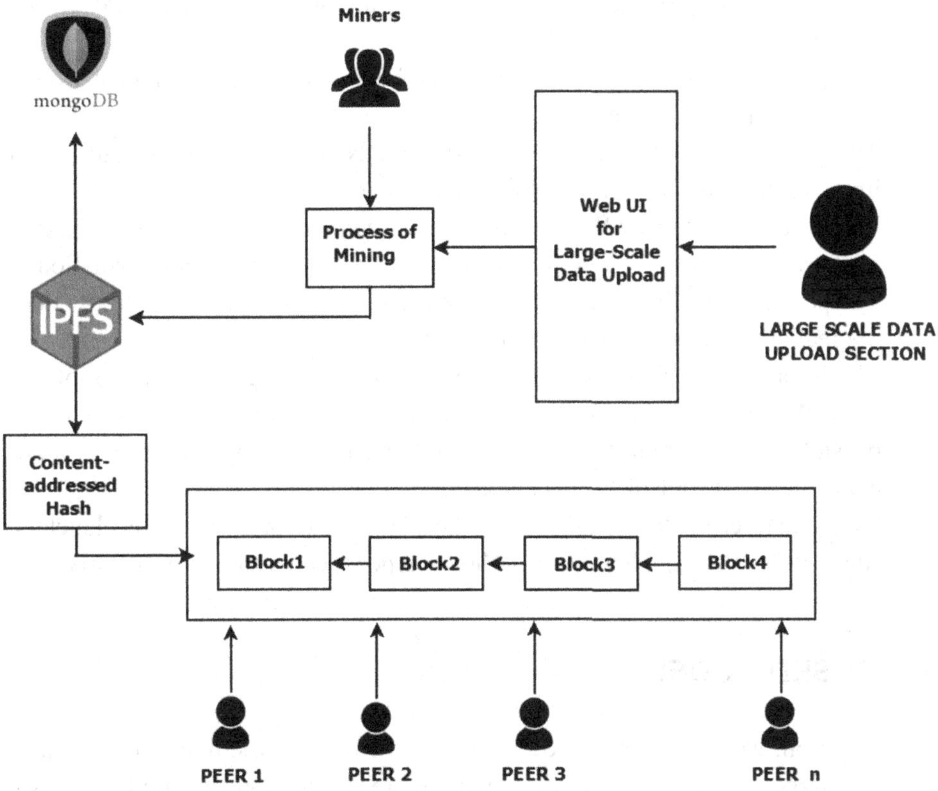

As shown in Figure 1, the work of centralized storage has been explored. The user upload section is provided to each of the peers in-network to share the large scale data and information. Each user is having the authority to access the information from the centralized source. However, the model heavily depends on centralized or third party authority. The existing model is also vulnerable in terms of an attack like DoS (Denial of service attack) where a set of information or complete information can be compromised by sending multiple requests by an adversary; this issue can lead to the single point of failure. To access the stored data from the centralized storage, each time the user has to take permission from the centralized storage. The complete structure describes various issues that need to be managed like data storage, data access, and data privacy.

CONTRIBUTION OF THE CHAPTER

The contribution of the chapter is as follows:

1. The DSSB provides the dissemination of mined block among the peers.
2. The immutability of the critical event (transactions) of a block in the DSSB is maintained
3. The privacy of the critical information and the reduced size of information is stored into the DSSB network by content-addressed hash
4. The Large-Scale data is hash is stored in the NoSQL (MongoDB) storage to improve the audibility in the blockchain network.
5. The security of the DSSB information is maintained by the nodes (peers) registration process (only authorized peers can see the critical information).
6. The permissioned blockchain structure has been designed in such a way that, the malicious peers cannot manipulate the information
7. The information of distributed ledger is shared among all the peers of the network; hence making DoS (denial of service) attack by an adversary is not possible. To distribute the consistent information among the peers, we are using a PoW (Proof-of-Work) algorithm.
8. We have stored the large scale data in the distributed storage i.e., interplanetary file systems (IPFS) where only authorized peers can access the information.

PROPOSED MODEL

In this section, we have showcased our model DSSB with the notion of efficient storage of large scale data which is shown in Figure 2. The proposed model consists of five different parts such as a user or peer upload section, mining approach to validate the transaction, content-addressed hash creation, persistent storage of records in the MongoDB storage, and finally the on-chain (distributed ledger) storage of content-addressed hash. In the peer upload section, a large scale file can be uploaded into the blockchain network. The upload section can be accessed by the peer after the registration into the network. The unauthorized peer cannot access the upload section. The Mining process is performed by using consensus algorithm Proof-of-Work (PoW) to maintain consistency in the blockchain network. The mining approach also validates the transactions which are uploaded by the peer upload section. The content-addressed hash creation is maintained to reduce the size of the distributed ledger of a blockchain network. The content-addressed hash only takes a fixed hash value of 46 bytes storage irrespective of any file size. The content-addressed hash ensures scalability in the network owing to the least storage size (46 bytes). In the

DSSB model, we have proposed content-addressed hash storage for better privacy of the peer information into the network. To maintain the persistent storage in the DSSB model, we have proposed NoSQL (MongoDB) which ensures the availability of the data. The NoSQL becomes suitable to the blockchain storage owing to its JSON (JavaScript Object Notation) based storage.

Figure 2. DSSB Model for large-scale data sharing using Blockchain, NoSQL, and IPFS based Decentralized Storage

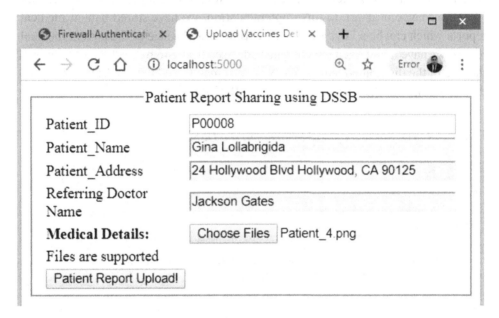

The peers of the network can access the details of the distributed ledger after the consensus resolved technique. The consensus resolve approach is maintained in the DSSB model, to ensure the security in the network.

IMPLEMENTATION OF PROPOSED MODEL (DSSB)

The implementation of our proposed DSSB model is carried out in the MongoDB and IPFS distributed file-sharing system where each transaction is represented into the blockchain network with their content-addressed hash value against the original size of a transaction. In this section, we have addressed the various issues of existing systems like centralization (data storage), data privacy, and dissemination of data. To maintain the persistent storage and auditability of the transactions, we have used

NoSQL (MongoDB) studio 3T storage structure. The experimental setup consists of python anaconda, python flask. The setup is performed on Intel(R) Xeon(R) W-2175 CPU @ 2.50GHZ running Window x64- based processor with 128 GB of RAM and 2 TB of local storage. To develop the complete blockchain model, we have used python anaconda, python flask programming language. In this section, we have implemented as our model (DSSB) proposed in five different parts like peer upload section for large-scale data, miner section(verification of data), content-addressed hash (privacy of data), persistent storage of hash in NoSQL (auditability of data), and finally content-addressed hash storage into the blockchain network (the provenance of data). In this implementation, we have stored patient medical reports which can be a large size of data. To reduce the size of the patient medical report, we have maintained the content-addressed hash (46 bytes storage) to reduce the size of the distributed ledger. We have also maintained the persistent storage of data using MongoDB 3T studio in our DSSB model.

Figure 3. Large file size upload by peers in the DSSB Model

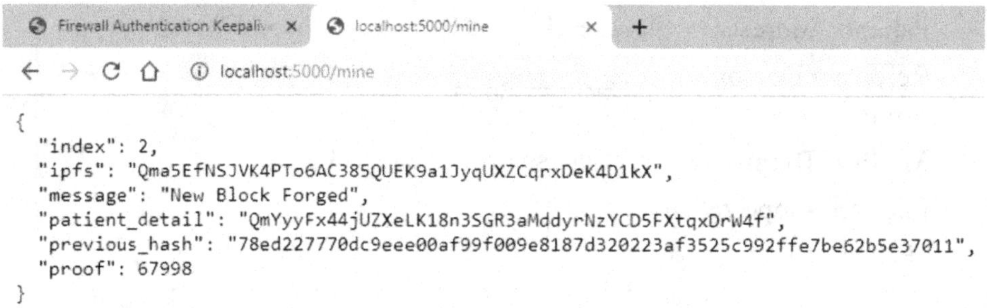
Firewall Authentication Keepaliv
localhost:5000/mine
localhost:5000/mine
{
"index": 2,
"ipfs": "Qma5EfNSJVK4PTo6AC385QUEK9a1JyqUXZCqrxDeK4D1kX",
"message": "New Block Forged",
"patient_detail": "QmYyyFx44jUZXeLK18n3SGR3aMddyrNzYCD5FXtqxDrW4f",
"previous_hash": "78ed227770dc9eee00af99f009e8187d320223af3525c992ffe7be62b5e37011",
"proof": 67998
}

As shown in Figure 3, we have implemented the peer large size data upload section. In this section registered peer (hospital or patient) can upload the medical reports of the patient into the distributed ledger (main-chain) of the network. The uploaded reports can be accessed by the other peers (hospitals) when a patient gets transferred from one hospital to another hospital. The DSSB, model ensures the patient information privacy using content-addressed hash after upload of the original reports. This upload section provides a user-friendly environment to share the data.

Figure 4, Figure 5, and Figure 6 describe the mining process in the DSSB model. To perform the mining process we have used a proof-of-work consensus approach. The consensus approach validates the transactions which are uploaded by the peers into the DSSB model. The PoW consensus maintains the consistency in the network. The other peers in the network maintain the same consensus to access the complete records of the chain using a consensus resolve technique. In the mining process, we are creating an index or block number of the transactions, ipfs hash, or content-addressed hash of the patient reports. We are creating the PDF file to store the uploaded details of the patient like patient_id, patient_name, patient_address, referring doctor name, and maintaining their hash in the patient_details. This hash storage ensures the privacy of patient- information into the distributed ledger of the DSSB model. The previous hash is maintained to ensure the integrity of the subsequent block. In this DSSB model, each block is attached with their subsequent block using the previous hash that shows the tempered-proof storage (changing in one block is difficult because other subsequent blocks also need to be changed). The proof-of-work is stored as proof in our model, which maintains the consistency in the network.

Figure 4. Process of mining to validate the transactions in the DSSB Model

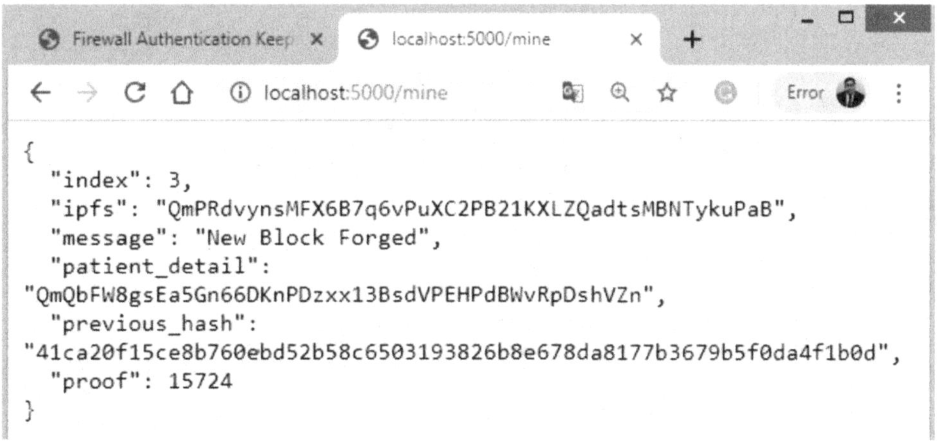
Firewall Authentication Keep
localhost:5000/mine
localhost:5000/mine
Error
{
"index": 3,
"ipfs": "QmPRdvynsMFX6B7q6vPuXC2PB21KXLZQadtsMBNTykuPaB",
"message": "New Block Forged",
"patient_detail":
"QmQbFW8gsEa5Gn66DKnPDzxx13BsdVPEHPdBWvRpDshVZn",
"previous_hash":
"41ca20f15ce8b760ebd52b58c6503193826b8e678da8177b3679b5f0da4f1b0d",
"proof": 15724
}

Figure 5. Process of mining to validate the transactions in the DSSB Model

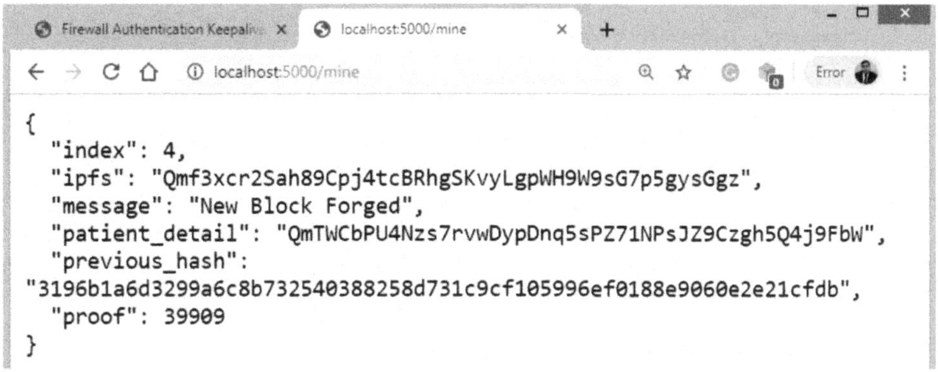
Firewall Authentication Keepaliv
localhost:5000/mine
localhost:5000/mine
Error
{
"index": 4,
"ipfs": "Qmf3xcr2Sah89Cpj4tcBRhgSKvyLgpWH9W9sG7p5gysGgz",
"message": "New Block Forged",
"patient_detail": "QmTWCbPU4Nzs7rvwDypDnq5sPZ71NPsJZ9Czgh5Q4j9FbW",
"previous_hash":
"3196b1a6d3299a6c8b732540388258d731c9cf105996ef0188e9060e2e21cfdb",
"proof": 39909
}

Figure 6. Process of mining to validate the transactions in the DSSB Model

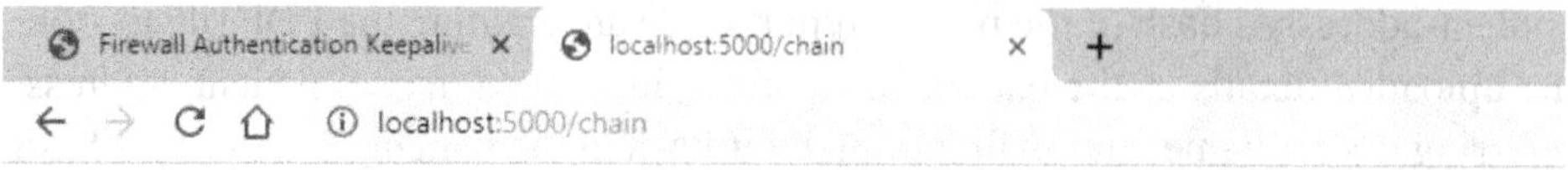

```
{
  "chain": [
    {
      "index": 1,
      "ipfsh": "1",
      "patient_detail": "1",
      "previous_hash": "1",
      "proof": 100,
      "timestamp": 1570049009.4231339,
      "transactions": []
    },
    {
      "index": 2,
      "ipfsh": "Qma5EfNSJVK4PTo6AC385QUEK9a1JyqUXZCqrxDeK4D1kX",
      "patient_detail": "QmYyyFx44jUZXeLK18n3SGR3aMddyrNzYCD5FXtqxDrW4f",
      "previous_hash": "78ed227770dc9eee00af99f009e8187d320223af3525c992ffe7be62b5e37011",
      "proof": 67998,
      "timestamp": 1570049359.0547223,
      "transactions": []
    },
    {
      "index": 3,
      "ipfsh": "QmPRdvynsMFX6B7q6vPuXC2PB21KXLZQadtsMBNTykuPaB",
      "patient_detail": "QmQbFW8gsEa5Gn66DKnPDzxx13BsdVPEHPdBWvRpDshVZn",
      "previous_hash": "41ca20f15ce8b760ebd52b58c6503193826b8e678da8177b3679b5f0da4f1b0d",
      "proof": 15724,
      "timestamp": 1570049576.5583746,
      "transactions": []
    },
    {
      "index": 4,
      "ipfsh": "QmaT38yBJ12aX4r6adZSzHToBiTf5L6qyehXqeapVr6u9E",
      "patient_detail": "QmWDmX5tbFmLXzmV28HX6maNwVF2RaAXH2W4CwEYXJtDyb",
      "previous_hash": "36bff721e87230add8aa2aadd02299ad70ff27a518578da62872bff844df8356",
      "proof": 33230,
      "timestamp": 1570049704.1373596,
      "transactions": []
    },
    {
      "index": 5,
      "ipfsh": "QmXn1amwjmCd7JFyTii5t1H66xRdeW6Dfsnrg6b6bLghkL",
      "patient_detail": "QmNwE8BWmtHVy6cPDBkcJe46jhBkQfqUURY6rBVZ6btMqC",
      "previous_hash": "2d41604c7a05d25bcd8221283e15f906fc4405b04e1117c1a3ceeafdc0f478a9",
      "proof": 66909,
      "timestamp": 1570049821.779329,
      "transactions": []
    }
  ],
  "length": 5
}
```

As shown in Figure 7, the lists of transactions are shown into the distributed ledger (main-chain) of the DSSB model. Each transaction consists of an index, ipfs hash or content-addressed hash, patient details, previous hash, proof, and timestamp. The timestamp ensures the provenance of the information like when this transaction was uploaded to the distributed ledger. The timestamp provides a history of the information in the chain. In our DSSB model, we are using distributed ledger (main-chain) into the port number 5000 shown in Figure 7. The same chain gets disseminated to other peers after the consensus resolve approach. The proof-of-work is maintained while the access of the transactions by the other peers in the network.

Figure 7. List of transactions (large file size hash) in the distributed ledger of DSSB Model

As shown in Figure 8, we have implemented the permissioned blockchain model to maintain the authentication of the peer node. This process also mitigates the malicious attack on the DSSB model owing to authorized access to transactions. The peer node (http://127.0.0.1:6009/nodes/register) is registered in our proposed model to access the list of transactions from a distributed ledger. To access the content from the distributed ledger, we have used a content-addressed approach that ensures the privacy of the transaction. The registration process of the peer nodes (patients or hospitals) in the proposed model authenticates the peers in DSSB and also ensures security during transaction access. The malicious nodes cannot access the transactions (private information of patients) from the distributed ledger owing to

Figure 8. Adding new peer in the DSSB Model

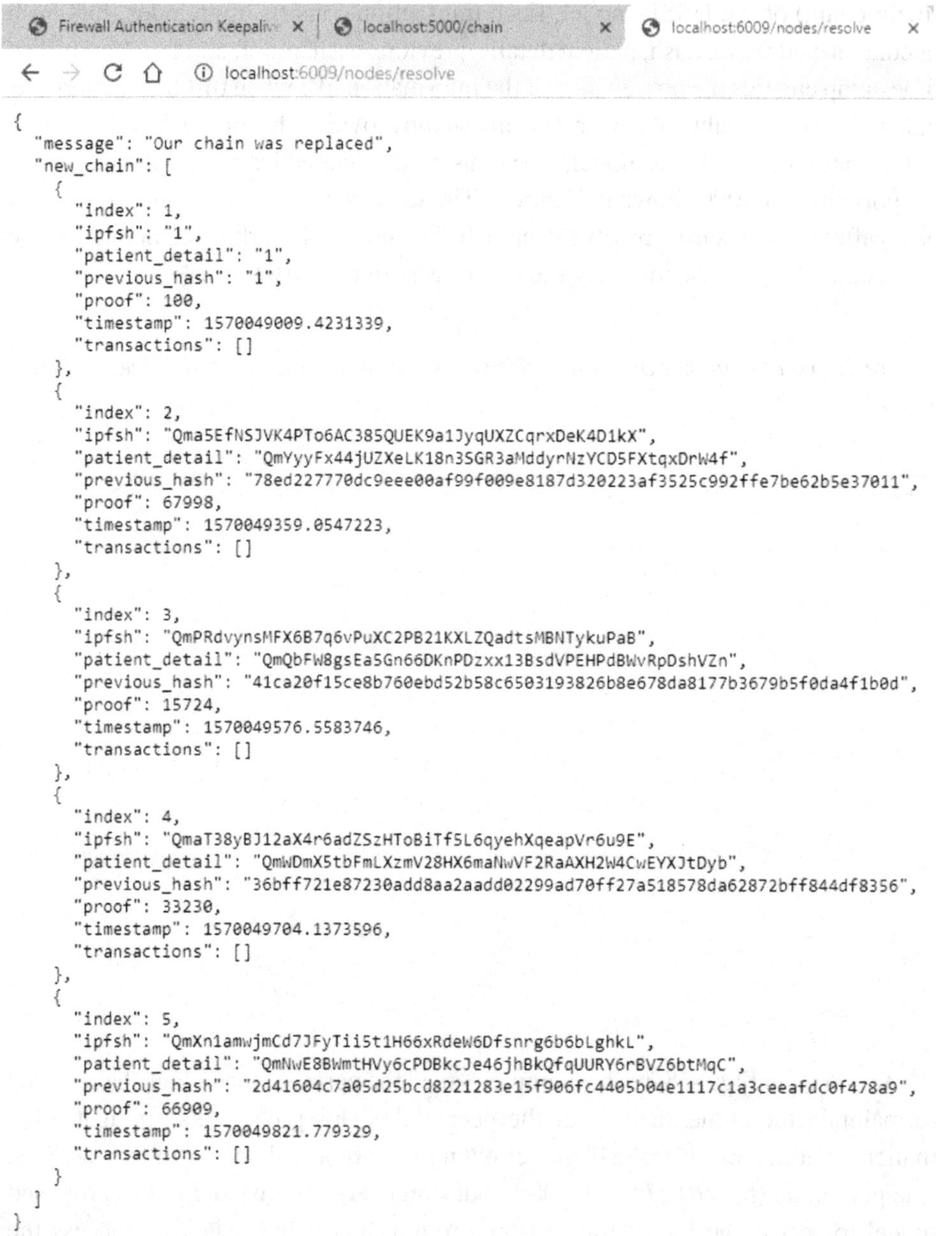
Firewall Authentication Keepaliv
localhost:5000/chain
localhost:6009/nodes/resolve
localhost:6009/nodes/resolve
{
"message": "Our chain was replaced",
"new_chain": [
{
"index": 1,
"ipfsh": "1",
"patient_detail": "1",
"previous_hash": "1",
"proof": 100,
"timestamp": 1570049009.4231339,
"transactions": []
},
{
"index": 2,
"ipfsh": "Qma5EfNSJVK4PTo6AC385QUEK9a1JyqUXZCqrxDeK4D1kX",
"patient_detail": "QmYyyFx44jUZXeLK18n3SGR3aMddyrNzYCD5FXtqxDrW4f",
"previous_hash": "78ed227770dc9eee00af99f009e8187d320223af3525c992ffe7be62b5e37011",
"proof": 67998,
"timestamp": 1570049359.0547223,
"transactions": []
},
{
"index": 3,
"ipfsh": "QmPRdvynsMFX6B7q6vPuXC2PB21KXLZQadtsMBNTykuPaB",
"patient_detail": "QmQbFW8gsEa5Gn66DKnPDzxx13BsdVPEHPdBWvRpDshVZn",
"previous_hash": "41ca20f15ce8b760ebd52b58c6503193826b8e678da8177b3679b5f0da4f1b0d",
"proof": 15724,
"timestamp": 1570049576.5583746,
"transactions": []
},
{
"index": 4,
"ipfsh": "QmaT38yBJ12aX4r6adZSzHToBiTf5L6qyehXqeapVr6u9E",
"patient_detail": "QmWDmX5tbFmLXzmV28HX6maNwVF2RaAXH2W4CwEYXJtDyb",
"previous_hash": "36bff721e87230add8aa2aadd02299ad70ff27a518578da62872bff844df8356",
"proof": 33230,
"timestamp": 1570049704.1373596,
"transactions": []
},
{
"index": 5,
"ipfsh": "QmXn1amwjmCd7JFyTii5t1H66xRdeW6Dfsnrg6b6bLghkL",
"patient_detail": "QmNwE8BWmtHVy6cPDBkcJe46jhBkQfqUURY6rBVZ6btMqC",
"previous_hash": "2d41604c7a05d25bcd8221283e15f906fc4405b04e1117c1a3ceeafdc0f478a9",
"proof": 66909,
"timestamp": 1570049821.779329,
"transactions": []
}
]
}

the registration process of the peers. The registered peer node (http://127.0.0.1:6009/nodes/register) can access the distributed ledger (main chain) which is deployed on (http://127.0.0.1:5000/chain) by agreeing the consensus (PoW) approach of the proposed model on registered port number 6009. To access similar transactions from the distributed ledger (main chain) we have applied consensus resolve technique in the DSSB model (http://localhost:6009/nodes/resolve) shown in Figure 9. In the DSSB model, multiple peers can register to share the patient report into the distributed ledger (main chain). We have applied the process of registration to ensure security in a model from the malicious attack. We have also disseminated the distributed ledger among the peers of the DSSB, to address the issue of centralized storage and single point of failure. The decentralized storage of distributed ledger (main-chain) on various sides of peers (patients or hospitals) ensures the availability of the content in DSSB. The dissemination of the distributed ledger among various peers ensures the content recovery if the distributed chain gets corrupted by the malicious peers. Moreover, the DSSB model does not allow access of distributed ledger (main-chain) content to outside peers of the network owing to the feature of consortium blockchain (unauthorized user cannot access the network).

Figure 9. List of transactions accessed by peers after registration in the DSSB Model

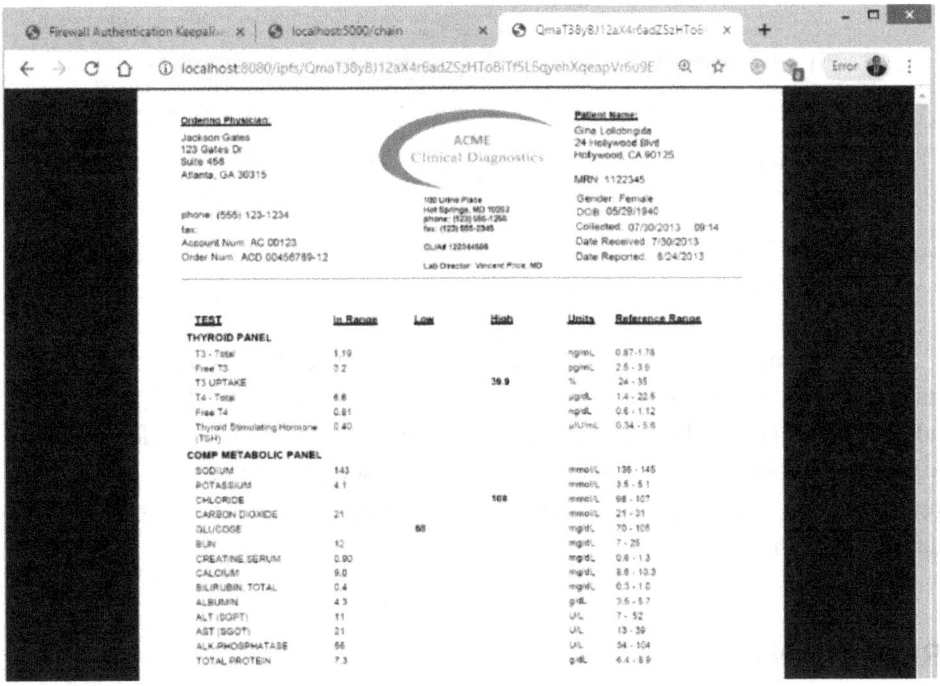

As shown in Figure 9, we have applied a consensus resolve technique to access a similar chain by the peer http://localhost:6009/nodes/resolve in the DSSB model. As we can see a similar distributed ledger is shared with the peer (6009). The distributed ledger (main chain 5000 port) is replaced to the peer side with the same number of block and their contents. The consistency of the block in DSSB is maintained during distributed ledger (main chain) content accessed by peers owing to the feature of consensus (PoW) approach.

Figure 10. Content-addressed hash to access the transaction in DSSB Model

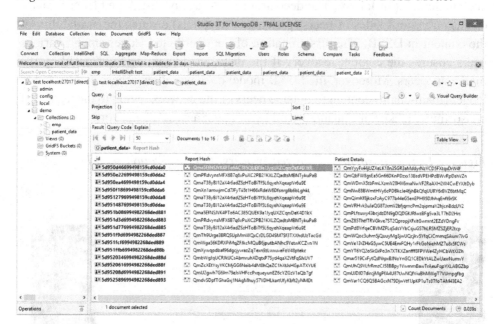

As shown in Figure 10, the patient report is accessed by using content-addressed hash which is already stored into the distributed ledger of DSSB. The content-addressed hash can only be accessed by the already registered peer node. In Figure 10, the patient report has been shared by the peer node into the DSSB model. The registered peers can access the patient details and patient reports by using the content addressed hash technique.

RESULT ANALYSIS

In this section, we have stored the patient details in MongoDB studio 3T. We have implemented the persistence storage of all the transactions using the NoSQL (JSON) structure. The NoSQL is implemented for the query-based system so that registered peers can access the details by writing the NoSQL query which is shown in a query (1). In-studio 3T, we have designed a collection patient_data which consists of all the details of distributed ledger (main-chain) and these details can be accessed by registering into the DSSB model. In patient_data collection, we are storing a content-addressed hash of each patient report including the details of the patients for the auditability purpose. In our proposed model, we have computed both patient details hash and patient report hash which is content-addressed. The content-addressed hash is applied to minimize the storage size of the chain.

Figure 11. List of the stored hash in MongoDB

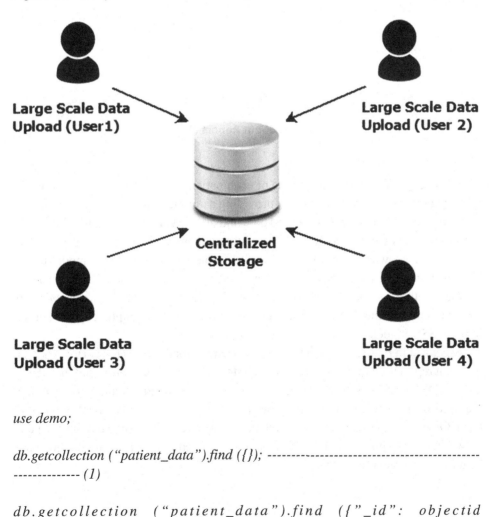

use demo;

db.getcollection ("patient_data").find ({}); -- -------------- (1)

db.getcollection ("patient_data").find ({"_id": objectid ("5d950f18699498159cd0dda6")}) --- (2)

Figure 12. Upload and Download Time in DSSB model (Varying file Size)

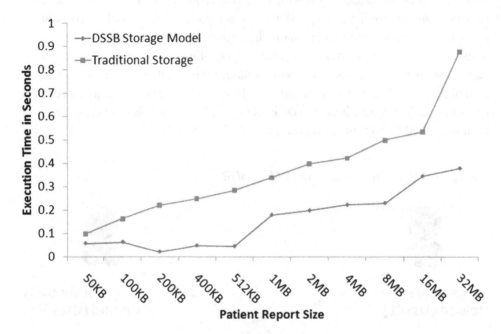

The query (1) provides the details of each patient which is shown in Figure 11. In the patient_data collection, we are providing a unique **id** for each transaction that mitigates the redundancy in the stored data and also to validate the auditability. The registered peers can access the details of the patient by their unique **id** provided in-studio 3T shown in a query (2). We have implemented the DSSB model using NoSQL to provide query-based record access and efficient storage. If the changes are made into the studio 3T, then it can be easily identified from the chain owing to the timestamp of the transactions. The timestamp approach improves auditability in the DSSB model.

As shown in Figure 12, we have computed the upload time of the varying size of a patient report with traditional centralized storage (Mysql) and proposed the DSSB model (DHT and NoSQL Storage). As we can see in the graph and conclude that the upload time is efficient from traditional storage owing to a content-addressed hash. Owing to the less upload time the patient reports can be shared quickly in the network. The proposed model (DSSB) can be utilized in real-time applications for better improvement in scalability.

Figure 13. Block Mining Time in DSSB model (Varying file Size)

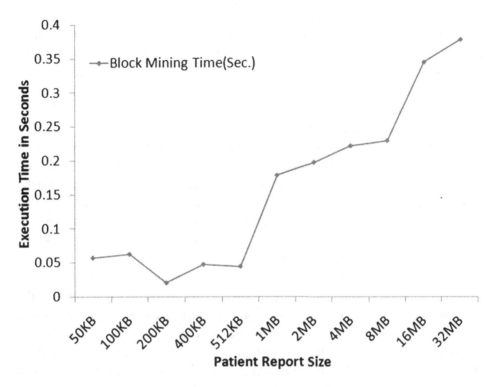

As shown in Figure 13, we have computed the block mining time for varying sizes of the reports in the DSSB model. As we can see in the graph and conclude that the upload time is gradually increasing as the patient report size is increasing. However, the 200KB and 400KB report sizes are average sizes in healthcare. The execution time is slightly decreasing for 200 KB of report size comparing to 50KB and 100KB of report size. The execution time in the mining process of 400KB size of reports is almost similar to 50KB and 100 KB of report size. Thus our proposed model DSSB is efficient in terms of block mining and verifications of the average report size of the patient.

CONCLUSION

In this chapter, we have implemented the hybrid storage DSSB model which provides stores large scale data storage into the blockchain network. To implement this we have used IPFS distributed file storage scheme to generate a content-addressed hash of the files irrespective of the original size. The content-addressed hash only contains

46 bytes of storage on the blockchain network that ensures a greater reduction in the size of a distributed ledger. To store the persistent transactions, we have used MongoDB studio 3T. The MongoDB provides a query-based infrastructure where registered peers can see the records of an individual as well as complete records. Currently, all the blockchain-based applications are maximum allows 100KB files storage. We are the first to manage the large size of data into the blockchain network. The existing model of blockchain is using centralized storage for large-scale data storage. However, centralized storage is prone to mutability, security, privacy, and availability issues due to a single point of failure. The DSSB ensures availability, privacy, and security in the network. To maintain privacy in the network, we have used content-addressed hash for the private information (patient report). To maintain the security in the network, we have designed a consortium blockchain structure so that only authorized peers can access the model. To maintain availability in the network, we have used distributed file storage using IPFS. In the IPFS if one of the peers exists, then the files can be easily accessed. Moreover, the IPFS maintains the distributed hash table (DHT) that ensures version control. The version control minimizes the redundancy in the storage physically. A similar version of files mapped with the same hash in the DHT. This process improves the physical storage infrastructure in our DSSB model. Thus, the DHT storage scheme can be also applied in the real-time blockchain-based application to improve the storage for large scale data. We have implanted the DSSB model using permissioned blockchain (consortium) that ensure the privacy in the network like who will access what content from the distributed ledger.

REFERENCES

Abe, R. (2018). *Mitigating Bitcoin Node Storage Size By DHT*. Academic Press.

Al-mamun, A., Li, T., Sadoghi, M., & Zhao, D. (2018). In-memory Blockchain : Toward Efficient and Trustworthy Data Provenance for HPC Systems. *2018 IEEE International Conference on Big Data (Big Data)*, 3808–3813. 10.1109/BigData.2018.8621897

Ali, S., Wang, G., Bhuiyan, Z. A., & Jiang, H. (2020). Secure Data Provenance in Cloud-centric Internet of Things via Blockchain Smart Contracts. *2018 IEEE SmartWorld, Ubiquitous Intelligence & Computing, Advanced & Trusted Computing, Scalable Computing & Communications, Cloud & Big Data Computing, Internet of People and Smart City Innovation (SmartWorld/SCALCOM/UIC/ATC/CBDCom/ IOP/SCI)*, 991–998. doi:10.1109/SmartWorld.2018.00175

Arslan, S. S., & Goker, T. (n.d.). *Compress-Store on Blockchain : A Decentralized Data Processing and Immutable Storage for Multimedia Streaming*. Academic Press.

Bandara, E., Ng, W. E. E. K., Zoysa, K. D. E., & Fernando, N. (2018). Mystiko — Blockchain Meets Big Data. *2018 IEEE International Conference on Big Data (Big Data)*, 3024–3032. 10.1109/BigData.2018.8622341

Bartoletti, M., Lande, S., Pompianu, L., & Bracciali, A. (2017). *A general framework for blockchain analytics*. Academic Press.

Benet, J. (n.d.). *IPFS - Content Addressed, Versioned, P2P File System* (Draft 3).

Bhuiyan, Z. A., Wang, T., & Wang, G. (2018). *Blockchain and Big Data to Transform the Healthcare*. Academic Press.

Bragagnolo, S., Marra, M., Polito, G., & Boix, E. G. (2019). *Towards Scalable Blockchain Analysis*. doi:10.1109/WETSEB.2019.00007

Cheney, J. (2011). A formal framework for provenance security. *2011 IEEE 24th Computer Security Foundations Symposium*, 281–293. 10.1109/CSF.2011.26

Colloquium, J. N., & Zrt, B. E. (2017). *Blockchain : solving the privacy and research availability tradeoff for EHR data*. Academic Press.

Dai, M., Zhang, S., Wang, H., & Jin, S. (2018). A Low Storage Room Requirement Framework for Distributed Ledger in Blockchain. *IEEE Access: Practical Innovations, Open Solutions, 6*, 22970–22975. doi:10.1109/ACCESS.2018.2814624

Dang, H., Tuan, T., Dinh, A., Loghin, D., Chang, E., Lin, Q., & Ooi, C. (2019). *Towards Scaling Blockchain Systems via Sharding*. Academic Press.

Dika, A., & Nowostawski, M. (2018). Security Vulnerabilities in Ethereum Smart Contracts. *2018 IEEE International Conference on Internet of Things (IThings) and IEEE Green Computing and Communications (GreenCom) and IEEE Cyber, Physical and Social Computing (CPSCom) and IEEE Smart Data (SmartData)*, 955–962. 10.1109/Cybermatics_2018.2018.00182

Dorri, A., Steger, M., & Kanhere, S. S. (n.d.). *SpeedyChain : A framework for decoupling data from blockchain for smart cities*. Academic Press.

Gao, W., Hatcher, W. G., & Yu, W. (2018). A Survey of Blockchain : Techniques, Applications, and Challenges. *2018 27th International Conference on Computer Communication and Networks (ICCCN)*, 1–11. 10.1109/ICCCN.2018.8487348

Gattermayer, J., & Tvrdik, P. (2017). *Blockchain-based multi-level scoring system for P2P clusters*. doi:10.1109/ICPPW.2017.50

Hanley, M. (2018). Managing Lifetime Healthcare Data on the Blockchain. *2018 IEEE SmartWorld, Ubiquitous Intelligence & Computing, Advanced & Trusted Computing, Scalable Computing & Communications, Cloud & Big Data Computing, Internet of People and Smart City Innovation (SmartWorld/SCALCOM/UIC/ATC/ CBDCom/IOP/SCI)*, 246–251. doi:10.1109/SmartWorld.2018.00077

Hua, J., Wang, X., Kang, M., Wang, H., & Wang, F. (2018). Blockchain Based Provenance for Agricultural Products : A Distributed Platform with Duplicated and Shared Bookkeeping. *2018 IEEE Intelligent Vehicles Symposium (IV)*, 97–101. 10.1109/IVS.2018.8500647

Ismail, L., Box, P. O., Ain, A., Hameed, H., Ain, A., Alshamsi, M., … Aldhanhani, N. (2019). *Towards a Blockchain Deployment at UAE University : Performance Evaluation and Blockchain Taxonomy*. Academic Press.

Kang, J., Yu, R., Huang, X., Wu, M., Maharjan, S., Xie, S., & Zhang, Y. (2019). Blockchain for Secure and Efficient Data Sharing in Vehicular Edge Computing and Networks. *IEEE Internet of Things Journal*, *6*(3), 4660–4670. doi:10.1109/ JIOT.2018.2875542

Khqj, V. W., Dqg, Q., Qjlqhhulqj, R., Dqg, H. R. I., Dqg, Q., Dqg, H. R. I., ... Vwhp, W. K. H. V. (2018). %. *ORFNFKDLQ*, *1–5*. Advance online publication. doi:10.1109/WI.2018.000-8

Kim, B. Y. (2018). *Data Managing and Service Exchanging on IoT Service Platform Based on Blockchain with Smart Contract and Spatial Data Processing*. Academic Press.

Li, D., Du, R., Fu, Y., & Au, M. H. (2019). Meta-Key: A Secure Data-Sharing Protocol Under Blockchain-Based Decentralized Storage Architecture. *IEEE Networking Letters*, *1*(1), 30–33. doi:10.1109/LNET.2019.2891998

Li, R., Song, T., Mei, B., Li, H., Cheng, X., Sun, L., ... Worth, F. (2018). *Blockchain For Large-Scale Internet of Things Data Storage and Protection*. Advance online publication. doi:10.1109/TSC.2018.2853167

Li, W., & Sforzin, A. (n.d.). *Towards Scalable and Private Industrial Blockchains*. Academic Press.

Liu, J., Tang, H., Sun, R., Du, X., & Guizani, M. (2019). Lightweight and Privacy-Preserving Medical Services Access for Healthcare Cloud. *IEEE Access: Practical Innovations, Open Solutions*, *7*, 106951–106961. doi:10.1109/ ACCESS.2019.2931917

Liu, S., Wu, J., & Long, C. (2018). IoT Meets Blockchain : Parallel Distributed Architecture for Data Storage and Sharing. *2018 IEEE International Conference on Internet of Things (IThings) and IEEE Green Computing and Communications (GreenCom) and IEEE Cyber, Physical and Social Computing (CPSCom) and IEEE Smart Data (SmartData)*, 1355–1360. 10.1109/Cybermatics_2018.2018.00233

Liu, Y., Wang, K., Member, S., Lin, Y., Xu, W., & Member, S. (2019). *LightChain : A Lightweight Blockchain System for Industrial Internet of Things.* doi:10.1109/TII.2019.2904049

Lu, Z., Wang, Q., Qu, G., Member, S., Zhang, H., & Liu, Z. (2019). *A Blockchain-Based Privacy-Preserving Authentication Scheme for VANETs*. Academic Press.

Maiyya, S., Zakhary, V., & Abbadi, A. El. (2018). *Database and Distributed Computing Fundamentals for Scalable, Fault-tolerant, and Consistent Maintenance of Blockchains*. Academic Press.

Nygaard, R. (n.d.). *Distributed Storage System based on Permissioned Blockchain.* Academic Press.

Sel, D., Zhang, K., & Jacobsen, H. (n.d.). *Towards Solving the Data Availability Problem for Sharded Ethereum*. Academic Press.

Selvanathan, N. (2018). Comparative Study on Decentralized Cloud Collaboration (DCC). *2018 3rd International Conference for Convergence in Technology (I2CT)*, 1–6.

Stoykov, L., Zhang, K., & Jacobsen, H. (n.d.). *Demo : VIBES : Fast Blockchain Simulations for Large-scale Peer-to-Peer Networks*. Academic Press.

Wang, Q., Wang, H., & Zheng, B. (n.d.). *An efficient distributed Storage Strategy for Blockchain*. Academic Press.

Wang, R. (2019). *A Video Surveillance System Based on Permissioned Blockchains and Edge Computing*. Academic Press.

Wang, S., Wang, X., & Zhang, Y. (2019). A Secure Cloud Storage Framework With Access Control Based on Blockchain. *IEEE Access: Practical Innovations, Open Solutions, 7*, 112713–112725. doi:10.1109/ACCESS.2019.2929205

Wang, Z. (2018). Data Sharing and Tracing Scheme Based on Blockchain. *2018 8th International Conference on Logistics, Informatics and Service Sciences (LISS)*, (61662009), 1–6.

Wu, S. (n.d.). *Electronic Medical Record Security Sharing Model Based on Blockchain*. Academic Press.

Xu, J., Xue, K., Member, S., Li, S., & Tian, H. (2019). Healthchain : A Blockchain-based Privacy Preserving Scheme for Large-scale Health Data. *IEEE Internet of Things Journal,* 1. doi:10.1109/JIOT.2019.2923525

Yang, R., Yu, F. R., Si, P., & Member, S. (2019). Integrated Blockchain and Edge Computing Systems : A Survey, Some Research Issues and Challenges. *IEEE Communications Surveys and Tutorials*, *21*(2), 1508–1532. doi:10.1109/ COMST.2019.2894727

Zhang, X., & Chen, X. (2019). Data Security Sharing and Storage Based on a Consortium Blockchain in a Vehicular Ad-hoc Network. *IEEE Access: Practical Innovations, Open Solutions*, *7*, 58241–58254. doi:10.1109/ACCESS.2018.2890736

Zheng, X., Mukkamala, R. R., Vatrapu, R., & Ordieres-mer, J. (2018). *Blockchain-based Personal Health Data Sharing System Using Cloud Storage*. doi:10.1109/ HealthCom.2018.8531125

Chapter 6
Application of Deep Learning in Biological Big Data Analysis

Rohit Shukla
Department of Biotechnology and Bioinformatics, Jaypee University of Information Technology, India

Arvind Kumar Yadav
Department of Biotechnology and Bioinformatics, Jaypee University of Information Technology, India

Tiratha Raj Singh
ⓘ https://orcid.org/0000-0003-1109-5626
Department of Biotechnology and Bioinformatics and Centre for Excellence in Healthcare technologies and Informatics (CEHTI), Jaypee University of Information Technology, India

ABSTRACT

The meaningful data extraction from the biological big data or omics data is a remaining challenge in bioinformatics. The deep learning methods, which can be used for the prediction of hidden information from the biological data, are widely used in the industry and academia. The authors have discussed the similarity and differences in the widely utilized models in deep learning studies. They first discussed the basic structure of various models followed by their applications in biological perspective. They have also discussed the suggestions and limitations of deep learning. They expect that this chapter can serve as significant perspective for continuous development of its theory, algorithm, and application in the established bioinformatics domain.

DOI: 10.4018/978-1-7998-3444-1.ch006

INTRODUCTION

The generation of massive amount of data in this era is a good process in the biological systems and contributes for big data. The big data can be of any type like epigenome, genome, proteome, transcriptome, and metabolome, etc. The big data is defined by its four key characteristics first is volume and others are variety, velocity, and variability. The structure of big data is defined by three types: first is structured, next is unstructured and the last is semi-structured (Mirza et al., 2019). The biological data is very complex as compared to other data because the regulation of one gene or protein depends on the behavior of other genes or regulatory element proteins. The one entity in biological data can regulate many entities and vice versa. In recent years the vast amount of biological data is generated due to the technology advancement towards the high throughput sequencing, medical image processing, genome-wide association studies, gene expression analysis, protein binding motifs and expression studies, pathway and network level analyses, and structural investigations of biological entities etc. These types of data need a complete workflow for the analysis. As earlier described, the biological systems are very complex and not regulated by one entity. Hence in the case of genome-wide association studies, scientists focus on the genetic variants which are associated with the measured phenotypes while only one phenotype is not involved in the disease. It is a very complex process and several elements participate in the disease cascade so by the analysis of one gene or protein or a single type of data, we cannot analyze all the disease spreading factors (C. Xu & Jackson, 2019). Therefore the analysis of all the factors simultaneously can give a better measurement of the disease causing and spreading factors (Zitnik et al., 2019). The other and major challenge regarding the big data is its dimensionality. The big data have high dimensions described by high-resolution data, while in the case of biological data the samples which are collected from the different patients are limited and much less than the number of variables due to its high costs or limited resources like Alzheimer disease patients or replicates of sequencing so they lead to data sparsity, multicollinearity, multiple testing, and overfitting (Altman & Krzywinski, 2018).

The extraction of meaningful information from this complex biological dataset is a challenge in computational biology. Traditionally these types of data were analyzed using various platforms through several statistical and machine learning techniques. Nowadays, the integration of these techniques can handle a large amount of data. With the invention of computation capability in terms of storage and processing, we need to design machine learning-based algorithms which can efficiently extract the meaningful information from the vast amount of data. In that case, deep learning is a part of machine learning and is a very innovative technology that can extract the features on the basis of data characteristics and can also classify the data (Tang, Pan,

Yin, & Khateeb, 2019). Machine learning techniques uses a lot of data as a training set for understanding the fundamental patterns, building the models and on the basis of this information, it makes the best fit model for predicting the hidden patterns and information. For Systems biology, proteomics, genomics and several other domains, few well known algorithms like Hidden Markov Model, Random Forest, Bayesian Networks, Support Vector Machine (SVM) and Gaussian Networks were already used (Larranaga et al., 2006). The conventional machine learning performance is heavily based on the feature's identification which is generated from the data. These features are designed by human engineers who have extensive domain expertise in machine learning. The feature selection is a very critical task because we have to select the appropriate features for the appropriate tasks. Sometimes feature selection can be wrong and it can hinder the whole results. To overcome this drawback, deep learning being evolved as a recently emerging and effective technique. By entering "Deep learning in big data analysis" keyword in Pubmed, we got 134 entries as on dated 09/10/2019. Additionally, it is also responsible for the advancements in the various fields where Artificial Intelligence (AI) community has struggled for many years (LeCun, Bengio, & Hinton, 2015). Several advancements in the deep learning capability describe speech recognition and image processing (Chorowski, Bahdanau, Serdyuk, Cho, & Bengio, 2015). The deep learning also has a key role in language translation (Luong, Pham, & Manning, 2015) and natural language processing (NLP) (Kiros et al., 2015), etc.

THE BASIC CONCEPT OF DEEP LEARNING

The basic idea behind a neural network is the same in the entire concept such as processing of data and feature extraction for generating the results while the assumptions and theories are slightly different. During the forward pass, the input in the first layer activates the network, so by using the weighted connection it spread the activation function to the first layer, and finally, it generates the prediction of reconstructed results. During the backward pass, the weights of connections are tuned by minimizing the difference between the predicted and the real data (Cao et al., 2018).

Basic Framework of Artificial Neural Network

The neural network is frequently utilized in machine learning and it belongs to the information processing modules class. It is a multilayer structure where a basic building block unit called neurons is connected with each other in between the layer while the neuron is not connected in the same layer as shown in **Figure 1.**

Equation 1 describes the processing of inputs in each hidden layer via a connection function in **Figure 1**.

$$h_{W,b}(X) = f(W^T X + b) \dots\dots\dots\dots\dots\dots\dots\dots\dots\dots\dots\dots (1)$$

W and *b* represent the weight and bias respectively. During the activation of all input layer neurons, the weight matrix of respective input neurons is multiplied and then the one bias is summed up with the output and then these values are feed into the adjacent hidden layer. The direct connection between two neurons in the same layer is not established so the information between the input-output is repeated in the hidden layers.

Here the activation function is used for the quantification of the connection between two neighboring neurons in the two hidden layers. The function $W^T X + b$ denoted in equation (1) is the combination of the inputs of the activation function. The output of this function is feed to the next neuron for the new input. Subsequent to the connection formula, the former input feature can be extracted for the next layer; by this means the features can be well-extracted and refined further. The activation function selection significantly decides the performance of feature extraction. Prior to the training of the constructed model, the raw input data is divided randomly into three datasets like first is the training set second is the test set and last is the validation set. The last set (validation set) is usually the experimental data that is used for the validation of the dataset as shown in **Figure 2**.

Learning by Training, Validation, and Testing

Generally, the training of a neural network is described by a process in which it attains self parameters for the processing of network or weights to meet the pre-specified performance criteria. By this training, the model is completely trained and can be further used for classification or regression purposes. As shown in **Figure 2**, the complete dataset which is collected from the experimental observations or automatic methods is divided into a training set, test set, and validation set. These datasets were used for the models training, validation and followed by performance comparison. The characteristics of the model parameters can be tuned normally in several learning paradigms like rectification functions and appropriate activation functions in the initial batches training of the data samples. From here the predicted model or trained network should be validated by using the other datasets for increasing the high robustness and good predictability. This is a process that is mostly referred to the model testing and training (Tang et al., 2019).

Figure 1. The figure shows the general architecture of a deep learning model. It has two hidden layers where X denotes the input layer node and the hidden layer nodes are denoted by H. The output layer is denoted by the Y and f (·) denotes an activation function. W and b represent the weight and bias respectively.

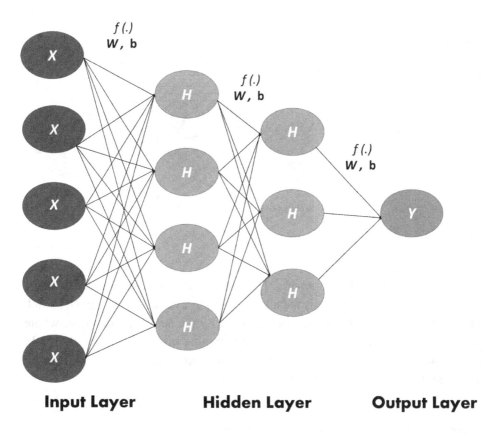

Input Layer   **Hidden Layer**   **Output Layer**

Activation and Loss Function

When the training of a neural network is completed, then it can perform the classification or regression of the given test dataset, although it is a true fact that there is a key difference between the experimental and predicted value. This difference can be minimized by model optimization for better performance. Inside the certain layer, reduction of errors requiring scaling it back within a present range before reaching the next layer of neurons. The activation term defines the neurons output control in active or inactive status, by using various non-linear functions like tanh, rectified linear unit (ReLU) and logistic (Sigmoid or soft step) (LeCun et al., 2015).

Additionally, the loss function is also defined here for the quantification of the total difference between the accurate and the predicted values by using the fine-

Figure 2. Analysis procedure of deep learning method. It covers various aspects like data preparation for training set, model construction, fine-tuning of hyperparameter (in training loop), prediction and performance evaluation. Principally, it still follows the necessary schema in machine learning.

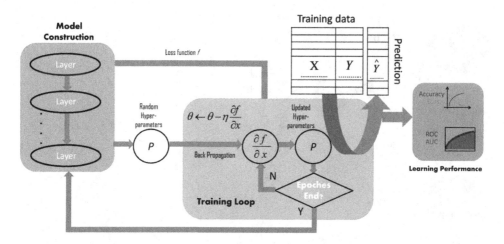

tuning in the backpropagation process. This process acts as an ending threshold for the optimization of parameters by means of iteratively evaluating the trained model. Throughout the diverse layers in each neuron with the activation function, whole hyper-parameter space is searched during the training procedure till the threshold ending, compare and find the combination of an optimal parameter by minimizing the present loss function (Tang et al., 2019).

ADVANCED ALGORITHMS AND THEIR BIOLOGICAL APPLICATIONS

The advancement in the computational hardware and graphics processing unit (GPU) resulting in the advancement in the computation of the massive amount of data to understand the pattern of the data by using the deep learning approaches. In the below section we will discuss several advanced techniques that are currently being used for deep learning by using the high-end computations.

Recurrent Neural Network

It is a type of deep learning model that is more advanced and different from the traditional neural networks. If we compare the Recurrent Neural Network (RNN) with the traditional network models, the RNN can unfold horizontally while it has only one hidden layer, and the using memory (previous results) are utilized by the multi-vertical-groups.

As shown in **Figure 3**, the *Hn* (hidden layer neuron) is described by Equation (2)

$$Hn = \sigma_1(W_{1,n}^T H_{n-1} + W_{2,n}^T X_n + b_{1,n})\dots\dots\dots\dots\dots\dots\dots\dots\dots(2)$$

Here, $W_{1,n}$ and $W_{2,n}$ showing the weight matrix, bias matrix is represented by $b_{1,n}$ and activation function is represented by σ(.) (usually tanh(.)). Hence, the part of output will be generated by each layer from the current hidden layer of neuron with the weight matrix $W_{3,n}$ and bias $b_{2,n}$ defined by Equation (3),

$$\hat{Y}_n = \sigma_2(W_{3,n}H_n + b_{2,n})\dots\dots\dots\dots\dots\dots\dots\dots\dots(3)$$

And the total loss L_{total} will be the sum of the loss functions from each hidden layer, defined as below,

$$L_{total} = \sum_{n=1}^{N} L_n = \sum_{n=1}^{N} L(\hat{Y}, Y)\dots\dots\dots\dots\dots\dots\dots\dots(4)$$

Therefore, the three weights $W_{1,n}$, $W_{2,n}$ and $W_{3,n}$ decides the fine-tuning of RNN back-propagation. While the setting of multi-parameters in weight adds the optimization burden, as compared to Convolutional Neural Network (CNN) the RNN performs worse in the case of fine-tuning. Although it is an ensemble with CNN in various applications like image processing, dimension reduction and video processing (Hu & Lu, 2018).

In a recent study, the authors proposed a combination of RNN-CNN architecture "DeepCpG" on DNA methylation data in a single cell, for the betterment of the prediction of CpG status in the genome-wide analysis; simultaneously the model's interpretable parameters shed light on the connection among sequence composition and methylation variability (Angermueller, Lee, Reik, & Stegle, 2017). Moreover, as compared to conventional models like SVM and logistic regression the RNN can outperform and it can be implemented in the GPUs so it can use the high-performance computing environment (Ang. Li, Serban, & Negrut, 2017). The structural characteristics of RNN make the capability of this algorithm to handle a large amount of sequential data like genomic sequences and DNA arrays (T. Xu, Zhang, Huang, Zhang, & Metaxas, 2016). While the limitation of the RNN is that it cannot interact with the hidden neuron which is far from the current one. For solving the problem of long-time dependence issues in RNN the two recently improved derivatives of RNN, GRU (Gated Recurrent Unit) and LSTM (Long Short-Term Memory) were introduced. These both share a similar architecture with the various gates which are used for the modeling of their memory center (Tang et al., 2019). **Figure 4** represents that the current memory output is influenced by the association of three terms like its current input feature, the context (namely the previous influence) and the inner action towards the input.

Figure 3. The descriptive architecture of RNN, where X, Y, and W are and the Li denotes the loss function between the actual Yi and predicted $\hat{Y}_i$ (i ∈ N)

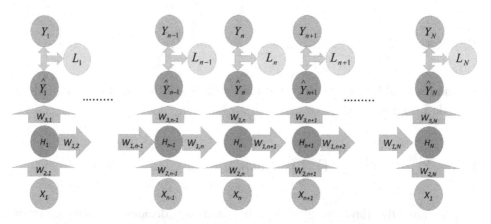

As depicted in **Figure 4**, the red track acts as an input gate for transferring it's all past features, and accessible for any newly added features. The mixture of an input gate and their previous hidden layer neurons are depicted by the orange track. The green track decides that what to skip, specifically resetting the activation function nearby the o, and what should be updated to the red track. The yellow track inner influence is integrated by the output gate of the blue track and it decides the output of the currently hidden neurons and it also decides which content should be passed to the next hidden neuron. The Sekhon *et al* recently proposed an attention-based architecture called DeepDiff, which utilized the LSTM modules hierarchy for the prediction of histone modifications cooperation's simultaneously, and the cell-type-specific gene expression can also be effectively predicted by this architecture (Sekhon, Singh, & Qi, 2018).

Figure 4. The structure of the LSTM network and its general information flow chart

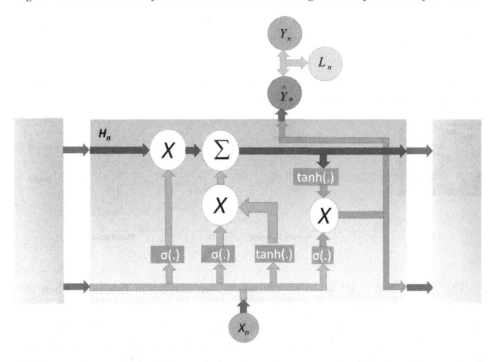

Convolutional Neural Network

The Convolutional neural network (ConvNet or CNN) is a novel architecture or algorithm for information processing in the form of multiple arrays. The general principle of CNN is based on that the reduction in parameters without affecting the CNN learning process and the backpropagation algorithm is used to train for the CNN convolution kernel's parameters (Hu & Lu, 2018). The CNN is especially used for the image-related applications, where it can greatly handle with the image processing and pixel scanning, hence the CNN accelerates the performance of optimized algorithm into practice (Esteva et al., 2017). The CNN architecture is made up of the linear convolution operation, followed by nonlinear activators, classifier of deep neural network and pooling layers as shown in **Figure 5**. The input image in CNN was processed by several filters and after that, the output of this stage is subsample for the new input towards the next layer, and these processes like sub-sampling and convolution are repeated till to obtain the high-level features, namely shapes of figures can be obtained. For obtaining the higher-level feature, CNN should have more layers as depicted in **Figure 5**. During the CNN feature learning process, the 2D image is scanned in the convolution process with a given pattern, and the matching degree is calculated in each step, and finally, the patterns which are present in the scanned region is identified by the pooling (Angermueller, Parnamaa, Parts, & Stegle, 2016). The activation function is used for passing the inputs of the weighted sum for non-linear transformation.

Figure 5. The general architecture and evaluation procedure of a CNN model, which illustrates a classification procedure for an apple on a tree

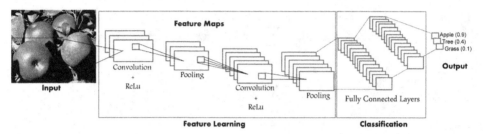

The binary output (0 or 1) is returned by an activation function, when the accumulation of neurons exceeds the present threshold the information is passed to the next layers due to the activation of neurons else the neuron is deactivated. Several activation functions like ReLU, softmax, leaky, sigmoid and tanh are commonly used (LeCun et al., 2015; Schmidhuber, 2015). The dense layer is fed by the concatenated and vectorized pixel information which is known as fully connected layers and used for further classification. The final decision is taken by the fully connected layers where the probability is returned by the CNN which defines that the particular object in the input image belongs to a specific type (Tang et al., 2019).

The loss layer is the next layer to the fully connected layer and it is used for the weight adjustment of the weight throughout the network. The inconsistency of the actual and predicted values and model performance is measured by the loss function. When the loss function is decreased then the model performance is increased. For an output vector y_i and an input $x = (x_1, x_2, \ldots, x_n)$, the mapping loss function $L(\cdot)$ between x and y is defined as,

$$L(y_i, \hat{y}_i) = \frac{1}{n} \sum_{i=1, j=1}^{n,k} \phi[y_i, f(x_i, \sigma_i, \omega_{ij}, b_i)] \quad \ldots\ldots\ldots\ldots\ldots\ldots\ldots\ldots\ldots(5)$$

Where, ϕ is the empirical risk for each output, $\hat{y}$ is the ith prediction, n is the number of total training. The weights ω_{ij} are counted by k and activation function σ_i bias is denoted by b_i.

Due to the association of CNN with the GPU's card and its novel performance in computer vision, CNN uses continuously increasing in the field of biomedical image processing (Hua, Hsu, Hidayati, Cheng, & Chen, 2015). The MRI (magnetic resonance imaging) images, CT (computed tomographic) scans, brain EPV (enlarged perivascular space) detection, and stroke diagnosis image features can better extract by using convolution-pooling structure (Dubost et al., 2019). The DeepChrome a discriminative CNN framework is developed for the gene expression prediction by using the features of histone modification. The deep learning model outperforms traditional Random Forests and SVM on 56 cell types from the REMC database (Singh, Lanchantin, Robins, & Qi, 2016). CNN can also be combined with the other models of deep learning, like RNN to predict the imaging content, where image encoding is done by CNN and the corresponding image description is generated by the RNN (Angermueller et al., 2016).

Autoencoder

The autoencoder is an advance artificial neural network that uses unsupervised learning to extract the key features using data-driven learning (W. Yang et al., 2018). In the case of high-dimensional data, loading all the raw data into a network is a time consuming and infeasible process hence by reducing the data dimensionality or data compression is a key task for the preprocessing of the data. The information can be compressed and encoded in autoencoder in the shortcode from the input layer, then after specific processing, the information is decoded as the output which closely matches the original input. The basic model structure and the processing steps are illustrated in **Figure 6A**.

The encoder algorithm consists of two major steps, first is the convolution and second is the pooling which is shown in **Figure 6B** while two complete opposite steps (deconvolution and unspooling) are used in the decoder which is depicted in **Figure 6C**. Both steps are used for compressing the data while the most important features are preserved in two ways. By using the rectangle window the data is continuously scanned by the convolution, like if we take an example of 3×3 size window; the windows moves towards the next position after every scan, namely pixel, by the replacement of the old elements with the new element, simultaneously with convolution operation. Subsequent to the convolution and whole scanning the pooling is utilized to deeper compress on redundancy.

Figure 6. The descriptive figure of an autoencoder model. (A) The general architecture of an autoencoder model which comprises an input, hidden and output layers; (B) encoding processing steps; (C) Decoding processing steps.

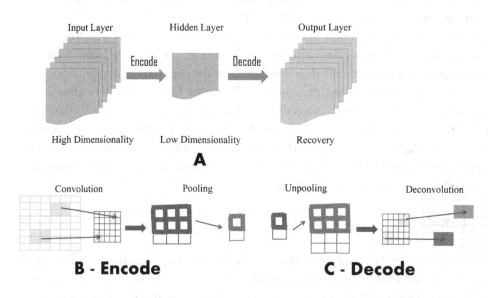

The autoencoder is similar to the traditional principal component methods in the way of data dimension reduction while it can extract more effective and robust data features due to its non-linear alteration in hidden layers. From the given input x, the main features were extracted by the model and generate $\hat{x} = Wb$, where W denotes weight and b denotes the bias vectors. Usually, the input and output cannot fit precisely, which can be calculated through a loss function is the mean squared error (MSE) as depicted in Equation (6).

$$L(W,b) = \frac{1}{m} \sum_{i=1}^{m} (\hat{x} - x)^2 \dots\dots\dots\dots\dots\dots\dots\dots(6)$$

So by the iterative optimization, the loss L is minimized in the learning process.

The denoising of the corrupted data and admirable performance in the dimension reduction a recently introduced algorithm called sparse autoencoder (SAE) is frequently discussed and Equation (7) showed the SAE loss function.

$$L_{SAE} = L(W,b) + \beta \sum_{k} KL(\rho \parallel \hat{\rho}_k) \dots\dots\dots\dots\dots\dots\dots\dots(7)$$

In the equation (7) the KL-divergence is referred by *KL*, the neurons activation level is denoted by ρ, generally fixed as 0.05 in sigmoid condition, indicates most of the neurons are inactive ρ_k represents the neuron k average activation level and the regularization coefficient is designated by β.

$$KL(\rho \| \hat{\rho}_k) = \rho \log \frac{\rho}{\hat{\rho}_k} + (1-\rho) \log \frac{1-\rho}{1-\hat{\rho}_k} \dots\dots\dots\dots\dots\dots\dots\dots\dots(8)$$

Where the level of average activation for a test sample is represented by $\hat{\rho}_k$ and $x^{(i)}$ is the *i-th* test sample in Equation (9).

$$\hat{\rho}_k = \frac{1}{m} \sum \left[a_j(x^{(i)}) \right] \dots\dots\dots\dots\dots\dots\dots\dots\dots\dots\dots(9)$$

The deep autoencoder where several autoencoders are stacked is used for the high dimensional data. This architecture of deep autoencoder may lead to a disappearance gradient, due to its gradient-based and backpropagation learning. The current solutions include adopting ReLu activation and dropout (Krizhevsky, Sutskever, & Hinton, 2017). The greedy layer-wise training is used to acquire the model weights during the configuration and pertaining and after that, the backpropagation algorithm is used for the fine-tuning of the network (Tang et al., 2019).

The SAE and DAE (denoising autoencoder) are the variants of the autoencoder which are proposed recently. The high-resolution histopathological images of breast cancer are analyzed for proposing the stacked sparse autoencoder (SSAE) (J. Xu et al., 2016). The secondary structure of the protein, solvent accessible surface area (SASA) and local backbone angles are predicted by using the SAE algorithm with three iterations (Heffernan et al., 2015). Miotto *et al.* used the stack of DAEs and predicted the key features from the large electronic health care records (EHR) dataset (Miotto, Li, Kidd, & Dudley, 2016).

Deep Belief Network

The Deep Belief Network (DBN) is a generative graphical model and composed of multiple Restricted Boltzmann Machines (RBM) or contains the autoencoders stacked on top of each other, and here each hidden layer acts as a subnetwork and acts as visible layer for the next layer (G. E. Hinton, Osindero, & Teh, 2006).

Figure 7 shows the RBM and DBN main network structure. **Figure 7** showed the construction relation between the two models.

Figure 7. The descriptive network structure of RBM and DBN. (A) The structure of RBM. (B) Take the hidden layer of the trained RBM to function as the visible layer of another RBM. (C) The structure of a DBN. It stacks several RBMs on top of each other to form a DBN.

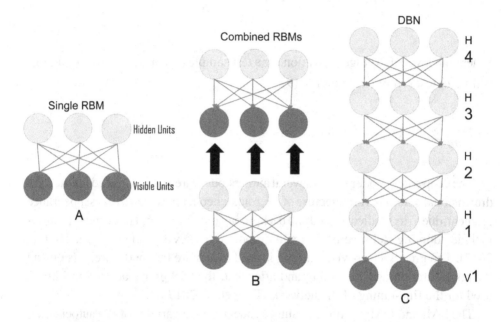

For the initialization of the network weights, the unsupervised greedy approach is used as layer by layer in DBS training, independently; then it can utilize the wake-sleep or backpropagation algorithm during fine-tuning. During the fine-tuning for traditional backpropagation, several problems can be encountered by DBN: (1) for the training it requires label data; (2) slower learning rate; (3) for acquiring the local optimum tending to inappropriate parameters.

DBN was used for lung nodules classification using CT scan image data (Hua et al., 2015) and emotion classification using biomedical signal data (W.-L. Zheng, 2014). By the abstraction of high level features the DBN is also used in the exploitation of a combination of resting-state fMRI (rs-fMRI), gray matter, and white matter data (Akhavan Aghdam, Sharifi, & Pedram, 2018). Meanwhile, DBN and CNN were compared to confirm that deep learning has better discriminative results and holds promise in the medical image diagnosis (Hua et al., 2015).

APPLICATION OF DEEP LEARNING IN BIOLOGICAL DATA ANALYSIS

Meanwhile, deep learning has clearly demonstrated its power in promoting the bioinformatics field. The deep learning is a popular and widely used continuously growing field in several domains of bioinformatics like structure prediction etc. (S. Wang et al., 2019), sequence analysis (R. Umarov, Kuwahara, Li, Gao, & Solovyev, 2019), biomedical image processing and diagnosis (Y. Guo, Liu, Bakker, Guo, & Lew, 2018), biomolecular property and function prediction (Zou, Tian, Gao, & Li, 2019), and biomolecule interaction prediction and systems biology (Smaili, Gao, & Hoehndorf, 2019).

In the case of sequence analysis, the noncoding sequence variants effects were predicted by using the deep learning (Panigrahi & Singh, 2013), for the modeling of the binding affinity landscape of the transcription factor (M. Wang et al., 2018), and peptide sequencing (Tran, Zhang, Xin, Shan, & Li, 2017). It is also used for the modeling of various regulatory events in the pos-transcriptional process like polyadenylation (Leung, Delong, & Frey, 2017), alternative splicing (Leung, Xiong, Lee, & Frey, 2014), identification of promoter (Sagar & Yadav, 2011), transcription start site (R. Umarov, Kuwahara, Li, Gao, & Solovyev, 2018), noncoding RNA identification (C. Yang et al., 2018) and transcript boundaries identification (Shao, Ma, & Wang, 2017).

Deep learning is also used to predict the protein structure during the interaction with other molecules (Fout, Byrd, Shariat, & Ben-Hur, 2017). The structure of membrane protein and protein contact maps were also predicted by deep learning (S. Wang et al., 2019). The drug designing (Kumar et al., 2018) is an emerging field which used various type of machine learning techniques and predicts the potential compounds from a lot of compounds (Shukla, Munjal, & Singh, 2019; Shukla & Singh, 2019). In the case of biomolecular property and function prediction, the deep learning is used for the prediction of details functions and Enzyme Commission number (EC numbers) (Y. Li, Wang, et al., 2018), the protein gene ontology is also predicted by deep learning (Kulmanov, Khan, Hoehndorf, & Wren, 2018).

The deep learning is an emerging field for the early diagnosis of the disease by the biomedical image processing. In a recent study, the authors have developed an efficient method that can identify skin cancer like a dermatologist (Esteva et al., 2017). A method is recently proposed which can automatically predict the level of fluorescence from the transmitted light images of unlabeled biological samples (Christiansen et al., 2018). Finally, cell imaging data is also analyzed by the deep learning method (Godinez, Hossain, Lazic, Davies, & Zhang, 2017). In the field of Systems Biology (Gupta, Singh, Shukla, & Misra, 2013) and biomolecules interaction prediction, the deep learning is a widely used method for the modeling of whole-cell and to model the hierarchical structure (Ma et al., 2018). The polypharmacy effects (Bansal, Srivastava, & Singh, 2018) are also modeled by the multi-model graph convolutional networks by the advantage of deep learning.

LIMITATIONS AND SUGGESTIONS FOR THE DEEP LEARNING PERSPECTIVE

In this section, we have discussed a few of the problems encountered in deep learning.

Lack of Data

The deep learning is totally dependent on the data and the learning also depends upon the data representation (Kermany et al., 2018). For the deep learning model building with excellent performance, we need more amount of data as compared to shallow algorithms. In most of the biological data, it is enough to predict a confident deep learning model (Marx, 2013) while in some rare cases it cannot be enough (Kermany et al., 2018). There are three ways to handle these difficulties. In the first case, the data is used for the transfer learning and collected from the similar type of tasks, while the amount of real data cannot be increased by the related task of data and the better mapping function can be learned by the help of this data and the better representation of original input can boost the model performance (Yosinski, Clune, Bengio, & Lipson, 2014). On the other hand, we can also use a well-trained model from another similar task and fine-tune the last one or two layers using the limited real data. Secondly, we can perform data augmentation (Perez & Wang, 2017). In the third condition, we can use the simulated data also for increasing the amount of training data. Sometimes, if the physical process behind the problem is well-known, we can build simulators based on the physical process, which can result in as much simulated data as we want. The recent study (Y. Li, Xu, et al., 2018) gives us an example of handling the data requirement for deep learning using simulation.

Overfitting

The model complexity in the deep learning model is very high, and all these vast amounts of parameters are related to each other in a very complex manner. For the training data, these models are getting the high risk of overfitted and are not capable to generalize well on the testing data set. The data overfitting problem is associated with every deep learning model, which should be fully measured and properly checked when adapting any of the deep learning methods. The recent studies (Y. Li, Ding, & Gao, 2019) suggest, serious overfitting issues can be managed by the help of implicit bias of deep learning training process although some novel techniques are also required to handle the overfitting issues. The various algorithms are proposed for removing the deep learning overfitting model that can be divided into three parts. Batch normalization (Ioffe & Szegedy, 2015), dropout and weight decay (Krogh & Hertz, 1992) are the most important techniques which act on the model architecture and model parameters. The model inputs such as data corruption and data augmentation are regulated by the second category (Van Der Maaten, Chen, Tyree, & Weinberger, 2013). Due to the insufficient amount of training data, the deep learning models are likely to favor the overfitting problem hence the actual distribution may not be reflected by learned distribution. The increment of data can increase the amount of training data explicitly and the data corruption (Van Der Maaten et al., 2013) is marginalized and the problem can be solved with the help of without augmenting the data explicitly. Recently, a technique (Pereyra, Tucker, Chorowski, Kaiser, & Hinton, 2017) was proposed to control the model by penalizing the over-confident outputs, which was shown to be capable to regulate both CNN and RNN.

Imbalanced Data

In the case of biological data sets the negative data set is much more as compared to the positive set and it represents the data imbalance (P. Yang, Zhang, Zhou, & Zomaya, 2011). In the case of a special type of enzyme family, the number will be less as compared to the non-enzyme proteins (Y. Li, Wang, et al., 2018). This problem also occurs in the poly(A) site prediction (Xiao et al., 2016), transcription starting site prediction (R. K. Umarov & Solovyev, 2017), etc. The undesired results can be obtained due to the use of imbalanced data. The whole data which have 1 positive sample with the 99 negative samples will be predicted as a negative. While in the case of model accuracy it showed a good score of 99% and the result will be wrong if the performance is evaluated on a small dataset. For solving this issue the following techniques can be used. Firstly for the evaluation of prediction results and loss we need to use the right criteria. Additionally, we have to develop such a type of model for imbalanced data which can predict the novel performance in the small dataset also. As a result, we should use AUC as the criteria and the corresponding loss (S. Wang, Sun, & Xu, 2015). In the second case, if the cross-entropy loss is still used, then the user can use the weighted cross-entropy loss which gives the penalty to the model if the model is used for the small data set and performs terribly. In the meantime, the user can downsample the larger classes or upsample the smaller classes during the model training. The hierarchical label space is often found in the biological systems so the models are built on the basis of each hierarchical level for maintaining the data balanced as shown in a recent study (Y. Li, Wang, et al., 2018).

Interpretability

In the case of bioinformatics, useful information like patterns of sequence and motifs can be identified by using the deep learning model. In the case of DNA-protein binding affinity prediction using a deep learning model, we will also try to find which motifs of DNA or protein are important for the binding affinity (Dai et al., 2017). In the case of disease diagnosis if we will build a deep learning model, so our interest is not lying only for the prediction and diagnosis while we will be interested to know, how of the model for disease cause and progression (Choi et al., 2017). To gain that, we can allocate an example-specific significance score for all part of a specific example. In that's direction, the backpropagation-based or perturbation-based approaches can be used by scientists (Chen et al., 2015). The input part is changed in the case of Perturbation-based approaches (R. K. Umarov & Solovyev, 2017) and its impact is observed in the model's output. This idea has high computational complexity while it is easy to understand. Backpropagation-based methods (Shrikumar, Greenside, & Kundaje, 2019) transmit backward the signal from the output layer to the input layer for checking the significant score of different parts of the input. These types of methods are under active development because they proved their usefulness (Sundararajan, Taly, & Yan, 2017). To read the detailed discussion about the methods which are used in bioinformatics and deep learning model interpretability, the reader can refer to (Lipton, 2017).

Uncertainty Scaling

The confidence score which is an important parameter in any application scenario is used for preventing the believing misleading and unreliable predictions. For the prediction, if we use the machine learning methods, we frequently do not just want a final predicted label but also want a confidence score for every query from the model, showing how confident the model is sure about the prediction. The uncertainty scaling is an important parameter in the healthcare because it can assist in the evaluation of the reality of machine learning-based methods for disease diagnosis and an automatic clinical decision (Leibig, Allken, Ayhan, Berens, & Wahl, 2017). The probability score from the direct deep learning Softmax output is usually not in the right scale since deep learning models can output overconfident prediction (Pereyra et al., 2017). For gaining a reliable probability score, the post-scaling is necessary to perform for the Softmax output. Various methods has been developed and suggested for the output of probability score in the right scale, like histogram binning (Zadrozny & Elkan, 2001), legendary Platt scaling (Platt, 1999), Bayesian Binning into Quantiles (BBQ) (Naeini, Cooper, & Hauskrecht, 2015) and isotonic regression (Zadrozny & Elkan, 2002). In a recent study, they showed that temperature scaling is a much better method as compared to other methods for the deep learning methods (C. Guo, Pleiss, Sun, & Weinberger, 2017).

Catastrophic Forgetting

The catastrophic forgetting is defined in the simple term that the new knowledge cannot incorporate into the plain deep learning model without interfering with the learned knowledge (Kirkpatrick et al., 2017). Like if we take an example of a flower classification model, which can classify the 1000 types of flowers, the 1001st class of flowers comes in if the model is fine-tuned with the newly added data, the performance of the fine-tuned model will be unacceptable for the older classes (Y. Li, Li, et al., 2018). The biological data is not constant and with the newly added techniques, it is increasing day by day. If we take the example of protein data bank (PDB), entries in the year 2000 were 13,590 and increased to 158,787 in 2019. The Swiss-Prot is a database that has all the protein sequences and entries in the year 2000 were 100,000 sequences and increased to 561,568 in 2019. The three types of machine learning methods are available which is used for the understanding of human brain neurophysiological theories (Zenke, Gerstner, & Ganguli, 2017), which are free of catastrophic forgetting. The method EWC (Kirkpatrick et al., 2017) is based on regularizations is the first type of method. The iCaRL (Y. Li, Li, et al., 2018) is the second method based on rehearsal training methods and dynamic neural network architecture. The dual memory system based model is the last type of model (G. E. Hinton & Plaut, 1987).

Reducing Computational Requirements and Model Compression

The deep learning models have lots of parameters for their training and are very complex in nature. These are computationally very expensive and require a lot of memory power for gaining the well-trained models and for the accurate result prediction or productive usage of the models (Y. Cheng, Wang, Zhou, & Zhang, 2019). In the case of healthcare data, the doctors evaluate the patients in multiple ways hence data is in heterogeneous nature and it makes the data more complex with the much larger size (Dinov, 2016), resulting in the increase in computational demand (Esteva et al., 2019). Analysis of large scale bioinformatics data using deep-learning is computationally expensive that needs to develop new hardware such as GPUs and FPGAs (Zhang et al., 2015) and new methods. The new methods are divided into four categories. The first type is reducing the unnecessary or redundant parameters by using parameter pruning which is not significantly contributing to the model's performance including the famous DeepCompression (Han, Mao, & Dally, 2016).

In the second type, the model is trained by the distilled knowledge from the larger model as a more compact model by using knowledge distillation (G. Hinton, Vinyals, & Dean, 2015). The compact convolutional filter is used in the third category for saving the parameters (Cohen & Welling, 2016). The informative parameters are estimated in the last category for preserving the low-rank factorization.

Comparison of Various Deep Learning Methods:

There are numerous deep learning algorithms that have been applied in the analysis of biological big data. These algorithms facilitate to move forward in the analysis of various domains such as biomedical image and signal processing. Here, we have compiled some recent works that applied different deep learning methods on various signal and image datasets (**Table 1**). We believe that this will give significant insight to readers to choose appropriate deep learning approaches in their research domain.

CONCLUSION

In this chapter, we tried to summarize the basic and essential concepts of deep learning. The detailed description of deep learning techniques and their applications were discussed in sequence analysis, biomedical image analysis, and many more domains. We have reviewed the various typical deep learning models such as CNN, RNN, autoencoder, and DBN. We emphasized the specific application in biological and other scenarios, like data feature and model applicability, are the important factors in designing a suitable deep learning approach for extracting the knowledge from the biological data. Recent deep learning studies suggest that the selection of specific deep learning models either classical or derivatives of the classical network models including CNN, RNN, autoencoder, and DBN are making hindrances in the result in deep learning applications. After describing the various deep learning variants architecture and its applications we have described the limitations and suggestions to improve the deep learning techniques for wide applications.

The deep learning is achieving high success in the various fields with the extraordinary innovations day by day, some even argued that deep learning can bring another wave like the internet. The deep learning is shaping our future of the societies and our lives with the long term efforts to its full extent. With the progressive success of this field, we should not overestimate the deep learning for the Artificial Intelligence agency or academia, and a lot of problems remained to solve due to its nature.

Table 1. Comparison of different deep-learning methods and their performance on various signal and image datasets

Type of method	Biomedical signal processing			Biomedical image processing		
	Research topic	Author	Results	Research topic	Author	Results
CNN	Discriminate brain activity	(Spampinato et al., 2017)	Accuracy 86.9%	Classification of lung nodules	(Hua et al., 2015)	Sensitivity 73.3% Specificity 78.7%
	Heartbeat classification	(Acharya, Oh, et al., 2017)	Accuracy 94.03%	Response prediction of neoadjuvant chemotherapy	(Ypsilantis et al., 2015)	Accuracy 73.4%
	Heartbeat classification	(Kiranyaz, Ince, & Gabbouj, 2016)	Accuracy 99%	Hierarchical image classification	(Y. Guo et al., 2018)	Accuracy 76.01%
	Congestive heart failure detection	(Y. Zheng, Liu, Chen, Ge, & Zhao, 2014)	Accuracy 94.67%	-	-	-
	Arrhythmia detection	(Acharya, Fujita, et al., 2017)	Accuracy 92.50.67%	-	-	-
RNN	Sleep apnea detection	(M. Cheng, Sori, Jiang, Khan, & Liu, 2017)	Accuracy 90%	Hierarchical image classification	(Y. Guo et al., 2018)	Accuracy 75.09%
	Emotion recognition	(Alhagry, Fahmy, & El-Khoribi, 2017)	Accuracy 85%	-	-	-
DNN	Heartbeat classification	(Luo, Li, Wang, & Cuschieri, 2017)	Accuracy 97.5%	Brain decoding	(Koyamada, Shikauchi, Nakae, Koyama, & Ishii, 2015)	Accuracy 50.74%
DBN	Emotion classification	(W.-L. Zheng, 2014)	Accuracy 87.62%	Classification of lung nodules	(Hua et al., 2015)	Sensitivity 73.4% Specificity 82.2%
	Motor imagery	(J. Li & Cichocki, 2014)	Accuracy 96%	-	-	-
Autoencoder	Sleep state identification	(Fraiwan & Lweesy, 2017)	Accuracy 80.4%	Diagnosis of Alzheimer's Disease (AD)	(Suk & Shen, 2013)	Accuracy 95.9%
	Fetal-ECG signal reconstruction	(Muduli, Gunukula, & Mukherjee, 2016)	Accuracy 99.67%	-	-	-

In conclusion, we tried to summarize all the efforts which have been made in recent years to develop new techniques of deep learning and their use in biological data analysis. We anticipate that this chapter will provide an insight into the deep learning techniques and their applications in the biological big data analysis to the students, academicians, and researchers globally.

REFERENCES

Acharya, U. R., Fujita, H., Lih, O. S., Hagiwara, Y., Tan, J. H., & Adam, M. (2017). Automated Detection of Arrhythmias Using Different Intervals of Tachycardia ECG Segments with Convolutional Neural Network. *Inf. Sci.*, *405*, 81–90. doi:10.1016/j.ins.2017.04.012

Acharya, U. R., Oh, S. L., Hagiwara, Y., Tan, J. H., Adam, M., Gertych, A., & Tan, R. S. (2017). A deep convolutional neural network model to classify heartbeats. *Computers in Biology and Medicine*, *89*, 389–396. doi:10.1016/j.compbiomed.2017.08.022 PMID:28869899

Akhavan Aghdam, M., Sharifi, A., & Pedram, M. M. (2018). Combination of rs-fMRI and sMRI Data to Discriminate Autism Spectrum Disorders in Young Children Using Deep Belief Network. *Journal of Digital Imaging*, *31*(6), 895–903. doi:10.100710278-018-0093-8 PMID:29736781

Alhagry, S., Fahmy, A. A., & El-Khoribi, R. A. (2017). Emotion Recognition based on EEG using LSTM Recurrent Neural Network. *International Journal of Advanced Computer Science and Applications, 8.*

Altman, N., & Krzywinski, M. (2018). The curse(s) of dimensionality. *Nature Methods*, *15*(6), 399–400. doi:10.103841592-018-0019-x PMID:29855577

Angermueller, C., Lee, H. J., Reik, W., & Stegle, O. (2017). DeepCpG: Accurate prediction of single-cell DNA methylation states using deep learning. *Genome Biology*, *18*(1), 67. doi:10.118613059-017-1189-z PMID:28395661

Angermueller, C., Parnamaa, T., Parts, L., & Stegle, O. (2016). Deep learning for computational biology. *Molecular Systems Biology*, *12*(7), 878. doi:10.15252/msb.20156651 PMID:27474269

Bansal, A., Srivastava, P. A., & Singh, T. R. (2018). An integrative approach to develop computational pipeline for drug-target interaction network analysis. *Scientific Reports*, *8*(1), 1–9. doi:10.103841598-018-28577-6 PMID:29980766

Cao, C., Liu, F., Tan, H., Song, D., Shu, W., Li, W., Zhou, Y., Bo, X., & Xie, Z. (2018). Deep Learning and Its Applications in Biomedicine. *Genomics, Proteomics & Bioinformatics*, *16*(1), 17–32. doi:10.1016/j.gpb.2017.07.003 PMID:29522900

Chen, T., Li, M., Li, Y., Lin, M., Wang, N., Wang, M., … Zhang, Z. (2015). *MXNet: A Flexible and Efficient Machine Learning Library for Heterogeneous Distributed Systems*. Retrieved from https://arxiv.org/abs/1512.01274

Cheng, M., Sori, W. J., Jiang, F., Khan, A., & Liu, S. (2017). Recurrent Neural Network Based Classification of ECG Signal Features for Obstruction of Sleep Apnea Detection. *2017 IEEE International Conference on Computational Science and Engineering (CSE) and IEEE International Conference on Embedded and Ubiquitous Computing (EUC), 2*, 199–202. 10.1109/CSE-EUC.2017.220

Cheng, Y., Wang, D., Zhou, P., & Zhang, T. (2019). *A Survey of Model Compression and Acceleration for Deep Neural Networks*. Retrieved from https://arxiv.org/abs/1710.09282

Choi, E., Bahadori, M. T., Kulas, J. A., Schuetz, A., Stewart, W. F., & Sun, J. (2017). *RETAIN: An Interpretable Predictive Model for Healthcare using Reverse Time Attention Mechanism*. Retrieved from https://arxiv.org/abs/1608.05745

Chorowski, J., Bahdanau, D., Serdyuk, D., Cho, K., & Bengio, Y. (2015). Attention-based models for speech recognition. In Advances in Neural Information Processing Systems, (pp. 577–585). Neural Information Processing Systems Foundation.

Christiansen, E. M., Yang, S. J., Ando, D. M., Javaherian, A., Skibinski, G., Lipnick, S., … Finkbeiner, S. (2018). In Silico Labeling: Predicting Fluorescent Labels in Unlabeled Images. Cell, 173, 792-803.

Cohen, T., & Welling, M. (2016). Group Equivariant Convolutional Networks. *International Conference on Machine Learning*, 2990–2999.

Dai, H., Umarov, R., Kuwahara, H., Li, Y., Song, L., & Gao, X. (2017). Sequence2Vec: A novel embedding approach for modeling transcription factor binding affinity landscape. *Bioinformatics (Oxford, England), 33*(22), 3575–3583. doi:10.1093/bioinformatics/btx480 PMID:28961686

Dinov, I. D. (2016). Volume and Value of Big Healthcare Data. *Journal of Medical Statistics and Informatics, 4*(1), 4. doi:10.7243/2053-7662-4-3 PMID:26998309

Dubost, F., Adams, H., Bortsova, G., Ikram, M. A., Niessen, W., Vernooij, M., & de Bruijne, M. (2019). 3D regression neural network for the quantification of enlarged perivascular spaces in brain MRI. *Medical Image Analysis, 51*, 89–100. doi:10.1016/j.media.2018.10.008 PMID:30390514

Esteva, A., Kuprel, B., Novoa, R. A., Ko, J., Swetter, S. M., Blau, H. M., & Thrun, S. (2017). Dermatologist-level classification of skin cancer with deep neural networks. *Nature*, *542*(7639), 115–118. doi:10.1038/nature21056 PMID:28117445

Esteva, A., Robicquet, A., Ramsundar, B., Kuleshov, V., DePristo, M., Chou, K., Cui, C., Corrado, G., Thrun, S., & Dean, J. (2019). A guide to deep learning in healthcare. *Nature Medicine*, *25*(1), 24–29. doi:10.103841591-018-0316-z PMID:30617335

Fout, A., Byrd, J., Shariat, B., & Ben-Hur, A. (2017). Protein Interface Prediction using Graph Convolutional Networks. In I. Guyon, U. V. Luxburg, S. Bengio, H. Wallach, R. Fergus, S. Vishwanathan, & R. Garnett (Eds.), Advances in Neural Information Processing Systems (Vol. 30, pp. 6530–6539). Curran Associates, Inc.

Fraiwan, L., & Lweesy, K. (2017). Neonatal sleep state identification using deep learning autoencoders. *2017 IEEE 13th International Colloquium on Signal Processing Its Applications (CSPA)*, 228–231.

Godinez, W. J., Hossain, I., Lazic, S. E., Davies, J. W., & Zhang, X. (2017). A multi-scale convolutional neural network for phenotyping high-content cellular images. *Bioinformatics (Oxford, England)*, *33*(13), 2010–2019. doi:10.1093/bioinformatics/btx069 PMID:28203779

Guo, C., Pleiss, G., Sun, Y., & Weinberger, K. Q. (2017). *On Calibration of Modern Neural Networks*. Retrieved from https://arxiv.org/abs/1706.04599

Guo, Y., Liu, Y., Bakker, E. M., Guo, Y., & Lew, M. S. (2018). CNN-RNN: A large-scale hierarchical image classification framework. *Multimedia Tools and Applications*, *77*(8), 10251–10271. doi:10.100711042-017-5443-x

Gupta, M. K., Singh, D. B., Shukla, R., & Misra, K. (2013). A comprehensive metabolic modeling of thyroid pathway in relation to thyroid pathophysiology and therapeutics. *OMICS: A Journal of Integrative Biology*, *17*(11), 584–593. doi:10.1089/omi.2013.0007 PMID:24044365

Han, S., Mao, H., & Dally, W. J. (2016). *Deep Compression: Compressing Deep Neural Networks with Pruning, Trained Quantization and Huffman Coding*. Retrieved from https://arxiv.org/abs/1510.00149

Heffernan, R., Paliwal, K., Lyons, J., Dehzangi, A., Sharma, A., Wang, J., Sattar, A., Yang, Y., & Zhou, Y. (2015). Improving prediction of secondary structure, local backbone angles, and solvent accessible surface area of proteins by iterative deep learning. *Scientific Reports*, *5*(1), 11476. doi:10.1038rep11476 PMID:26098304

Hinton, G., Vinyals, O., & Dean, J. (2015). *Distilling the Knowledge in a Neural Network*. Retrieved from https://arxiv.org/abs/1503.02531

Hinton, G. E., Osindero, S., & Teh, Y.-W. (2006). A fast learning algorithm for deep belief nets. *Neural Computation, 18*(7), 1527–1554. doi:10.1162/neco.2006.18.7.1527 PMID:16764513

Hinton, G. E., & Plaut, D. C. (1987). Using Fast Weights to Deblur Old Memories. In *Proceedings of the 9th Annual Conference of the Cognitive Science Society*, (pp. 177–186). Erlbaum.

Hu, Y., & Lu, X. (2018). Learning spatial-temporal features for video copy detection by the combination of CNN and RNN. *Journal of Visual Communication and Image Representation, 55*, 21–29. doi:10.1016/j.jvcir.2018.05.013

Hua, K.-L., Hsu, C.-H., Hidayati, S. C., Cheng, W.-H., & Chen, Y.-J. (2015). Computer-aided classification of lung nodules on computed tomography images via deep learning technique. *OncoTargets and Therapy, 8*, 2015–2022. PMID:26346558

Ioffe, S., & Szegedy, C. (2015). *Batch Normalization: Accelerating Deep Network Training by Reducing Internal Covariate Shift*. Retrieved from https://arxiv.org/abs/1502.03167

Kermany, D. S., Goldbaum, M., Cai, W., Valentim, C. C. S., Liang, H., Baxter, S. L., McKeown, A., Yang, G., Wu, X., Yan, F., Dong, J., Prasadha, M. K., Pei, J., Ting, M. Y. L., Zhu, J., Li, C., Hewett, S., Dong, J., Ziyar, I., ... Zhang, K. (2018). Identifying Medical Diagnoses and Treatable Diseases by Image-Based Deep Learning. *Cell, 172*(5), 1122–1131.e9. doi:10.1016/j.cell.2018.02.010 PMID:29474911

Kiranyaz, S., Ince, T., & Gabbouj, M. (2016). Real-Time Patient-Specific ECG Classification by 1-D Convolutional Neural Networks. *IEEE Transactions on Biomedical Engineering, 63*(3), 664–675. doi:10.1109/TBME.2015.2468589 PMID:26285054

Kirkpatrick, J., Pascanu, R., Rabinowitz, N., Veness, J., Desjardins, G., Rusu, A. A., ... Hadsell, R. (2017). *Overcoming catastrophic forgetting in neural networks*. Retrieved from https://arxiv.org/abs/1612.00796

Kiros, R., Zhu, Y., Salakhutdinov, R., Zemel, R. S., Torralba, A., Urtasun, R., & Fidler, S. (2015). *Skip-Thought Vectors*. Retrieved from https://arxiv.org/abs/1506.06726

Koyamada, S., Shikauchi, Y., Nakae, K., Koyama, M., & Ishii, S. (2015). *Deep learning of fMRI big data: A novel approach to subject-transfer decoding*. Retrieved from https://arxiv.org/abs/1502.00093

Krizhevsky, A., Sutskever, I., & Hinton, G. E. (2017). ImageNet Classification with Deep Convolutional Neural Networks. *Communications of the ACM*, *60*(6), 84–90. doi:10.1145/3065386

Krogh, A., & Hertz, J. A. (1992). A Simple Weight Decay Can Improve Generalization. In J. E. Moody, S. J. Hanson, & R. P. Lippmann (Eds.), Advances in Neural Information Processing Systems (Vol. 4, pp. 950–957). Morgan-Kaufmann.

Kulmanov, M., Khan, M. A., Hoehndorf, R., & Wren, J. (2018). DeepGO: Predicting protein functions from sequence and interactions using a deep ontology-aware classifier. *Bioinformatics (Oxford, England)*, *34*(4), 660–668. doi:10.1093/bioinformatics/btx624 PMID:29028931

Kumar, A., Mehta, V., Raj, U., Varadwaj, P. K., Udayabanu, M., Yennamalli, R. M., & Singh, T. R. (2018). Computational and in-vitro validation of natural molecules as potential Acetylcholinesterase inhibitors and neuroprotective agents. *Current Alzheimer Research*. PMID:30543170

Larranaga, P., Calvo, B., Santana, R., Bielza, C., Galdiano, J., Inza, I., Lozano, J. A., Armañanzas, R., Santafé, G., Pérez, A., & Robles, V. (2006). Machine learning in bioinformatics. *Briefings in Bioinformatics*, *7*(1), 86–112. doi:10.1093/bib/bbk007 PMID:16761367

LeCun, Y., Bengio, Y., & Hinton, G. (2015). Deep learning. *Nature*, *521*(7553), 436–444. doi:10.1038/nature14539 PMID:26017442

Leibig, C., Allken, V., Ayhan, M. S., Berens, P., & Wahl, S. (2017). Leveraging uncertainty information from deep neural networks for disease detection. *Scientific Reports*, *7*(1), 1–14. doi:10.103841598-017-17876-z PMID:29259224

Leung, M. K. K., Delong, A., & Frey, B. J. (2017). Inference of the Human Polyadenylation Code. *bioRxiv*, 130591.

Leung, M. K. K., Xiong, H. Y., Lee, L. J., & Frey, B. J. (2014). Deep learning of the tissue-regulated splicing code. *Bioinformatics (Oxford, England)*, *30*(12), i121–i129. doi:10.1093/bioinformatics/btu277 PMID:24931975

Li, A., Serban, R., & Negrut, D. (2017). Analysis of a Splitting Approach for the Parallel Solution of Linear Systems on GPU Cards. *SIAM Journal on Scientific Computing*, *39*(3), C215–C237. doi:10.1137/15M1039523

Li, J., & Cichocki, A. (2014). Deep Learning of Multifractal Attributes from Motor Imagery Induced EEG. In C. K. Loo, K. S. Yap, K. W. Wong, A. Teoh, & K. Huang (Eds.), *Neural Information Processing* (pp. 503–510). Springer International Publishing. doi:10.1007/978-3-319-12637-1_63

Li, Y., Ding, L., & Gao, X. (2019). *On the Decision Boundary of Deep Neural Networks*. Retrieved from https://arxiv.org/abs/1808.05385

Li, Y., Li, Z., Ding, L., Pan, Y., Huang, C., Hu, Y., … Gao, X. (2018). *SupportNet: Solving catastrophic forgetting in class incremental learning with support data*. Retrieved from https://arxiv.org/abs/1806.02942

Li, Y., Wang, S., Umarov, R., Xie, B., Fan, M., Li, L., & Gao, X. (2018). DEEPre: Sequence-based enzyme EC number prediction by deep learning. *Bioinformatics (Oxford, England)*, *34*(5), 760–769. doi:10.1093/bioinformatics/btx680 PMID:29069344

Li, Y., Xu, F., Zhang, F., Xu, P., Zhang, M., Fan, M., Li, L., Gao, X., & Han, R. (2018). DLBI: Deep learning guided Bayesian inference for structure reconstruction of super-resolution fluorescence microscopy. *Bioinformatics (Oxford, England)*, *34*(13), i284–i294. doi:10.1093/bioinformatics/bty241 PMID:29950012

Lipton, Z. C. (2017). *The Mythos of Model Interpretability*. Retrieved from https://arxiv.org/abs/1606.03490

Luo, K., Li, J., Wang, Z., & Cuschieri, A. (2017). *Patient-Specific Deep Architectural Model for ECG Classification*. Academic Press.

Luong, M.-T., Pham, H., & Manning, C. D. (2015). *Effective Approaches to Attention-based Neural Machine Translation*. Retrieved from https://arxiv.org/abs/1508.04025

Ma, J., Yu, M. K., Fong, S., Ono, K., Sage, E., Demchak, B., Sharan, R., & Ideker, T. (2018). Using deep learning to model the hierarchical structure and function of a cell. *Nature Methods*, *15*(4), 290–298. doi:10.1038/nmeth.4627 PMID:29505029

Marx, V. (2013). Biology: The big challenges of big data. *Nature*, *498*(7453), 255–260. doi:10.1038/498255a PMID:23765498

Miotto, R., Li, L., Kidd, B. A., & Dudley, J. T. (2016). Deep Patient: An Unsupervised Representation to Predict the Future of Patients from the Electronic Health Records. *Scientific Reports*, *6*(1), 26094. doi:10.1038rep26094 PMID:27185194

Mirza, B., Wang, W., Wang, J., Choi, H., Chung, N. C., & Ping, P. (2019). Machine Learning and Integrative Analysis of Biomedical Big Data. *Genes*, *10*(2), 10. doi:10.3390/genes10020087 PMID:30696086

Muduli, P. R., Gunukula, R. R., & Mukherjee, A. (2016). A deep learning approach to fetal-ECG signal reconstruction. *2016 Twenty Second National Conference on Communication (NCC)*, 1–6. 10.1109/NCC.2016.7561206

Naeini, M. P., Cooper, G. F., & Hauskrecht, M. (2015). Obtaining Well Calibrated Probabilities Using Bayesian Binning. *Proceedings of the ... AAAI Conference on Artificial Intelligence. AAAI Conference on Artificial Intelligence*, 2901–2907.

Panigrahi, P. P., & Singh, T. R. (2013). Computational studies on Alzheimer's disease associated pathways and regulatory patterns using microarray gene expression and network data: Revealed association with aging and other diseases. *Journal of Theoretical Biology*, *334*, 109–121. doi:10.1016/j.jtbi.2013.06.013 PMID:23811083

Pereyra, G., Tucker, G., Chorowski, J., Kaiser, Ł., & Hinton, G. (2017). *Regularizing Neural Networks by Penalizing Confident Output Distributions*. Retrieved from https://arxiv.org/abs/1701.06548

Perez, L., & Wang, J. (2017). *The Effectiveness of Data Augmentation in Image Classification using Deep Learning*. Retrieved from https://arxiv.org/abs/1712.04621

Platt, J. C. (1999). *Probabilistic Outputs for Support Vector Machines and Comparisons to Regularized Likelihood Methods. In Advances in Large Margin Classifiers*. MIT Press.

Sagar, M., & Yadav, A. K. (2011). Computer-aided vaccine design for liver cancer using epitopes of HBx protein isolates from HBV substrains. *International Journal of Bioinformatics Research and Applications*, *7*(3), 299–316. doi:10.1504/IJBRA.2011.041740 PMID:21816717

Schmidhuber, J. (2015). Deep learning in neural networks: An overview. *Neural Networks*, *61*, 85–117. doi:10.1016/j.neunet.2014.09.003 PMID:25462637

Sekhon, A., Singh, R., & Qi, Y. (2018). DeepDiff: DEEP-learning for predicting DIFFerential gene expression from histone modifications. *Bioinformatics (Oxford, England)*, *34*(17), i891–i900. doi:10.1093/bioinformatics/bty612 PMID:30423076

Shao, M., Ma, J., & Wang, S. (2017). DeepBound: Accurate identification of transcript boundaries via deep convolutional neural fields. *Bioinformatics (Oxford, England)*, *33*(14), i267–i273. doi:10.1093/bioinformatics/btx267 PMID:28881999

Shrikumar, A., Greenside, P., & Kundaje, A. (2019). *Learning Important Features Through Propagating Activation Differences*. Retrieved from https://arxiv.org/abs/1704.02685

Shukla, R., Munjal, N. S., & Singh, T. R. (2019). Identification of novel small molecules against GSK3β for Alzheimer's disease using chemoinformatics approach. *Journal of Molecular Graphics & Modelling, 91*, 91–104. doi:10.1016/j.jmgm.2019.06.008 PMID:31202091

Shukla, R., & Singh, T. R. (2019). Virtual Screening, Pharmacokinetics, Molecular dynamics and binding free energy analysis for small natural molecules against Cyclin-dependent kinase 5 for Alzheimer's disease. *Journal of Biomolecular Structure & Dynamics*, 1–22. doi:10.1080/07391102.2019.1696890 PMID:30688165

Singh, R., Lanchantin, J., Robins, G., & Qi, Y. (2016). DeepChrome: Deep-learning for predicting gene expression from histone modifications. *Bioinformatics (Oxford, England), 32*(17), i639–i648. doi:10.1093/bioinformatics/btw427 PMID:27587684

Smaili, F. Z., Gao, X., & Hoehndorf, R. (2019). OPA2Vec: Combining formal and informal content of biomedical ontologies to improve similarity-based prediction. *Bioinformatics (Oxford, England), 35*(12), 2133–2140. doi:10.1093/bioinformatics/bty933 PMID:30407490

Spampinato, C., Palazzo, S., Kavasidis, I., Giordano, D., Souly, N., & Shah, M. (2017). Deep Learning Human Mind for Automated Visual Classification. *2017 IEEE Conference on Computer Vision and Pattern Recognition (CVPR)*, 4503–4511. 10.1109/CVPR.2017.479

Suk, H.-I., & Shen, D. (2013). Deep learning-based feature representation for AD/MCI classification. Medical Image Computing and Computer-Assisted Intervention: *MICCAI ... International Conference on Medical Image Computing and Computer-Assisted Intervention, 16*, 583–590. 10.1007/978-3-642-40763-5_72

Sundararajan, M., Taly, A., & Yan, Q. (2017). *Axiomatic Attribution for Deep Networks*. Retrieved from https://arxiv.org/abs/1703.01365

Tang, B., Pan, Z., Yin, K., & Khateeb, A. (2019). Recent Advances of Deep Learning in Bioinformatics and Computational Biology. *Frontiers in Genetics, 10*, 214. doi:10.3389/fgene.2019.00214 PMID:30972100

Tran, N. H., Zhang, X., Xin, L., Shan, B., & Li, M. (2017). De novo peptide sequencing by deep learning. *Proceedings of the National Academy of Sciences of the United States of America, 114*(31), 8247–8252. doi:10.1073/pnas.1705691114 PMID:28720701

Umarov, R., Kuwahara, H., Li, Y., Gao, X., & Solovyev, V. (2018). *PromID: Human promoter prediction by deep learning*. Retrieved from https://arxiv.org/abs/1810.01414

Umarov, R., Kuwahara, H., Li, Y., Gao, X., & Solovyev, V. (2019). Promoter analysis and prediction in the human genome using sequence-based deep learning models. *Bioinformatics (Oxford, England)*, *35*(16), 2730–2737. doi:10.1093/bioinformatics/bty1068 PMID:30601980

Umarov, R. K., & Solovyev, V. V. (2017). Recognition of prokaryotic and eukaryotic promoters using convolutional deep learning neural networks. *PLoS One*, *12*(2), e0171410. doi:10.1371/journal.pone.0171410 PMID:28158264

Van Der Maaten, L., Chen, M., Tyree, S., & Weinberger, K. Q. (2013). Learning with Marginalized Corrupted Features. *Proceedings of the 30th International Conference on International Conference on Machine Learning*, 28, I–410–I–418.

Wang, M., Tai, C. E. W., & Wei, L. (2018). DeFine: Deep convolutional neural networks accurately quantify intensities of transcription factor-DNA binding and facilitate evaluation of functional non-coding variants. *Nucleic Acids Research*, *46*(11), e69. doi:10.1093/nar/gky215 PMID:29617928

Wang, S., Fei, S., Wang, Z., Li, Y., Xu, J., Zhao, F., & Gao, X. (2019). PredMP: A web server for de novo prediction and visualization of membrane proteins. *Bioinformatics (Oxford, England)*, *35*(4), 691–693. doi:10.1093/bioinformatics/bty684 PMID:30084960

Wang, S., Sun, S., & Xu, J. (2015). *AUC-maximized Deep Convolutional Neural Fields for Sequence Labeling*. Retrieved from https://arxiv.org/abs/1511.05265

Xiao, M.-S., Zhang, B., Li, Y.-S., Gao, Q., Sun, W., & Chen, W. (2016). Global analysis of regulatory divergence in the evolution of mouse alternative polyadenylation. *Molecular Systems Biology*, *12*(12), 890. doi:10.15252/msb.20167375 PMID:27932516

Xu, C., & Jackson, S. A. (2019). Machine learning and complex biological data. *Genome Biology*, *20*(1), 76. doi:10.118613059-019-1689-0 PMID:30992073

Xu, J., Xiang, L., Liu, Q., Gilmore, H., Wu, J., Tang, J., & Madabhushi, A. (2016). Stacked Sparse Autoencoder (SSAE) for Nuclei Detection on Breast Cancer Histopathology Images. *IEEE Transactions on Medical Imaging*, *35*(1), 119–130. doi:10.1109/TMI.2015.2458702 PMID:26208307

Xu, T., Zhang, H., Huang, X., Zhang, S., & Metaxas, D. N. (2016). Multimodal Deep Learning for Cervical Dysplasia Diagnosis. In S. Ourselin, L. Joskowicz, M. R. Sabuncu, G. Unal, & W. Wells (Eds.), *MICCAI 2016* (pp. 115–123). Springer International Publishing. doi:10.1007/978-3-319-46723-8_14

Yang, C., Yang, L., Zhou, M., Xie, H., Zhang, C., Wang, M. D., & Zhu, H. (2018). LncADeep: An ab initio lncRNA identification and functional annotation tool based on deep learning. *Bioinformatics (Oxford, England)*, *34*(22), 3825–3834. doi:10.1093/bioinformatics/bty428 PMID:29850816

Yang, P., Zhang, Z., Zhou, B. B., & Zomaya, A. Y. (2011). Sample Subset Optimization for Classifying Imbalanced Biological Data. In *Proceedings of the 15th Pacific-Asia Conference on Advances in Knowledge Discovery and Data Mining - Volume Part II*, (pp. 333–344). Berlin: Springer-Verlag. 10.1007/978-3-642-20847-8_28

Yang, W., Liu, Q., Wang, S., Cui, Z., Chen, X., Chen, L., & Zhang, N. (2018). Down image recognition based on deep convolutional neural network. *Information Processing in Agriculture*, *5*(2), 246–252. doi:10.1016/j.inpa.2018.01.004

Yosinski, J., Clune, J., Bengio, Y., & Lipson, H. (2014). How transferable are features in deep neural networks? In Z. Ghahramani, M. Welling, C. Cortes, N. D. Lawrence, & K. Q. Weinberger (Eds.), Advances in Neural Information Processing Systems (Vol. 27, pp. 3320–3328). Curran Associates, Inc.

Ypsilantis, P.-P., Siddique, M., Sohn, H.-M., Davies, A., Cook, G., Goh, V., & Montana, G. (2015). Predicting Response to Neoadjuvant Chemotherapy with PET Imaging Using Convolutional Neural Networks. *PLoS One*, *10*(9), e0137036. doi:10.1371/journal.pone.0137036 PMID:26355298

Zadrozny, B., & Elkan, C. (2001). Obtaining Calibrated Probability Estimates from Decision Trees and Naive Bayesian Classifiers. In *Proceedings of the Eighteenth International Conference on Machine Learning*, (pp. 609–616). San Francisco, CA: Morgan Kaufmann Publishers Inc.

Zadrozny, B., & Elkan, C. (2002). Transforming Classifier Scores into Accurate Multiclass Probability Estimates. In *Proceedings of the Eighth ACM SIGKDD International Conference on Knowledge Discovery and Data Mining*, (pp. 694–699). New York, NY: ACM. 10.1145/775047.775151

Zenke, F., Gerstner, W., & Ganguli, S. (2017). The temporal paradox of Hebbian learning and homeostatic plasticity. *Current Opinion in Neurobiology*, *43*, 166–176. doi:10.1016/j.conb.2017.03.015 PMID:28431369

Zhang, C., Li, P., Sun, G., Guan, Y., Xiao, B., & Cong, J. (2015). Optimizing FPGA-based Accelerator Design for Deep Convolutional Neural Networks. In *Proceedings of the 2015 ACM/SIGDA International Symposium on Field-Programmable Gate Arrays*, (pp. 161–170). New York, NY: ACM. 10.1145/2684746.2689060

Zheng, W.-L. (2014, September 8). *EEG-based emotion classification using deep belief networks.* Retrieved December 13, 2019, from Wei-Long Zheng website: https://weilongzheng.github.io/publication/zheng2014eeg/

Zheng, Y., Liu, Q., Chen, E., Ge, Y., & Zhao, J. L. (2014). Time Series Classification Using Multi-Channels Deep Convolutional Neural Networks. In F. Li, G. Li, S. Hwang, B. Yao, & Z. Zhang (Eds.), *Web-Age Information Management* (pp. 298–310). Springer International Publishing. doi:10.1007/978-3-319-08010-9_33

Zitnik, M., Nguyen, F., Wang, B., Leskovec, J., Goldenberg, A., & Hoffman, M. M. (2019). Machine Learning for Integrating Data in Biology and Medicine: Principles, Practice, and Opportunities. *An International Journal on Information Fusion, 50,* 71–91. doi:10.1016/j.inffus.2018.09.012 PMID:30467459

Zou, Z., Tian, S., Gao, X., & Li, Y. (2019). mlDEEPre: Multi-Functional Enzyme Function Prediction With Hierarchical Multi-Label Deep Learning. *Frontiers in Genetics, 9,* 9. doi:10.3389/fgene.2018.00714 PMID:30723495

Chapter 7
Building Better India:
Powered by Blockchain

Swarup Roy Chowdhury
Sabre Corporation, India

Suman Saha
Jaypee University of Information Technology, India

ABSTRACT

We can name many industries that are still based on the same working practices and business models that they have had for a long time – maybe since they started. Despite the wealth of modern technology now available, public infrastructure, a critical component for the well-being of the society, is still an industry based on the paperwork, letters, emails, manual approvals, and a large amount of guess work. It involves a lot of manual effort and is also error prone. It is really very hard for the stakeholders and end users to get an update on the progress of the project, which impacts them directly or indirectly. The authors intend to develop a groundbreaking blockchain platform that can meet the needs of all the different stakeholders involved in creating and providing a better infrastructure. They plan to automate the entire process by using smart contracts to minimize paperwork for the government officials. This will not only eliminate the errors that can happen during manual execution but will also provide a real-time update to all the stakeholders in making the process more transparent.

DOI: 10.4018/978-1-7998-3444-1.ch007

INTRODUCTION

Blockchain technology (BCT) has gained popularity because of it's wider acceptance in the recent past as the technology has developed platforms for various applications in almost all areas (Okada et al., 2017; Lemieux, 2017; Xu, 2017; Glaser, 2017). Some of the most important features of the open blockchain technology include - global nature and scope, decentralized and distributed character, built-in transparency and independence of trusted parties. These features are particularly important in countries vulnerable to corruption and in which there is a general distrust in government on the part of citizens and businesses. However, as our use cases show, most countries can benefit from the global reach and openness that the open blockchain technology offers.

The specific aim of this chapter is to discuss how and in what ways the blockchain technology can be used as an infrastructure for specific areas in government (Xu, 2017; Glaser & Bezzenberger, 2015; Saltzer, 1984). There are many paper contracts written between the governments, brokers, contractors that often won't be in place until the infrastructure is built. It is based on the experience of the people building this or some historical data that might be there in the government records. The risk can change significantly while an infrastructure like a flyover is being built or as simple as a tarred road is being laid. It may sustain damage due to soil conditions or adverse weather conditions or even due to lack of expertise of the contractor being hired for delivering the project (Lemieux, 2017; Xu, 2017; Lemieux, 2016). We intend to develop a ground-breaking platform using blockchain that can meet the needs of all the different parties involved in creating a better infrastructure for the country. We plan to automate the entire process by using smart contracts to minimize paperwork for government officials (Lindman, 2017; Phillip, 2004; Huckle, 2016).

The core strength of blockchain lies in its ability to connect every party involved in the work and have the data stored in the database which is visible to everyone but is also secured completely (Zyskind et al., 2015). The solution will be applied across the entire infrastructure arena including the end consumers - the citizens of India. The visibility of near real-time data connected directly to smart contracts will also help in decision-making, security, and transparency with third parties such as regulators and auditors who will also be able to view the data stored in the database. Developing the platform requires a connected effort across all facets of the workstream. We want to gain a deep understanding of the practical needs of the community through workshops with everyone involved in the process of building the infrastructure. We had an initial set of design thinking workshop to understand the actual problem. Based on that we have come up with a high-level architecture for this solution to work in an end-to-end fashion. We recommend having a detailed design thinking workshop to get the specific requirements that will help in achieving the right solution (Zhu & Zhou, 2016; Kianmajd et al., 2016).

We also recommend the solution will be built in an iterative agile fashion. Product Owner should be the key player of managing and maintaining the product backlog while being in constant discussion with the users of this platform. This will ensure we have a Minimum Viable Product (MVP) going out in the first quarter for the users to try out and provide feedback (Koshy et al., 2014). This approach will help to build the right solution iteratively and fail fast (if at all).

We have organized the chapter in such a way that it provides all the ingredients to implement this solution. Starting with a detailed high-level architecture with deep insights into each of the areas of the architecture is the backbone of the chapter. This is backed by a case study to provide even more insights on how the solution can be achieved on a practical basis. We will end the chapter with a conclusion and scope for future work so that the solution can benefit society.

HIGH-LEVEL ARCHITECTURE

We plan to utilize the blockchain platform to support and build full-fledged capabilities for government projects to function most efficiently and transparently possible (Ron & Shamir, 2012. We plan to build this platform to cater to individual users (B2C) as well as Enterprises (B2B) across three areas. We plan to divide it into 3 areas – Users, Platform, and Enterprise. The capabilities we depicted as part of each area are all indicative of reference architecture (Biswas et al., 2016). We plan to use the cloud because of its inherent in-built capability of elasticity, performance, and networking characteristics (Banerjee et al., 2017).

Let us explain three areas one by one in detail.

USER AREA

They can be anyone starting from Government Officials, Suppliers, and Contractors to even individual workers and citizens as well. The User Area will primarily have the actors who can be in WAN using the Internet or in cloud systems or edge services.

Edge Services

We plan to use Edge service – the component that will be exposed to the public internet and which will act as a gateway to allow the data to flow safely from the actors in the user area to the blockchain platform. End-user applications are also supported by the Edge Services. Edge service includes the following which will help in efficiently serving the inbound traffic:

Figure 1. High-level architecture

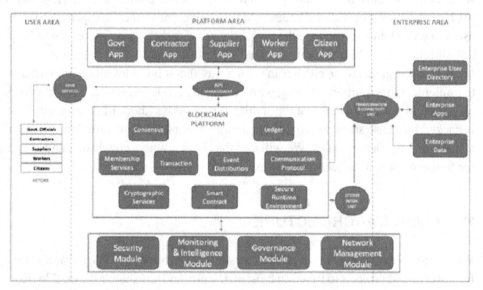

Domain Name System (DNS) - The DNS will resolve the URL from the user area to the IP address of the server hosting the service in the blockchain platform which is designed to serve the request (Kondor et al., 2014; Crosby et al., 2016; Johnson, 2001).

Firewall -Firewalls will help in providing network security and will also monitor and control incoming and outgoing network traffic based on preconfigured security rules. It will help in establishing a barrier between our blockchain platform (trusted internal network) and the user area (untrusted external network). Network firewalls will help in filtering the inbound traffic from the user area.

Content Delivery Networks (CDN) - The CDNs will help the participants in the user area with enhanced response time by providing distributed systems of servers deployed across the country. This will minimize the response time for serving the requests by the blockchain platform to geographically distributed users. This will ensure that content is always highly available and displayed to users with minimum response time (Ralph, & Samaniego, 2016; Sarah, 2016; Lemieux, 2016).

Load Balancers - We will use a load balancer which will act as a reverse proxy and distributes traffic from the user area into our platform. Load balancers will also help to increase the capacity (concurrent users) and reliability of the platform. This will also help in keeping the platform always available without a single point of failure (Christidis & Devetsikiotis, 2016; Hon, 2016; Hashemi, 2016).

Requests received by load balancers will be distributed to a particular server in our platform based on one of the configured algorithm shown below.

- Round robin
- Weighted round-robin
- Least connections
- Least response time

Users

Users are the actors of our blockchain platform who will perform operations on our blockchain platform by creating and distributing blockchain applications. Below is the list of the users:

Government Officials – Government officials will publish the tenders, sign, and approve the contracts.

Contractors – Contractors work on tenders, upload the tenders, and on successful win, sign the contract.

Suppliers – Suppliers will supply the materials, upload the invoices against the contract for proper billing, tax payment, and audit.

Workers – Workers and their supervisors will upload their plan of work and job cards to ensure online tracking monitoring and reporting is possible to check the progress of the project and also monitor the health of the project.

Citizens – Citizens operate in a business network and will interact with this blockchain platform using an application.

Now that we have defined the actors, let us define how they will access the platform and the constituent components of this platform.

PLATFORM AREA

Apps

To leverage the core capabilities of the blockchain platform intuitively and seamlessly, we plan to develop applications that will provide business capabilities to the users of our platform. Apps will be designed for the end-users to present the capabilities to the users in such a way that enhances their ease of use. We plan to implement some applications for authorization and controlling these applications which will be in the control of administrators, operators and auditors (Zyskind, et al., 2015; Aitzhan et al., 2016; Zhang et al., 2016; Kosba, et al., 2016). These applications can be in the form of web applications or mobile applications that will run on the end-user device(s). They will connect to the blockchain platform through Edge Service. These apps will work on REST-based APIs which will interface with our core blockchain platform using the APIs offered by the blockchain platform.

This will be broadly categorized into two areas:

Standard in-built apps - We plan to provide a few standard applications which will help in start leveraging the capabilities of the blockchain platform.

Customized apps – Users (mostly administrators) will have the provision to build their customized apps as per their needs. This would reduce the dependency on the core team and will help in reducing the operation cost.

API Management Layer

Standard API Management capabilities will be used. This will help developers and end-users to rapidly enable solutions.

The apps will interface with the blockchain platform through the API management layer. Our blockchain platform will provide various APIs which the apps can use to interact with the platform components to achieve their business goals.

Blockchain Platform

The Blockchain platform we are planning to build will support all the essential capabilities required for this solution (Meiklejohn, et al., 2013; Reynolds et al., 2017; Liu, et al., 2017).

Ledger -Each Ledger entry is typically maintained as the block in the blockchain platform so that no one can tamper the entries. Ledger generally holds cryptographically linked blocks in the sequence that are used to store transaction details.

But ledgers are everywhere. Ledgers do more than just recording transactions. Here as we will need a **consensus** about **facts** hence we will use a ledger to record facts related to the project – be it recording the authenticity of materials used or the progress of the project updated by various stakeholders working on the project.

Consensus –Consensus component as the name suggests will enable the consensus process which will be used by the nodes within the blockchain platform to agree on the validity and order of the transactions that will be appended to the ledger when the transactions take place. This will be achieved by the component by maintaining a single ledger which will be replicated across the network and thus providing consistency.

Smart Contract -Smart contracts on the blockchain platform allows the automatic execution of agreements autonomously and securely. Smart contracts will help in eliminating the manual work that is needed when contracts are executed like maintaining, enforcing, and sending confirmation that it is successfully executed. This will ease a lot of overhead from the government officials, contractors, suppliers, workers and help in providing run-time updates to all the stakeholders including the citizens of the country (Polyzo, & Fotiou, 2017; Pinzon, 2016).

Smart contracts in blockchain are nothing but computer programs that will execute in any secure node within the blockchain platform. Smart contracts have business logic which involves terms of the contract and conditions that are agreed between the participants.

There are primarily two types of contract – Complete Contract and Incomplete Contract. In a complete contract, we generally denote what will happen when there is a contingency. On the other hand, in an incomplete contract, we need to have a provision to allow the terms of the contract to be renegotiated in case of events that we did not anticipate at the time of writing the contract. Incomplete contracts also explain why some exchanges take place in contracts and why others take place outside of the contract, and provide a further guide to questions. Executing a complete contract is a herculean task, while incomplete contracts take a lot of time and effort. It allows every stakeholder in the contract including citizens of the country to operate where before only government officials could operate.

There is something called smart contract code which helps in identifying a recorded transaction in the blockchain platform and the information associated with the same. Smart contracts will be written in the programming language that will be supported by the blockchain platform.

A smart contract code will be stored in the Ledger. A transaction will invoke smart contract functions, which can be either stateful or stateless and will perform the business logic written in the contract. The smart contract code will have the provision to access external information and systems which will interface with the help of the system integration component.

Smart contracts help in making the right decisions by automating the relationships. For this to happen, all the possible outcomes must be specified in the contract beforehand.

Membership Services - These services will be used to provide privacy, confidentiality, audibility, and identity within the blockchain platform (Dennis & Owenson, 2016; Stankovic, 2014; Zhao et al, 2016).

Membership service will apply only to the permissioned blockchains on the platform. This will only allow specific actors to submit transactions to the platform purely based on authorization defined in the platform. In this kind of blockchain, the actors may be given different roles permitting them to perform a specific set of operations.

On the other hand, non-permissioned blockchain does not authorize and users can submit transactions or attempt to accumulate them into acceptable blocks.

Transactions –The records that get generated are known as transactions which will get appended to the ledger so that nobody can tamper the records. Transactions can be of any form such as government contracts, government tenders, any form of commercial paper, invoice, job card, etc. Any change to the transactions should also be logged and should have a consensus by the related parties.

Event Distribution -Effective distribution of events to the key stakeholders who are registered (either by self or by the platform) is a very important part of the solution. Events are generally the notifications to the users which denote any changes or operations that occurred in the blockchain platform. Events can trigger for various reasons like when a smart contract executes or say a ledger block is created/modified/deleted.

The event distribution module will assign listeners so that it receives the events from the blockchain platform. There will be event producers who will publish the event to the blockchain platform and there will be event consumers subscribed for these events and will consume the events. In the case of broadcast, the sender in the blockchain platform will send messages to all the members who are connected. The message will be sent in the same order as it is broadcasted by the publisher.

Communication Protocol –It is a mechanism using which the systems communicate with each other within the blockchain platform. We intend to use peer-to-peer protocols for communicating with the nodes within this blockchain platform.

Secure Runtime Environment –A secure environment will be required when a blockchain transaction will trigger smart contract functions during run time. This will host an environment blockchain business logic will reside. We will be hosting each smart contract within Ethereum Virtual Machine (EVM) which will provide a secure environment for the smart contracts to run.

Cryptographic Services - This component will provide the blockchain platform to the cryptographic algorithms like hash functions and digital signatures. Hash functions will be used to protect the ledger from any modifications. If anyone changes the information in the ledger this will trigger the hash to be re-computed, but this will be different from the previously computed hash stored in the ledger. Every time a new transaction happens, a new hash is computed.

Digital signatures ensure that the receiver receives the transactions without anyone modifying the transactions. This also ensures that the transactions are from the actual senders which are signed with the private keys and not by any hacker.

System Integration Unit

To integrate our two major system areas - blockchain platform and enterprise systems, we would need a system integration module. We plan to use API adapters and ESB (enterprise service bus) connections to achieve this.

Transformation and Connectivity Unit

We would need a mechanism to filter, or aggregate, or modify data or even transfer in the format we desire as moves between the blockchain platform and enterprise area. This capability enables secure communication and connections to the enterprise area.

In our proposed architecture, the transformation and connectivity components are hosted between the blockchain platform and the enterprise area. This component includes the following capabilities:

- **Transformation -** Transforms data going to and from the enterprise area.
- **Enterprise Data Connectivity -** Enables blockchain components to connect securely to the data in the enterprise area. Examples are gateway tunnels and VPN.
- **Enterprise Secure Connectivity –**This integrates with the enterprise area data security systems to authenticate and authorize access to components in the enterprise area.

ENTERPRISE AREA

The enterprise area will be comprised of the following components:

Enterprise Applications

There will be a provision for the enterprise to create applications and use them which will in turn communicate with the blockchain platform to achieve business outcomes. These enterprise applications will interact with smart contracts. The smart contract will obtain data from the enterprise application, send data to the enterprise application, or request services from the enterprise application.

Enterprise User Directory

This is used to store user information which will be in turn used to provide authentication, authorization. This is used to control access to various services within the enterprise area.

Enterprise Data

The data and metadata including systems of record for enterprise applications will all be considered as Enterprise Data. This data may be generated directly by the enterprise applications or indirectly by the data repositories which will be providing a feedback loop in the analytical system for blockchain systems. Enterprise data can be classified into three main types:

Transactional Data –Any data that is generated by the business transactions and which adhere to a sequence or related processes may be financial or logistics related. Transactional data can originate from reference data or master data repositories and even from distributed data storage systems as well.

Application Data –We classify application data as that data which is produced by enterprise applications functionally or operationally. Typically, the data has been improved or augmented to add value and drive insight.

Log Data - Data generated from the log files for enterprise applications is classified as Log data in our platform.

FOUNDATIONAL MODULES

Security Module - Security of the blockchain area will be maintained by the security module which will ensure in applying the security policy and standards needed to secure the blockchain platform. The security module will not only address IT (information technology) but will also take care of OT (operations technology). We plan to use public-key cryptography and the Secure Hash Algorithm (SHA) for this.

Monitoring and Intelligence Module - This module's primary responsibility is to provide monitoring, analytics, and automation tools. This will help in monitoring the platform and take necessary actions to manage and maintain the platform in good health and ensuring 100% uptime.

Governance Module - To have proper procedures and policies to govern the operation of the blockchain area we will be having the Governance module. All network participants will agree on the rules set-up by the governance module.

Blockchain Network Management Module - This module will help in providing visibility of the blockchain platform operations like business process metrics and other information needed to manage this network. It will also help in providing a management interface using which configurations and other parameters can be updated by the administrations.

CONTEXT AND OPTIONS

In this section, we will talk about a few additional components which will be used in our blockchain platform.

Blockchain storage - We will be using a blockchain platform to record transactions. But only a small amount of the transaction data is stored in the blockchain ledger. The remaining data related to the transaction is much larger and needs to be stored separately. But there should be a reference to this data to the ledger entry to get to the right context. This will help in avoiding overcrowding the ledger with large data volume.

In our case, say an order is placed for goods by a contractor to a supplier. The complete order will be a large document that will include all the details including the items that are ordered, the quantity ordered its price and other information like details of the customer, where to deliver (delivery location), and so on. The ledger will only have order number (primary key), customer identity, and the total cost, plus the security token (such as a hash) related to the transaction. Other details related to the order will be stored separately in the Order table in the database. Both will be linked together by the Order ID.

Ledger Storage - Any transactions that happen in our blockchain platform will be physically stored in the Ledger.

Data Storage - All the data that is generated by the platform during the transactions need to be stored separately. Depending on its nature, data generated can be of many forms. If it is relational data, we will use a SQL database (Oracle / MySQL) to store the same. If it is document-oriented, we will use the NoSQL database (MongoDB / Elasticsearch) to store it. There is a chance that we can have object storage service as well.

Needless to mention, that the choice of data storage will be dependent on the nature of the data objects and the operations that will be performed on them. Considering the diversity of data sets we will have, we need to have all forms of data storage mechanisms. As we will be using data storage, so we need to consider the option of data backup and replication which is an important aspect of data storage. For standard databases like Oracle and others, they will have this mechanism in-built. But if we are using the non-standard ones which do not have this mechanism, we need to build the same.

Permissions - Permissionless networks are open to any anyone and verification of the transactions happens against the rules which are pre-defined and already exist in the blockchain platform. This is a very useful feature as we would want anyone in our country (citizens of India) to view the transactions in the ledger so that they know all the details starting from the progress of the project to even the authenticity of the materials used for the infrastructure being built. On the other hand, permissioned networks are only restricted to the users who are actively involved in the project like Government Officials, Suppliers, and Contractors. On this variant, designated business users can view the transactions which are relevant to them and they are allowed to perform those operations which have been provisioned for them.

This will be a huge step forward in the participating economy.

Interaction Options - We will provide two ways for the users to interact with our blockchain platform. They are command-line interfaces and software development kits (SDK).

Command Line Interface (CLI) - Blockchain developers and administrators will use the command-line interface to interact with the blockchain platform for performing various activities. They can use this for executing a simple command, importing or exporting data, and managing the accounts of users. They should also have the capability to monitor the health of the platform.

Software Development Kit (SDK) - We will provide Software Development SDKs for the users using which they should be able to develop, test, debug, and deploy blockchain applications.

We will provide a set of tools as part of this SDK which will help blockchain application developers to create and deploy the applications which in turn will interact with our platform to achieve business goals.

CASE STUDY

The case study depicts a typical runtime flow below how government officials can use this platform. The scenario illustrates the flow starting from the invitation of tender till the job completion with constant monitoring on the progress of job with the ability to track the quality of materials used for this job and health of the project for its timely completion.

1. Government official access the blockchain platform using the "Government App"
   a. Government official raise an invitation for tender
   b. They key-in the details related to the tender in the app.
   c. They will also set the last date for the invitation.

    d.   If required, this app can be enhanced by the administrator to add relevant details

    e.   This platform is used by the Roads Department as well as Sewage Department. In that case, two child apps can be created from this master app. The administrator can host the app post proper testing into the apps area of the platform.

    f.   The invitation will be sent to the Contractors email-id and to their corresponding apps whoever has registered for receiving the notification.

2.   Contractors access the "Contractor App"

    a.   Once they receive the notification, they can either choose not to respond or respond with their proposal

    b.   The contractor who choose to apply for the tender, will key-in all the details in their app against the invite which will have a unique tender_invitation_id

3.   Below are the actions were taken by the Government app when they receive the tender from individual contractors.

    a.   The government app will store all the tenders as valid tenders received from the contractors within the set the last date and will send an acknowledgment to the contractor.

    b.   The government app will reject all the tenders received after the last day of submission and will send an error message to the contractor for proper reasons.

4.   Upon receiving the request to access the blockchain platform, edge services route the request to the security gateway.

5.   All the requests that land into the Blockchain platform via an API management layer need to have security, privacy, and protection for blockchain users. This is provided by the Hyperledger Fabric Membership Services.

6.   Once Government finalise the tender, notification is sent to the contractor who won the bid. The contractors who did not win the bid are also notified.

7.   The contractor who won the bid – the app will have an option enabled to add the suppliers and start the work by tracking the same.

8.   Suppliers will access the blockchain platform with the "Supplier App".

    a.   The contractor who took up the work will ask the required suppliers to install the app and in-turn the contractor will enable the supplier job against tender_id.

    b.   The supplier will start procuring the materials and upload in the app. The authenticity and quality of the materials used by the supplier will be tracked using the Ethereum component of the blockchain platform.

9.   There will be a "Worker App" for the workers to upload their daily job details.

    a.   This will help in assessing the progress of the work by various charts and monitoring tools.

b. In case the worker is not qualified enough to use the app, the "Contractor App" will have an option to enter the job details for an individual worker.

10. Citizens can also check the status of each of project's status via "Citizen App"

a. This app will help citizen to check the status of any government project (Road construction, Flyovers, Metro Rail, sub-urban railways, Sewage System, Drinking water, Building schools or colleges) presently in execution or even executed in the past.

b. They can check the progress of the project with its expected time of completion.

c. They can also check the materials used to the level from where it was procured and the quality and authenticity of the material – Smart Contract system of blockchain will be used to provide this capability.

d. They will have an option to rate the quality of the project and provide comments.

11. Hyperledger Fabric Membership Services is enabled by the Security services check proper user identity by providing authentication and authorization along with other related capabilities.

12. Finally, server-side blockchain business logic is triggered as when transactions take place but definitely within a secure environment.

Figure 2. Use case diagram

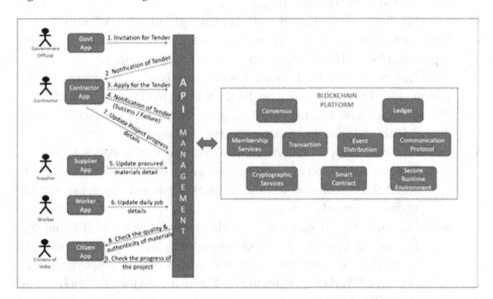

CONCLUSION

Blockchain technology (BCT) has become very popular these days for its potential to provide platforms for various applications in almost all areas. Some of the most important features of the open blockchain technology are its global nature and scope; it's a decentralized and distributed character, its built-in transparency and independence of trusted parties. These features are particularly important in countries vulnerable to corruption and in which there is a general distrust in government on the part of citizens and businesses. However, as our use cases show, how most countries can benefit from the global reach and openness that this platform offers.

In this chapter, we demonstrated possible ways the blockchain technology can be used as a platform for specific areas in government. There are many paper contracts written between the governments, brokers, contractors that often won't be in place until the infrastructure is built. It's all based on experience and historical examples. The risk can change significantly while an infrastructure like a flyover or a simple tarred road is being laid. It may sustain damage due to soil conditions or adverse weather conditions or even due to the lack of expertise of the contractor being hired for delivering the project. We tried to develop a groundbreaking blockchain-enabled platform that can meet the needs of all the different parties involved in creating a better infrastructure for the country. Our architecture can automate the entire process by using smart contracts to minimize paperwork for government officials.

The Blockchain revolution will see an economy dominated by human capitalism and a greater individual economy. Our contribution is that we have a clear understanding of a model that can be deployed to provide clarity to the disruption in government projects.

FUTURE WORK

To take it to the next level, we intend to build this platform iteratively. First, we plan to get the MVP (Minimum Viable Product) rolled out for the users to try out. Then based on the feedback, we can maintain a product backlog and iteratively implement them. This will help us to evolve the platform by considering all aspects of the users so that it is usable for them.

REFERENCES

Aitzhan, N. (2016). Security and Privacy in Decentralized Energy Trading Through Multi-Signatures, Blockchain and Anonymous Messaging Streams. *IEEE Transactions on Dependable and Secure Computing*. doi:10.1109/TDSC.2016.2616861

Banerjee, M., & Lee, J., & Choo, & K-K. (2017). A blockchain future to Internet of Things security: A position paper. *Digital Communications and Networks, 4.* Advance online publication. doi:10.1016/j.dcan.2017.10.006

Biswas, K., & Muthukkumarasamy, V. (2016). *Securing Smart Cities Using Blockchain Technology.* . doi:10.1109/HPCC-SmartCity-DSS.2016.0198

Christidis, K., & Devetsikiotis, M. (2016). Blockchains and Smart Contracts for the Internet of Things. *IEEE Access: Practical Innovations, Open Solutions, 4,* 2292–2303. doi:10.1109/ACCESS.2016.2566339

Crosby, M., Nachiappan, Pattanayak, P., Verma, S., & Kalyanaraman, V. (2016). BlockChain Technology: Beyond Bitcoin. *Applied Innovation Review, 2,* 6-19.

Dennis, R. M., & Owenson, G. (2016). *Rep on the block: A next generation reputation system based on the blockchain.* . doi:10.1109/ICITST.2015.7412073

Glaser, F. (2017). Pervasive Decentralisation of Digital Infrastructures: A Framework for Blockchain Enabled System and Use Case Analysis. *50th Hawaii International Conference on System Sciences.*

Glaser, F., & Bezzenberger, L. (2015). Beyond Cryptocurrencies - A Taxonomy of Decentralized Consensus Systems. *23rd European Conference on Information Systems (ECIS).*

Hashemi, S. H., Faghri, F., Rausch, P., & Campbell, R. H. (2016). World of Empowered IoT Users. In IoTDI (pp. 13-24). IEEE Computer Society. doi:10.1109/IoTDI.2015.39

Hon, W. K., Palfreyman, J., & Tegart, M. (2016). Distributed Ledger Technology & Cybersecurity. In *European Union Agency For Network And Information Securit.* ENISA.

Huckle, S., Bhattacharya, R., White, M., & Beloff, N. (2016). Internet of Things, blockchain and shared economy applications. *Procedia Computer Science, 98,* 461-466.

Johnson, D., Menezes, A., & Vanston, S. (2001). The elliptic curve digital signature algorithm (ecdsa). *International Journal of Information Security, 1*(1), 36–63. doi:10.1007102070100002

Kianmajd, P., Rowe, J., & Levitt, K. (2016, April). Privacy-preserving coordination for smart communities. In *2016 IEEE Conference on Computer Communications Workshops (INFOCOM WKSHPS)* (pp. 1045-1046). IEEE. 10.1109/INFCOMW.2016.7562245

Kondor, D., Pósfai, M., Csabai, I., & Vattay, G. (2014). Do the rich get richer? An empirical analysis of the Bitcoin transaction network. *PLoS One, 9*(2), e86197. doi:10.1371/journal.pone.0086197 PMID:24505257

Kosba, A., Miller, A., Shi, E., Wen, Z., & Papamanthou, C. (2016). Hawk: The Blockchain Model of Cryptography and Privacy-Preserving Smart Contracts. *Proceedings of the 2016 IEEE Symposium on Security and Privacy SP '16*. 10.1109/SP.2016.55

Koshy, P., Koshy, D., & McDaniel, P. (2014). *An Analysis of Anonymity in Bitcoin Using P2P Network Traffic.* . doi:10.1007/978-3-662-45472-5_30

Lemieux, V. (2017). A typology of blockchain recordkeeping solutions and some reflections on their implications for the future of archival preservation. *Big Data, IEEE International Conference on Big Data*, 2271-2278.

Lemieux, V. L. (2016). Trusting records: Is Blockchain technology the answer? *Records Management Journal, 26*(2), 110–139. doi:10.1108/RMJ-12-2015-0042

Lemieux, V. L. (2016). Trusting records: Is Blockchain technology the answer? *Records Management Journal, 26*(2), 110–139. doi:10.1108/RMJ-12-2015-0042

Lindman, J., Rossi, M., & Tuunainen, V. (2017). Opportunities and risks of Blockchain Technologies in payments – a research agenda. In *Proceedings of the 50th Hawaii International Conference on System Sciences*. HICSS/IEEE Computer Society. DOI: 10.24251/HICSS.2017.185

Liu, B., Yu, X. L., Chen, S., Xu, X., & Zhu, L (2017). *Blockchain Based Data Integrity Service Framework for IoT Data.* doi:10.1109/ICWS.2017.54

Mattila, J., & Seppälä, T., & Lähteenmäki, I. (2018). Who Holds the Reins? Banks in the Crossfire of Global Platforms. ETLA Reports 86. The Research Institute of the Finnish Economy.

Meiklejohn, S., Pomarole, M., Jordan, G., Levchenko, K., McCoy, D., Voelker, G. M., & Savage, S. (2013). Damon McCoy, Geoffrey M. Voelker, Stefan Savage, A Fistful of Bitcoins: Characterizing Payments Among Men with No Names. *Communications of the ACM, 59*(4), 86–93. doi:10.1145/2896384

Okada, H., Yamasaki, S., & Bracamonte, V. (2017). Proposed classification on blockchains based on authority and incentive dimensions. *2017 19th International Conference on Advanced Communication Technology (ICACT)*.

Phillip, R. (2004). Nonce-Based Symmetric Encryption. *International Workshop on Fast Software Encryption*.

Pinzon, R. C., & Rocha, C. (2016). Double-spend Attack Models with Time Advantange for Bitcoin. *Electronic Notes in Theoretical Computer Science, 329*(C), 79–103. doi:10.1016/j.entcs.2016.12.006

Polyzos, G. C., & Fotiou, N. (2017). *Blockchain-Assisted Information Distribution for the Internet of Things.* Advance online publication. doi:10.1109/IRI.2017.83

Ralph, D., & Samaniego, M. (2016). Blockchain as a Service for IoT. *2016 IEEE International Conference on Internet of Things (iThings) and IEEE Green Computing and Communications (GreenCom) and IEEE Cyber Physical and Social Computing (CPSCom) and IEEE Smart Data (SmartData)*.

Reynolds, P., & Irwin, A. S. M. (2017). Tracking digital footprints: Anonymity within the bitcoin system. *Journal of Money Laundering Control., 20*(2), 172–189. doi:10.1108/JMLC-07-2016-0027

Ron, D. & Shamir, A. (2012). Quantitative Analysis of the Full Bitcoin Transaction Graph. *IACR Cryptology ePrint Archive, 2012*, 584.

Saltzer, J. H., Reed, D. P., & Clark, D. D. (1984). End-to-end arguments in system design. *ACM Trans. Comput. Syst. TOCS, 2*(4), 277–288. doi:10.1145/357401.357402

Sarah, U. (2016). Blockchain Beyond Bitcoin. *Communications of the ACM, 59*(11), 15–17. doi:10.1145/2994581

Stankovic, J. A. (2014). Research Directions for the Internet of Things. *Internet of Things Journal, IEEE., 1*(1), 3–9. doi:10.1109/JIOT.2014.2312291

Xu, X., Weber, I., Staples, M., Zhu, L., Bosch, J., Bass, L., ... Rimba, P. (2017). A Taxonomy of Blockchain-Based Systems for Architecture Design. *2017 IEEE International Conference on Software Architecture*.

Zhang, J., Xue, N., & Huang, X. (2016). A Secure System For Pervasive Social Network-based Healthcare. *IEEE Access.* . doi:10.1109/ACCESS.2016.2645904

Zhao, J. L., Fan, S., & Jiaqi, Y. (2016). Overview of business innovations and research opportunities in blockchain and introduction to the special issue. *Financial Innovation, 2*(1), 28. Advance online publication. doi:10.118640854-016-0049-2

Zhu, H., & Zhou, Z. Z. (2016). Analysis and outlook of applications of blockchain technology to equity crowdfunding in China. *Financ Innov*, 2(1), 29. doi:10.118640854-016-0044-7

Zyskind, G., Nathan, O., & Pentland, A. S. (2015). Decentralizing Privacy: Using Blockchain to Protect Personal Data. In *Proceedings of the 2015 IEEE Security and Privacy Workshops (SPW '15)*. IEEE Computer Society. 10.1109/SPW.2015.27

Chapter 8
Blockchain–Based Digital Rights Management Techniques

Nguyen Ha Huy Cuong
Vietnam-Korea University of Information and Communication Technology,
University of Da-Nang, Vietnam

Gautam Kumar
https://orcid.org/0000-0002-8230-4432
CMR Engineering College, India

Vijender Kumar Solanki
https://orcid.org/0000-0001-5784-1052
CMR Institute of Technology (Autonomous), Hyderabad, India

ABSTRACT

The usage of information is essential for data-driven capabilities in artificial intelligence. The data-driven AI techniques lead to several security and privacy concerns. Among various digital techniques, digital rights management is required as one of collaboration scheme that ensures the security and privacy of intellectual rights. Though a number of researchers have proposed various security techniques, none of them have proposed an efficient and effective privacy procedure for digital rights. Recently, blockchain technique is considered as one of the major security methods to ensure a transparent communication among individuals. It can be used by various applications such as industries, marketing, transportation systems, etc. The aim of this chapter is to propose an ensured resource allocation algorithm that validates the scheme by comparing various security measures against previous approaches. Further, the proposed phenomenon ensures the transparency on security and privacy due to its integration.

DOI: 10.4018/978-1-7998-3444-1.ch008

INTRODUCTION

Organizations started focusing on data driven Artificial Intelligence (AI) designing systems by aiming a sophisticated and collaborative development of applications [Darabant and Darabant], [Walsh]. The collaboration process in AI helps to build the engineering processes by reusable AI objects and specialization systems such as deep learning methods and data set models. The reusable objects have been developed or gathered by including a third party process for designing the final system or application. The potential advantages of using these processes are the reduced time and development process and components access that enable several engineering processes for higher AI performance. In addition, the interesting features are supported by the expansion of AI pipelines [Song], and data revelation tools such as Orange [Xiao], open source machine learning techniques and the materialize of several data marketplaces [Knapp], [Singhal].

Further, the collaborative schemes, however, comes at a price. It inflicts at least three primary challenges on the designing process. Initially, the intrinsic usage of data hoists various privacy anxieties. These threats become even higher regarding the trait of datasets being communal. After that, Data-driven artificial intelligence techniques aim at recognizing the unidentified relationships within the data. Though, when using typical security enforcing techniques such anonymous schemes or restriction in information collection, then it can't be barred that intrinsic relationships inside the data sets are not deleted or captured. Therefore, as a result, these data sets are fetching of no worth. Whilst such typical concepts are of high cost for specific purposes might bang the AI objects usability in general. Therefore, a quandary for the general notion of alliance based on reusability occurs. Then, the reuse of objects in collaborative schemes necessitates trust amongst the users and developers. This trust assortments from comply with licenses among developers to authorizing supremacy on objects as requisite by individuals and societies, e.g. GDPR-like and enabling GDPR concepts on the usage of information and objects in Europe. Therefore, this chapter goal is to address these primary challenges by providing the insight to the security and privacy necessities in collaborative development. In addition, it will offer an initial classification of privacy and Digital Rights Management (DRM) and the attacks against AI objects in the pipeline. Further, the chapter discusses the need of transparency while sharing the data or ensuring the privacy among various individuals. Furthermore, the usage of Blockchain technology in digital marketing for AI objects collaboration processes. Finally, the chapter highlighted the GDPR act and its potential insinuation for Bonseyes such as AI marketplaces and illustrates potential behavior of disobey the DRM connected with the artefacts. It further delineated a Blockchain security architecture to avoid the attacks.

In today's world, network system and cloud computing organizations are crucial factors in the development and operation of IoT applications. 2017, in according to the appraisal of the Asian Cloud Computing Association ACCA also known as cloud asia and, resource provision, a significant service in Cloud Computing, is flattering a major insist in scientific request. Most of the traditional cloud computing structures in Vietnam have been ensuring services with various challenges and issues as listed below:

i.   The price of translation involves services offered through remote information centers and is construct on practical servers borrowed from overseas, so the price is very costly.
ii. The ease of use of human income to provide the action of the entire structure is unsecured and insufficient.
iii. Cloud computing capital often emerge as the only admission point for all computing servers, so there is no assurance for consumer about reliable time and design .
iv. Cloud centers have not build service stipulation systems that must have superior characterstics of suppleness in security recovery, scalability and system congestion.

In current years, with the notice of the government, the whole nation, from big cities to distant areas of the nation and in approximately every house, everybody is involved in the rebellion of knowledge 4.0. Through the real survey, we can see that with the benefit of the nation as an undeveloped economy linked with military, the district have also made decisions to endorse smart farming, agriculture 4.0. Some plant variety were also plant in farms from average to some tens of hectares, mainly Pomelo trees. With the benefits of discussion, it is very appropriate for Pomelos that has high enlargement and efficiency after various years of caring and planting. However, the issue faced by the supportive members is to relate high knowledge in farming such as habitual irrigation replica. In addition, the model of traceability also countenance difficulty such as the price of employ technology repair packages. In this chapter, we present answer to hold virtual server navy and provide effectual solutions in given that capital for remote needs (farmers) and virtual server infrastructures. The solution convene the following specific supplies with technical answer to make sure anti-conflict capital, that are as follows:

- Technical solution to shun congestion
- Technical solution to make sure abridged price for users
- Technical solution for confidential cloud
- Architecture for replica that offer heterogeneous income

Section 2 presents some related work. Section 3 presents resource allocation artificial intelligent algorithms. Section 4 in turn elaborates the experimental setup and contrast the experimental results.

RELATED WORK

This section illustrates the number of privacy and security techniques in digital rights using various machine learning and Blockchain techniques. We initially discuss various security and privacy schemes using machine learning techniques and then will elaborate the usage of Blockchain technique in digital rights.

Digital Rights

The Information system, indistinguishable relation current requirements, often through the input schemes for virtual machines that need resources like Walsh's colleagues and study, suggest two different classes through utility systems, through information. Autonomous and automatic scenes; whilst author Yazir and colleagues use controllers to continously adjust the use of resources to meet user's satisfaction. Yazir have proposed an approach to ensure adaptive resources with a intellectual of giving preference to traditional resource request registration system. Meanwhile Qiang and authors have proposed a liable solution of automatic multidimensional provisioning and a proff to overcome the demand for the agent nodes (NA) with this system that solved the drawbacks of scattered clusters or nodes. However, the authors also pointed out the limitations on the in abilities to accomodate the responses altogether for the entire system to operate effectively, that is a combination that cannot be revovered. In the [Stillwell] study and the publication of survey on ensuring infrastructure systems based on open source computing infrasturcture, proposed optimal algorithm and allotment of the ability to require spirit Activation permits maximum use of physical resources. Meanwhile Zhen Xiao and his authors have proposed a load balancing scheme with a smart object management approach. The author in [Singhal] claimed that traditional resource delivery schemes are processor obkects that depend on resource management and cores processes. The solutions are in proposed through these techniques, highlightes on resource-based systems that demand on process system to be flexible and responsible to resource effectively. It can be seen that there are several different approaches in the direction of resource research, the proposed results have benefits but still issues and difficulties present. Therefore, there is no proposal that best requires the service quality for virtualized resources. Further, in the Cloud Computing environment with various information Centers, they are diversed across all geographic networks. These virtual servers are pooled from physical linked through a networked system that built on a diverse and integrated hardware networks. The study of technical results to ensure resources requires on the virtual networks on the heterogeneous dispersion system is also required in research by world researchers and domestic.

[Farinaz and Potkonjak] have proposed an integrated circuit unique identification process for securing the CAD based protocols. The authors have presented various integrated circuit metering techniques to ensure a digital right management and low overhead analysis.

In recent days, organizations are looking for various fraud detection techniques to prevent from digital threats. It is very difficult to provide a security to a company because of its very complex database management system. [Shirbhate et al.] have proposed a security technique that initially kept all the marketing secrets with their financial details to prevent from fraud transactions. The authors have illustrated the database structure along with its various security techniques. They have proposed an algorithm to find a covert channel among individuals by investigating various tools.

Further, the management started receiving much attention because of the rapid expansion of distributed and internet technologies such as digital rights and multimedia privacy. Digital marketing have been proposed as a viable solution by various authors to ensure privacy to digital rights. [Lai et al.] have proposed robust watermarking techniques by applying an evolutionary and transformation domain schemes. The proposed framework is validated and experimented among various security concerns such as image processing threats and perceptual qualities simultaneously.

The prediction of stock markets is considered as a challenging task in AI techniques. The challenge is due to investor's guidance to determine when is the right time to sell or buy anything. In the current days, there exist various machine learning schemes to predict stock markets such as artificial neural networks (ANN), support vector machine (SVM) and genetic algorithms (GA). Amongst them, ANN is considered as the most usable technique. [Boonpeng and Jeatrakul] have understood the use of ANN schemes for stock market predictions during the year of 2006 and 2013.

Furthermore, [Lin et al.] have proposed a digital marketing content using mobile trading scheme on the basis of digital right concepts. The authors have provided that using their proposed phenomenon, not only providers may transmit the digital content but also consumers may purchase their telecommunication companies using their personal devices. The proposed schemes supported the content in both visited and home domain. Further, the proposed phenomenon provided the non-repudiation, authentication and confidentially features.

Blockchain in Digital Right

With the increase value of distributed penetration and energy challenges and opportunities, traditionally, the centralized transaction mode has low efficiency, maintenance cost and untimely settlement. Therefore, it is very difficult to adapt the small scale distribution trading methods based on Blockchain technique. [Jin et al] have initially reviewed the history of Blockchain mechanism with the combination of various distributed features and requirements analysis of trading markets. Further, the authors have constructed the models and mechanisms for building trading security constraints. Finally, a distributed trading method based on Blockchain technique is proposed to provide smart contracts and proof of works for distributed transactions. The distributed trading method is further explained through ethereum to realize their correction corrections.

In order to provide an economic analysis of Blockchain business, a game theory technique is used to model competitive market over centralized third party system. In this market, the mediators are the platforms to deliver their services. [Lee et al.] have proposed a non-cooperative 2-stage dynamic game to incentivize the Blockchain platform, further; the authors have modeled the competition among platforms to attract clients by providing an equilibrium analysis. The proposed method is validated against quality of service by providing non-increasing services with the increase of participants.

The economy of digital marking is entirely based upon trust and security. Blockchain technology is considered as one of the viable solution that provides a trust worthy and reliable network for non-financial and financial transactions. Blockchain electric vehicles benefitted Blockchain. In order to provide a feasible ability of charging and owner's privacy, [Firoozjaei et al.] have proposed Blockchain based electric vehicles that are most trustful to share the credits in EV marketing's. The authors have introduced interconnection positions to preserve owner's privacy and evaluated their privacy and security protection based on vehicle charging scenarios.

The aim of this chapter to propose a resource allocation AI algorithm along with Blockchain technology to ensure the security and privacy issues in digital rights.

RESOURCE ALLOCATION INTELLIGENT ALGORITHM

Technological proceeds in communications, computing, consumer electronics and their junction have outlined in phenomenal augment in the quantity of digital information that have been stored, generated, distributed, and addicted. The term "information or content" is broadly defined as any packaged and processed digital record, such as digital video, audio, animation, graphics, text, images, or any grouping of these sorts. The explosive augments in the consumption and generation of digital information has raised various questions about the privileges of the data producer, creator, and dispenser as well as the responsibilities and rights of the buyer. The rules leading the suitable use of records are also open to query.

The term DRM is broadly defined to a set of techniques, policies, and tools that direct the correct use of digital information. A high level view content flow from the inventor to the customer via the creator. The record creator is mainly anxious with the actual information that leaves into the data.

This could be defined as raw information that needs to be practiced further with esteem to remaining to certain set-ups, the suitable addition of various kinds of quality enhancement, media, additions of possible particular effects, and origin and calculation of meta data such as information about the record. The creator of the record performs the essential dispensation and produces the packaged information. The packaged information is in a appearance that is appropriate for expenditure and for the tracing and organization of information usage. The customer is the final user of the information.

A DRM organization acts as an important role in various processes that are concerned in the flow of information. Very broadly, it assists the inventor to identify the desired possession rights of the information. It facilitates the creator to gain suitable metadata from the information and specify the creator's rights.

It permits the customer to identify the preferred information and the several options in the use of information. It also permits the creator to watch the record usage and track payment record.

There are various privacy and security techniques to watch appropriate information to prevent from illegal usage. The choice of a meticulous scheme depends on the information type, needs, application and lenience to unsuitable use of information. It must be unspoken, however, that no information defense and watching scheme assurance absolute privacy and full proof operation. There is forever the option that attractive features and functionalities of a DRM method will be circumvented. The operation and design of the DRM ought to take these issues into account.

Major functionalities of DRM scheme is simply refer to put a DRM that direct the suitable use of information. The major features of this system are frequent. They include assisting the packaging of raw information into a fitting form for easy sharing and tracking, defensive the information for tamper-proof broadcast, protecting information from unauthorized usage, and facilitate stipulation of appropriate rights, that describe the modes of information consumption. The DRM schemes must also aid the delivery of information offline on DVDs and CDs; deliver information on-demand over peer-to-peer systems, the Internet or enterprise systems; and ensure number of ways of formative the legitimacy of information and of interpretation devices. Supporting imbursement over the Internet for information usage is another function of DRM as long as suitable remuneration for information creators and producer. The DRM scheme must also watch the usage of information and provide that they are in agreement with the rights, trace payment and make sure they are in accord with the usage of information, and direct privacy and security issues suitably.

In addition, a DRM scheme should ease the personalization of the information, tailoring information to certain favorites of the customer; be interoperable; behind various formats of information in a transparent way; and should grip several levels of information granularity. The Granularity of a DRM scheme is defined as the size of the chunk or unit of information or record that can be separately delivered, selected, and inspired such as a section from a book, a meticulous track/song from an audio book, or a sight from a video).

Among the major preferred features of a DRM scheme are ease of use by information inventor, creator, and patrons; robustness to the circumvention of rules usage; fairness of information usage policies; transparency in the use of information from a variety of information services and providers; fair duty for various types of information innovation and consumption; income of payments and pricing such as micropayments. The below algorithm determine the resource allocation process using AI algorithm.

Resource Allocation Artificial Intelligent Algorithm

Input: W[c_i ; m_i ; n_i ; d_i ;]

Output: Resource Allocation t_i

1. Do

2. Job.Insert (t_i)

3. k←0; max_k= input

4. While (Read.isfree()=true do

5. Ready.Insert (Job.delete(ti));

6. J-cur←Readly.delete(ti);

7. J-cur.Status = Assigned;

8. for each j ∈ Ri do;

9. If(usedbyi[j]=0) send request (ti) to pj end for;

10. Else if respone = Succes;

11. Return result

12. Else wait (2k++) if (Timeout Or k = max_k);

13. Return fail

14. While (True)

15. Close 3

Further, the proposed algorithm is integrated with blockchain network where each and every record is linked with the blockchain in order to maintain the transparency and strict the privacy and security issues of content delivery among customers and producers. Different Blockchain network is maintained among producers and consumers to reduce the complexity, storage and communication overheads where each and every record of content delivery is also stored inside Blockchain network along with their database.

EXPERIMENTATION AND ANALYSIS OF PROPOSED ALGORITHM

In this section, we have illustrated the validity of proposed phenomenon using resource allocation process through some experimental results as depicted in Table [1]. We applying the scheduling with the greedy algorithm to request resources for 10 cases of given CPU capability p = {10%, 20%, 30%}, we realize that it is possible If the success rate between requests to create a virtual server, the ability to create VMs is 20% higher than the given capacity of the CPU. As for the 10% CPU capabilities, there is no significant difference and between the ability to perform and not be implemented is the same. At the ability of the CPU 30%, we can see a clear difference that the ability to create unsuccessful is very high than 160% when the ability to create only 60.10%. Initially, we necessitate generating 6 virtual machines with the results fined as depicted below:

Table 1. Resource allocation process

CPU Access/ Scheduling Algorithms	CPU Accessibility in 10% Differences	CPU Accessibility in 20% Differences	CPU Accessibility in 30% Differences
No For/Wait Non create VM	23.95	45.65	160
Used For/Wait Non generate VM	14.05	28.40	78.46
Generate VM	15.21	23.27	60.10

The table [2] presents the result of productively generating 7 virtual machines requisite through Cloudlet, symbolized by VM ID 1 to VM ID 7. preliminary time is considered as 0.1 ms and ending time is defined as 85 ms for virtual machines VM ID 1 and 175 ms for VM ID 7 virtual equipment with various different situation such as: if we enhance the number of machines requisite, as well as assign physical servers on numerous D information centers various materials. In figure 1, In test case 2 after 4 machines were generated in the second middle, next to the difficult center 3 generated 2 machines. In the third test middle 2 also generated 4, then the middle 3 generated 2, the middle 4 generated 1. With the limited ability of the laptop we experienced, it can make up to 8 machines with 4 information centers.

Table 2. Results of successful creation

CPU Access Scheduling Algorithms	CPU Accessibility in 10% Differences	CPU Accessibility in 20% Differences	CPU Accessibility in 30% Differences
No For/ Wait Non create VM	0.15%	0.37%	10.71%
Used For/ Wait Non generate VM	0.46%	1.26%	6.09%
Generate VM	5.46%	7.40%	55.99%

The application of scheduling with greedy algorithm combined with deadlock detection algorithm in distributed resource provisioning with the requirement of providing resources for 10 contracts with the given CPU capacity is given. (p = {10%, 20%, 30%}), we realize that the probability of success between the requirements of creating a virtual server to create a VM is very high with a given ability of 30% CPU. As for the 10% and 20% CPU, the probability of success is not much different but with the possibility of success much higher than the probability of failure.

Figure 1. A Time contract graph with the aptitude of each CPU to give virtual server formation resources

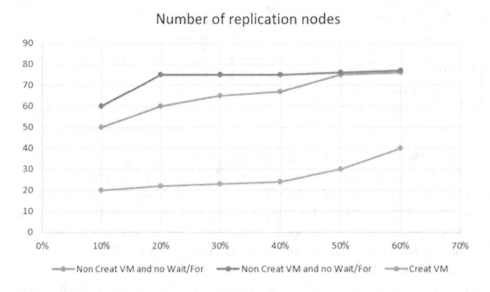

CONCLUSION

Depending upon a successful transaction among agents, digital rights are to be considered as a very important system to provide security among individuals. This chapter have proposed an efficient resource allocation proposed solution to ensure privacy and security among various solutions. Further, to ensure a transparent communication and interaction among transactions, Blockchain technique can be considered as a most vital technology. The authors in this paper have used a Blockchain mechanism with resource allocatopn process with AI based techniques. The proposed results are successfully validated against various security measures and showed the outperformance of proposed phenomenon against various traditional approaches. The integration of AI and Blockchain technique ensured a lot of privacy and security during transaction in digital rights.

REFERENCES

Boonpeng, S., & Jeatrakul, P. (2014), Enhance the performance of neural networks for stock market prediction: An analytical study. *Ninth International Conference on Digital Information Management.* 10.1109/ICDIM.2014.6991352

Darabant, A. S., & Darabant, L. (2011). Clustering methods in data fragmentation. *Romanian Journal of Information Science and Technology*, *4*(1), 81–87.

Farinaz, K., & Potkonjak, M. (2007). CAD-based Security, Cryptography, and Digital Rights Management. *44th ACM/IEEE Design Automation Conference.*

Firoozjaei, M. D., Ghobbani, A., & Kim, H. (2019). EVChain: A Blockchain-based Credit Sharing in Electric Vehicles Charging. *IEEE International Conference on Privacy, Security and Trust.* 10.1109/PST47121.2019.8949026

Jin, X., Bai, C., Zhang, Z., Zhao, S., Wang, H., Yan, Z., Zhang, Lu., & Chen, S. (2019). Blockchain-enabled Transactive Method in Distributed Systems Considering Security Constraints. *IEEE Congress on Evolutionary Computation.* 10.1109/CEC.2019.8790069

Knapp, E. (1987). Deadlock Detection in Distributed Databases. *ACM Computing Surveys*, *19*(4), 3030–3327. doi:10.1145/45075.46163

Lai, C. C., Chen, H. C., & Yeh, G. M., Ouyang, (2011), A robust digital image watermarking using transformation domain and evolutionary computation techniques. *Int'l Conference on Machine Learning and Cybernetics*, 4. 10.1109/ICMLC.2011.6016997

Lee, H., Sung, K., Lee, K., & Min, S. (2018). Economic Analysis of Blockchain Technology on Digital Platform Market. *IEEE 23rd Pacific Rim International Symposium on Dependable Computing (PRDC).* 10.1109/PRDC.2018.00020

Lin, C. C., & Chiang, P. H. A Mobile Trading Scheme for Digital Content Based on Digital Rights. *Eighth International Conference on Intelligent Systems Design and Applications.* 10.1109/ISDA.2008.205

Shirbhate, D., & Gupta, S.R., (2015). Digital forensic techniques for finding the hidden database using analytical strategies. In *Int'l Conference on Information Processing.* IEEE. 10.1109/INFOP.2015.7489344

Singhal, M. (1989). Deadlock detection in distributed systems. *IEEE Computer*, *22*(11), 37–48. doi:10.1109/2.43525

Song, Y., Sun, Y., & Shi, W. (2013). A Two-Tiered On-Demand Resource Allocation Mechanism for VM-Based Data Centers. *IEEE Transactions on Services Computing*, *6*(1), 116–129. doi:10.1109/TSC.2011.41

Stillwell, M., Vivien, F., & Casanova, H. (2012). Virtual Machine Resource Allocation for Service Hosting on Heterogeneous Distributed Platforms. *IEEE International Symposium on Parallel and Distributed Processing (IPDPS)*. 10.1109/IPDPS.2012.75

Walsh, W. E., Tesauro, G. J., Kephart, J. O., & Das, R. (2004). Utility Functions in Autonomic Systems. In *1st International Conference on Autonomic Computing (ICAC 2004)*, (pp. 17-19). Academic Press.

Xiao, Z., Song, W., & Chen, Q. I. (2013). Dynamic Resource Allocation Using Virtual Machines for Cloud Computing Environment. *IEEE Transactions on Parallel and Distributed Systems*, *24*(6), 1107–1117. doi:10.1109/TPDS.2012.283

Chapter 9
Understanding Blockchain:
Case Studies in Different Domains

Hemraj Saini
iD https://orcid.org/0000-0003-2957-1491
Jaypee University of Information and Technology, India

Geetanjali Rathee
Jaypee University of Information Technology, India

Dinesh Kumar Saini
iD https://orcid.org/0000-0002-5140-1731
Sohar University, Oman

ABSTRACT

In this chapter, the authors have detailed the need of blockchain technology along with its case studies in different domains. The literature survey is described that describes how blockchain technology is rising. Further, a number of domains where blockchain technology can be applied along with its case studies have been discussed. In addition, the authors have considered the various use cases with their recent issues and how these issues can be resolved using the blockchain technology by proposing some new ideas. A proposed security framework in certain applications using blockchain technology is presented. Finally, the chapter is concluded with future directions.

DOI: 10.4018/978-1-7998-3444-1.ch009

INTRODUCTION

Blockchains have pulled in overall consideration lately and is characterized as an immutable, successive chain of records called blocks. The record contains transactions, documents or some other information, and are fastened together utilizing hashes. It is executed and overseen by a peer-to-peer network (Christin, N., 2011; Iansiti, M., & Lakhani, K. R., 2017; Swan, M., 2015; Cachin, C., 2016) of computers (also called peer nodes) spread everywhere throughout the globe. Blockchain likewise called distributed ledger which utilizes independent PCs (nodes) to record, share and synchronize transactions in their particular electronic ledgers, rather than keeping information incorporated on a server as in a customary record (Nandwani, K., 2018). A Schematic outline of the blockchain is depicted in Figure 1. Blockchains have the potential to disrupt any industry that employs the use of a trusted middleman and gives direct control back to the end-user. In any case, similarly, as with any technological revolution and the paradigm shift that joins it is a procedure of trial and error. What works and what does not and we are as of now in that stage with blockchain advancements. 99% of the business sectors are filled by an unadulterated hypothesis (Peters, M. A., 2017). There are no completely useful blockchain items that can oblige the requests of the majority. Blockchains must be less expensive, snappier, simpler to utilize and similarly as versatile, if not more thus, than the present frameworks set up. The coming of the web drove the technological revolution of the 90's and the industrial upheaval was in the late eighteenth century (Peters, M. A., 2017). These quantum jumps in human capacity and accomplishment change our whole reality and disturb pretty much every settled industry. They change the manner in which we travel, cooperate, communicate, business with one another. All that we once knew is flipped on its head and life gets improved, making things a lot less demanding and progressively productive. The same is the appearance of blockchain technology where the component of trust is the whole sudden put under the control of target numbers and PCs.

Blockchain is the initial step at placing trust into PCs. It sounds kind of terrifying where it would state that however, the seasons of Skynet and eliminators are far away and except if we create methods for keeping self-aware robots from turning into a reality, at that point we ought to be safe. Blockchain technology is still without a doubt so in its earliest stages. Blockchains are moderate, user-unfriendly, unscalable, and costly. For instance, DApps created on ethereum require the end-user to initially buy ethereum and afterward pay a transaction fee each time they accomplish something in the DApp. Then again, EOS expects developers to buy over the top expensive RAM to build up a DApp while the users get transaction fees, simply after the user gets some EOS, downloads an EOS wallet from Github, make a key pair and sends EOS to that key pair. Not to speak to the average consumer who could think less about decentralization. The fact of the matter is that blockchain technology needs to develop before mainstream adoption happens. A blockchain that takes care of enormous real-world problems, finds a harmony among decentralization and administration while giving speed, scalability, cost viability, and overall smooth user experience will be the blockchain that ascents above them all. 2018 was an incredibly dynamic year for blockchain and cryptocurrencies (Houben, R., & Snyers, A., 2018). Numerous jumps in advancement were made and blockchain is entering the worldwide awareness increasingly every day. The subject of mass selection is when, not in the event that it occurs. We unquestionably observe this occurrence very soon, however as things remain at the present minute, the blockchain space still makes them develop agonies to traverse.

Figure 1. Schematic outline of Blockchain

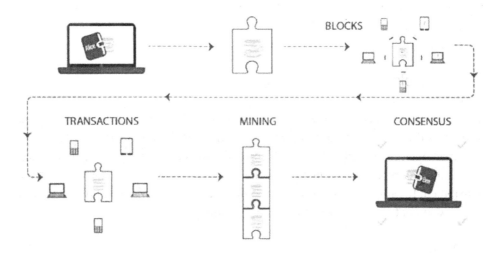

Key Advantages of Blockchain

A. Distributed

Blockchain enables a wide assortment of PCs to partake in a network, circulating the processing power. For instance, Amazon purchases and keeps up a private arrangement of computing power for AWS, nobody, however, Amazon can contribute this. Interestingly the blockchain association Ethereum permits nearly anybody to contribute their PC to their system, just by introducing their product. Distribution decreases the chance of altering, extortion, and tampering. With more hubs ready to partake, frameworks are difficult to "takedown" by means of customary brute force network attacks.

B. Trustless

Blockchain enables advanced exchanges to occur between gatherings who don't confide in one another. Envision a digital coin stored in a document on your PC. You may read the document an endless number of times. The estimation of this digital currency would near zero. Previously, focal experts (banks) have gone about as records, tracking the number of coins every one of us has access as a bought together to evade the issue of duplication. By distributing the Ledger to numerous nodes, and synchronizing the ledger through Consensus, blockchain permits parties who don't confide in one another, to trust that the exchange is genuine and not useless. After some time, trust can be expanded further, by means of shared procedures and permanent records of exchanges. This encourages a monstrous scope of potential digital transactions that couldn't have occurred before without a focal specialist overseeing them.

C. Immutable

When a transaction is concurred and shared over the distributed system it turns out to be near difficult to fix. Indeed, after some time, it ends up increasingly hard to fix. In an open record, like Bitcoin, this implies you can investigate the blockchain and find the number of Bitcoins in anyone's record, or follow where reserves were distributed. In different situations, this could be utilized to follow supply chains, or check who got to specific documents on a system.

D. Decentralized

Blockchain likewise underpins the decrease in centralized monopolies infrastructures or "middlemen" and expels costs. By distributing systems, blockchain can discover economies of scale, without single incorporated speculation. This builds rivalry in the market, by bringing down the hindrances to the passage, putting pressure on all members to turn out to be progressively effective. In addition, enabling peers to transact with no prerequisite for trust upsets the present business practices of associations who encourage trust for example Banks. Transactions straightforwardly between peers may prompt a decrease in "middle man" steps, further expanding business sector effectiveness.

Challenges of Blockchain

Wasteful

Each node runs the blockchain so as to keep up Consensus over the blockchain. This gives outrageous dimensions of adaptation to non-critical failure, guarantees zero downtime, and makes the information stored on the blockchain perpetually unchangeable and restriction safe. Yet, this is inefficient, as every node rehashes a task to achieve consensus consuming electricity and time in transit. This makes calculation far slower and more costly than on a customary single PC. There are numerous activities that look to diminish this cost concentrating on elective methods for looking after Consensus, for example, Proof-of-Stake.

Network speed/cost

Blockchain systems expect nodes to run. However, the same numbers of the systems are new, they do not have the number of nodes to encourage broad utilization. This absence of resource shows as:

- Higher costs—as hubs look for higher prizes for finishing transactions in a supply and demand situation
- Slower transactions—as hubs organize transactions with higher prizes, backlogs of transactions develop.

After some time, effective public blockchain networks should incentivize nodes, while making ideal expenses for clients, with transactions finished in a significant time allotment. This balance is key to the financial matters of each blockchain.

The size of the block

Every transaction or "block" added to the chain builds the span of the database. As each hub needs to keep up the chain to run, the computing necessities increase with utilization. For substantial public usage of blockchain this has one of two effects:

- Smaller ledger—Only one out of every odd node can convey a full copy of the blockchain, conceivably influencing immutability, consensus, etc.
- More centralized— There is a high obstruction to a passage to turn into a node, empowering a bigger measure of centralization in the network, with greater players ready to take more control.

Neither of these situations is alluring, without thinking about the full ramifications, as it will probably influence the utilization cases for blockchain variations.

Speculative markets

Numerous blockchains are run utilizing token/currency models to support advancement or deal with the financial matters of nodes. For instance, Ether (ETH) is the currency used to pay for computing power (or Gas) on the Ethereum organizes. In this manner, ETH is a cash for computing power.

Customary currencies like USD, GBP, EUR (additionally called Fiat currencies) are commonly connected to the estimation of their particular economies for example GBP to the UK. These economies are very much created, directed and stable. In any case, because of the possibly troublesome nature of Blockchains, individuals have taken to guessing on the estimation of the digital economies they create.

As these business sectors are liable to restricted guidelines and are exceedingly theoretical they are inclined to quick variance and control, spiking transaction value. This presents specific dangers while transacting from Fiat currencies into blockchain currencies. For instance, 1 ETH may cost ~$200 today, yet ~$180 tomorrow, a 10% price fluctuation (Ametrano, F. M., 2016). While this can make vast rewards, it likewise introduces high degrees of vulnerability for undertakings created on public blockchain innovation.

Hard and Soft Forks

Numerous blockchains and currencies decentralize their basic leadership. For instance, Bitcoin enables nodes to "signal" support for upgrades deeply software that runs the system. This permits the blockchain to stay away from bringing together basic decision making, yet in addition, it presents challenges when communities are partitioned about the best course.

At the point when nodes change their software, there is potential for a "Fork" in the chain. Nodes working the new software won't acknowledge indistinguishable transactions from nodes working the former one. This makes another blockchain, with a similar history as the one it is based on.

Forks make noteworthy uncertainty, as they can possibly piece the intensity of the blockchain arrange into loads of variations. They are additionally prone to be essential, as, without the ability to refresh the software, the blockchain is probably not going to be future proof.

Immutable Smart Contracts

When the smart contact is added to the blockchain, it ends up permanent, in that it can't be changed. In the event that there are imperfections in the code that might be misused by hackers, they are there until the end of time. This isn't a worry when a smart contract isn't being utilized, however as smart contacts carry on like records, they can be utilized to store a lot of significant worth.

This can make situations where hackers can abuse code defects to send the substance of smart contracts to their very own records. As the blockchain is permanent, these transactions are extremely difficult to fix, which means a lot of significant worth might be lost until the end of time.

Solutions of Weaknesses of Blockchain

All the weaknesses of the blockchain can be removed using three different consensus protocols named proof-of-work, proof-of-stake and proof-of-useful-work (Vukolić, M., 2015; Yu, B., Liu, J., Nepal, S., Yu, J., & Rimba, P., 2019; Baldominos, A., & Saez, Y., 2019; Zheng, Z., Xie, S., Dai, H., Chen, X., & Wang, H., 2017). A brief summary of these three protocols is given below.

Proof-of-work

A self-explanatory pictorial representation of proof-of-work is shown in Figure 2.

Proof-of-stake (virtual mining)

A self-explanatory pictorial representation of proof-of-stake is shown in Figure 3.

Proof-of-useful-work

A self-explanatory pictorial representation of proof-of-useful-work is shown in Figure 4.

Table 1 represents the comparison of proof-of-stake and proof-of-work and proof-of-useful-work.

CASE STUDIES

Beyond the simple applications, bitcoin has transcended the environment in the cloud, ensuring data privacy and other major issues. For the future of blockchain, it has great potential in empowering the citizens of developing countries in different sectors like healthcare, identity management, and other commercial uses. Some of the following case studies represent the strength of blockchain.

Figure 2. Proof-of-work

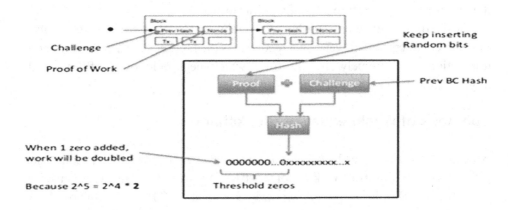

Figure 3. Proof-of-stake

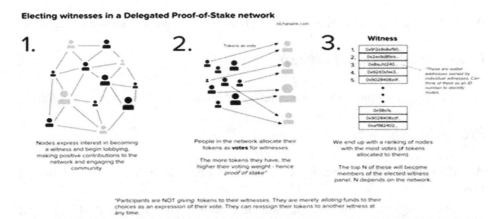

A. Proposed Decentralized Voting Application

Our application determines the vote count of the voter for certain people who are to be selected. Firstly, in this application, we determine the illegibility of the voters using blind signatures. For high availability and result immutability of privacy using double private blockchain and using bitcoin logic to redesign transactions and new protocols to cast a vote. The proposed system contains:

Figure 4. Proof-of-useful-work

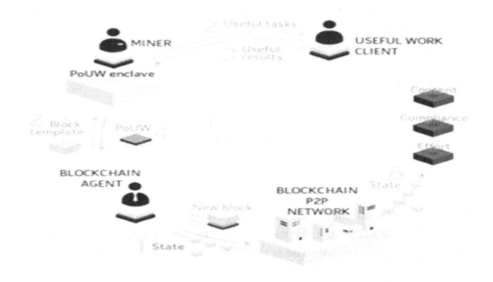

Table 1. Proof-of-stake, Proof-of-work, and proof-of-useful-work

Proof-of-work (PoW)	Proof-of-stake (PoS)	Proof-of-useful-work (PoUW)
Power-hungry, enough energy to power a small country is required to secure the blockchain.	ECO-friendly, minimum recourses required to secure the blockchain	Very much power-hungry
Incentivizes centralized mining farms.	Truly decentralized mining.	Truly decentralized mining.
Advanced technical knowledge required.	Very little technical knowledge required.	Very little technical knowledge required, mining scheme requires training deep learning models
It requires constant tweaking and monitoring.	Set it and forget it.	Set it and forget it.

- Anonymity
- Check flag for voter's illegibility
- Voting integrity with the system.

- Vote Verification

Different Phases in the System

Publishing phase

It's a dummy approach to publicize the system and generating candidate ballots. The Authority has eligible bling signature which is communicated securely to prevent any attacks like DOS, Men-in-the-middle Attack

Login phase

After the publishing phase, the voter's will login and then verification will be done for eligibility. This phase also deals with the impersonation and EIDs establishment.

EID generation phase

This phase will be used to generate the public-private key for electronic identity. For every identity made, an EID password will be established in order to prevent tampering and impersonation. The generation of OTP can also be done.

Voting phase

For the generation of Blockchain transactions, our Voting phase ensures data consistency and isolation as depicted in Figure 5.

Blind signatures

These digital signatures (Seo, J. H., 2019) are heavily used in our application for transactions working for eligible voters sign and extract public and private keys and encrypt them in Ballot. The Ballot is sent to Electoral Authority (admin) and verifies the source of the ballot, removes the outer envelope and Encrypts the keys and sends back to the eligible voter.

System Protocol

This phase depicts the working of the voting application using different phases as per the sequence provided in Figure 6.

Figure 5. Implementing blind signatures

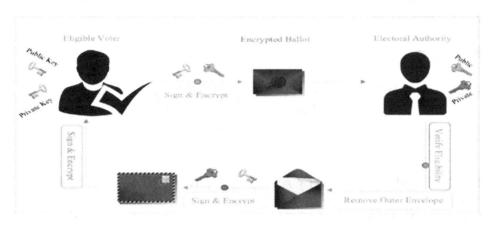

Figure 6. Proposed complete Solution

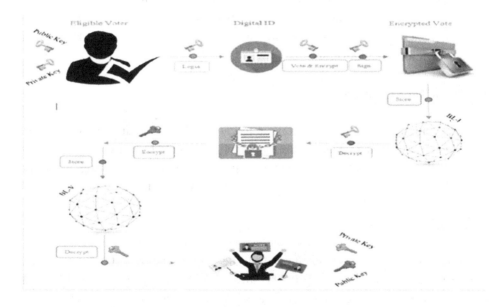

Threat Model

Various models have been taken in care for the full functionality of the Blockchain without any foreboding of threat initiation. As Blockchain helps with decentralization, and impenetrable security level, various threats are seldom to be seen. Some of the most common threats (Saini, H. Rao, Y.S., Panda, T. C., 2012; Rathee, G., Saini,

H., 2016) are DDoS Attack, Sybil Attack, Freak Attack, Malwares, Cross-Site Scripting (XSS), etc.

Evaluation

After the completion of the project, we will study all the sufficient properties of the proposed system design and these are the availability of the project, integrity with the OS and web page, uniqueness, accuracy, and election secrecy.

SOME OTHER SECURITY ANALYSIS AND LEGAL ISSUES

Security Analysis

DDoS

For the application to fail under DDOS Attack, the attacker must perform it on every node in the network. But tampering with the boot nodes will eventually inform the institution and the location could be found out. For locating failed blocks, we can use a fault-tolerance algorithm

Authentication Vulnerability

As the value of the hash will be unique to each and every individual or eligible voter, there is seldom a chance of multiple voting process by the voters. This will not only help with the ease to finalize the output result with incrementing by +1 but also eradicates out the total chances of the system malfunctioning.

Sybil Attacks

The consensus algorithms implemented in the project are prone to these attacks. Furthermore, with the incoming of the strong cryptography features and limited access to the ledger, Blockchain solves today's most often security problems

Legal Issues

Transparency

No method of transparency can be offered to the voters in today's electoral scheme. Without some other tech involvement, transparency in the system is a very tedious task with the formulation of a new law by government officials.

Voter Privacy

Voter privacy in pen and paper scheme is meandering which may involve leakage of voter credentials and vote to the party or the candidate. To satisfy the privacy, initiation of the non-traceable vote will be prominent to implement.

Remote Voting

To prevent coercion resistance in the election, remote voting could be of good use. If the results can be used in websites or mobile applications, there is no chance of misconfigured results, but on the negative side, people with good hacking skills can take down the host website and different threats can be introduced. We can use Blockchain features to subdue these effects.

Comparison

Traditional Blockchain Solution

In the traditional Blockchain solution, we can observe the common implementation of litecoin, dash, ripple and many other programming languages based bitcoin implementation. There is less privacy needed even though implemented in a suitable domain of programming languages.

Proposed Blockchain Solution

The platform implements all the solutions in ethereum, solidity and other bitcoin consensus protocols using of RSA algorithm implemented with the generation of private keys. The main idea of proposing this blockchain solution for the voting system is to make the electoral system cheaper and quicker. By doing this, the barrier between voters and officials to be elected will be an endgame. Furthermore, with ease in operation, we can assure a direct form of democracy as people will be in more ease to use it and give a better result in return without any involvement of a central agency. We also implemented a simple voting application using smart contracts (solidity, ethereum) for the proper conduct of system execution while maintaining security features like privacy and authentication verification. By comparing with the current process of the electoral system, we can observe that blockchain technology has a new future for democratic countries where most of it is pen and paper-based. Using the ethereum private blockchain, we can transmit hundreds of transactions in one second, for countries with bigger democracy, this system can provide a well-executed result with seldom chances of result tampering. The use of modern hash algorithms makes the data fetching impenetrable and isolated within each and every block. Decentralization has made the platform much more secret and private than that of centralized systems. Our proposed system will ensure that all the blockchain concepts will be executed properly resulting in a better approach to implement the platform practically in the provinces or the region. The pros and cons of our solution are represented in Table 2.

Table 2. Traditional Blockchain Solution Vs Proposed Blockchain Solution

Traditional blockchain solution	Proposed blockchain solution
Operated with decentralized property	Operated with decentralized property
Programming tools: Native Programming Languages (Java, Python, C++, ASP.NET, C#)	Programming tools: Ethereum, Solidity, web3.js
Time of Transaction: Minutes	Time of Transaction: Seconds
Implementing client-server architecture and RDBMS	Facilitates P2P architecture and smart contracts; no RDBMS required

B. Proposed e-Waste Management System

India is the fifth-biggest maker of the e-waste on the planet amazingly has not many arrangements with regards to reusing and appropriately arranging e-waste (Terazono, A., et al., 2006). Therefore, e-waste is an inevitable problem, but this problem can be stopped before it turns into a disaster. The current solutions are not enough to properly dispose of e-waste, the present scenario can be changed very easily if the proposed solution is applied to it.

The proposed e-waste Management system depends upon resourceful contracts made by utilizing blockchain progression. Bringing government work environments, clients and assistants on the corresponding blockchain stage will incite improved checking and higher transparency at the same time. Blockchain will empower the appropriate maintenance of records of the electrical and electronic supplies launched in the technical market by various makers and retailers (Gupta, N., & Bedi, P., 2018). This will empower smart contracts to verifiably choose collectors and disapprove of inappropriate collectors at whatever point required. In a similar manner, we provide the inclusion of clients as individuals from this blockchain. Offering motivations to lure clients to channelize their e-garbage to the formal part can fill in as the hidden stage in lessening the nature of the tangled division in e-waste management. Also, collection centers, as well as recycling units, are being included in our proposed system. These bright contracts will help control the initial point and extent of e-waste collected, delivered and reused all over in the framework.

Table 3. List of all the nodes

S.No	Node	Description
1.	Producer(PR)	A node association with Ethereum arranges a producer/provider/ merchant of EEE in India.
2.	Retailer(RT)	A node associated with the Ethereum arranges the largescale purchaser of the EEE from PR and pitches to the clients.
3.	Collection Centre(CC)	Spot where the E-waste is briefly put away by the PR, which is gathered by RT from clients. Proprietors of CC are associated with Ethereum organize as nodes.
4.	Recycling Unit(RU)	A Government Certified Unit where E-waste from CC is reused in a situation well-disposed way. The proprietors of RU are additionally associated with Ethereum organize.

Table 4. List of other participants in e-waste management

S. No.	Participant	Description
1.	Government's Agency(GA)	An initial point on the Ethereum organizes as in-charge of composing and keeps up savvy contracts for the EWM framework.
2.	Consumer(CS)	A hub on the Ethereum arranges that utilizes the EEEs for their very own advantage.

In our proposal, we use Ethereum blockchain to approve Electronic Wate Management in India. Table 3 and Table 4 represent the list of all types of nodes used in the solution and list of other participants in e-waste management respectively. The center addressing GAs manages the smart contract for coordinating the surge of e-garbage across over multiple accomplices and CSs. GAs endorse only those PRs and RTs who will join this e-waste administrator blockchain. Owners of CCs and RUs, who wish to set up their associations in our country, ought to similarly transform into a bit of this EWMB. CSs will benefit from this project by getting pre-portrayed spurring powers for channelizing their e-squander to real accomplices present on the blockchain. The splendid contract made by GAs will contain the following components that will track the activities of every part. The complete flow diagram of our e-waste management system is depicted in Figure 7.

Figure 7. e-waste Management System

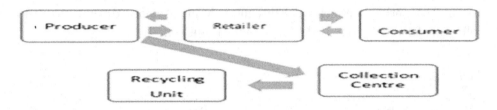

Table 5. Traditional Blockchain Solution Vs Proposed Blockchain Solution

Current Solution	Proposed Solution
Local market using ends up in black market recycling units use toxic chemicals, and use child labor.	E-waste recycling unit is trackable, easy to manage the operations, and easy for the administration to use.
The capital generated from this solution is often miscalculated and is often very less from what it should be. Most of the capital earned from this process ends up in the hands of illegal recycling unit owners.	The capital generated through this system Will be properly calculable and this would Help the government generate more capital from E-waste.
User is mostly in dark and not aware where their E-waste ends and unfortunately, most of them don't even care about what happens to their E-waste. At least the user should be aware of how much their E-waste is worth.	Through our proposed Solution users and manufacturers of the E-waste would have an insight where their E-waste ends up. It would be a more responsible and manageable operation for the manufacturing side.
The current situation of E-waste recycling exposes a lot of workers to toxic chemicals Like lead, mercury, etc. And these units also don't have proper equipment and techniques to deal with generated this E-waste.	Although the use of Hazardous chemicals cannot be stopped, it can be reduced. Recycling E-waste is Manageable through our solution. If proper recycling units are set up properly. This solution will bring proper standards in the E-waste recycling industry.

Utilizing of blockchain, all the participating parties can be easily connected to each other and will be able to track and use this proposed solution to efficiently manage E-waste management and the government to generate appropriate capital from this recycling of the E-waste through our proposed solution. Clients and makers of the E-waste would have a knowledge where their E-waste winds up. It would be a progressively mindful and reasonable activity for the assembling side.

In order to fulfill this goal, the government needs to associate with the cooperative authorities who are supposed to handle the process. Also, the awareness also plays a very important role in order to get the people on the track of the recycling process. For this to happen, the government needs to take it seriously (Nandwani, K., 2018).

Despite the fact that the utilization of Hazardous synthetic can't be halted yet can be diminished. At last, as Blockchain is public to everyone and is able to access where the E-waste went and who handled this information would be very useful for government and manufacturing companies to plan and efficiently manage E-waste and also be responsible for proper recycling E-waste. A comparative analysis is given in Table 5.

C. Decentralized Kickstarter Crowdfunding

Kickstarter is an application as depicted in Figure 8 that allows investors, no matter big or small to invest in projects they see on the application, again, the projects can also be of varying sizes and require a varying amount of investments. This is a very useful and unique application as the investors are paying the project owner some amount of money in return for the stocks, or profits or whatever their agreement is and the owner gets the required funding to start his business.

A very important feature of kickstarter is that it only allows money to be transferred from an investor to an owner when a certain threshold limit is touched that has been set by the owner in order to start his project. This is something that needs to be taken special care of. Now, like all applications and especially the applications that involve money kickstarter hits certain road bumps and problems. The biggest issue with kickstarter is the fact that money is not tracked. Once the investor gives his money to the owner, he can do whatsoever he wishes with that money, he can use it for his personal use or he can be honest and use it for the project as he mentioned before. Another problem with it is that as the project owner can also work with fiat money in the physical world, it is nearly impossible to know how much money did he actually make and what share of it is to be given to the investor.

The proposed kickstarter clone will be hosted on the RinkebyTestnet which is a free Ethereumtestchain, the same code can then be shifted to the real Ethereum Blockchain with minimal effort. This would allow us to test the application as if it was hosted live and not spend any Ether doing it either. The application we tend to build will be nearly the same as kickstarter when it comes to features and procedures to be followed to host your project on it or be an investor on the application. The frontend will be nearly identical to the real kickstarter application in terms of general usage. Where the difference lie is in the use of smart contracts to restrict the usage of money invested and in the participation of the investors every time the owner wants to spend money. If the owner wants to spend money, he will issue a request in the application and the smart contract will make sure that 51% of voters have voted favorably for the spending of money and only then that money will be moved from the project account to the account destined for. This will nullify the possibility of the project owner using project money for personal usage and benefits. Also, the investors will be able to track and know where there invested money is being used.

Figure 8. A generic model for Kickstarter

In order to be an investor in the first place, a certain amount of money have to be donated by the investor. Once that is done, that money will be submitted to the project account and that investor will be added to a list of investors for that project and will get his voting rights for any spending in the future.

The project owner is the only one who can make spending requests on the application and can need to make genuine requests as otherwise the investors will vote NO and that transaction will be canceled. As the money will be in the account of the project account (that is possible using a contract account instead of externally owned account), the owner cannot spend money on his own and has to abide by the rules.

Once the request is approved, that money will be transferred to whatever destination address was. This will solve both the major problems –money tracking and proper usage of money. Table 6 represents the comparison of the traditional and proposed blockchain solution.

Table 6. Comparison of a traditional and proposed blockchain solution

Traditional solution	Proposed block-chain solution
Centralized controlled	Decentralized controlled
Integrity: Not always possible	Integrity: every user can be sure that the data they are retrieving is uncorrupted and unaltered since the moment it was recorded
Transparency: same as Integrity	Transparency: every user can verify how the blockchain has been appended over time
The traditional application uses a traditional database, on which a client can perform four functions on data: Create, Read, Update, and Delete.	The blockchain is designed to be an append-only structure. A user can only add more data, in the form of additional blocks. All previous data is permanently stored and cannot be altered.
Traditional application incurs transaction cost.	A blockchain carries no transaction cost. (An infrastructure cost yes, but no transaction cost.)
Selected users can see the data.	All participants see consistent data.
Scalability is a major issue	Blockchain simplifies the processes and thus scalability is not an issue.

Issuing and Verifying College Degree using Blockchain

It is easy to use, yet the secure application of issuing and verifying college degrees. Authorized personal can issue the degrees in blockchain, and anyone can verify its existence or validity.

Figure 9. Generic Architecture

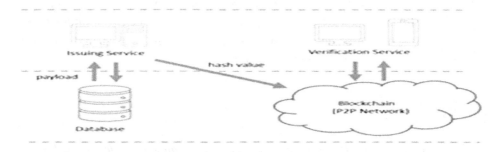

The goal is to create a De-centralised application for issuing and verifying college degrees using blockchain. Following are the goals for the setup process for building the application which is also depicted in Figure 9:

- Setup the development environment.
- Learn how to write a contract, push degree data (pdf) into the block, compiling it and deploying it to our development environment.
- Interact with the smart-contract on the blockchain.
- Propose a simple and easy to use applications to deploy degrees on the blockchain.

Advantages of the proposed approach can be as follows-

- No central authority or a third party required. All the functionality and working will be taken by the peer to peer networks.
- There is no way of tampering of college degree's as concepts of "PROOF OF WORK" and "PROOF OF STAKE" are highly maintained.
- No individual can try and change the data in the degrees present in the block.

For the basic idea, we will go with the smart contracts and object-oriented programming in Solidity.

CONCLUSION

In this manuscript, we have reviewed the state-of-art of the blockchain technique along with its case studies in various fields. Further, we have described various blockchain uses cases and explored the different applications in the blockchain with a significant proposed scenario. The aim of this paper is to point out the significance of blockchain in various fields. Further, we have defined how blockchain technology could be helpful in various fields having a decentralized network. In our future work, we will propose a solution corresponding to the above IIoT blockchain discussion with some analyzed and evaluated parameters.

REFERENCES

Ametrano, F. M. (2016). *Hayek money: The cryptocurrency price stability solution.* Available at SSRN 2425270

Baldominos, A., & Saez, Y. (2019). *Coin. AI: A Proof-of-Useful-Work Scheme for Blockchain-based Distributed Deep Learning.* arXiv preprint arXiv:1903.09800

Cachin, C. (2016, July). Architecture of the hyperledger blockchain fabric. In *Workshop on distributed cryptocurrencies and consensus ledgers* (*Vol. 310*, p. 4). Academic Press.

Christin, N. (2011). Peer-to-peer networks: Interdisciplinary challenges for interconnected systems. In *Information Assurance and Security Ethics in Complex Systems: Interdisciplinary Perspectives* (pp. 81–103). IGI Global. doi:10.4018/978-1-61692-245-0.ch005

Gupta, N., & Bedi, P. (2018, September). E-waste Management Using Blockchain based Smart Contracts. In *2018 International Conference on Advances in Computing, Communications and Informatics (ICACCI)* (pp. 915-921). IEEE. 10.1109/ICACCI.2018.8554912

Houben, R., & Snyers, A. (2018). *Cryptocurrencies and blockchain: Legal context and implications for financial crime, money laundering and tax evasion*. Academic Press.

Iansiti, M., & Lakhani, K. R. (2017). The truth about blockchain. *Harvard Business Review*, *95*(1), 118–127.

Nandwani, K. (2018). *Squaring the Blockchain Circle*. Available at: https://kunalnandwani.com/books/

Peters, M. A. (2017). Technological unemployment: Educating for the fourth industrial revolution. *Journal of Self-Governance and Management Economics*, *5*(1), 25–33. doi:10.22381/JSME5120172

Rathee, G., & Saini, H. (2016). Security Concerns with Open Research Issues of Present Computer Network. *International Journal of Computer Science and Information Security*, *14*(4), 406–432.

Saini, H. Rao, Y.S., Panda, T. C. (2012). Cyber-Crimes and their Impacts: A Review. *International Journal of Engineering Research and Applications, 2*(2), 202-209.

Seo, J. H. (2019). Efficient Digital Signatures from RSA without Random Oracles. *Information Sciences*.

Swan, M. (2015). *Blockchain: Blueprint for a new economy.* O'Reilly Media, Inc.

Terazono, A., Murakami, S., Abe, N., Inanc, B., Moriguchi, Y., Sakai, S. I., ... Wong, M. H. (2006). Current status and research on E-waste issues in Asia. *Journal of Material Cycles and Waste Management, 8*(1), 1–12. doi:10.100710163-005-0147-0

Vukolić, M. (2015, October). The quest for scalable blockchain fabric: Proof-of-work vs. BFT replication. In *International workshop on open problems in network security* (pp. 112-125). Springer.

Yu, B., Liu, J., Nepal, S., Yu, J., & Rimba, P. (2019). Proof-of-QoS: QoS Based Blockchain Consensus Protocol. *Computers & Security*, *87*, 101580. doi:10.1016/j.cose.2019.101580

Zheng, Z., Xie, S., Dai, H., Chen, X., & Wang, H. (2017, June). An overview of blockchain technology: Architecture, consensus, and future trends. In *2017 IEEE International Congress on Big Data (BigData Congress)* (pp. 557-564). IEEE.

Chapter 10
Integrating Blockchain and IoT in Supply Chain Management:
A Framework for Transparency and Traceability

Madumidha S.
Sri Krishna College of Technology, India

SivaRanjani P.
Kongu Engineering College, India

Venmuhilan B.
Sri Krishna College of Technology, India

ABSTRACT

Internet of things(IoT) is the conception of interfacing the devices to the internet to make life more efficient. It comprises the large amount of data in its network where it fails to assure complete security in the network. Blockchain is a distributed ledger where it mainly focuses on the data security. Every block in the blockchain network is connected to its next block, which prevents threats like large data loss. In the area of agri-food supply chain, where IoT plays a very important role, there occurs data integrity issues or data tampering. This can lead to improper supply chain management, timely shortage of goods, food spoilage, etc. So the traceability of agri-food supply chain is necessary to ensure food safety and to increase the trust between all stakeholders and consumers. Many illegal activities can be prevented, and cold chain monitoring can be achieved by bringing in transparency and traceability.

DOI: 10.4018/978-1-7998-3444-1.ch010

INTRODUCTION

The 21st century is all about technology that increases the need for transformation in day-to-day life. People from all over the world are ready to accept the modern tools and technologies by using a remote for controlling devices to voice notes. In the past decade, technologies like Augmented Reality and the Internet of Things played a vital role in humans. Now there is a new addition to the pack called Blockchain Technology (Aung, M. M., & Chang, Y. S.; (2014)). One reason why the modern world is seeing more and more wealth created is that the economics and markets are connected via ever more sophisticated routes of global trade. Whether be it by air, sea, or road, billions worth of goods are being taken from continent to continent every single day, to satisfy demand and meet supply quotas. However, while new methods of storage and route tweaks are still developed to further propel this vital aspect of the global economy, the sheer volume of transport information processed on a daily basis means there is huge inaccuracy of data when trying to monitor an individual product's journey. Major business leaders are dependent on physical supply chains that have long pushed for additional transparency, price-efficiency and data insight, beginning at the creation of a product to its final destination (Storøy, J., Thakur, M., & Olsen, P.; (2013)).

SUPPLY CHAIN MANAGEMENT (SCM)

A supply chain is an entire network of entities, directly or indirectly interlinked and independent in serving the same consumer or customer. It comprises vendors that supply raw material, the producer who convert the material into products, warehouses that store the products, distribution center that deliver to the retailers, and retailers who bring the product to the ultimate user. Figure 1 explains the management of the flow of goods, services, and information involving the storage and movement of raw materials, building products as well as full-fledged finished goods from one point to another are known as supply chain management. Supply chain management includes integrated planning as well as the execution of different processes within the supply chain (Khan, M. A., & Salah, K.; (2018)). These processes include:

- Material flow
- Information flow
- Financial capital flow

Importance of Supply Chain Management

- SCM activities can improve customer service. Effective supply chain management can ensure customer satisfaction by making certain the necessary products are available at the correct location at the right time. By delivering products to consumers on time and providing fast services and support SCM increases customer satisfaction (Mao, D. et al. (2019)).
- SCM decreases overall production costs for the companies. The reduced supply chain costs can greatly increase a business's profits and cash flow.
- SCM can help ensure human survival by improving healthcare, protecting humans from climate extremes and sustaining human life.
- The supply chain is also vital to the delivery of electricity to homes and businesses, providing the energy needed for light, heat, air conditioning, and refrigeration.

Figure 1. Traditional Supply Chain Management

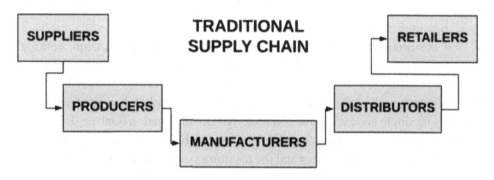

- The main drawbacks of Traditional Supply chain are:
- Product safety cannot be assured at any stage.
- The detailed information about the origin of the product will not be available at the customer end.
- Limited transparency and Lack of traceability (hard to track down).
- Controllability-Lifespan of control.
- Information is stored in Centralized databases.

CENTRALIZED VS DECENTRALIZED

Data Monarchy vs Data Democracy

A centralized System is where the information is stored and maintained in a single centralized server. Figure 2 describes the centralized networks run the very real risk of being attacked, altered or held for ransom. This is because centralized networks store all of their data in one place. By keeping all of your information in one place, it increases its vulnerability to malicious behavior (Peck, M. E. (2017)).

The Disadvantage of a Centralized Database

- Since all the data are stored at the same location, if multiple users try to access it simultaneously it creates a problem. This will reduce the efficiency of the system (Thakur, M., & Hurburgh, C. R. (2009)).
- All the data in the database will be destroyed if there are no data recovery measures in the system when the system fails.
- If the centralized system fails it will stop the entire system from working. This is called a Single point of failure (SPOF).

In a decentralized System, there is no single entity control. A key attribute is that typically no single node will have complete system information (Galvez, J. F., et al., (2018). Here the decisions are not made by the centralized server. Every node makes its own decisions for its behavior and the resulting system behavior is the aggregate response. If parts of a network failure, the rest of the network will still be functional and safe. So, decentralized networks are more secure. This is not just because they use cryptography, but because the information is not all in one place (Madumidha, S et al., (2018), Bogner, A et al., (2016), Tian, F. (2017)). When information is in one place, the system is at a much greater threat to malicious attacks, server failure, and even upgrades will temporarily shut down a centralized server.

Advantage of Decentralized and Distributed System

- No third party can access the user's information
- No single point of failure
- Transparent-where everyone in the network can see the transaction that has taken place on the network
- Secure
- Cheap transactions globally
- Quick transactions globally

Figure 2. Centralized, Decentralized and Distributed database Visualization

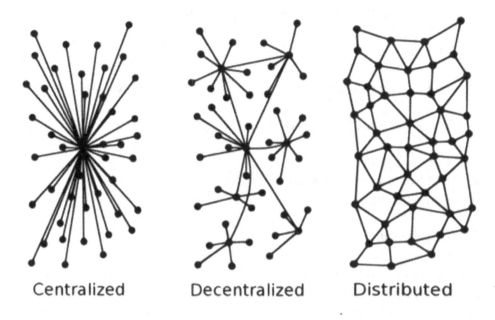

Centralized   Decentralized   Distributed

BLOCKCHAIN

A blockchain is a secure, decentralized, immutable public ledger that records every transaction, chronologically, on the network. A linked list of blocks where each block defines a set of transactions. The blockchain is the underlying technology upon which cryptocurrencies and DApps (Decentralised applications that run on a distributed computer system) are built (JoSEP, A. D et al., (2010)). Blockchains update regularly, confirming transactions. Once a transaction has been confirmed and listed in the blockchain, it is impossible to change or tamper with. This makes blockchains extremely secure and highly resistant to fraudulent behavior or human error. Blockchain technology is set to disrupt industries all over the world in the coming years – especially industries where there are a high number of intermediary or third-party companies (Li, D., Kehoe, D., & Drake, P.; (2006)).

Blocks

A collection of data containing multiple transactions over a given period of time on the blockchain network. It contains two parts-the header and the data(the Transactions) (Schneider, M.; (2017), Chinaka, M.; (2016), Lucena, P. et al.; (2018)). The header of a block connects the transactions any change in any transaction will result in a change at the block header. The headers of a subsequent block are connected in a chain-the entire blockchain that needs to be updated if you want to make any change in the blockchain (Holmberg, A., & Åquist, R.; (2018)).

Chain

The cryptographic connection which keeps blocks together using a 'hash' function.

Blockchain is the combination of three Technologies

- Cryptography
- P2P Networks(decentralized)
- Game Theory

Cryptography

Cryptography is simply taking unencrypted data or a message, such as a piece of text, and encrypting it using a mathematical algorithm, known as a cipher. For Bitcoin this is SHA-256. In applying this algorithm plain text becomes unreadable without the correct unlocking script (Caro, M. P et al., (2018), Li, C., & Zhang, L. J. (2017)). Asymmetric cryptography is the most secure form of cryptography, which is the form of cryptography that Bitcoin uses. For asymmetric cryptography verification, it needs two keys to do so. This is not the case for symmetrical cryptography. Asymmetric cryptography, therefore, needs a public key and a private key. Asymmetric cryptography is also called "Public-key cryptography". Once a public key is matched to the private key the information, is made intelligible for its owner. Matching the keys is executed with the programmed script. Unlike symmetric key algorithms that rely on one key to both encrypt and decrypt, asymmetric algorithms require a specific key, to perform specific functions. The public key is used to encrypt and the private key is used to decrypt (Zheng, Z.; (2017).

Cryptographic Hash Function

Cryptographic hashing is a fundamental part of blockchain technology and is directly responsible for producing immutability – one of blockchain's most important features. Figure 3 explains about hashing is a computer science term that means taking an input string of any length and producing a fixed-length output. It doesn't matter if the input to a certain hash function is 3 or 100 characters, the output will always be the same length. Cryptographic hash functions have the following properties:

- Deterministic: No matter how many times you give the function a specific input, it will always have the same output.
- Irreversible: It is impossible to determine an input from the output of the function.
- Collision resistance: No two inputs can ever have the same output.

The cryptographic hashing also enables immutability for blockchain. Every new block of data contains a hash output of all the data in the previous block. A blockchain is made up of a series of blocks with a new block always added to its last. Each block contains zero or more transactions and some additional metadata. Blocks achieve immutability by including the result of the hash function of the previous block.

SHA-256

Figure 3. Cryptographic Hashing Function

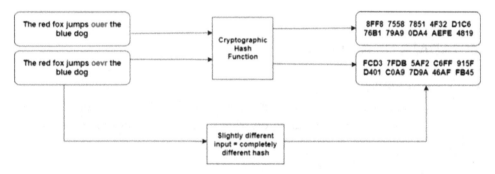

Hash algorithms are computational functions. The input data is condensed to a fixed size. The result is the output called a hash, or a hash value. Hashes identify, compare or run calculations against files and strings of data. To add to an extent blockchain, the program must first solve for the target-hash for it to accept the new block of data. Presently SHA-256 is the most secure hashing function. This function expresses the possible combinations of values that result from the given input data. SHA stands for Secure Hashing Function, and 256 expresses the numerical quantity of the fixed bit length. This means that the target is correct 256 bit, and as mentioned, Bitcoin uses a 65-hexadecimal hash value. Using the SHA-256 function makes it (nearly) impossible to duplicate a hash because there are just too many combinations to try and process. Therefore, this requires a significant amount of computational work; So much so that personal computers no longer mine Bitcoin. Presently miners require Application Specific Integrated Circuits or ASIC. Achieving this target has the probability of 2^256, if you remember your exponents, you will deduce this is an incredibly difficult variable to hit.

Furthermore, using this hash function means that such a hash is intentionally computationally impractical to reverse and as the intentional result that requires a random or brute-force method to solve for the input. Consider the following, if the player has 1 six-sided dice, he has a 1 in 6 chance of rolling a 6. However, the more sides dice has (say 256 sides), his chances of rolling a 6 get a whole lot lower (that's 1 in 256: which is still better than your odds of using brute-force on an extent hash). A hash rate is then the speed at which hashing operations take place during the mining process. If the hash rate gets too high and miners solve the target has too quickly, increasing the potential for a collision, and indicating that the difficulty of the hash needs to be adjusted accordingly. For example, every 10 minutes, at present, new Bitcoin is mined.

Collision Resistance: SHA-256 is collision-resistant because of the large amount of data, so arriving the same target-hash at the same time is nearly impossible. This is also a result of using a target with high min-entropy.

METADATA OF A BLOCK

- **Genesis block:**
    - The first block in the blockchain network is known as the 'genesis' block. It is the foundation on which additional blocks are sequentially

Figure 4. Blockchain – Metadata of a Block

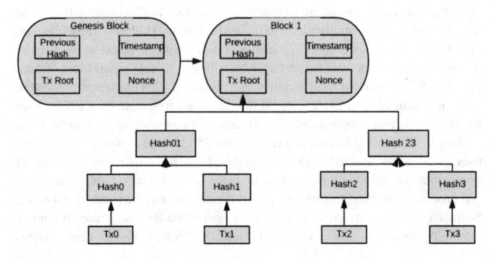

added to form a chain of blocks. The genesis block is also referred to as block zero.

- **Previous Hash:**
  - This hash address points to the previous block. Every block inherits from the previous block. New block's hash is created by the use of the previous block's hash.
- **Transaction Details:**
  - Details of all the transactions that need to occur.
- **Nonce:**
  - The nonce is abbreviated as "number only used once," in a Bitcoin block is a 32-bit (4-byte). An arbitrary number is given in cryptography to differentiate the block's hash address. Miners (who validates new transactions and record them on the public ledger) adjust the value of the nonce so that the hash of the block will be less than or equal to the current target of the network.
- **Hash Address of the Block:**
  - All of the above (i.e., preceding hash, transaction details, and nonce) are transmitted through a hashing algorithm. The output consists of a 256-bit, 64character length value, which is called the unique 'hash address'. It is referred to as the hash of the block.
- **Timestamp:**
  - Timestamp in the blockchain is used as evidence or proof exists and it keeps proof for notarization. The process will prove that a certain document exists, for some time. Any unauthorized and unauthenticated modification can be detected easily under this and from when the document is being in existence.

This process involves two steps:

1. Hashing the documents.
2. Recording data into the blockchain.

In Blockchain, a single document can be hashed and stored very easily. But it's not practically possible with large-sized digital files to get stored and kept in the blockchain. So every data has to be hashed and stored into the blockchain. The main logic behind data hashing is that blockchain offers limited space and it is very costly to have large space and transaction costs, another reason is document privacy and data security. Hashing helps the documents to be cryptographically stored into blockchain with a timestamp. Large data can be stored by building a Merkle tree. On hashing, the data one time will promise the same output. Hash value always has a fixed length no matter how huge the data is. Any change in hash value will result in a tampered result. After hashing the data recorded into blockchain will especially create a particular space for the hashed document and stored into blockchain with a timestamp. Once the transaction is done it can return a transaction ID. And ID will contain transaction details, block number, timestamp and nonce which will help later verification process of a particular action. The verification process can be done easily with minimal steps since a small size hashed value is stored into the blockchain, it won't take much space and time in retrieving.

- **Merkle Root Tree:**
  A tree is a computer science term for storing data in a hierarchical tree-like structure where bits of data are called nodes. There is a single root (top) node that has "child" nodes linked under it, which themselves have child nodes, and so on. A Merkle tree (or hash tree) is a tree that uses cryptographic hash functions to store hash outputs instead of raw data in each node. Each leaf node consists of a cryptographic hash of its original data, and every parent node is a hash of the combination of its child node hashes. Merkle root trees are structures used to validate huge amounts of data efficiently. They cannot only verify that the data received from other peers in a peer-to-peer network like Bitcoin or Ethereum (blockchain-based distributed computing platform) are unaltered but also that the blocks being sent are legitimate. Merkle roots, however, can be understood as the signature of all the transactions included within a single block. In Bitcoin, for example, the Merkle root can be found in the block header (along with the hash of the previous block, the timestamp, and the nonce). Most Merkle Trees are binary, however, there are non-binary Merkle Trees employed by other blockchain platforms. Ethereum is an example of a blockchain that uses non-binary a Merkle Tree.

HOW DO BLOCKCHAINS WORK?

- Figure 5 explain someone requests a transaction or exchange of data or currency.
- The request is shared on the decentralized, peer-to-peer network. The network is made up of independent computers which are called nodes.
- The network of participating nodes validates the transaction using the required computing algorithms.
- Transactions include any of the following: cryptocurrencies, smart-contracts, records, among others.

Figure 5. Blockchain Process

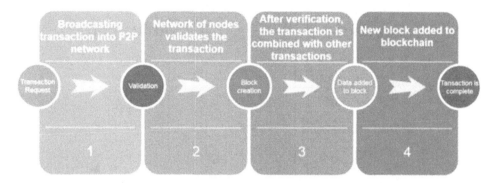

- To make new blocks cryptographic algorithms are applied. The block of data includes the original transaction. Once it is added to the blockchain the block cannot be altered.
- After the network verifies the transaction, the miner adds a new block to the digital ledger. The new block is combined with the other blocks of data.
- The transaction is complete. This means the data is successfully transferred to its new owner, (in the case of a cryptocurrency). Otherwise, there is just a new block of data on the chain.

Digital Signature

Digital signatures are one amongst the most aspects of guaranteeing security and integrity of the info that's recorded onto a blockchain. They are a standard part of blockchain protocols that are used for securing transactions and blocks of transactions, conveyance of information, contract management and the other cases where identifying and preventing any external tampering is very important. Digital signatures utilize Asymmetric cryptography that means that info is often shared with anyone, through the employment of a public key.

Digital signatures are distinctive to the signer and are created by utilizing 3 algorithms:

- A key generation algorithmic program, providing a private and public key.
- A signing algorithm merges information private key to create a signature.
- An algorithm that verifies signatures and determines whether the message is authentic or not based on the message, the public key, and signature.

Figure 6. Digital Signature Signing and Verification

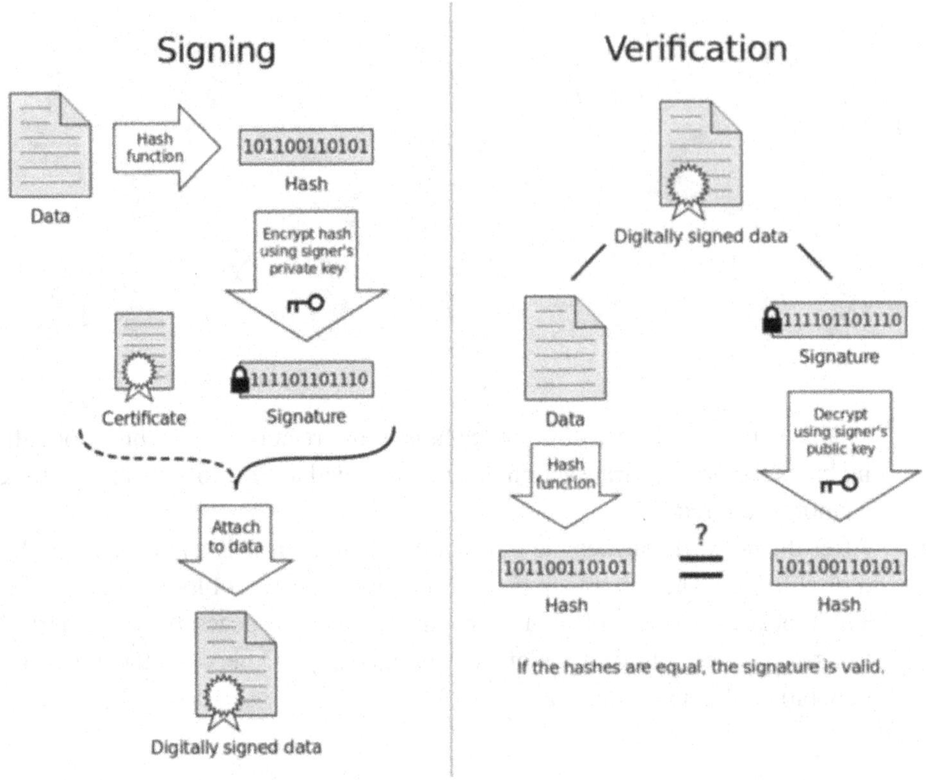

The key options of these algorithms are:

- Making it impossible to figure out the private key based on the public key or info that it has encrypted.
- Ensuring the authenticity of a signature based on the message and also the private key, verified through public key

PEER-TO-PEER NETWORK - DECENTRALIZED & DISTRIBUTED NETWORK

Every node of the network in Figure 7 is a client as well as server, holding identical copies of the application state. The process is by design very democratic, not only because it relies on multiple participants, but because there are few benefits to undermining the system. If a proposed block does not meet the parameters of the consensus, it will not be approved and added to the chain.

Figure 7. Peer to Peer Network

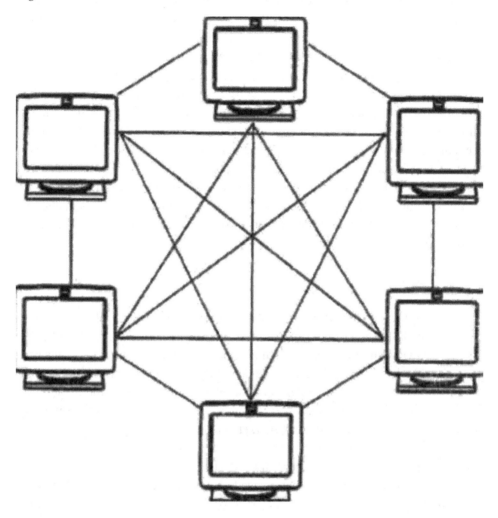

Features of Peer-to-Peer Networks

- Each peer is equal in authority.
- Peers give computing resources to the network to use the network.
- Sometimes peers are referred to as nodes. Generally, running a node puts the user in control of his network data.
- No single party owns or controls the network.
- Each user is essentially a server.
- It's almost impossible to hack because the network is distributed across many different computers.
- The more users, the more powerful the network becomes.

Each node is an autonomous computer. It is, therefore, the node's job to maintain connection and communication with the network. These nodes are rewarded for their work with transaction fees. At present, there is no set standard for the cost of a transaction. Transaction fees are dictated by the supply and demand of the network. As a result, they can be very volatile. Each computer then maintains a list of peers it communicates with. This list is only a subset of all nodes that make up the entire network. Each computer must regularly verify that those peers are still available. This is done by sending peers a small message, often called "ping." When their peers on the network approve the request other computers are added to the system. The new node's address is then added to the connected network. When a node joins the peer-to-peer system, it typically establishes connections to many different nodes for the sake of redundancy and security. Doing so ensures that the connection to the system as a whole is maintained, as individual nodes will inevitably disconnect or shut down.

- Peer control:

    ◦ In the distributed network of a blockchain-algorithm, all participating nodes supervise all other nodes. The nodes both contribute and peer-review simultaneously. Each node verifies transactions and creates new blocks. They also receive, review, and validate the blocks created by other nodes. And so the system takes care of itself. And so long as no individual has exponentially more power than any other, it is fairly egalitarian, but driven by market demand.

Working of peer-to-peer Network in Blockchain:

All nodes receive all the information needed to validate and add transaction data. Nodes process new transaction data they receive. The blocks created by other nodes are processed immediately on arrival at the node's inbox. Valid transaction data alone are added to the blockchain-data-structure. All nodes take part in a race for solving the hash puzzle. Due to the nature of the hash puzzle, it is unpredictable which node will solve it first. They are informed when a node solves the hash puzzle of a new block. All nodes receive the newly created block and recognize the winner of the race for solving the hash puzzle. The nodes of the system review and verify newly created blocks and ensure that only correct blocks are accepted. They add new blocks to their copy of the blockchain-data-structure and hence grow the transaction history. The collectively maintained transaction history is kept free of invalid transactions and hence maintains integrity. No transaction data will be added twice. No valid transaction will get lost even if previously processed blocks are reprocessed. The system can perform ex-post validity checks on the transaction history and correct it retrospectively. Nodes have an incentive to process transactions and to create new blocks quickly. They also have an incentive to inform all other nodes about a new block because earning a reward depends on having transactions examined and accepted by all other nodes. Nodes have an incentive to work correctly, to avoid accepting any invalid transaction data or producing invalid blocks. Nodes have an incentive to review and revalidate blocks and transactions in a retrospective way.

GAME THEORY

Game Theory is the study of strategic decision making. Nodes of P2P network validates transactions by consensus, following economic incentive mechanisms like Proof of Work or Proof of Stake, etc.

Consensus Mechanism

- The blockchain-algorithm is a sequence of programmed instructions that govern how nodes process new transaction data and blocks. This is known as the "consensus mechanism".
- The validity of each block is evaluated based on two distinct groups of validation rules:
  ◦ Validation of the transaction data
  ◦ Validation of the block headers
- The validation rules for block headers are based on the formal and semantic correctness of the block headers. That means that there is no ambiguity of the data in the block header. This is crucial, as it is part of the validation process; invalid data will stop the transaction.
- A central element of validating block headers is the verification of the proof of work or the hash puzzle respectively. Only blocks whose headers contain a correct solution of its hash puzzle are processed further. Every block whose header fails the verification of its proof of work is discarded immediately.

Blockchain miners try to solve a mathematical puzzle, which is referred to as a proof of work problem and so on. Whoever solves it first gets a reward. In Blockchain technology, the process of adding transactional details to the present digital/public ledger is called 'mining.' Mining involves generating the hash of a block transaction, which is tough to forge, which ensures the safety of the entire Blockchain without needing a central system.

Proof of Work

The miners figure out a series of cryptographic puzzles to 'mine' a block so that it can be added to the chain. This procedure requires a massive amount of energy from the individual and an equally large amount of computational usages. It should be noted that the puzzles have been purposefully designed to be hard, as well as taxing on the system. When a miner ends up solving a puzzle, they present their mined block to the network for authentication. Verifying whether or not the presented block belongs to the chain is a fairly uncomplicated task.

Proof of Stake

Proof of stake makes the mining process into virtual and will employ validators as replacements for miners. This is how this particular procedure will work: The validators will need to lock up a portion of their coins as stake. Following this, they will proceed to start validating the blocks, meaning that when they uncover a block that they believe can be added to the chain, they will verify it by placing a bet on it. When the block get conjoined validators will then be given a reward that is correspondent to their bets.

Some other consensus mechanisms are proof of Burn, Delegated proof of stake, delegated Byzantine fault tolerance, proof of elapsed time, proof of capacity, proof of Activity and so on.

Other components of Blockchain:

- **Node:**
  - A copy of the ledger operated by a member of the blockchain network
- **Coin:**
  - The purpose of a coin is to act like money – to allow transactions of products and services to occur. Depending on the coin, it is a store of value, unit of account or medium of transfer
- **Token:**
  - A means of payment, but it has some added layer of functionality. Holders of tokens often get value from them beyond speculative returns, such as being able to vote on certain business decisions or technical changes, earn dividend payments for holding or staking tokens, or to get discounts on, or access to, services.
- **Cryptocurrencies:**
  - They are secured digital currencies using cryptography and built using blockchain technology. Ex.bitcoin
- **DApps:**

   ○ DApps are 'Decentralised Applications'. Applications, like Bitcoin or Ethereum, Hyperledger that are built on a decentralized blockchain.

Blockchain Platforms

- **Bitcoin:**
  - ○ Bitcoin was launched in 2009. It is the most famous blockchain network that offers crypto-currency transactions. The bitcoin blockchain has a 1MB block limit. It takes 10 minutes to mine, or create, a new block on the bitcoin blockchain.
- **Ethereum:**
  - ○ Ethereum was launched in 2015. It is an open-source blockchain platform. It does not have any block limit. It introduces smart contracts for decentralized applications (Dapps). Ethereum can serve as both a public and private blockchain network. The number of transactions that are put into a block is decided by the validators. Each block is mined in 12-14 seconds and the number of transactions per second is around 15.
- **Hyperledger:**
  - ○ It is mainly designed for enterprise applications. It is an open-source, private blockchain network.

SUPPLY CHAIN INTEGRATION

Supply chain processes and records are other areas that can gain from blockchain applications and a shared ledger. Now IBM is working on blockchain solutions to supply chain problems. Because blockchain relies on a shared immutable ledger, record management and traceability can be significantly improved. Food distributors are one of the main industries that are invested in blockchain and supply chain. Food distribution has the most opportunity to gain from blockchain applications. Currently records keeping and tracing product is error-prone and time-consuming because many processes have yet to be digitized. That means that keeping track of the movement of a product, for instance, food is very difficult. Not only does this pose concerns for efficiency, but it creates a serious issue for health concerns. The distributor must work quickly to isolate the spoiled food as well as alert the public once a food item is recalled. However, if all levels and handlers of a product are recorded on a shared network, it is very easy to isolate where the tainted food came from. They will also be able to isolate where and when the product was purchased. Currently, we must trust food labels alone. However, if blockchain were incorporated into supply chain processes, consumers could learn all about the processes of their products.

Use of Smart Contracts

A Traditional contract is not efficient for blockchain technology. The traditional supply chain consists of a large number of paper documents which result in a lack of transparency. Smart contracts are a type of self-executing contract with the terms of agreement residing in the lines of code. To be more specific, these agreement terms are those that are between a buyer and a seller. Both the code and the agreements exist across a distributed and decentralized blockchain network. Figure 8, these contracts allow for the execution of transactions and agreements among dissimilar, anonymous parties. On top of that, it is without a need for a central authority, a legal system, or any external enforcement. They essentially make all transactions traceable, transparent, and above all else, irreversible. The primary goal of these contracts is to boost the overall transparency of the transaction. All the while it reduces fees and eases any potential for conflict over a lack of performance. Unlike traditional contracts, however, smart contracts have absolutely no room for interpretation. This is due to all of the terms being predetermined and conditions executed automatically. Every smart contract is assigned with a unique address of 20 bytes. The contract code can never be changed once the contract is deployed into the blockchain, the user can only send a transaction to the contract's address. This transaction will be executed by every consensus node in the network to reach a consensus on its output.

- The benefits of using a smart contract include:

  ○ Turning legal obligations into more of an automated process
  ○ Guaranteeing a higher-level degree of security for parties involved in a contract
  ○ Reducing the conventional reliance on intermediates and any other form of middlemen
  ○ Lowering transaction costs

Figure 8. Smart Contract Flow Diagram

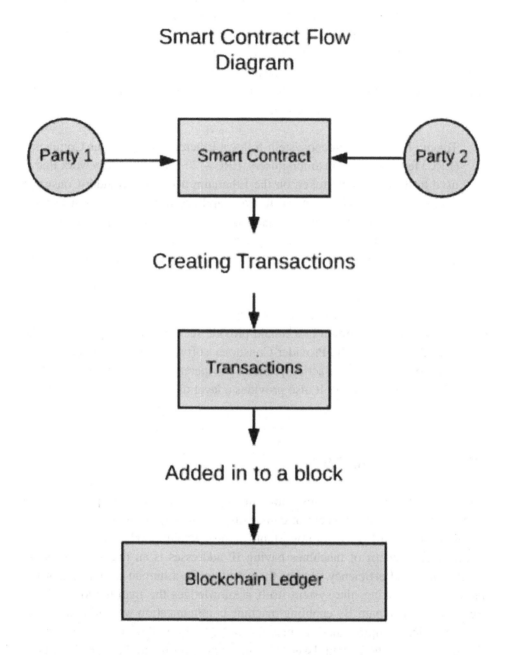

METHODS OF TOKEN IN BLOCKCHAIN

The Ethereum Platform is an open-source project that determines with two networks. One is a user account, which controls in a private key and address. Second is a

Smart Contract account that is controlled by code which is built inside. The code is compiled and ran using Ethereum Virtual Machines (EVM), which runs on individual nodes. The interaction between contracts is called transactions. The transactions update the state of smart contracts allowing for the state to be changed and viewed transparently from interacting with individual smart contracts. On top of the Ethereum network, the "Producer-Consumer" Network is built to globally access real-time transaction execution.

- Token: The Ethereum ecosystem follows Ethereum Request for Comments (ERC) feedback system among users. ERC – 20 is a token framework that is used to build a digital token on the Ethereum network. Provider-Consumer exploits the ERC-721 proposal to track and create assets that will provide asset and non-fungible token standard. This standard helps in integrating with Provider-Consumer with the current Ethereum Platform. All the digital assets are created on its own with the help of the ERC-721 standard.
- Steps in transferring an asset
  ○ Using a phone app
  ○ IoT devise that triggers a transaction
- The tokens in Ethereum blockchain provide security that is approved in the ERC-20 contract. The Provider-Consumer software assigns private keys to execute the whole transaction process. To operate on different phones ERC-721 contracts are used. It also provides a level of abstraction for IoT devices and users.

INTERNET OF THINGS

Internet of Things (IoT), makes communication between objects possible. The Internet of things is the concept of connecting the devices to the internet to make it more efficient. IoT plays an important role in tracking goods and sensing food spoilage. The benefit of machines having IP addresses is an overall increase in effectiveness and efficiency. Rather than waiting on a human to notice that the dishwasher is leaking, the system itself acknowledges the malfunction and can even manage its repair. By enabling machine communication we will continue to see a significant improvement in manufacturing and distribution, as it is a more effective check of the system. Issues are noted and returned to the manufacturer to implement the improvement. For example, smart thermostats regulate temperature more effectively than a human, and as we move towards automated vehicles, we will also see greater communication between traffic infrastructure and the vehicles themselves. Naturally, the IoT requires shared data so that machine communication is executed effectively. The needs of the human user are then tracked by the machine and sent to the manufacturer.

Gas and Payment

Ether is a cryptocurrency of Ethereum which is used for the transaction. Gas is the unit used to measure the fees required for a particular computation. With every transaction, a sender sets a gas limit and gas price. Gas price is the amount of Ether in which the user willing to spend on every unit of gas, and "gwei" is the unit that is applied to measure gas. The smallest unit of Ether is "Wei", where 10^{018} Wei =1 Ether. One gwei is 1,000,000,000 Wei. gas limit represents the maximum amount of Wei that the sender is willing to pay for executing a transaction. For example, let's say the sender sets the gas limit to 50,000 and a gas price to 20 gwei. This implies that the sender is willing to spend at most 50,000 x 20 gwei = 1,000,000,000,000,000 Wei = 0.001 Ether to execute that transaction. All the money spent on gas by the sender is sent to the miner's address. Not only is the gas used to pay for computation steps, but it is also used to pay for storage usage. Imposing fees prevents users from overtaxing the network.

Blockchain in supply chain overall process:

- Figure 9 explains the Provider-Consumer Solution provides blockchain a most efficient structure of a database having a public ledger that includes digital information on the products, people, or events that can be accessed or inspected by many users. With the help of blockchain, there is a chance to
  - Increase Transparency
  - Reduce Error
  - Prevents product delays
  - Eliminate unethical and illegal activities
  - Better management
  - Increase the trust between consumer and supplier
- · The customer demands are increasing every day and to meet that we need an improved supply chain. Also for a better marketing environment, we can make use of Blockchain technology in supply chains.
- Ether:

Ether is not meant to be a unit of currency on a peer-to-peer payment network; rather, it acts as the "fuel" or "gas" that powers the Ethereum network. Ethereum is an open-source platform that runs smart contracts. Smart contracts are self-executing when certain conditions are met. The smart contract execution requires computational resources that must be paid for in some way: this is where ether comes in. Ether is the crypto-fuel or currency allowing smart contracts to run. It provides the reward for nodes to validate blocks on the Ethereum blockchain, which contains the smart contract code. 5 ethers are created whenever the block is validated and awarded to the successful node. A new block is generated roughly every 15–17 seconds.

- The **timestamp** plays a vital role in the supply chain given various time-based competitive issues, such as lead time, delivery, and food spoilage concerns. The timestamp is also expository to traceability and information transparency

- The supplier uploads the data about the food product like its harvested date, price. The Food product is then tagged with RFID chip. The tags are placed on any items, ranging from individual parts to delivery labels. Inside the RFID tag, it consists of a microchip and antennae. Identifying information Special printers are used to print the tags which wirelessly load the identifying information to the tags. The information on the tags can be used for multiple tasks. When RFID scanners scan the item, information is read from the tag which could include some necessary information that could be very effective in maintaining Supply chain such as:
  ◦ ID number
  ◦ Serial numbers for individual product
  ◦ Location logs
  ◦ Bin location of a product
  ◦ Order status
  ◦ Its components

- The information can be updated and sent through any RFID receiver and the information is not limited to just holding the ID and serial numbers. The information that RFID can provide will be matched with the system. To track shipment and stock locations automatically as the product moves through warehouses and Trucks. Implementation of RFID to these systems can ensure that both correct products and the correct qualities of the product are collected at both points, thereby eliminating errors. Coupled with the IoT the product information can be tracked at all stages of shipment and storage, increasing accuracy, efficiency, and accountability.

- The fully utilized RFID-enabled supply chain network can determine the product's location.

- After RFID tags are attached by the supplier, then the producer gets information about the food product and adds QR code to packaging.

- Then the product moves from producer to distributor, in which the distributor automatically receives a notification about the receipt of food products. Then Distributors choose suiting 3PL (Third Party Logistics) based on fully available data on the customer, delivery date and other user information. Then

Figure 9. Supply Chain Process using RFID

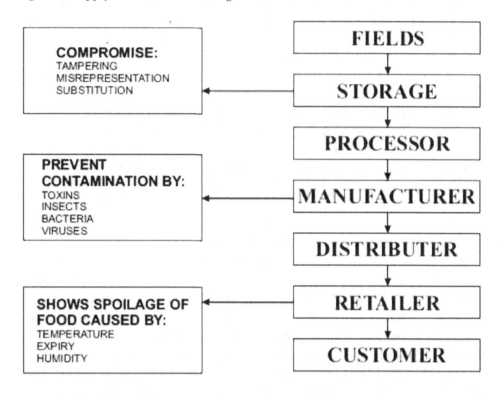

3PL (distribution, warehouse and fulfillment services) is informed about the origin and destination of food products. It flexibly optimizes network flows. Now the retailer runs a machine learning-based forecasting and also provides an app for end customers.

- The product information will remain the same. Then the product is ready for sale, it moves to market by retailers. The store has full transparency in delivery time. They adopt orders, promos, etc. accordingly. All these transactions take place in a Smart Contract. Now at each process involved in the production, each organization scans the RFID and updates the details using a mobile app to the blocks which are stored in the cloud. So the cloud also plays a major role in storing blocks. The verification, validation, transactions, etc., all are done through the app or website. A mobile app and a website serve as a platform for communication.

- Data Protection: Ethereum Blockchain platform ensures that the user's data is encrypted which means it is a difficult task to modify data. You can also save a cryptographic signature of a file on the Blockchain. This would give users a way to ensure a file is tamper-proof without needing to save the entire file on the Blockchain. To achieve the privacy of users, pseudonyms are used. Pseudonyms are virtual identities that can be derived, for example, from a public key that is associated with a person's real identity. To achieve the confidentiality of transactions, encryption is used. The encryption of transaction payload guarantees the transaction data is available only to authorized parties.

- Blockchain Technology will start to work when the genesis block is created, the details are stored in that and the first transaction made is also added to it. Customers Scan the QR code via an app and can view the details of the products from its origin, aging, duration, and expiry and so on.

Result Analysis

The solution mainly aims at bringing in maximum security and traceability in the process involved in supplying a product. Here the Ethereum framework is used for implementation. Studying the performance of Ethereum and Hyperledger Fabric (existing work), Ethereum is more suitable for the supply chain in terms of its execution time, throughput and latency. Table 1 compares the performance of Ethereum and Hyperledger Fabric networks. Here performance is measured by the amount of data moving between nodes. Compare to the Hyperledger Fabric, Ethereum has the lowest latency delay of 14.55s but its execution time is about 17.8s. This shows that the proposed work is efficient in implementing supply chain management using Ethereum.

Table 1. compares the performance of Ethereum and Hyperledger Fabric Networks

Parameters	Ethereum	Hyperledger Fabric
Execution time	17.8	20
CPU Load (in percentage)	46.78	18.32
Latency (in seconds)	14.55	17.46

Benefits of Blockchain in the Supply Chain

- The reduction of error-prone paperwork.
- Improved accuracy through automation.
- Increased accountability through distributed networks.
- Immutable public ledgers.

- Improved production and manufacturing.
  - Automating the purchase process:
- With blockchains, automatic contracts (smart contracts) can be set up. Once the users agreed conditions are met, these smart contracts automatically execute their terms– shipment authorization, service payment, etc.
  - Improving transaction flow:
- Validation times for transactions between producers and clients (like signatures, orders, payments, contracts, etc.) are drastically reduced. It provides virtual real-time management of flows and relationships with business partners.
  - Being more reactive:
- Blockchains can help you detect fraud by identifying problems from the very start of the transaction (inconsistencies with validation, suspicious identity of a party, etc.). An alert is instantly sent when it comes to product recovery.
  - Securing the supply chain:
- Imputing a tag(RFID) to each product recorded in a blockchain enables provider to secure his supply chain. Origin, place of storage, property certificates, records, authenticity: all the necessary information is in a single ledger(public ledger in the blockchain)
  - Ensuring integral traceability:
- Blockchains ensure the traceability of flows and goods by recording all transactions made by users. These records are indestructible and constitute tamper-proof evidence that guarantees the integrity of information.
  - Streamlining internal documents:
- The validity of data shared among participants of the network prevents the creation of multiple versions of a document. Each party involved in the transaction thus has access to the same data.

CONCLUSION

Blockchain shows a significant scope to benefit today's today's supply chain. Currently, blockchain is actively improving a multitude of issues, including, maintaining and developing cryptocurrencies, eliminating middle-men, increasing data protection through cryptographic processes, decreasing error-prone records, and developing self-executing smart-contracts. Although blockchains alone will not be able to tackle all the challenges of the supply chain and logistics, they will contribute to securing transactions, fighting fraud and limiting errors. For now, it is not possible to handle data from large infrastructures that need to be processed by the millisecond. Only single or double-digit transactions can be processed per second by the blocks in a blockchain, but these results may be improved in the future. As proof, Walmart and some multinational food retailers came together to work with IBM on developing a blockchain dedicated to their activity. In the future, we are more likely to see a decrease in centralized servers and an increase in decentralized networks. That means that users will have more access to better information.

REFERENCES

Armbrust, M., Fox, A., Griffith, R., Joseph, A. D., Katz, R., Konwinski, A., Lee, G., Patterson, D., Rabkin, A., Stoica, I., & Zaharia, M.JoSEP. (2010). A view of cloud computing. *Communications of the ACM, 53*(4), 50–58. doi:10.1145/1721654.1721672

Aung, M. M., & Chang, Y. S. (2014). Traceability in a food supply chain: Safety and quality perspectives. *Food Control, 39*, 172–184. doi:10.1016/j.foodcont.2013.11.007

Bogner, A., Chanson, M., & Meeuw, A. (2016, November). A decentralized sharing app running a smart contract on the ethereum blockchain. In *Proceedings of the 6th International Conference on the Internet of Things* (pp. 177-178). ACM.

Caro, M. P., Ali, M. S., Vecchio, M., & Giaffreda, R. (2018, May). Blockchain-based traceability in Agri-Food supply chain management: A practical implementation. In *2018 IoT Vertical and Topical Summit on Agriculture-Tuscany (IOT Tuscany)* (pp. 1-4). IEEE.

Chinaka, M. (2016). *Blockchain technology-Applications in improving financial inclusion in developing economies: a Case study for small scale agriculture in Africa* (Ph.D. dissertation). Sloan School Manage., Massachusetts Inst. Technol., Cambridge, MA, USA.

Galvez, J. F., Mejuto, J. C., & Simal-Gandara, J. (2018). Future challenges on the use of blockchain for food traceability analysis. *Trends in Analytical Chemistry, 107*, 222–232. doi:10.1016/j.trac.2018.08.011

Holmberg, A., & Åquist, R. (2018). *Blockchain technology in food supply chains: A case study of the possibilities and challenges with the implementation of a blockchain technology supported framework for traceability* (M.S. thesis). Fac. Health, Science Technology, Karlstad Univ., Karlstad, Sweden.

Khan, M. A., & Salah, K. (2018). IoT security: Review, blockchain solutions, and open challenges. *Future Generation Computer Systems, 82*, 395–411. doi:10.1016/j. future.2017.11.022

Li, C., & Zhang, L. J. (2017, June). A blockchain-based new secure multi-layer network model for the Internet of Things. In *2017 IEEE International Congress on the Internet of Things (ICIOT)* (pp. 33-41). IEEE. 10.1109/IEEE.ICIOT.2017.34

Li, D., Kehoe, D., & Drake, P. (2006). Dynamic planning with wireless product identification technology in food supply chains. *International Journal of Advanced Manufacturing Technology, 30*(9-10), 938–944. doi:10.100700170-005-0066-1

Lucena, P., Binotto, A. P., Momo, F. S., & Kim, H. (2018). *A case study for grain quality assurance tracking based on a blockchain business network.* Available: https://arxiv.org/abs/1803.07877

Madumidha, S., SivaRanjani, P., Rajesh, S., & Sivakumar, S. (2018). Blockchain security for Internet of Things: A literature survey. *International Journal of Pure and Applied Mathematics, 119*(16), 3677–3686.

Mao, D., Hao, Z., Wang, F., & Li, H. (2019). Novel Automatic Food Trading System Using Consortium Blockchain. *Arabian Journal for Science and Engineering, 44*(4), 3439–3455. doi:10.100713369-018-3537-z

Peck, M. E. (2017). Blockchains: How they work and why they'll change the world. *IEEE Spectrum, 54*(10), 26–35. doi:10.1109/MSPEC.2017.8048836

Schneider, M. (2017). *Design and prototypical implementation of a blockchain-based system for the agriculture sector* (M.S. thesis). Fac. Bus., Econ. Inform., Univ. Zurich, Zürich, Switzerland.

Storøy, J., Thakur, M., & Olsen, P. (2013). The TraceFood Framework–Principles and guidelines for implementing traceability in food value chains. *Journal of Food Engineering, 115*(1), 41–48. doi:10.1016/j.jfoodeng.2012.09.018

Thakur, M., & Hurburgh, C. R. (2009). Framework for implementing a traceability system in the bulk grain supply chain. *Journal of Food Engineering, 95*(4), 617–626. doi:10.1016/j.jfoodeng.2009.06.028

Tian, F. (2017, June). A supply chain traceability system for food safety based on HACCP, Blockchain & Internet of things. In *2017 International Conference on Service Systems and Service Management* (pp. 1-6). IEEE.

Zheng, Z., Xie, S., Dai, H., Chen, X., & Wang, H. (2017, June). An overview of blockchain technology: Architecture, consensus, and future trends. In *2017 IEEE International Congress on Big Data (BigData Congress)* (pp. 557-564). IEEE.

Chapter 11
Electronic Voting Application Powered by Blockchain Technology

Geetanjali Rathee
Jaypee University of Information Technology, India

Hemraj Saini
iD https://orcid.org/0000-0003-2957-1491
Jaypee University of Information Technology, India

ABSTRACT

India is the largest democracy in the world, and in spite of that, it faces various challenges on a daily basis that hinder its growth like corruption and human rights violations. One of the ugliest phases of corruption and political mayhem is visible during the election process where no stone is kept unturned in order to gain power. However, it is the common citizen who suffers most in terms of clarity as well as security when it comes to his/her vote. Blockchain can play a very important role in ensuring that the voters registering their votes are legit and the counting of votes is not manipulated in any way. It is also needed in today's times where the world is available to people in their smart phones to also give them the opportunity to register their votes hassle free via their smart phones without having to worry about the system getting hacked. Therefore, in this chapter, the proposed layout will be based on a smart contract, using Ethereum software to create an e-voting app. In this chapter, the authors have proposed a secure e-voting framework through blockchain mechanism.

DOI: 10.4018/978-1-7998-3444-1.ch011

INTRODUCTION

Lately, Blockchains have pulled in overall consideration. A Blockchain is characterized as an immutable, successive chain of records called blocks. The record can contain transactions, documents or some other information, and are fastened together utilizing hashes (Iansiti & Lakhani, 2017; Crosby et al., 2016). It is executed and overseen by a peer-to-peer network of computers (also called peer nodes) spread everywhere throughout the globe. Blockchain likewise called distributed ledger which utilizes independent PCs (nodes) to record, share and synchronies transactions in their particular electronic ledgers, rather than keeping information incorporated on a server as in a customary record.

Figure 1. Schematic outline of e-voting using Blockchain

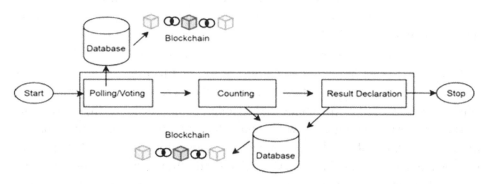

Blockchains have the potential to disrupt any industry that employs the use of a trusted middleman and give direct control back to the end user. In any case, similarly as with any technological revolution and the paradigm shift that joins it, there is a procedure of trial and error. What works and what does not and we are as of now in that stage with Blockchain advancements (Zyskind, & Nathan, 2015; Eyal et al. 2016; Pilkington, 2016). 99% of the business sectors are filled by unadulterated hypothesis. There are no completely useful Blockchain items that can oblige the requests of the majority. Blockchains must be less expensive, snappier, simpler to utilize and similarly as versatile, if not more thus, than the present frameworks set up. The coming of the web drove the technological revolution of the 90's and the industrial upheaval was in the late eighteenth century. These quantum jumps in human capacity and accomplishment change our whole reality and disturb pretty much every settled industry. They change the manner in which we travel, cooperate, communicate, business with one another, even think. All that we once knew is flipped on its head and life gets improved, making things a lot less demanding and progressively productive. The same is the appearance of Blockchain technology where the component of trust is the whole sudden put under the control of target numbers and PCs. Blockchain is the initial step at placing trust into PCs. Sounds kind of terrifying and we would state that it is. Rest guaranteed however, the seasons of skynet and eliminators are far away and except if we create methods for keeping self-aware robots from turning into a reality, at that point we ought to be safe. In a vibrant and large democracy like India which holds the title of conducting the biggest electoral practice in the world, issues of political mayhem and electoral malpractice are becoming grim year after year with this once considered a holy festival of our republic touching its low ebb (Cachin, 2016; Rathee et al. 2019). It is needed to ensure fair and free election across the globe in democratic countries, by allowing voters safety to cast their free decisions. In democratic countries, voting is a process where people choose their government by making their decisions through registration and cast their votes (Tsang & Wei, V.K, 2005; Christian & Carter, 2005). However, it is much necessary to avoid manipulations and provide integrity during voting process. Further, security and privacy of voters during their voting casts where paper based scheme was used before introduction of EVM. The EVMs or Electronic Voting Machines came into being, that had marvelous advantages over paper ballots however, voters have to cast their votes at polling stations only (Zissis & Lekkas, 2011; Moynihan, 2004; Keller, 2006). Elections anywhere in the world are a very daunting affair where individuals use every kind of manipulation to gain seats in the office. In India especially, some of the risks involved is voter manipulation, spreading of fake news, hacking and extreme files of violence basing damage to property and life. EVM counters many such issues for example Bogus voting, cost saving and providing faster result but there is still room for expansion and more security. Blockchain can play a very important role in ensuring that the voters registering their votes are legit and the vote counts are not manipulated in any way. Further, it is desired in current times where the world is accessible to people in their smart phones to also offer them the chance to register and cast their votes irritate free via their smart phones without worrying about the system receiving hacked. Blockchain is a distributed ledger that stores information in the form of blocks where each block associated to the next via cryptography (Yavuz, 2018; Goguen & Meseguer, 1984). It is distributed, decentralized and immutable that makes it nearly unfeasible to tamper with. When blockchain is applied in the procedure of voting will have a proper user account for every valid Voter ID holder and will therefore nullify the risk of a single person voting multiple times. Also, once every individual has an application in their smart phones, it is not requisite to stand in long line in the polling stations and panicking any kind of poll aggression. It will provide a kind of transparency that will not let the results be questioned and provide a new poise to the voters as depicted in Figure 1.

Figure 2. Proof-of-work using Blockchain in voting application

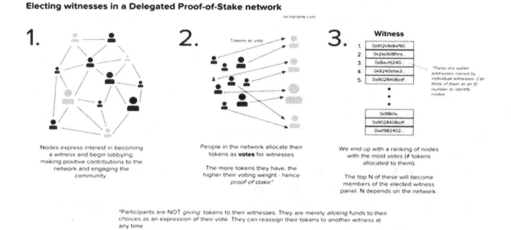

Blockchain technology is still without a doubt so in its earliest stages. Blockchains are moderate, user unfriendly, unscalable, and costly. For instance, DApps created on Ethereum require the end user to initially buy Ethereum and afterward pay a transaction fee each time they accomplish something in the DApp. Then again, EOS expects developers to buy over the top expensive RAM to build up a DApp while the users get transaction fee, simply after the user gets some EOS, downloads an EOS wallet from github, makes a key pair and sends EOS to that key pair. Not to speaking to the average consumer who could think less about decentralization. The fact of the matter being that Blockchain technology needs to develop before mainstream adoption happens (Hjálmarsson, 2018; Aitzhan, & Svetinovic, 2016). UI will be absolutely critical thus will administrations. A Blockchain that takes care of an enormous real-world problems, finds a harmony among decentralization and administration while giving speed, scalability, cost viability, and an overall smooth user experience will be the Blockchain that ascents above them all. 2018 was an incredibly dynamic year for Blockchain and crypto currencies. Numerous jumps in advancement were made and Blockchain is entering the worldwide awareness increasingly every day (Wüst & Gervais, 2018; Taylor et al. 2019). The subject of mass selection is when, not in the event that it occurs. We unquestionably observe this occurrence very soon, however as things remain at the present minute, the Blockchain space still makes them develop agonies to traverse. All the weaknesses of the Blockchain can be removed using three different consensus protocols named proof-of-work, proof-of-stake and proof-of-useful-work. A brief summary of these three protocols are given in Figure 2.

The proposed layout is based on a smart contract, using Ethereum to generate an e-voting app. The users have to create an account with proper confirmation done via id and other biometric schemes. Every transmission done via this account which in this case will be registering vote will be verified by a miner. The miner further has taken into account the voter's permanent address depends on voter id and thereby conveying that vote to a vote pool of that constituency. Every vote registered will be done via biometric schemes and the miner will verify the authenticity of the vote. This will counter the issue of bogus votes. Biometric data will remain in the peer to peer network and will be very difficult to obtain otherwise. Once the election date of the electorate has passed and there is any other vote registered, the miner may cancel the request. Similarly, if the biometric authentication has failed for the user, the request will be cancelled by the miner.

The remaining organization of the paper is defined as follows. Section II illustrates the literature work. The e-voting application using blockchain technology is described in section III. Further, the performance metrics of e-voting application is presented in section IV. Finally, section V concludes the paper.

RELATED WORK

This section illustrates the number of security methods in voting procedures proposed by several scientists/researchers. For instance, Salahuddin et al., 2018 have projected an agile and softwarized system for providing a secure, flexible and cost efficient, privacy IoT deployment system in smart healthcare services and applications. Further, kang et al., 2019 have proposed a blockchain enables security system by addressing the security and privacy issues among Internet-of-Vehicles (IoV). They have proposed a two-stage solution that is data verification and miners selection by designing a reputation based voting approach and past summary interactions. The selection of miners is done by analyzing behavior of each device and consulting their previous interaction before including them in communication process. The proposed reputation and blockchain based approach was simulated over different data sharing results in IoV. Though, wireless networks ensured a vital role in the support of IoT solutions, however, the comparison is not adopting them properly. The reason of not adopting the IoT with wireless networks is various privacy and security challenges. Though researchers have proposed various security solutions to avoid these limitations.

She et al., 2019 have projected trusted approach using blockchain technique to identify the malicious behavior of communicating nodes in wireless environment. They have proposed a trust based scheme with the integration of blockchain to provide transparency and immediate identification of malicious devices. Further, the authors have realized the detection of malicious devices through smart contracts and node's quadrilaterals. The simulated graphs depicted the efficiency that is able to trace and identify every single malicious behavior in real time environment. Moreover, the management and efficiency enhancements, several oil and gas companies have shifted towards digitalization by simply adopting blockchain. In addition, Lu et al., 2019 have reviewed the importance and usage of blockchain in oil and gas industries in several aspects such as trading, management, supervision and cyber security. Finally the authors have also highlighted the usage of blockchain at just in their initial levels because of their new systems, transformations and techniques.

Lamas et al., 2019 focused on reviewing various blockchain integrated applications by emphasizing on their security and privacy challenges. They have discussed various business models creating and car economy disruption and their solutions with blockchain integration. In addition, they have highlighted the threats, strengths and weaknesses by recommending various companies and guidelines in futuristic developments. Further, Jarodi et al., 2019 have focused on only one application of blockchain i.e. industries by highlighting or discussing various challenges, benefits and opportunities in other use cases also. They have highlighted various implementation requirements for integrating the blockchain technique in industries. The authors have integrated the blockchain usage in financial areas where digital payments for verifying the financial transactions deployed on various proxy nodes are integrated through blockchain mechanism. They have projected several probability based metrics for realizing the rigorous operations and demonstrated the feasibility with near field communication on raspberry pi mobile wallets and mining nodes applications. For reducing the redundancies and inconsistencies in voting phenomenon, e-voting has altered traditional voting schemes. However, the e-voting further leads to several security and privacy issues with the growth of time. Shahzad & Crowcroft, 2019 have applied blockchain in voting procedures by block sealing to provide transparency. The proposed approach described the hash utility, information accumulation, polling generation, creation, sealing in blocks till the declaration of results. The proposed scheme has claimed the security and management of issues by ensuring an enhanced digital voting approach. Kdhetri & Voas, 2018 have projected a blockchain based e-voting process by increasing the access rights to voters and reducing the access rights to other entities. The registered voters are allowed to casts their votes through online such as computer based or smart phones through blockchain. The authors have presented a proof id of each voter's to ensure transparency during votes. The proposed scheme is further highlighting various potential challenges. Further, Anjum et al., 2017 have discussed and illustrated several blockchain use cases to highlight their importance in today's era. They have tracing of products, smart healthcare, industries and other verification processes. Though the continuous increment of shifts in health services, information is secured by limiting their access rights and applies crypto schemes to further identify privacy and security concerns. Further, the authors Esposito et al., 2018 have projected the blockchain usage that may clearly provide the security in health services over the clouds. In addition, Espocito et al., 2018 have described the potential issues with their future perspectives.

PROPOSED SOLUTION

Our application determines the vote count of the voter for certain people who are to be selected. Firstly, in this application, we determine the illegibility of the voters using blind signatures. For high availability and result immutability of privacy using double private block chain and using bit coin logic to redesign transactions and new protocols to cast a vote. The proposed system will contain 1) Anonymity, 2) Check flag for voter's illegibility, 3) Voting integrity with the system and 4) Vote Verification.

Different Phases in the System

Publishing phase

It's a dummy approach to publicize the system and generating candidate ballots. The Authority has eligible bling signature which are communicated securely to prevent any attacks like DOS, Men-in-the-middle Attack

Login phase

After the publishing phase, the voters will login and then verification will be done for eligibility. This phase also deals with the impersonation and EIDs establishment.

EID generation phase

This phase will be used to generate public private key for electronic identity. For every identity made, an EID password will be established in order to prevent tampering and impersonation. Generation of OTP can also be done.

Voting phase

For the generation of Block chain transactions, our Voting phase will ensure data consistency and isolation.

Figure 3. Implementing blind signatures

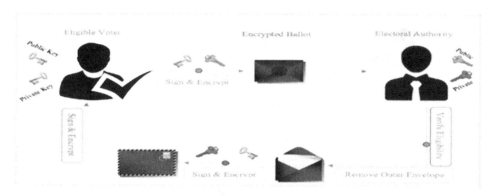

Blind signatures

These digital signatures are heavily used in our application for transactions working. Eligible voter sign and extract public and private keys and encrypt them in Ballot. This Ballot is sent to Electoral Authority (admin) and verifies the source of the ballot, removes outer envelope and Encrypt the keys and sends back to the eligible voter as depicted in Figure 3.

System Protocol

This phase depicts the working of voting application using different phase.

Threat Model

Various models have been taken in care for the full functionality of the Block chain without any foreboding of threat initiation. As Block chain helps with Decentralization, and impenetrable security level, various threats are seldom to be seen. Some of the most common threats are DDoS Attack, Sybil Attack, Freak Attack, Malwares, Cross Site Scripting (Xss) etc. the compete proposed solution of e-voting through blockchain is depicted in Figure 4.

Evaluation

After the completion of the project, we will study all the sufficient properties of the proposed system design and these are availability of the project, Integrity with the OS and web page, Uniqueness, Accuracy, and Election secrecy.

Figure 4. Proposed complete Solution

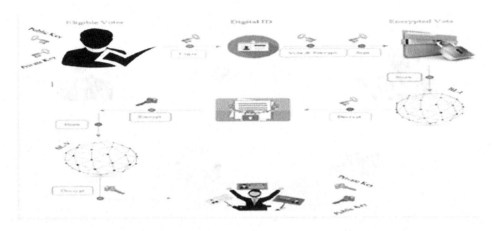

Some Other Security Analysis and Legal Issues

Security Analysis

i. DDoS: For the application to fail under DDOS Attack, the attacker must perform it on every node in the network. But tampering with the boot nodes will eventually inform the institution and the location could be found out. For locating failed blocks, we can use fault tolerance algorithm

ii. Authentication Vulnerability: As the value of the hash will be unique to each and every individual or eligible voter, there is seldom chance of multiple voting process by the voters. This will not only helps with the ease to finalize the output result with incrementing by +1, but also eradicates out the total chances of the system malfunctioning.

iii. Sybil Attacks: The consensus algorithms implemented in the project are prone to these attacks. Furthermore, with the incoming of the strong cryptography features and limited access to the ledger, Block chain solves today's most often security problems

Legal Issues

i. Transparency: No method of transparency can be offered to the voters in today's electoral scheme. Without some other tech involvement, the transparency In the system is a very tedious task with formulation of new law by government officials.

ii.   Voter Privacy: Voter privacy in pen and paper scheme is meandering which may involve leakage of voter credentials and vote to the party or the candidate. To satisfy the privacy, initiation of non-traceable vote will be prominent to implement.

iii.   Remote Voting: To prevent coercion resistance in the election, remote voting could be of good use. If the results can be used in websites, or mobile applications, there is no chance of misconfigured results, but on the negative side, people with good hacking skills can take down host website and different threats can be introduced. This requires security. We can use Block chain features to subdue these affects.

Comparison

Traditional Blockchain Solution: In the traditional Blockchain solution, we can observe the common implementation of lit coin, dash, ripple and many other programming languages based bit coin implementation. There is less privacy though, if implemented in suitable domain of programming languages.

Proposed Blockchain Solution: Our platform implements all the solution in Ethereum, solidity and other bitcoin consensus protocols to be in use, usage of RSA algorithm can also be implemented with the generation of private keys. Table 1 depicts the comparison among traditional and proposed blockchain voting application.

As the scope of this paper does not end till execution as more functionality can also be appended such as login-logout scenarios, more data related storage for large count of voters.

Table 1. Traditional Blockchain Solution Vs Proposed Blockchain Solution

Traditional blockchain solution	Proposed blockchain solution
Operated with decentralized property	Operated with decentralized property
Programming tools: Native Programming Languages (Java, Python, C++, ASP.NET, C#)	Programming tools: Ethereum, Solidity, web3.js
Time of Transaction: Minutes	Time of Transaction: Seconds
Implementing client server architecture and RDBMS	Facilitates P2P architecture and smart contracts; no RDBMS required

The main idea of proposing this Blockchain solution for voting system is to make electoral system cheaper and quicker. By doing this, the barrier between voter and officials to be elected will be an endgame. Furthermore, with the ease in operation, we can assure a direct form of democracy as people will be in more ease to use it and give a better result in return without any involvement of central agency. In the report, we implemented a simple voting application using smart contracts (solidity, Ethereum) for proper conduct of system execution while maintaining security features like privacy and authentication verification. By comparing with the current process of electoral system, we can observe that block chain technology has a new future for democratic countries where most of it are pen and paper based. Using the Ethereum private block chain, we can transmit hundreds of transaction in one second, for countries with bigger democracy; this system can provide well executed result with seldom chances of result tampering. With the use of modern hash algorithms makes the data fetching impenetrable and isolated within each and every block. Decentralization has made the platform much more secret and private than that of centralized systems. Our proposed system will ensure that all the block chain concepts will be executed properly resulting in better approach to implement the platform practically in the provinces or the region.

PERFORMANCE ANALYSIS

System State

For providing the verification and validation of proposed approach, the numerically simulated results are verified over NS2. The analyzed metrics are analyzed against various security measures over various metrics. Though, security analysis of e-voting is considered to be a very challenging task. In this manuscript, we have proposed a blockchain based voting method which not only ensures node's security but also provides transparency in the network. In the proposed voting frameworks, network simulator version 2.5 having predefined various nodes is executed. 500*500 network area is generated having various numbers of nodes. Further, for verifying the security procedures, nodes metrics are measured where most of them are hacked by various attackers. The malevolent devices are further added on probability basis. The response time and accuracy based on malevolent node prediction is analyzed against varying number of nodes. The execution of proposed framework is accomplished for one minute.

Evaluated Performance Metrics

Number of measuring parameters such as response time, accuracy, number of processed request and resource utilization are evidenced on mentioned test bed. The depicted figures represent proposed and traditional mechanisms over certain metrics. The depicted graphs 5 and 6 shows the accuracy and response time of

Figure 5. Accuracy to predict malevolent nodes

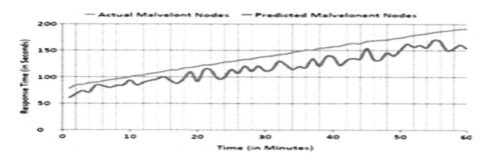

detected malicious nodes over varying number of nodes. Proposed scheme close to 83% accuracy against malevolent system is predicted. In addition, it is supposed the response time of proposed approach augments better results than traditional mechanisms. Traditional approaches are not able to productively able to guarantee transparency that may further cover way to reduce response time and accuracy of individuals who cast their voters and voting counts. Whilst proposed mechanism that is based on Blockchain that successfully able to remove and detect the malicious activities of devices.

Figure 6. Response Time with presence of malicious devices

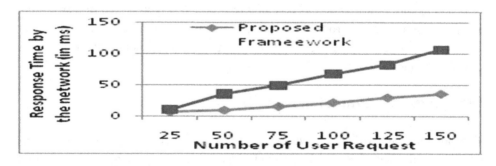

In addition, the transparent feature of proposed approach provides the trust among polling/ voting procedures. The framework analysis is further measured against resource utilization as revealed in Figure 7, 8. All the depicted figures clearly realistic that the nodes augmentation is linear and the processed requests also enhances linearly.

Proposed scheme is close to 83% accuracy for the malicious devices prediction which may be further enhanced if simulation runs for longer time. Further, it is alleged that proposed scheme response time from sensors will augment as depicted in Figure 7 shows better values than existing system.

Figure 7. Resource Utilization in Fog Environment 1

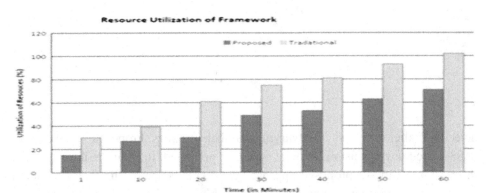

Here, traditional schemes are not efficient to identify or able to eliminate malevolent nodes from the environment that further escort to increase in response time of the traditional system. However, in proposed phenomenon that detects any malevolent node and able to instantly remove it from the network so that it does not obstruct the performance. This analysis further results in improved response time and resources utilization as revealed in Figure 6, Figure 7. Moreover, Figure 8 depicts the number of processed request by the proposed system regarding linear trend for all three networks. It can be clearly practical augmentation is linear the proposed requests also lead to linear time.

Discussion on Evaluated Results

The proposed and traditional voting schemes have been detected over various numbers of devices. The simulation evaluation is victorious where various several results over certain metrics were recorded. The evaluation of simulation conduction was victorious where numbers of concerned results against several parameters were recorded. The proposed blockchain based voting approach behaves as preferred having an optimized analyzed metrics over traditional procedures. In addition, the accuracy of Blockchain based on voting scheme enabled framework reached to 83% that can be further improved and superior over increased period of time. Moreover, remaining metrics such as response time, processed request during malicious environment provides better results. The removal and detection of malevolent nodes in proposed scheme is entirely based on Blockchain technique to provide transparency and security among all the devices. Any alteration and change in polling process may immediately change the remaining polling stations and authorized individual's information.

Figure 8. Number of processed request by each network through a linear line

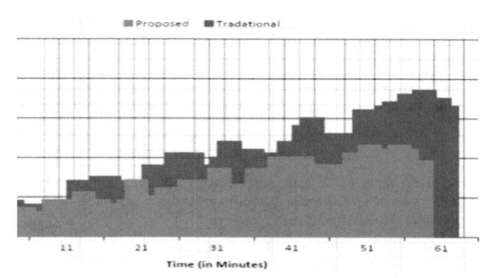

CONCLUSION

This manuscript has proposed a secure online voting mechanism based on Blockchain approach. The proposed framework provides the security by intimating and capturing each and every illegal and legal activity of the voters and counting EVM's. The proposed Blockchain voting framework has considerably enhanced the accuracy, response time, number of processed request and resource utilization against traditional mechanisms in the presence of malicious nodes. Furthermore, the simulated results of proposed scheme show 83% accuracy compared to traditional voting procedures. The real time situation where EVM can instantly detect the malevolent activity and blocked will be reported in future directions.

REFERENCES

Aitzhan, N. Z., & Svetinovic, D. (2016). Security and privacy in decentralized energy trading through multi-signatures, blockchain and anonymous messaging streams. *IEEE Transactions on Dependable and Secure Computing, 15*(5), 840–852. doi:10.1109/TDSC.2016.2616861

Al-Jaroodi, J., & Mohamed, N. (2019). Blockchain in Industries: A Survey. *IEEE Access: Practical Innovations, Open Solutions, 7*, 36500–36515. doi:10.1109/ACCESS.2019.2903554

Anjum, A., Sporny, M., & Sill, A. (2017). Blockchain standards for compliance and trust. *IEEE Cloud Computing, 4*(4), 84–90. doi:10.1109/MCC.2017.3791019

Cachin, C. (2016), July. Architecture of the hyperledger blockchain fabric. *Workshop on distributed cryptocurrencies and consensus ledgers, 310*, 1-4.

Christian Schaupp, L., & Carter, L. (2005). E-voting: From apathy to adoption. *Journal of Enterprise Information Management, 18*(5), 586–601. doi:10.1108/17410390510624025

Crosby, M., Pattanayak, P., Verma, S., & Kalyanaraman, V. (2016). Blockchain technology: Beyond bitcoin. *Applied Innovation, 2*(71), 6–10.

Esposito, C., De Santis, A., Tortora, G., Chang, H., & Choo, K. K. R. (2018). Blockchain: A panacea for healthcare cloud-based data security and privacy? *IEEE Cloud Computing, 5*(1), 31–37. doi:10.1109/MCC.2018.011791712

Eyal, I., Gencer, A. E., Sirer, E. G., & Van Renesse, R. (2016). Bitcoin-ng: A scalable blockchain protocol. *13th USENIX Symposium on Networked Systems Design and Implementation*, 45-59.

Fraga-Lamas, P., & Fernández-Caramés, T. M. (2019). A Review on Blockchain Technologies for an Advanced and Cyber-Resilient Automotive Industry. *IEEE Access: Practical Innovations, Open Solutions, 7*, 17578–17598. doi:10.1109/ACCESS.2019.2895302

Goguen, J. A., & Meseguer, J. (1982). Security policies and security models. In *1982 IEEE Symposium on Security and Privacy* (pp. 11-11). IEEE. 10.1109/SP.1982.10014

Hjálmarsson, F. Þ., Hreiðarsson, G. K., Hamdaqa, M., & Hjálmtýsson, G. (2018). Blockchain-based e-voting system. In *2018 IEEE 11th International Conference on Cloud Computing (CLOUD)* (pp. 983-986). IEEE.

Iansiti, M., & Lakhani, K. R. (2017). The truth about blockchain. *Harvard Business Review*, *95*(1), 118–127.

Kang, J., Xiong, Z., Niyato, D., Ye, D., Kim, D. I., & Zhao, J. (2019). Towards Secure Blockchain-enabled Internet of Vehicles: Optimizing Consensus Management Using Reputation and Contract Theory. *IEEE Transactions on Vehicular Technology*, *68*(3), 2906–2920. Advance online publication. doi:10.1109/TVT.2019.2894944

Keller, A. M., Mertz, D., Hall, J. L., & Urken, A. (2006). Privacy issues in an electronic voting machine. In *Privacy and Technologies of Identity* (pp. 313–334). Springer. doi:10.1007/0-387-28222-X_18

Kshetri, N., & Voas, J. (2018). Blockchain-enabled e-voting. *IEEE Software*, *35*(4), 95–99. doi:10.1109/MS.2018.2801546

Lu, H., Huang, K., Azimi, M., & Guo, L. (2019). Blockchain technology in the oil and gas industry: A review of applications, opportunities, challenges, and risks. *IEEE Access: Practical Innovations, Open Solutions*, *7*, 41426–41444. Advance online publication. doi:10.1109/ACCESS.2019.2907695

Moynihan, D. P. (2004). Building secure elections: E-voting, security, and systems theory. *Public Administration Review*, *64*(5), 515–528. doi:10.1111/j.1540-6210.2004.00400.x

Pilkington, M. (2016). 11 Blockchain technology: principles and applications. *Research handbook on digital transformations*, 225.

Rathee, G., Sharma, A., Iqbal, R., Aloqaily, M., Jaglan, N., & Kumar, R. (2019). A blockchain framework for securing connected and autonomous vehicles. *Sensors (Basel)*, *19*(14), 3155–3165. doi:10.339019143165 PMID:31323870

Salahuddin, M. A., Al-Fuqaha, A., Guizani, M., Shuaib, K., & Sallabi, F. (2018). *Softwarization of Internet of Things infrastructure for secure and smart healthcare*. arXiv preprint arXiv:1805.11011

Shahzad, B., & Crowcroft, J. (2019). Trustworthy Electronic Voting Using Adjusted Blockchain Technology. *IEEE Access: Practical Innovations, Open Solutions*, *7*, 24477–24488. doi:10.1109/ACCESS.2019.2895670

She, W., Liu, Q., Tian, Z., Chen, J. S., Wang, B., & Liu, W. (2019). Blockchain Trust Model for Malicious Node Detection in Wireless Sensor Networks. *IEEE Access: Practical Innovations, Open Solutions*, *7*, 38947–38956. doi:10.1109/ACCESS.2019.2902811

Taylor, P. J., Dargahi, T., Dehghantanha, A., Parizi, R. M., & Choo, K. K. R. (2019). *A systematic literature review of blockchain cyber security.* Digital Communications and Networks. doi:10.1016/j.dcan.2019.01.005

Tsang, P. P., & Wei, V. K. (2005). April. Short linkable ring signatures for e-voting, e-cash and attestation. In *International Conference on Information Security Practice and Experience* (pp. 48-60). Springer. 10.1007/978-3-540-31979-5_5

Wüst, K., & Gervais, A. (2018). June. Do you need a Blockchain? In *2018 Crypto Valley Conference on Blockchain Technology (CVCBT)* (pp. 45-54). IEEE. 10.1109/CVCBT.2018.00011

Yavuz, E., Koc, A. K., Çabuk, U. C., & Dalkılıç, G. (2018). March. Towards secure e-voting using ethereum blockchain. In *2018 6th International Symposium on Digital Forensic and Security (ISDFS)* (pp. 1-7). IEEE.

Zissis, D., & Lekkas, D. (2011). Securing e-Government and e-Voting with an open cloud computing architecture. *Government Information Quarterly*, 28(2), 239–251. doi:10.1016/j.giq.2010.05.010

Zyskind, G., & Nathan, O. (2015). May. Decentralizing privacy: Using blockchain to protect personal data. 2015 IEEE Security and Privacy Workshops, 180-184.

Compilation of References

Aazam, M., & Huh, E.-N. (2015). Dynamic resource provisioning through Fog micro datacenter. In *Pervasive Computing and Communication Workshops (PerCom Workshops), 2015 IEEE International Conference on*. IEEE.

Abe, R. (2018). *Mitigating Bitcoin Node Storage Size By DHT*. Academic Press.

Achariya, D., & Kauser, A. (2016). Survey on Big Data Analytics: Challenges, Open Research Issues and Tools. *International Journal of Advanced Computer Science and Applications*, 7(2), 511–518.

Acharya, U. R., Fujita, H., Lih, O. S., Hagiwara, Y., Tan, J. H., & Adam, M. (2017). Automated Detection of Arrhythmias Using Different Intervals of Tachycardia ECG Segments with Convolutional Neural Network. *Inf. Sci.*, *405*, 81–90. doi:10.1016/j.ins.2017.04.012

Acharya, U. R., Oh, S. L., Hagiwara, Y., Tan, J. H., Adam, M., Gertych, A., & Tan, R. S. (2017). A deep convolutional neural network model to classify heartbeats. *Computers in Biology and Medicine*, *89*, 389–396. doi:10.1016/j.compbiomed.2017.08.022 PMID:28869899

Acito, F., & Khatri, V. (2014). Business analytics: Why now and what next? *Business Horizons*, *57*(5), 565–570. doi:10.1016/j.bushor.2014.06.001

Ahlawat, K., Chug, A., & Singh, A. P. (2019). Benchmarking framework for class imbalance problem using novel sampling approach for big data. *International Journal of System Assurance Engineering and Management. Springer*, *10*(4), 824–835. doi:10.100713198-019-00817-6

Ahlawat, K., Chug, A., & Singh, A. P. (2019). Empirical Evaluation of Map Reduce Based Hybrid Approach for Problem of Imbalanced Classification in Big Data. *International Journal of Grid and High Performance Computing*, *11*(3), 23–45. doi:10.4018/IJGHPC.2019070102

Aitzhan, N. (2016). Security and Privacy in Decentralized Energy Trading Through Multi-Signatures, Blockchain and Anonymous Messaging Streams. *IEEE Transactions on Dependable and Secure Computing*. doi:10.1109/TDSC.2016.2616861

Akhavan Aghdam, M., Sharifi, A., & Pedram, M. M. (2018). Combination of rs-fMRI and sMRI Data to Discriminate Autism Spectrum Disorders in Young Children Using Deep Belief Network. *Journal of Digital Imaging*, *31*(6), 895–903. doi:10.100710278-018-0093-8 PMID:29736781

Akter, S., & Wamba, S. F. (2016). Big data analytics in E-commerce: A systematic review and agenda for future research. *Electronic Markets*, *26*(2), 173–194. doi:10.100712525-016-0219-0

Alhagry, S., Fahmy, A. A., & El-Khoribi, R. A. (2017). Emotion Recognition based on EEG using LSTM Recurrent Neural Network. *International Journal of Advanced Computer Science and Applications, 8.*

Alhamad, M., Dillon, T., & Chang, E. (2010). Sla-based trust model for cloud computing. *2010 13th international conference on network-based information systems*, 321-324. 10.1109/NBiS.2010.67

Ali, S., Wang, G., Bhuiyan, Z. A., & Jiang, H. (2020). Secure Data Provenance in Cloud-centric Internet of Things via Blockchain Smart Contracts. *2018 IEEE SmartWorld, Ubiquitous Intelligence & Computing, Advanced & Trusted Computing, Scalable Computing & Communications, Cloud & Big Data Computing, Internet of People and Smart City Innovation (SmartWorld/SCALCOM/ UIC/ATC/CBDCom/IOP/SCI)*, 991–998. doi:10.1109/SmartWorld.2018.00175

Al-Jaroodi, J., & Mohamed, N. (2019). Blockchain in Industries: A Survey. *IEEE Access: Practical Innovations, Open Solutions*, *7*, 36500–36515. doi:10.1109/ACCESS.2019.2903554

Al-Jarrah, O. Y., Yoo, P. D., Muhaidat, S., Karagiannidis, G. K., & Taha, K. (2015). Efficient Machine Learning for Big Data: A Review. *Big Data Research*, *2*(3), 87–93. doi:10.1016/j. bdr.2015.04.001

Al-mamun, A., Li, T., Sadoghi, M., & Zhao, D. (2018). In-memory Blockchain : Toward Efficient and Trustworthy Data Provenance for HPC Systems. *2018 IEEE International Conference on Big Data (Big Data)*, 3808–3813. 10.1109/BigData.2018.8621897

Altman, N., & Krzywinski, M. (2018). The curse(s) of dimensionality. *Nature Methods*, *15*(6), 399–400. doi:10.103841592-018-0019-x PMID:29855577

Ametrano, F. M. (2016). *Hayek money: The cryptocurrency price stability solution*. Available at SSRN 2425270

Amirian, P., van Loggerenberg, F., Lang, T., Thomas, A., Peeling, R., Basiri, A., & Goodman, S. N. (2017). Using big data analytics to extract disease surveillance information from point of care diagnostic machines. *Pervasive and Mobile Computing*, *42*, 470–486. doi:10.1016/j. pmcj.2017.06.013

Angermueller, C., Lee, H. J., Reik, W., & Stegle, O. (2017). DeepCpG: Accurate prediction of single-cell DNA methylation states using deep learning. *Genome Biology*, *18*(1), 67. doi:10.118613059-017-1189-z PMID:28395661

Angermueller, C., Parnamaa, T., Parts, L., & Stegle, O. (2016). Deep learning for computational biology. *Molecular Systems Biology*, *12*(7), 878. doi:10.15252/msb.20156651 PMID:27474269

Anjum, A., Sporny, M., & Sill, A. (2017). Blockchain standards for compliance and trust. *IEEE Cloud Computing*, *4*(4), 84–90. doi:10.1109/MCC.2017.3791019

Arslan, S. S., & Goker, T. (n.d.). *Compress-Store on Blockchain : A Decentralized Data Processing and Immutable Storage for Multimedia Streaming.* Academic Press.

Aung, M. M., & Chang, Y. S. (2014). Traceability in a food supply chain: Safety and quality perspectives. *Food Control, 39*, 172–184. doi:10.1016/j.foodcont.2013.11.007

Azzedin, F., & Maheswaran, M. (2002). Integrating trust into grid resource management systems. *2002 Proceedings International Conference on Parallel Processing*, 47-54. 10.1109/ICPP.2002.1040858

Azzedin, F., & Maheswaran, M. (2002). Towards trust-aware resource management in grid computing systems. *2002 2nd IEEE/ACM International symposium on Cluster Computing and the Grid (CCGRID'02)*, 452-452.

Baldominos, A., & Saez, Y. (2019). *Coin. AI: A Proof-of-Useful-Work Scheme for Blockchain-based Distributed Deep Learning.* arXiv preprint arXiv:1903.09800

Bandara, E., Ng, W. E. E. K., Zoysa, K. D. E., & Fernando, N. (2018). Mystiko — Blockchain Meets Big Data. *2018 IEEE International Conference on Big Data (Big Data)*, 3024–3032. 10.1109/BigData.2018.8622341

Banerjee, M., & Lee, J., & Choo, & K-K. (2017). A blockchain future to Internet of Things security: A position paper. *Digital Communications and Networks, 4*. Advance online publication. doi:10.1016/j.dcan.2017.10.006

Bansal, A., Srivastava, P. A., & Singh, T. R. (2018). An integrative approach to develop computational pipeline for drug-target interaction network analysis. *Scientific Reports, 8*(1), 1–9. doi:10.103841598-018-28577-6 PMID:29980766

Bari, M. D., Shroff, S., & Thomas, M. (2013). SentiML: functional annotation for multilingual sentiment analysis. *Proceedings of the 1st International Workshop on Collaborative Annotations in Shared Environment: Metadata, Vocabularies and Techniques in the Digital Humanities.* 10.1145/2517978.2517994

Bartoletti, M., Lande, S., Pompianu, L., & Bracciali, A. (2017). *A general framework for blockchain analytics.* Academic Press.

Bechini, A., Matteis, A. D. D., Marcelloni, F., & Segatori, A. (2016). Spreading Fuzzy Random Forests with MapReduce. *International Conference on Systems, Man, and Cybernetics*, 2641-2646.

Benet, J. (n.d.). *IPFS - Content Addressed, Versioned, P2P File System* (Draft 3).

Bhuiyan, Z. A., Wang, T., & Wang, G. (2018). *Blockchain and Big Data to Transform the Healthcare.* Academic Press.

Biswas, K., & Muthukkumarasamy, V. (2016). *Securing Smart Cities Using Blockchain Technology.* . doi:10.1109/HPCC-SmartCity-DSS.2016.0198

Bogner, A., Chanson, M., & Meeuw, A. (2016, November). A decentralized sharing app running a smart contract on the ethereum blockchain. In *Proceedings of the 6th International Conference on the Internet of Things* (pp. 177-178). ACM.

Boonpeng, S., & Jeatrakul, P. (2014), Enhance the performance of neural networks for stock market prediction: An analytical study. *Ninth International Conference on Digital Information Management.* 10.1109/ICDIM.2014.6991352

Bouazizi, M., & Ohtsuki, T. (2015). Opinion mining in twitter: how to make use of sarcasm to enhance sentiment analysis. *2015 IEEE/ACM International Conference on Advances in Social Networks Analysis and Mining*, 1594–1597. 10.1145/2808797.2809350

Bouazizi, M., & Ohtsuki, T. (2016). Sentiment analysis: From binary to multi-class classification: A pattern-based approach for multi-class sentiment analysis in Twitter. *2016 IEEE International Conference on Communications, ICC 2016*, 1–6. 10.1109/ICC.2016.7511392

Bragagnolo, S., Marra, M., Polito, G., & Boix, E. G. (2019). *Towards Scalable Blockchain Analysis.* doi:10.1109/WETSEB.2019.00007

Cachin, C. (2016, July). Architecture of the hyperledger blockchain fabric. In *Workshop on distributed cryptocurrencies and consensus ledgers* (*Vol. 310*, p. 4). Academic Press.

Cachin, C. (2016), July. Architecture of the hyperledger blockchain fabric. *Workshop on distributed cryptocurrencies and consensus ledgers*, *310*, 1-4.

Canuto, S., Gonçalves, M. A., & Benevenuto, F. (2016). Exploiting new sentiment-based meta-level features for effective sentiment analysis. *WSDM 2016 - Proceedings of the 9th ACM International Conference on Web Search and Data Mining*, 53–62. 10.1145/2835776.2835821

Cao, C., Liu, F., Tan, H., Song, D., Shu, W., Li, W., Zhou, Y., Bo, X., & Xie, Z. (2018). Deep Learning and Its Applications in Biomedicine. *Genomics, Proteomics & Bioinformatics*, *16*(1), 17–32. doi:10.1016/j.gpb.2017.07.003 PMID:29522900

Carbone, P., Katsifodimos, A., Sweden, S., Ewen, S., Markl, V., Haridi, S., & Tzoumas, K. (2015). *Apache Flink™: Stream and Batch Processing in a Single Engine.* Academic Press.

Caro, M. P., Ali, M. S., Vecchio, M., & Giaffreda, R. (2018, May). Blockchain-based traceability in Agri-Food supply chain management: A practical implementation. In *2018 IoT Vertical and Topical Summit on Agriculture-Tuscany (IOT Tuscany)* (pp. 1-4). IEEE.

Castelfranchi, C. (2004). Trust mediation in knowledge management and sharing. In *2004 International Conference on Trust Management.* Springer. 10.1007/978-3-540-24747-0_23

Chakraborty, K., & Bhattacharyya, S. (2018). *Comparative Sentiment Analysis on a Set of Movie.* doi:10.1007/978-3-319-74690-6

Chawda, R. K., & Thakur, G. (2016). Big data and advanced analytics tools. *2016 Symposium on Colossal Data Analysis and Networking, CDAN 2016.* 10.1109/CDAN.2016.7570890

Chen, T., Li, M., Li, Y., Lin, M., Wang, N., Wang, M., … Zhang, Z. (2015). *MXNet: A Flexible and Efficient Machine Learning Library for Heterogeneous Distributed Systems.* Retrieved from https://arxiv.org/abs/1512.01274

Cheney, J. (2011). A formal framework for provenance security. *2011 IEEE 24th Computer Security Foundations Symposium*, 281–293. 10.1109/CSF.2011.26

Cheng, Y., Wang, D., Zhou, P., & Zhang, T. (2019). *A Survey of Model Compression and Acceleration for Deep Neural Networks.* Retrieved from https://arxiv.org/abs/1710.09282

Cheng, M., Sori, W. J., Jiang, F., Khan, A., & Liu, S. (2017). Recurrent Neural Network Based Classification of ECG Signal Features for Obstruction of Sleep Apnea Detection. *2017 IEEE International Conference on Computational Science and Engineering (CSE) and IEEE International Conference on Embedded and Ubiquitous Computing (EUC)*, 2, 199–202. 10.1109/CSE-EUC.2017.220

Chinaka, M. (2016). *Blockchain technology-Applications in improving financial inclusion in developing economies: a Case study for small scale agriculture in Africa* (Ph.D. dissertation). Sloan School Manage., Massachusetts Inst. Technol., Cambridge, MA, USA.

Choi, E., Bahadori, M. T., Kulas, J. A., Schuetz, A., Stewart, W. F., & Sun, J. (2017). *RETAIN: An Interpretable Predictive Model for Healthcare using Reverse Time Attention Mechanism.* Retrieved from https://arxiv.org/abs/1608.05745

Choi, Y., Kim, Y., & Myaeng, S.-H. (2009). Domain-specific sentiment analysis using contextual feature generation. *Proceedings of the 1st International CIKM Workshop on Topic Sentiment Analysis for Mass Opinion*, 37–44. 10.1145/1651461.1651469

Chorowski, J., Bahdanau, D., Serdyuk, D., Cho, K., & Bengio, Y. (2015). Attention-based models for speech recognition. In Advances in Neural Information Processing Systems, (pp. 577–585). Neural Information Processing Systems Foundation.

Christian Schaupp, L., & Carter, L. (2005). E-voting: From apathy to adoption. *Journal of Enterprise Information Management*, 18(5), 586–601. doi:10.1108/17410390510624025

Christiansen, E. M., Yang, S. J., Ando, D. M., Javaherian, A., Skibinski, G., Lipnick, S., … Finkbeiner, S. (2018). In Silico Labeling: Predicting Fluorescent Labels in Unlabeled Images. Cell, 173, 792-803.

Christidis, K., & Devetsikiotis, M. (2016). Blockchains and Smart Contracts for the Internet of Things. *IEEE Access: Practical Innovations, Open Solutions*, 4, 2292–2303. doi:10.1109/ACCESS.2016.2566339

Christin, N. (2011). Peer-to-peer networks: Interdisciplinary challenges for interconnected systems. In *Information Assurance and Security Ethics in Complex Systems: Interdisciplinary Perspectives* (pp. 81–103). IGI Global. doi:10.4018/978-1-61692-245-0.ch005

Cohen, T., & Welling, M. (2016). Group Equivariant Convolutional Networks. *International Conference on Machine Learning*, 2990–2999.

Colloquium, J. N., & Zrt, B. E. (2017). *Blockchain : solving the privacy and research availability tradeoff for EHR data*. Academic Press.

Commonwealth Scientific and Industrial Research Organisation (CSIRO), Australia. (2011). *Phenonet: Distributed Sensor Network for Phenomics supported by High Resolution Plant Phenomics Centre*. CSIRO ICT Centre, and CSIRO Sensor and Sensor Networks TCP.

Coraddu, A., Oneto, L., Baldi, F., & Anguita, D. (2017). Vessels fuel consumption forecast and trim optimisation: A data analytics perspective. *Ocean Engineering, 130*(September), 351–370. doi:10.1016/j.oceaneng.2016.11.058

Crosby, M., Nachiappan, Pattanayak, P., Verma, S., & Kalyanaraman, V. (2016). BlockChain Technology: Beyond Bitcoin. *Applied Innovation Review, 2*, 6-19.

Crosby, M., Pattanayak, P., Verma, S., & Kalyanaraman, V. (2016). Blockchain technology: Beyond bitcoin. *Applied Innovation, 2*(71), 6–10.

Dai, H., Umarov, R., Kuwahara, H., Li, Y., Song, L., & Gao, X. (2017). Sequence2Vec: A novel embedding approach for modeling transcription factor binding affinity landscape. *Bioinformatics (Oxford, England), 33*(22), 3575–3583. doi:10.1093/bioinformatics/btx480 PMID:28961686

Dai, M., Zhang, S., Wang, H., & Jin, S. (2018). A Low Storage Room Requirement Framework for Distributed Ledger in Blockchain. *IEEE Access: Practical Innovations, Open Solutions, 6*, 22970–22975. doi:10.1109/ACCESS.2018.2814624

Dang, H., Tuan, T., Dinh, A., Loghin, D., Chang, E., Lin, Q., & Ooi, C. (2019). *Towards Scaling Blockchain Systems via Sharding*. Academic Press.

Dantu, K., Ko, S. Y., & Ziarek, L. (2017, April). RAINA: Reliability and adaptability in android for fog computing. *IEEE Communications Magazine, 55*(4), 41–45. doi:10.1109/MCOM.2017.1600901

Darabant, A. S., & Darabant, L. (2011). Clustering methods in data fragmentation. *Romanian Journal of Information Science and Technology, 4*(1), 81–87.

Dastjerdi & Buyya (Ed.). (2016). *Fog Computing: Helping the Internet of Things Realize its Potential*. IEEE Computer Society.

Dennis, R. M., & Owenson, G. (2016). *Rep on the block: A next generation reputation system based on the blockchain*. . doi:10.1109/ICITST.2015.7412073

Dev Mishra, A., & Beer Singh, Y. (2017). Big data analytics for security and privacy challenges. *Proceeding - IEEE International Conference on Computing, Communication and Automation, ICCCA 2016*, 50–53. 10.1109/CCAA.2016.7813688

Dika, A., & Nowostawski, M. (2018). Security Vulnerabilities in Ethereum Smart Contracts. *2018 IEEE International Conference on Internet of Things (IThings) and IEEE Green Computing and Communications (GreenCom) and IEEE Cyber, Physical and Social Computing (CPSCom) and IEEE Smart Data (SmartData)*, 955–962. 10.1109/Cybermatics_2018.2018.00182

Dinov, I. D. (2016). Volume and Value of Big Healthcare Data. *Journal of Medical Statistics and Informatics*, *4*(1), 4. doi:10.7243/2053-7662-4-3 PMID:26998309

Dorri, A., Steger, M., & Kanhere, S. S. (n.d.). *SpeedyChain : A framework for decoupling data from blockchain for smart cities*. Academic Press.

Dubost, F., Adams, H., Bortsova, G., Ikram, M. A., Niessen, W., Vernooij, M., & de Bruijne, M. (2019). 3D regression neural network for the quantification of enlarged perivascular spaces in brain MRI. *Medical Image Analysis*, *51*, 89–100. doi:10.1016/j.media.2018.10.008 PMID:30390514

Esposito, C., De Santis, A., Tortora, G., Chang, H., & Choo, K. K. R. (2018). Blockchain: A panacea for healthcare cloud-based data security and privacy? *IEEE Cloud Computing*, *5*(1), 31–37. doi:10.1109/MCC.2018.011791712

Esteva, A., Kuprel, B., Novoa, R. A., Ko, J., Swetter, S. M., Blau, H. M., & Thrun, S. (2017). Dermatologist-level classification of skin cancer with deep neural networks. *Nature*, *542*(7639), 115–118. doi:10.1038/nature21056 PMID:28117445

Esteva, A., Robicquet, A., Ramsundar, B., Kuleshov, V., DePristo, M., Chou, K., Cui, C., Corrado, G., Thrun, S., & Dean, J. (2019). A guide to deep learning in healthcare. *Nature Medicine*, *25*(1), 24–29. doi:10.103841591-018-0316-z PMID:30617335

Eyal, I., Gencer, A. E., Sirer, E. G., & Van Renesse, R. (2016). Bitcoin-ng: A scalable blockchain protocol. *13th USENIX Symposium on Networked Systems Design and Implementation*, 45-59.

Fan, W., & Perros, H. (2014). A novel trust management framework for multi-cloud environments based on trust service providers. *Knowledge-Based Systems*, *70*, 392–406. doi:10.1016/j.knosys.2014.07.018

Farinaz, K., & Potkonjak, M. (2007). CAD-based Security, Cryptography, and Digital Rights Management. *44th ACM/IEEE Design Automation Conference*.

Firoozjaei, M. D., Ghobbani, A., & Kim, H. (2019). EVChain: A Blockchain-based Credit Sharing in Electric Vehicles Charging. *IEEE International Conference on Privacy, Security and Trust*. 10.1109/PST47121.2019.8949026

Fog Computing and the Internet of Things: Extend the Cloud to Where the Things Are. (2015). Cisco White Paper.

Fout, A., Byrd, J., Shariat, B., & Ben-Hur, A. (2017). Protein Interface Prediction using Graph Convolutional Networks. In I. Guyon, U. V. Luxburg, S. Bengio, H. Wallach, R. Fergus, S. Vishwanathan, & R. Garnett (Eds.), Advances in Neural Information Processing Systems (Vol. 30, pp. 6530–6539). Curran Associates, Inc.

Fraga-Lamas, P., & Fernández-Caramés, T. M. (2019). A Review on Blockchain Technologies for an Advanced and Cyber-Resilient Automotive Industry. *IEEE Access: Practical Innovations, Open Solutions*, *7*, 17578–17598. doi:10.1109/ACCESS.2019.2895302

Fraiwan, L., & Lweesy, K. (2017). Neonatal sleep state identification using deep learning autoencoders. *2017 IEEE 13th International Colloquium on Signal Processing Its Applications (CSPA)*, 228–231.

Galar, M., Fernandez, A., Barrenechea, E., Bustince, H., & Herrera, F. (2012). A Review on Ensembles for the Class Imbalance Problem: Bagging-, Boosting-, and Hybrid-Based Approaches. *IEEE Transactions on Systems, Man and Cybernetics. Part C, Applications and Reviews, 42*(4), 463–484. doi:10.1109/TSMCC.2011.2161285

Galvez, J. F., Mejuto, J. C., & Simal-Gandara, J. (2018). Future challenges on the use of blockchain for food traceability analysis. *Trends in Analytical Chemistry, 107*, 222–232. doi:10.1016/j.trac.2018.08.011

Gambetta, D. (1988). Can We Trust Trust? In Trust: Making and Breaking Cooperative Relations. Basil Blackwell.

Gao, W., Hatcher, W. G., & Yu, W. (2018). A Survey of Blockchain : Techniques, Applications, and Challenges. *2018 27th International Conference on Computer Communication and Networks (ICCCN)*, 1–11. 10.1109/ICCCN.2018.8487348

García-gil, D., Ramírez-gallego, S., García, S., & Herrera, F. (2017). Open Access A comparison on scalability for batch big data processing on Apache Spark and Apache Flink. *Big Data Analytics*, 1–11. doi:10.118641044-016-0020-2

Gattermayer, J., & Tvrdik, P. (2017). *Blockchain-based multi-level scoring system for P2P clusters*. doi:10.1109/ICPPW.2017.50

Glaser, F. (2017). Pervasive Decentralisation of Digital Infrastructures: A Framework for Blockchain Enabled System and Use Case Analysis. *50th Hawaii International Conference on System Sciences*.

Glaser, F., & Bezzenberger, L. (2015). Beyond Cryptocurrencies - A Taxonomy of Decentralized Consensus Systems. *23rd European Conference on Information Systems (ECIS)*.

Godinez, W. J., Hossain, I., Lazic, S. E., Davies, J. W., & Zhang, X. (2017). A multi-scale convolutional neural network for phenotyping high-content cellular images. *Bioinformatics (Oxford, England), 33*(13), 2010–2019. doi:10.1093/bioinformatics/btx069 PMID:28203779

Goguen, J. A., & Meseguer, J. (1982). Security policies and security models. In *1982 IEEE Symposium on Security and Privacy* (pp. 11-11). IEEE. 10.1109/SP.1982.10014

Goyal, S. (2016). Sentimental analysis of twitter data using text mining and hybrid classification approach. *International Journal of Advance Research Ideas and Innovations in Technology, 2*(5), 1–9.

Grandison, T., & Sloman, M. (2002). Trust management formal techniques and system. *2002 Proceeding of Second IFIP Conference*, 1-10.

Guo, C., Pleiss, G., Sun, Y., & Weinberger, K. Q. (2017). *On Calibration of Modern Neural Networks*. Retrieved from https://arxiv.org/abs/1706.04599

Guo, Y., Liu, Y., Bakker, E. M., Guo, Y., & Lew, M. S. (2018). CNN-RNN: A large-scale hierarchical image classification framework. *Multimedia Tools and Applications, 77*(8), 10251–10271. doi:10.100711042-017-5443-x

Gupta, M. K., Singh, D. B., Shukla, R., & Misra, K. (2013). A comprehensive metabolic modeling of thyroid pathway in relation to thyroid pathophysiology and therapeutics. *OMICS: A Journal of Integrative Biology, 17*(11), 584–593. doi:10.1089/omi.2013.0007 PMID:24044365

Gupta, N., & Bedi, P. (2018, September). E-waste Management Using Blockchain based Smart Contracts. In *2018 International Conference on Advances in Computing, Communications and Informatics (ICACCI)* (pp. 915-921). IEEE. 10.1109/ICACCI.2018.8554912

Habib, S. M., Ries, S., & Muhlhauser, M. (2011). Towards a trust management system for cloud computing. *2011 IEEE 10th International Conference on Trust, Security and Privacy in Computing and Communications*, 933-939. 10.1109/TrustCom.2011.129

Halvard, S., Benatallah, B., Casati, F., & Toumani, F. (2007). Managing impacts of security protocol changes in service-oriented applications. *2007 Proceedings of the 29th international conference on Software Engineering*, 468-477.

Han, J., Kamber, M., & Pei, J. (2012). Classification: Basic Concepts. In Data Mining Concepts and Techniques (3rd ed., pp. 327-383). Waltham: MK.

Han, S., Mao, H., & Dally, W. J. (2016). *Deep Compression: Compressing Deep Neural Networks with Pruning, Trained Quantization and Huffman Coding*. Retrieved from https://arxiv.org/abs/1510.00149

Hanley, M. (2018). Managing Lifetime Healthcare Data on the Blockchain. *2018 IEEE SmartWorld, Ubiquitous Intelligence & Computing, Advanced & Trusted Computing, Scalable Computing & Communications, Cloud & Big Data Computing, Internet of People and Smart City Innovation (SmartWorld/SCALCOM/UIC/ATC/CBDCom/IOP/SCI)*, 246–251. doi:10.1109/SmartWorld.2018.00077

Hashemi, S. H., Faghri, F., Rausch, P., & Campbell, R. H. (2016). World of Empowered IoT Users. In IoTDI (pp. 13-24). IEEE Computer Society. doi:10.1109/IoTDI.2015.39

Hashem, I. A. T., Yaqoob, I., Anuar, N. B., Mokhtar, S., Gani, A., & Ullah Khan, S. (2015). The rise of "big data" on cloud computing: Review and open research issues. *Information Systems, 47*, 98–115. doi:10.1016/j.is.2014.07.006

Heffernan, R., Paliwal, K., Lyons, J., Dehzangi, A., Sharma, A., Wang, J., Sattar, A., Yang, Y., & Zhou, Y. (2015). Improving prediction of secondary structure, local backbone angles, and solvent accessible surface area of proteins by iterative deep learning. *Scientific Reports, 5*(1), 11476. doi:10.1038rep11476 PMID:26098304

Hesse, G., & Lorenz, M. (2016). Conceptual survey on data stream processing systems. *Proceedings of the International Conference on Parallel and Distributed Systems - ICPADS,* 797–802. 10.1109/ICPADS.2015.106

Hinton, G., Vinyals, O., & Dean, J. (2015). *Distilling the Knowledge in a Neural Network.* Retrieved from https://arxiv.org/abs/1503.02531

Hinton, G. E., Osindero, S., & Teh, Y.-W. (2006). A fast learning algorithm for deep belief nets. *Neural Computation, 18*(7), 1527–1554. doi:10.1162/neco.2006.18.7.1527 PMID:16764513

Hinton, G. E., & Plaut, D. C. (1987). Using Fast Weights to Deblur Old Memories. In *Proceedings of the 9th Annual Conference of the Cognitive Science Society,* (pp. 177–186). Erlbaum.

Hjálmarsson, F. Þ., Hreiðarsson, G. K., Hamdaqa, M., & Hjálmtýsson, G. (2018). Blockchain-based e-voting system. In *2018 IEEE 11th International Conference on Cloud Computing (CLOUD)* (pp. 983-986). IEEE.

Holmberg, A., & Åquist, R. (2018). *Blockchain technology in food supply chains: A case study of the possibilities and challenges with the implementation of a blockchain technology supported framework for traceability* (M.S. thesis). Fac. Health, Science Technology, Karlstad Univ., Karlstad, Sweden.

Hon, W. K., Palfreyman, J., & Tegart, M. (2016). Distributed Ledger Technology & Cybersecurity. In *European Union Agency For Network And Information Securit.* ENISA.

Houben, R., & Snyers, A. (2018). *Cryptocurrencies and blockchain: Legal context and implications for financial crime, money laundering and tax evasion.* Academic Press.

Hou, X., Li, Y., Chen, M., Wu, D., Jin, D., & Chen, S. (2016, June). Vehicular fog computing: A viewpoint of vehicles as the infrastructures. *IEEE Transaction., 65*(6), 3860–3873. doi:10.1109/TVT.2016.2532863

Hua, J., Wang, X., Kang, M., Wang, H., & Wang, F. (2018). Blockchain Based Provenance for Agricultural Products : A Distributed Platform with Duplicated and Shared Bookkeeping. *2018 IEEE Intelligent Vehicles Symposium (IV),* 97–101. 10.1109/IVS.2018.8500647

Hua, K.-L., Hsu, C.-H., Hidayati, S. C., Cheng, W.-H., & Chen, Y.-J. (2015). Computer-aided classification of lung nodules on computed tomography images via deep learning technique. *OncoTargets and Therapy, 8,* 2015–2022. PMID:26346558

Huang, W., Wang, H., Zhang, Y., & Zhang, S. (2017). A novel cluster computing technique based on signal clustering and analytic hierarchy model using hadoop. *Cluster Computing,* 1–8. doi:10.100710586-017-1205-9

Huckle, S., Bhattacharya, R., White, M., & Beloff, N. (2016). Internet of Things, blockchain and shared economy applications. *Procedia Computer Science, 98,* 461-466.

Hu, H., Wen, Y., Chua, T., & Li, X. (2014). Toward Scalable Systems for Big Data Analytics: A Technology Tutorial. *IEEE Access: Practical Innovations, Open Solutions*, 2, 652–687. doi:10.1109/ACCESS.2014.2332453

Hu, Y., & Lu, X. (2018). Learning spatial-temporal features for video copy detection by the combination of CNN and RNN. *Journal of Visual Communication and Image Representation*, 55, 21–29. doi:10.1016/j.jvcir.2018.05.013

Iansiti, M., & Lakhani, K. R. (2017). The truth about blockchain. *Harvard Business Review*, 95(1), 118–127.

Ioffe, S., & Szegedy, C. (2015). *Batch Normalization: Accelerating Deep Network Training by Reducing Internal Covariate Shift*. Retrieved from https://arxiv.org/abs/1502.03167

Ismail, L., Box, P. O., Ain, A., Hameed, H., Ain, A., Alshamsi, M., … Aldhanhani, N. (2019). *Towards a Blockchain Deployment at UAE University : Performance Evaluation and Blockchain Taxonomy*. Academic Press.

Issarny, V., Georgantas, N., Hachem, S., Zarras, A., Vassiliadist, P., Autili, M., Gerosa, M. A., & Hamida, A. B. (2011). Service-oriented middleware for the future internet: State of the art and research directions. *Springer Journal of Internet Services and Applications*, 2(1), 23–45. doi:10.100713174-011-0021-3

Jalali, F., Hinton, K., Ayre, R., Alpcan, T., & Tucker, R. S. (2016, May). Fog computing may help to save energy in cloud computing. *IEEE Journal on Selected Areas in Communications*, 34(5), 1728–1739. doi:10.1109/JSAC.2016.2545559

Janssen, M., van der Voort, H., & Wahyudi, A. (2017). Factors influencing big data decision-making quality. *Journal of Business Research*, 70, 338–345. doi:10.1016/j.jbusres.2016.08.007

Jin, X., Bai, C., Zhang, Z., Zhao, S., Wang, H., Yan, Z., Zhang, Lu., & Chen, S. (2019). Blockchain-enabled Transactive Method in Distributed Systems Considering Security Constraints. *IEEE Congress on Evolutionary Computation*. 10.1109/CEC.2019.8790069

Jin, X., Wah, B. W., Cheng, X., & Wang, Y. (2015). Significance and Challenges of Big Data Research. *Big Data Research*, 2(2), 59–64. doi:10.1016/j.bdr.2015.01.006

Johnson, D., Menezes, A., & Vanston, S. (2001). The elliptic curve digital signature algorithm (ecdsa). *International Journal of Information Security*, 1(1), 36–63. doi:10.1007102070100002

Joseph, A. D., Katz, R., Konwinski, A., Gunho, L., Patterson, D., & Rabkin, A. (2006). A view of cloud computing. *Communications of the ACM*, 53, 4.

Jurafsky, D., & Martin, J. H. (2019). Part-of-Speech Tagging. Speech and Language Processing.

Kang, J., Xiong, Z., Niyato, D., Ye, D., Kim, D. I., & Zhao, J. (2019). Towards Secure Blockchain-enabled Internet of Vehicles: Optimizing Consensus Management Using Reputation and Contract Theory. *IEEE Transactions on Vehicular Technology*, 68(3), 2906–2920. Advance online publication. doi:10.1109/TVT.2019.2894944

Kang, J., Yu, R., Huang, X., Wu, M., Maharjan, S., Xie, S., & Zhang, Y. (2019). Blockchain for Secure and Efficient Data Sharing in Vehicular Edge Computing and Networks. *IEEE Internet of Things Journal, 6*(3), 4660–4670. doi:10.1109/JIOT.2018.2875542

Kaur, R., Chauhan, V., & Mittal, U. (2018). Metamorphosis of data (small to big) and the comparative study of techniques (HADOOP, HIVE and PIG) to handle big data. *International Journal of Engineering & Technology, 7*(2.27), 1. doi:10.14419/ijet.v7i2.27.11206

Kaur, G., & Singla, A. (2016). Sentiment analysis of flipkart reviews using naive bayes and decision tree algorithm. *International Journal of Advanced Research in Computer Engineering & Technology, 5*(1), 148–153.

Keller, A. M., Mertz, D., Hall, J. L., & Urken, A. (2006). Privacy issues in an electronic voting machine. In *Privacy and Technologies of Identity* (pp. 313–334). Springer. doi:10.1007/0-387-28222-X_18

Kermany, D. S., Goldbaum, M., Cai, W., Valentim, C. C. S., Liang, H., Baxter, S. L., McKeown, A., Yang, G., Wu, X., Yan, F., Dong, J., Prasadha, M. K., Pei, J., Ting, M. Y. L., Zhu, J., Li, C., Hewett, S., Dong, J., Ziyar, I., ... Zhang, K. (2018). Identifying Medical Diagnoses and Treatable Diseases by Image-Based Deep Learning. *Cell, 172*(5), 1122–1131.e9. doi:10.1016/j.cell.2018.02.010 PMID:29474911

Khan, K. M., Malluhi, Q. (2010). Establishing trust in cloud computing. *IT Professional, 12*(5), 20-27.

Khan, M. A., & Salah, K. (2018). IoT security: Review, blockchain solutions, and open challenges. *Future Generation Computer Systems, 82*, 395–411. doi:10.1016/j.future.2017.11.022

Khqj, V. W., Dqg, Q., Qjlqhhulqj, R., Dqg, H. R. I., Dqg, Q., Dqg, H. R. I., ... Vwhp, W. K. H. V. (2018). %. *ORFNFKDLQ, 1–5*. Advance online publication. doi:10.1109/WI.2018.000-8

Kianmajd, P., Rowe, J., & Levitt, K. (2016, April). Privacy-preserving coordination for smart communities. In *2016 IEEE Conference on Computer Communications Workshops (INFOCOM WKSHPS)* (pp. 1045-1046). IEEE. 10.1109/INFCOMW.2016.7562245

Kim, B. Y. (2018). *Data Managing and Service Exchanging on IoT Service Platform Based on Blockchain with Smart Contract and Spatial Data Processing*. Academic Press.

Kiranyaz, S., Ince, T., & Gabbouj, M. (2016). Real-Time Patient-Specific ECG Classification by 1-D Convolutional Neural Networks. *IEEE Transactions on Biomedical Engineering, 63*(3), 664–675. doi:10.1109/TBME.2015.2468589 PMID:26285054

Kirkpatrick, J., Pascanu, R., Rabinowitz, N., Veness, J., Desjardins, G., Rusu, A. A., ... Hadsell, R. (2017). *Overcoming catastrophic forgetting in neural networks*. Retrieved from https://arxiv.org/abs/1612.00796

Kiros, R., Zhu, Y., Salakhutdinov, R., Zemel, R. S., Torralba, A., Urtasun, R., & Fidler, S. (2015). *Skip-Thought Vectors*. Retrieved from https://arxiv.org/abs/1506.06726

Knapp, E. (1987). Deadlock Detection in Distributed Databases. *ACM Computing Surveys, 19*(4), 3030–3327. doi:10.1145/45075.46163

Kondor, D., Pósfai, M., Csabai, I., & Vattay, G. (2014). Do the rich get richer? An empirical analysis of the Bitcoin transaction network. *PLoS One, 9*(2), e86197. doi:10.1371/journal.pone.0086197 PMID:24505257

Kosba, A., Miller, A., Shi, E., Wen, Z., & Papamanthou, C. (2016). Hawk: The Blockchain Model of Cryptography and Privacy-Preserving Smart Contracts. *Proceedings of the 2016 IEEE Symposium on Security and Privacy SP '16*. 10.1109/SP.2016.55

Koshy, P., Koshy, D., & McDaniel, P. (2014). *An Analysis of Anonymity in Bitcoin Using P2P Network Traffic*. . doi:10.1007/978-3-662-45472-5_30

Koyamada, S., Shikauchi, Y., Nakae, K., Koyama, M., & Ishii, S. (2015). *Deep learning of fMRI big data: A novel approach to subject-transfer decoding*. Retrieved from https://arxiv.org/abs/1502.00093

Kraemer, F. A., Braten, A. E., Tamkittikhun, N., & Palma, A. D. (2017). Fog Computing in Healthcare- A Review and Discussion. *IEEE Access: Practical Innovations, Open Solutions, 5*, 9206–9222. doi:10.1109/ACCESS.2017.2704100

Krawczyk, B. (2016). Learning from imbalanced data: Open challenges and future directions. *Progress in Artificial Intelligence, 5*(4), 221–232. doi:10.100713748-016-0094-0

Krizhevsky, A., Sutskever, I., & Hinton, G. E. (2017). ImageNet Classification with Deep Convolutional Neural Networks. *Communications of the ACM, 60*(6), 84–90. doi:10.1145/3065386

Krogh, A., & Hertz, J. A. (1992). A Simple Weight Decay Can Improve Generalization. In J. E. Moody, S. J. Hanson, & R. P. Lippmann (Eds.), Advances in Neural Information Processing Systems (Vol. 4, pp. 950–957). Morgan-Kaufmann.

Kshetri, N., & Voas, J. (2018). Blockchain-enabled e-voting. *IEEE Software, 35*(4), 95–99. doi:10.1109/MS.2018.2801546

Kulmanov, M., Khan, M. A., Hoehndorf, R., & Wren, J. (2018). DeepGO: Predicting protein functions from sequence and interactions using a deep ontology-aware classifier. *Bioinformatics (Oxford, England), 34*(4), 660–668. doi:10.1093/bioinformatics/btx624 PMID:29028931

Kumar, A., Mehta, V., Raj, U., Varadwaj, P. K., Udayabanu, M., Yennamalli, R. M., & Singh, T. R. (2018). Computational and in-vitro validation of natural molecules as potential Acetylcholinesterase inhibitors and neuroprotective agents. *Current Alzheimer Research*. PMID:30543170

Lai, C. C., Chen, H. C., & Yeh, G. M., Ouyang, (2011), A robust digital image watermarking using transformation domain and evolutionary computation techniques. *Int'l Conference on Machine Learning and Cybernetics, 4*. 10.1109/ICMLC.2011.6016997

Larranaga, P., Calvo, B., Santana, R., Bielza, C., Galdiano, J., Inza, I., Lozano, J. A., Armañanzas, R., Santafé, G., Pérez, A., & Robles, V. (2006). Machine learning in bioinformatics. *Briefings in Bioinformatics*, *7*(1), 86–112. doi:10.1093/bib/bbk007 PMID:16761367

LeCun, Y., Bengio, Y., & Hinton, G. (2015). Deep learning. *Nature*, *521*(7553), 436–444. doi:10.1038/nature14539 PMID:26017442

Lee, H., Sung, K., Lee, K., & Min, S. (2018). Economic Analysis of Blockchain Technology on Digital Platform Market. *IEEE 23rd Pacific Rim International Symposium on Dependable Computing (PRDC)*. 10.1109/PRDC.2018.00020

Leibig, C., Allken, V., Ayhan, M. S., Berens, P., & Wahl, S. (2017). Leveraging uncertainty information from deep neural networks for disease detection. *Scientific Reports*, *7*(1), 1–14. doi:10.103841598-017-17876-z PMID:29259224

Lei, X., Qian, X., & Zhao, G. (2016). Rating Prediction Based on Social Sentiment from Textual Reviews. *IEEE Transactions on Multimedia*, *18*(9), 1910–1921. doi:10.1109/TMM.2016.2575738

Lemieux, V. (2017). A typology of blockchain recordkeeping solutions and some reflections on their implications for the future of archival preservation. *Big Data, IEEE International Conference on Big Data*, 2271-2278.

Lemieux, V. L. (2016). Trusting records: Is Blockchain technology the answer? *Records Management Journal*, *26*(2), 110–139. doi:10.1108/RMJ-12-2015-0042

Leung, M. K. K., Delong, A., & Frey, B. J. (2017). Inference of the Human Polyadenylation Code. *bioRxiv*, 130591.

Leung, M. K. K., Xiong, H. Y., Lee, L. J., & Frey, B. J. (2014). Deep learning of the tissue-regulated splicing code. *Bioinformatics (Oxford, England)*, *30*(12), i121–i129. doi:10.1093/bioinformatics/btu277 PMID:24931975

Li, W., & Sforzin, A. (n.d.). *Towards Scalable and Private Industrial Blockchains*. Academic Press.

Li, Y., Ding, L., & Gao, X. (2019). *On the Decision Boundary of Deep Neural Networks*. Retrieved from https://arxiv.org/abs/1808.05385

Li, Y., Li, Z., Ding, L., Pan, Y., Huang, C., Hu, Y., ... Gao, X. (2018). *SupportNet: Solving catastrophic forgetting in class incremental learning with support data*. Retrieved from https://arxiv.org/abs/1806.02942

Li, A., Serban, R., & Negrut, D. (2017). Analysis of a Splitting Approach for the Parallel Solution of Linear Systems on GPU Cards. *SIAM Journal on Scientific Computing*, *39*(3), C215–C237. doi:10.1137/15M1039523

Li, C., & Zhang, L. J. (2017, June). A blockchain-based new secure multi-layer network model for the Internet of Things. In *2017 IEEE International Congress on the Internet of Things (ICIOT)* (pp. 33-41). IEEE. 10.1109/IEEE.ICIOT.2017.34

Li, D., Du, R., Fu, Y., & Au, M. H. (2019). Meta-Key: A Secure Data-Sharing Protocol Under Blockchain-Based Decentralized Storage Architecture. *IEEE Networking Letters*, *1*(1), 30–33. doi:10.1109/LNET.2019.2891998

Li, D., Kehoe, D., & Drake, P. (2006). Dynamic planning with wireless product identification technology in food supply chains. *International Journal of Advanced Manufacturing Technology*, *30*(9-10), 938–944. doi:10.100700170-005-0066-1

Li, J., & Cichocki, A. (2014). Deep Learning of Multifractal Attributes from Motor Imagery Induced EEG. In C. K. Loo, K. S. Yap, K. W. Wong, A. Teoh, & K. Huang (Eds.), *Neural Information Processing* (pp. 503–510). Springer International Publishing. doi:10.1007/978-3-319-12637-1_63

Lin, C. C., & Chiang, P. H. A Mobile Trading Scheme for Digital Content Based on Digital Rights. *Eighth International Conference on Intelligent Systems Design and Applications*. 10.1109/ISDA.2008.205

Lindman, J., Rossi, M., & Tuunainen, V. (2017). Opportunities and risks of Blockchain Technologies in payments – a research agenda. In *Proceedings of the 50th Hawaii International Conference on System Sciences*. HICSS/IEEE Computer Society. DOI: 10.24251/HICSS.2017.185

Lipton, Z. C. (2017). *The Mythos of Model Interpretability*. Retrieved from https://arxiv.org/abs/1606.03490

Li, R., Song, T., Mei, B., Li, H., Cheng, X., Sun, L., ... Worth, F. (2018). *Blockchain For Large-Scale Internet of Things Data Storage and Protection*. Advance online publication. doi:10.1109/TSC.2018.2853167

Liu, B., Yu, X. L., Chen, S., Xu, X., & Zhu, L (2017). *Blockchain Based Data Integrity Service Framework for IoT Data*. doi:10.1109/ICWS.2017.54

Liu, Y., Wang, K., Member, S., Lin, Y., Xu, W., & Member, S. (2019). *LightChain : A Lightweight Blockchain System for Industrial Internet of Things*. doi:10.1109/TII.2019.2904049

Liu, J., Tang, H., Sun, R., Du, X., & Guizani, M. (2019). Lightweight and Privacy-Preserving Medical Services Access for Healthcare Cloud. *IEEE Access: Practical Innovations, Open Solutions*, *7*, 106951–106961. doi:10.1109/ACCESS.2019.2931917

Liu, J., & Zio, E. (2019). *Integration of feature vector selection and support vector machine for classification of imbalanced data. Applied soft Computing Journal.* doi:10.1016/j.asoc.2018.11.045

Liu, S., Wu, J., & Long, C. (2018). IoT Meets Blockchain : Parallel Distributed Architecture for Data Storage and Sharing. *2018 IEEE International Conference on Internet of Things (IThings) and IEEE Green Computing and Communications (GreenCom) and IEEE Cyber, Physical and Social Computing (CPSCom) and IEEE Smart Data (SmartData)*, 1355–1360. 10.1109/Cybermatics_2018.2018.00233

Li, W., & Ping, L. (2009). Trust model to enhance security and interoperability of cloud environment. *2009 IEEE International Conference on Cloud Computing*, 69-79. 10.1007/978-3-642-10665-1_7

Li, W., Ping, L., & Pan, X., (2010). Use trust management module to achieve effective security mechanisms in cloud environment. *2010 International Conference on Electronics and Information Engineering, 1,* 1-14. 10.1109/ICEIE.2010.5559829

Li, Y., Wang, S., Umarov, R., Xie, B., Fan, M., Li, L., & Gao, X. (2018). DEEPre: Sequence-based enzyme EC number prediction by deep learning. *Bioinformatics (Oxford, England), 34*(5), 760–769. doi:10.1093/bioinformatics/btx680 PMID:29069344

Li, Y., Xu, F., Zhang, F., Xu, P., Zhang, M., Fan, M., Li, L., Gao, X., & Han, R. (2018). DLBI: Deep learning guided Bayesian inference for structure reconstruction of super-resolution fluorescence microscopy. *Bioinformatics (Oxford, England), 34*(13), i284–i294. doi:10.1093/bioinformatics/bty241 PMID:29950012

Ll, W-J., Wang, X. D., Fu, Y. G., & Fu, Z. X. (2005). Study on several trust models in grid environment. Fuzhou DaxueXuebao (ZiranKexue Ban). *Journal of Fuzhou University, 34*(2), 189–193.

Lopez, M. A., Lobato, A. G. P., & Duarte, O. C. M. B. (2016). A performance comparison of open-source stream processing platforms. *2016 IEEE Global Communications Conference, GLOBECOM 2016 - Proceedings.* 10.1109/GLOCOM.2016.7841533

López, V., Río, S. D., Benítez, J. M., & Herrera, F. (2015). Cost-sensitive linguistic fuzzy rule based classification systems under the MapReduce framework for imbalanced big data. *Fuzzy Sets and Systems, 258,* 5–38. doi:10.1016/j.fss.2014.01.015

Lu, Z., Wang, Q., Qu, G., Member, S., Zhang, H., & Liu, Z. (2019). *A Blockchain-Based Privacy-Preserving Authentication Scheme for VANETs.* Academic Press.

Lucena, P., Binotto, A. P., Momo, F. S., & Kim, H. (2018). *A case study for grain quality assurance tracking based on a blockchain business network.* Available: https://arxiv.org/abs/1803.07877

Lu, H., Huang, K., Azimi, M., & Guo, L. (2019). Blockchain technology in the oil and gas industry: A review of applications, opportunities, challenges, and risks. *IEEE Access: Practical Innovations, Open Solutions, 7,* 41426–41444. Advance online publication. doi:10.1109/ACCESS.2019.2907695

Luo, K., Li, J., Wang, Z., & Cuschieri, A. (2017). *Patient-Specific Deep Architectural Model for ECG Classification.* Academic Press.

Luong, M.-T., Pham, H., & Manning, C. D. (2015). *Effective Approaches to Attention-based Neural Machine Translation.* Retrieved from https://arxiv.org/abs/1508.04025

Madumidha, S., SivaRanjani, P., Rajesh, S., & Sivakumar, S. (2018). Blockchain security for Internet of Things: A literature survey. *International Journal of Pure and Applied Mathematics, 119*(16), 3677–3686.

Mahmood, Z. (2016). Data science and big data computing: Frameworks and methodologies. *Data Science and Big Data Computing: Frameworks and Methodologies.* doi:10.1007/978-3-319-31861-5

Maiyya, S., Zakhary, V., & Abbadi, A. El. (2018). *Database and Distributed Computing Fundamentals for Scalable, Fault-tolerant, and Consistent Maintenance of Blockchains.* Academic Press.

Ma, J., Yu, M. K., Fong, S., Ono, K., Sage, E., Demchak, B., Sharan, R., & Ideker, T. (2018). Using deep learning to model the hierarchical structure and function of a cell. *Nature Methods, 15*(4), 290–298. doi:10.1038/nmeth.4627 PMID:29505029

Mao, D., Hao, Z., Wang, F., & Li, H. (2019). Novel Automatic Food Trading System Using Consortium Blockchain. *Arabian Journal for Science and Engineering, 44*(4), 3439–3455. doi:10.100713369-018-3537-z

Marcu, O., Costan, A., Antoniu, G., & P, S. (2018). *KerA: Scalable Data Ingestion for Stream Processing.* doi:10.1109/ICDCS.2018.00152

Marjani, M., Nasaruddin, F., Gani, A., Karim, A., Hashem, I. A. T., Siddiqa, A., & Yaqoob, I. (2017). Big IoT Data Analytics: Architecture, Opportunities, and Open Research Challenges. *IEEE Access: Practical Innovations, Open Solutions, 5*(c), 5247–5261. doi:10.1109/ACCESS.2017.2689040

Marx, V. (2013). Biology: The big challenges of big data. *Nature, 498*(7453), 255–260. doi:10.1038/498255a PMID:23765498

Mattila, J., & Seppälä, T., & Lähteenmäki, I. (2018). Who Holds the Reins? Banks in the Crossfire of Global Platforms. ETLA Reports 86. The Research Institute of the Finnish Economy.

Mavridis, I., & Karatza, H. (2017). Performance evaluation of cloud-based log file analysis with Apache Hadoop and Apache Spark. *Journal of Systems and Software, 125*, 133–151. doi:10.1016/j.jss.2016.11.037

Meiklejohn, S., Pomarole, M., Jordan, G., Levchenko, K., McCoy, D., Voelker, G. M., & Savage, S. (2013). Damon McCoy, Geoffrey M. Voelker, Stefan Savage, A Fistful of Bitcoins: Characterizing Payments Among Men with No Names. *Communications of the ACM, 59*(4), 86–93. doi:10.1145/2896384

Michael, B. (2009). In clouds shall we trust? *IEEE Security and Privacy, 7*(5), 3–3. doi:10.1109/MSP.2009.124

Miotto, R., Li, L., Kidd, B. A., & Dudley, J. T. (2016). Deep Patient: An Unsupervised Representation to Predict the Future of Patients from the Electronic Health Records. *Scientific Reports, 6*(1), 26094. doi:10.1038rep26094 PMID:27185194

Mirza, B., Wang, W., Wang, J., Choi, H., Chung, N. C., & Ping, P. (2019). Machine Learning and Integrative Analysis of Biomedical Big Data. *Genes, 10*(2), 10. doi:10.3390/genes10020087 PMID:30696086

Mishra, R. K., & Mishra, R. K. (2018). The Era of Big Data, Hadoop, and Other Big Data Processing Frameworks. *PySpark Recipes*, 1–14. doi:10.1007/978-1-4842-3141-8_1

Mittal, M., Singh, H., Paliwal, K., & Goyal, L. M. (2017). Efficient Random Data Accessing in MapReduce. *International Conference on Infocom Technologies and Unmanned Systems (Trends and Future Directions)*, 552–556.

Moreno, J., Serrano, M. A., & Fernández-Medina, E. (2016). Main issues in Big Data security. *Future Internet*, *8*(3), 44. Advance online publication. doi:10.3390/fi8030044

Moynihan, D. P. (2004). Building secure elections: E-voting, security, and systems theory. *Public Administration Review*, *64*(5), 515–528. doi:10.1111/j.1540-6210.2004.00400.x

Muchahari, K. M., & Sinha, S. K. (2012). A new trust management architecture for cloud computing environment. *2012 International Symposium on Cloud and Services Computing*, *1*, 136-140. 10.1109/ISCOS.2012.30

Muduli, P. R., Gunukula, R. R., & Mukherjee, A. (2016). A deep learning approach to fetal-ECG signal reconstruction. *2016 Twenty Second National Conference on Communication (NCC)*, 1–6. 10.1109/NCC.2016.7561206

Mukherjee, M., Lie, S., & Wang, D. (2018). Survey of Fog Computing: Fundamental, Network Applications and Research Challenges. *IEEE Communication, Survey & Tutorials.*

Naeini, M. P., Cooper, G. F., & Hauskrecht, M. (2015). Obtaining Well Calibrated Probabilities Using Bayesian Binning. *Proceedings of the ... AAAI Conference on Artificial Intelligence. AAAI Conference on Artificial Intelligence*, 2901–2907.

Nandwani, K. (2018). *Squaring the Blockchain Circle*. Available at: https://kunalnandwani.com/books/

Nath, Gupta, Chakraborty, & Ghosh. (2018). *A Survey of Fog Computing and Communication: Current Researches and Future Directions, Networking and Internet Architecture*. Academic Press.

Ni, J., & Lin, X. (2018). Securing Fog Computing for Internet of Things Applications: Challenges and Solutions. *IEEE Communications Surveys and Tutorials*, *20*(1), 601–628. doi:10.1109/COMST.2017.2762345

Noor, T. H., & Quan, Z. S. (2010). Credibility-based trust management for services in cloud environments. *International Conference on Service-Oriented Computing*, 328-343.

Noor, T. H., & Quan, Z. S. (2011). Trust as a service: A framework for trust management in cloud environments. *International Conference on Web Information Systems Engineering*, 314-321. 10.1007/978-3-642-24434-6_27

Noor, T. H., Sheng, Q. Z., Zeadally, S., & Yu, J. (2012). Trust management of services in cloud environments: Obstacles and solutions. *ACM Computing Surveys*, *46*(1), 1–12. doi:10.1145/2522968.2522980

Nygaard, R. (n.d.). *Distributed Storage System based on Permissioned Blockchain*. Academic Press.

Okada, H., Yamasaki, S., & Bracamonte, V. (2017). Proposed classification on blockchains based on authority and incentive dimensions. *2017 19th International Conference on Advanced Communication Technology (ICACT).*

OpenIoT Consortium. (2012). *Open Source Solution for the Internet of Things into the Cloud.* Author.

Oussous, A., Benjelloun, F. Z., Ait Lahcen, A., & Belfkih, S. (2018). Big Data technologies: A survey. *Journal of King Saud University - Computer and Information Sciences, 30*(4), 431–448. doi:10.1016/j.jksuci.2017.06.001

Ozgur, C., Colliau, T., Rogers, G., Hughes, Z., & Myer-Tyson, E. B. (2017). MatLab vs. Python vs. R. *Journal of Data Science: JDS, 15*(3), 355–372.

Pang, B., & Lee, L. (2008). Opinion mining and sentiment analysis. In *Foundations and trends in information retrieval* (Vol. 2, pp. 1–2). Issues.

Panigrahi, P. P., & Singh, T. R. (2013). Computational studies on Alzheimer's disease associated pathways and regulatory patterns using microarray gene expression and network data: Revealed association with aging and other diseases. *Journal of Theoretical Biology, 334,* 109–121. doi:10.1016/j.jtbi.2013.06.013 PMID:23811083

Papalilo, E., & Freisleben, B. (2007). Managing behaviour trust in grids using statistical methods of quality assurance. *2007 Third International Symposium on Information Assurance and Security, 1,* 319-324. 10.1109/IAS.2007.51

Park, S.-H., & Ha, Y.-G. (2014). Large Imbalance Data Classification Based on MapReduce for Traffic Accident Prediction. *Eighth International Conference on Innovative Mobile and Internet Services in Ubiquitous Computing,* 45-49. 10.1109/IMIS.2014.6

Peck, M. E. (2017). Blockchains: How they work and why they'll change the world. *IEEE Spectrum, 54*(10), 26–35. doi:10.1109/MSPEC.2017.8048836

Perera, C., Zaslavsky, A., Christen, P., & Georgakopoulos, D. (2017, April). Sensing as a service model for smart cities supported by Internet of things. *Transactions on Emerging Telecommunications Technologies, 25*(1), 81–93. doi:10.1002/ett.2704

Pereyra, G., Tucker, G., Chorowski, J., Kaiser, Ł., & Hinton, G. (2017). *Regularizing Neural Networks by Penalizing Confident Output Distributions.* Retrieved from https://arxiv.org/abs/1701.06548

Perez, L., & Wang, J. (2017). *The Effectiveness of Data Augmentation in Image Classification using Deep Learning.* Retrieved from https://arxiv.org/abs/1712.04621

Perez, S. (2009). In Cloud We Trust? *ReadWriteWeb.* ww.readwriteweb.com/enterprise/2009/01/incloud-we-trust.php

Perwej, Y. (2017). An Experiential Study of the Big Data. *Science and Education, 4*(1), 14–25. doi:10.12691/iteces-4-1-3

Peters, M. A. (2017). Technological unemployment: Educating for the fourth industrial revolution. *Journal of Self-Governance and Management Economics, 5*(1), 25–33. doi:10.22381/JSME5120172

Phillip, R. (2004). Nonce-Based Symmetric Encryption. *International Workshop on Fast Software Encryption.*

Pilkington, M. (2016). 11 Blockchain technology: principles and applications. *Research handbook on digital transformations, 225.*

Pinzon, R. C., & Rocha, C. (2016). Double-spend Attack Models with Time Advantange for Bitcoin. *Electronic Notes in Theoretical Computer Science, 329*(C), 79–103. doi:10.1016/j.entcs.2016.12.006

Platt, J. C. (1999). *Probabilistic Outputs for Support Vector Machines and Comparisons to Regularized Likelihood Methods. In Advances in Large Margin Classifiers.* MIT Press.

Polyzos, G. C., & Fotiou, N. (2017). *Blockchain-Assisted Information Distribution for the Internet of Things.* Advance online publication. doi:10.1109/IRI.2017.83

Rajput, R., & Solanki, A. K. (2016). Review of sentimental analysis methods using lexicon based approach. *International Journal of Computer Science and Mobile Computing, 5*(2), 159–166.

Ralph, D., & Samaniego, M. (2016). Blockchain as a Service for IoT. *2016 IEEE International Conference on Internet of Things (iThings) and IEEE Green Computing and Communications (GreenCom) and IEEE Cyber Physical and Social Computing (CPSCom) and IEEE Smart Data (SmartData).*

Rathee, G., & Saini, H. (2016). Security Concerns with Open Research Issues of Present Computer Network. *International Journal of Computer Science and Information Security, 14*(4), 406–432.

Rathee, G., Sharma, A., Iqbal, R., Aloqaily, M., Jaglan, N., & Kumar, R. (2019). A blockchain framework for securing connected and autonomous vehicles. *Sensors (Basel), 19*(14), 3155–3165. doi:10.339019143165 PMID:31323870

Reynolds, P., & Irwin, A. S. M. (2017). Tracking digital footprints: Anonymity within the bitcoin system. *Journal of Money Laundering Control., 20*(2), 172–189. doi:10.1108/JMLC-07-2016-0027

Río, S. D., López, V., Benítez, J. M., & Herrera, F. (2015). *A MapReduce Approach to Address Big Data Classification Problems Based on the Fusion of Linguistic Fuzzy Rules. International Journal of Computational Intelligence Systems.* doi:10.1080/18756891.2015.1017377

Roman, R., Lopez, J., & Manbo, M. (2018, January). Mobile edge computing, Fog et al.: A survey and analysis of security threats and challenges. *Future Generation Computer Systems, 78*, 680–698. doi:10.1016/j.future.2016.11.009

Ron, D. & Shamir, A. (2012). Quantitative Analysis of the Full Bitcoin Transaction Graph. *IACR Cryptology ePrint Archive, 2012,* 584.

Rustamov, S., Mustafayev, E., & Clements, M. A. (2013). Sentiment analysis using Neuro-Fuzzy and hidden markov models of text. *Proceedings of IEEE Southeastcon.*

Sagar, M., & Yadav, A. K. (2011). Computer-aided vaccine design for liver cancer using epitopes of HBx protein isolates from HBV substrains. *International Journal of Bioinformatics Research and Applications, 7*(3), 299–316. doi:10.1504/IJBRA.2011.041740 PMID:21816717

Saini, H. Rao, Y.S., Panda, T. C. (2012). Cyber-Crimes and their Impacts: A Review. *International Journal of Engineering Research and Applications, 2*(2), 202-209.

Salahuddin, M. A., Al-Fuqaha, A., Guizani, M., Shuaib, K., & Sallabi, F. (2018). *Softwarization of Internet of Things infrastructure for secure and smart healthcare.* arXiv preprint arXiv:1805.11011

Saltzer, J. H., Reed, D. P., & Clark, D. D. (1984). End-to-end arguments in system design. *ACM Trans. Comput. Syst. TOCS, 2*(4), 277–288. doi:10.1145/357401.357402

Sandeep, R., Rajesh, B., & Debabrata, S. (2015). A Fog Based DSS Model for Driving Rule Violation Monitoring Framework on Internet of Things. *International Journal of Advance Science & Technology, 82*, 23–32. doi:10.14257/ijast.2015.82.03

Sandoval-Almazan, R., & Valle-Cruz, D. (2018). Facebook impact and sentiment analysis on political campaigns. *ACM International Conference Proceeding Series.* 10.1145/3209281.3209328

Sarah, U. (2016). Blockchain Beyond Bitcoin. *Communications of the ACM, 59*(11), 15–17. doi:10.1145/2994581

Sardari, S., Eftekhari, M., & Afsari, F. (2017). *Hesitant fuzzy decision tree approach for highly imbalanced data classification. In Applied Soft Computing.* Springer. doi:10.1016/j.asoc.2017.08.052

Sarkar, S., Chatterjee, S., & Misra, S. (2018, January). Assessment of the suitability of fog computing in the context of Internet of Things. *IEEE Trans. Cloud Comput., 6*(1), 46–59. doi:10.1109/TCC.2015.2485206

Sarkar, S., & Misra, S. (2016). Theoretical modelling of fog computing: A green computing paradigm to support IoT applications. *IET Netw., 5*(2), 23–29. doi:10.1049/iet-net.2015.0034

Schmidhuber, J. (2015). Deep learning in neural networks: An overview. *Neural Networks, 61*, 85–117. doi:10.1016/j.neunet.2014.09.003 PMID:25462637

Schneider, M. (2017). *Design and prototypical implementation of a blockchain-based system for the agriculture sector* (M.S. thesis). Fac. Bus., Econ. Inform., Univ. Zurich, Zürich, Switzerland.

Sekhon, A., Singh, R., & Qi, Y. (2018). DeepDiff: DEEP-learning for predicting DIFFerential gene expression from histone modifications. *Bioinformatics (Oxford, England), 34*(17), i891–i900. doi:10.1093/bioinformatics/bty612 PMID:30423076

Sel, D., Zhang, K., & Jacobsen, H. (n.d.). *Towards Solving the Data Availability Problem for Sharded Ethereum.* Academic Press.

Selvanathan, N. (2018). Comparative Study on Decentralized Cloud Collaboration (DCC). *2018 3rd International Conference for Convergence in Technology (I2CT)*, 1–6.

Selvi, S. T., Balakrishnan, P., Kumar, R., & Rajendar, K. (2007). Trust based grid scheduling algorithm for commercial grids. *2007 International Conference on Computational Intelligence and Multimedia Applications (ICCIMA 2007)*, *1*, 545-551. 10.1109/ICCIMA.2007.281

Seo, J. H. (2019). Efficient Digital Signatures from RSA without Random Oracles. *Information Sciences*.

Shahana, P., & Omman, B. (2015). Evaluation of features on sentimental analysis. *Procedia Computer Science*, *46*, 1585–1592. doi:10.1016/j.procs.2015.02.088

Shahzad, B., & Crowcroft, J. (2019). Trustworthy Electronic Voting Using Adjusted Blockchain Technology. *IEEE Access: Practical Innovations, Open Solutions*, *7*, 24477–24488. doi:10.1109/ACCESS.2019.2895670

Shao, M., Ma, J., & Wang, S. (2017). DeepBound: Accurate identification of transcript boundaries via deep convolutional neural fields. *Bioinformatics (Oxford, England)*, *33*(14), i267–i273. doi:10.1093/bioinformatics/btx267 PMID:28881999

She, W., Liu, Q., Tian, Z., Chen, J. S., Wang, B., & Liu, W. (2019). Blockchain Trust Model for Malicious Node Detection in Wireless Sensor Networks. *IEEE Access: Practical Innovations, Open Solutions*, *7*, 38947–38956. doi:10.1109/ACCESS.2019.2902811

Shirbhate, D., & Gupta, S.R., (2015). Digital forensic techniques for finding the hidden database using analytical strategies. In *Int'l Conference on Information Processing*. IEEE. 10.1109/INFOP.2015.7489344

Shrikumar, A., Greenside, P., & Kundaje, A. (2019). *Learning Important Features Through Propagating Activation Differences*. Retrieved from https://arxiv.org/abs/1704.02685

Shukla, R., Munjal, N. S., & Singh, T. R. (2019). Identification of novel small molecules against GSK3β for Alzheimer's disease using chemoinformatics approach. *Journal of Molecular Graphics & Modelling*, *91*, 91–104. doi:10.1016/j.jmgm.2019.06.008 PMID:31202091

Shukla, R., & Singh, T. R. (2019). Virtual Screening, Pharmacokinetics, Molecular dynamics and binding free energy analysis for small natural molecules against Cyclin-dependent kinase 5 for Alzheimer's disease. *Journal of Biomolecular Structure & Dynamics*, 1–22. doi:10.1080/07391102.2019.1696890 PMID:30688165

Siddiqui, T., Alkadri, M., & Khan, N. A. (2017). Review of Programming Languages and Tools for Big Data Analytics. *International Journal of Advanced Research in Computer Science*, *8*(5), 1112–1118.

Singhal, M. (1989). Deadlock detection in distributed systems. *IEEE Computer*, *22*(11), 37–48. doi:10.1109/2.43525

Singh, H., & Bawa, S. (2012). Evolution of Grid-GIS Systems. *International Journal of Computer Science and Telecommunications, 3*(3), 36–40.

Singh, H., & Bawa, S. (2016). Spatial Data Analysis with ArcGIS and MapReduce. *Proceedings of International Conference on Conference Computing, Communication and Automation.* 10.1109/CCAA.2016.7813687

Singh, R., Lanchantin, J., Robins, G., & Qi, Y. (2016). DeepChrome: Deep-learning for predicting gene expression from histone modifications. *Bioinformatics (Oxford, England), 32*(17), i639–i648. doi:10.1093/bioinformatics/btw427 PMID:27587684

Skogsrud, H., Motahari-Nezhad, H. R., Benatallah, B., & Casati, F. (2009). Modeling trust negotiation for web services. *Computer, 42*(2), 54–61. doi:10.1109/MC.2009.56

Smaili, F. Z., Gao, X., & Hoehndorf, R. (2019). OPA2Vec: Combining formal and informal content of biomedical ontologies to improve similarity-based prediction. *Bioinformatics (Oxford, England), 35*(12), 2133–2140. doi:10.1093/bioinformatics/bty933 PMID:30407490

Song, S., Hwang, K., & Kwok, Y-K. (2005). Trusted grid computing with security binding and trust integration. *Journal of Grid Computing, 1*(2), 53-73.

Song, S., Hwang, K., Zhou, R., & Kwok, Y.-K. (2005). Trusted P2P transactions with fuzzy reputation aggregation. *IEEE Internet Computing, 9*(6), 24–34. doi:10.1109/MIC.2005.136

Song, Y., Sun, Y., & Shi, W. (2013). A Two-Tiered On-Demand Resource Allocation Mechanism for VM-Based Data Centers. *IEEE Transactions on Services Computing, 6*(1), 116–129. doi:10.1109/TSC.2011.41

Spampinato, C., Palazzo, S., Kavasidis, I., Giordano, D., Souly, N., & Shah, M. (2017). Deep Learning Human Mind for Automated Visual Classification. *2017 IEEE Conference on Computer Vision and Pattern Recognition (CVPR)*, 4503–4511. 10.1109/CVPR.2017.479

Stankovic, J. A. (2014). Research Directions for the Internet of Things. *Internet of Things Journal, IEEE., 1*(1), 3–9. doi:10.1109/JIOT.2014.2312291

Stergiou, C., Psannis, K. E., Gupta, B. B., & Ishibashi, Y. (2018). Security, privacy & efficiency of sustainable Cloud Computing for Big Data & IoT. *Sustainable Computing: Informatics and Systems, 19*, 174–184. doi:10.1016/j.suscom.2018.06.003

Stillwell, M., Vivien, F., & Casanova, H. (2012). Virtual Machine Resource Allocation for Service Hosting on Heterogeneous Distributed Platforms. *IEEE International Symposium on Parallel and Distributed Processing (IPDPS).* 10.1109/IPDPS.2012.75

Storey, V. C., & Song, I. Y. (2017). Big data technologies and Management: What conceptual modeling can do. *Data & Knowledge Engineering, 108*(February), 50–67. doi:10.1016/j.datak.2017.01.001

Storøy, J., Thakur, M., & Olsen, P. (2013). The TraceFood Framework–Principles and guidelines for implementing traceability in food value chains. *Journal of Food Engineering*, *115*(1), 41–48. doi:10.1016/j.jfoodeng.2012.09.018

Stoykov, L., Zhang, K., & Jacobsen, H. (n.d.). *Demo : VIBES : Fast Blockchain Simulations for Large-scale Peer-to-Peer Networks*. Academic Press.

Suk, H.-I., & Shen, D. (2013). Deep learning-based feature representation for AD/MCI classification. *Medical Image Computing and Computer-Assisted Intervention: MICCAI ... International Conference on Medical Image Computing and Computer-Assisted Intervention*, *16*, 583–590. 10.1007/978-3-642-40763-5_72

Sundararajan, M., Taly, A., & Yan, Q. (2017). *Axiomatic Attribution for Deep Networks*. Retrieved from https://arxiv.org/abs/1703.01365

Swan, M. (2015). *Blockchain: Blueprint for a new economy*. O'Reilly Media, Inc.

Tang, B., Pan, Z., Yin, K., & Khateeb, A. (2019). Recent Advances of Deep Learning in Bioinformatics and Computational Biology. *Frontiers in Genetics*, *10*, 214. doi:10.3389/fgene.2019.00214 PMID:30972100

Taylor, P. J., Dargahi, T., Dehghantanha, A., Parizi, R. M., & Choo, K. K. R. (2019). *A systematic literature review of blockchain cyber security*. Digital Communications and Networks. doi:10.1016/j.dcan.2019.01.005

Teixeira, Hachem, Issarny, & Georgantas. (2011). Service oriented middleware for the internet of things: a perspective. In *Proceedings of the 2011 Springer European Conference on a Service-Based Internet*. Springer.

Terazono, A., Murakami, S., Abe, N., Inanc, B., Moriguchi, Y., Sakai, S. I., ... Wong, M. H. (2006). Current status and research on E-waste issues in Asia. *Journal of Material Cycles and Waste Management*, *8*(1), 1–12. doi:10.100710163-005-0147-0

Thakur, M., & Hurburgh, C. R. (2009). Framework for implementing a traceability system in the bulk grain supply chain. *Journal of Food Engineering*, *95*(4), 617–626. doi:10.1016/j.jfoodeng.2009.06.028

Tian, F. (2017, June). A supply chain traceability system for food safety based on HACCP, Blockchain & Internet of things. In *2017 International Conference on Service Systems and Service Management* (pp. 1-6). IEEE.

Tran, N. H., Zhang, X., Xin, L., Shan, B., & Li, M. (2017). De novo peptide sequencing by deep learning. *Proceedings of the National Academy of Sciences of the United States of America*, *114*(31), 8247–8252. doi:10.1073/pnas.1705691114 PMID:28720701

Triguero, I., Río, S. D., López, V., Bacardit, J., Benítez, J. M., & Herrera, F. (2015). ROSEFW-RF: The winner algorithm for the ECBDL'14 big data competition: An extremely imbalanced big data bioinformatics problem. *Knowledge-Based Systems*, *87*, 69–79. doi:10.1016/j.knosys.2015.05.027

Tsai, C. W., Lai, C. F., Chao, H. C., & Vasilakos, A. V. (2015). Big data analytics: A survey. *Journal of Big Data*, *2*(1), 1–32. doi:10.118640537-015-0030-3 PMID:26191487

Tsang, P. P., & Wei, V. K. (2005). April. Short linkable ring signatures for e-voting, e-cash and attestation. In *International Conference on Information Security Practice and Experience* (pp. 48-60). Springer. 10.1007/978-3-540-31979-5_5

Umarov, R., Kuwahara, H., Li, Y., Gao, X., & Solovyev, V. (2018). *PromID: Human promoter prediction by deep learning.* Retrieved from https://arxiv.org/abs/1810.01414

Umarov, R. K., & Solovyev, V. V. (2017). Recognition of prokaryotic and eukaryotic promoters using convolutional deep learning neural networks. *PLoS One*, *12*(2), e0171410. doi:10.1371/journal.pone.0171410 PMID:28158264

Umarov, R., Kuwahara, H., Li, Y., Gao, X., & Solovyev, V. (2019). Promoter analysis and prediction in the human genome using sequence-based deep learning models. *Bioinformatics (Oxford, England)*, *35*(16), 2730–2737. doi:10.1093/bioinformatics/bty1068 PMID:30601980

Vakilinia, S., Zhang, X., & Qiu, D. (2016). Analysis and optimization of big-data stream processing. *2016 IEEE Global Communications Conference, GLOBECOM 2016 - Proceedings*, 9–14. 10.1109/GLOCOM.2016.7841598

Van Der Maaten, L., Chen, M., Tyree, S., & Weinberger, K. Q. (2013). Learning with Marginalized Corrupted Features. *Proceedings of the 30th International Conference on International Conference on Machine Learning*, 28, I-410–I-418.

Varghese, B., Wang, N., Nikolopoulos, D. S., & Buyya, R. (2017). *Feasibility of fog computing.* Available: https://arxiv.org/pdf/1701.05451.pdf

Varshney, P., & Simmhan, Y. (2017). *Demystifying fog computing: Characterizing architectures, applications and abstractions.* Available: https://arxiv.org/pdf/1702.06331.pdf

Verma, D., Mohapatra, A., & Usmani, K. (2012). Light Weight Encryption Technique for Group Communication in Cloud Computing Environment. *International Journal of Computers and Applications*, *49*(8), 35–41. doi:10.5120/7649-0743

Vimercati, S. D. C., Foresti, S., Jajodia, S., Paraboschi, S., Psaila, G., & Samarati, P. (2012). Integrating trust management and access control in data-intensive web applications. *ACM Transactions on the Web*, *6*(2), 2, 6–12. doi:10.1145/2180861.2180863

Vohra, D. (2016). Practical Hadoop Ecosystem. *Practical Hadoop Ecosystem*, 339–347. doi:10.1007/978-1-4842-2199-0

Vukolić, M. (2015, October). The quest for scalable blockchain fabric: Proof-of-work vs. BFT replication. In *International workshop on open problems in network security* (pp. 112-125). Springer.

Wac, Bargh, Beijnum, Bults, Pawar, & Peddemors. (2009). Power- and delay-awareness of health telemonitoring services: The mobihealth system case study. *IEEE J. Sel. Areas Commun.*, *27*(4), 525-536.

Walsh, W. E., Tesauro, G. J., Kephart, J. O., & Das, R. (2004). Utility Functions in Autonomic Systems. In *1st International Conference on Autonomic Computing (ICAC 2004)*, (pp. 17-19). Academic Press.

Wang, Q., Wang, H., & Zheng, B. (n.d.). *An efficient distributed Storage Strategy for Blockchain.* Academic Press.

Wang, R. (2019). *A Video Surveillance System Based on Permissioned Blockchains and Edge Computing.* Academic Press.

Wang, S., Sun, S., & Xu, J. (2015). *AUC-maximized Deep Convolutional Neural Fields for Sequence Labeling.* Retrieved from https://arxiv.org/abs/1511.05265

Wang, Z. (2018). Data Sharing and Tracing Scheme Based on Blockchain. *2018 8th International Conference on Logistics, Informatics and Service Sciences (LISS)*, (61662009), 1–6.

Wang, M., Tai, C. E. W., & Wei, L. (2018). DeFine: Deep convolutional neural networks accurately quantify intensities of transcription factor-DNA binding and facilitate evaluation of functional non-coding variants. *Nucleic Acids Research*, 46(11), e69. doi:10.1093/nar/gky215 PMID:29617928

Wang, S., Fei, S., Wang, Z., Li, Y., Xu, J., Zhao, F., & Gao, X. (2019). PredMP: A web server for de novo prediction and visualization of membrane proteins. *Bioinformatics (Oxford, England)*, 35(4), 691–693. doi:10.1093/bioinformatics/bty684 PMID:30084960

Wang, S., Wang, X., & Zhang, Y. (2019). A Secure Cloud Storage Framework With Access Control Based on Blockchain. *IEEE Access: Practical Innovations, Open Solutions*, 7, 112713–112725. doi:10.1109/ACCESS.2019.2929205

Wang, X., & Matwin, S. (2014). A Distributed Instance-weighted SVM Algorithm on Large-scale Imbalanced Datasets. *International Conference on Big Data*, 45-51. 10.1109/BigData.2014.7004467

Wang, Y., & Yang, L. (2018). *A robust loss function for classification with imbalance datasets.* Neurocomputing. doi:10.1016/j.neucom.2018.11.024

Wu, S. (n.d.). *Electronic Medical Record Security Sharing Model Based on Blockchain.* Academic Press.

Wüst, K., & Gervais, A. (2018). June. Do you need a Blockchain? In *2018 Crypto Valley Conference on Blockchain Technology (CVCBT)* (pp. 45-54). IEEE. 10.1109/CVCBT.2018.00011

Wu, X., Zhu, X., Wu, G. Q., & Ding, W. (2014). Data Mining with Big Data. *IEEE Transactions on Knowledge and Data Engineering*, 26(1), 97–107. doi:10.1109/TKDE.2013.109

Xiao, M.-S., Zhang, B., Li, Y.-S., Gao, Q., Sun, W., & Chen, W. (2016). Global analysis of regulatory divergence in the evolution of mouse alternative polyadenylation. *Molecular Systems Biology*, 12(12), 890. doi:10.15252/msb.20167375 PMID:27932516

Xiao, Z., Song, W., & Chen, Q. I. (2013). Dynamic Resource Allocation Using Virtual Machines for Cloud Computing Environment. *IEEE Transactions on Parallel and Distributed Systems, 24*(6), 1107–1117. doi:10.1109/TPDS.2012.283

Xu, J., Xue, K., Member, S., Li, S., & Tian, H. (2019). Healthchain : A Blockchain-based Privacy Preserving Scheme for Large-scale Health Data. *IEEE Internet of Things Journal, 1.* doi:10.1109/JIOT.2019.2923525

Xu, C., & Jackson, S. A. (2019). Machine learning and complex biological data. *Genome Biology, 20*(1), 76. doi:10.118613059-019-1689-0 PMID:30992073

Xu, J., Xiang, L., Liu, Q., Gilmore, H., Wu, J., Tang, J., & Madabhushi, A. (2016). Stacked Sparse Autoencoder (SSAE) for Nuclei Detection on Breast Cancer Histopathology Images. *IEEE Transactions on Medical Imaging, 35*(1), 119–130. doi:10.1109/TMI.2015.2458702 PMID:26208307

Xu, T., Zhang, H., Huang, X., Zhang, S., & Metaxas, D. N. (2016). Multimodal Deep Learning for Cervical Dysplasia Diagnosis. In S. Ourselin, L. Joskowicz, M. R. Sabuncu, G. Unal, & W. Wells (Eds.), *MICCAI 2016* (pp. 115–123). Springer International Publishing. doi:10.1007/978-3-319-46723-8_14

Xu, X., Weber, I., Staples, M., Zhu, L., Bosch, J., Bass, L., ... Rimba, P. (2017). A Taxonomy of Blockchain-Based Systems for Architecture Design. *2017 IEEE International Conference on Software Architecture.*

Yang, Z., Yin, C., & Liu, Y. (2011). A cost-based resource scheduling paradigm in cloud computing. *2011 12th International Conference on Parallel and Distributed Computing, Applications and Technologies,* 417-422.

Yang, C., Huang, Q., Li, Z., Liu, K., & Hu, F. (2017). Big Data and cloud computing: Innovation opportunities and challenges. *International Journal of Digital Earth, 10*(1), 13–53. doi:10.108 0/17538947.2016.1239771

Yang, C., Yang, L., Zhou, M., Xie, H., Zhang, C., Wang, M. D., & Zhu, H. (2018). LncADeep: An ab initio lncRNA identification and functional annotation tool based on deep learning. *Bioinformatics (Oxford, England), 34*(22), 3825–3834. doi:10.1093/bioinformatics/bty428 PMID:29850816

Yang, C., Yu, M., Hu, F., Jiang, Y., & Li, Y. (2017). Utilizing Cloud Computing to address big geospatial data challenges. *Computers, Environment and Urban Systems, 61,* 120–128. doi:10.1016/j.compenvurbsys.2016.10.010

Yang, P., Zhang, Z., Zhou, B. B., & Zomaya, A. Y. (2011). Sample Subset Optimization for Classifying Imbalanced Biological Data. In *Proceedings of the 15th Pacific-Asia Conference on Advances in Knowledge Discovery and Data Mining - Volume Part II,* (pp. 333–344). Berlin: Springer-Verlag. 10.1007/978-3-642-20847-8_28

Yang, R., Yu, F. R., Si, P., & Member, S. (2019). Integrated Blockchain and Edge Computing Systems : A Survey, Some Research Issues and Challenges. *IEEE Communications Surveys and Tutorials, 21*(2), 1508–1532. doi:10.1109/COMST.2019.2894727

Yang, W., Liu, Q., Wang, S., Cui, Z., Chen, X., Chen, L., & Zhang, N. (2018). Down image recognition based on deep convolutional neural network. *Information Processing in Agriculture, 5*(2), 246–252. doi:10.1016/j.inpa.2018.01.004

Yao, J., Chen, S., Wang, C., Levy, D., & Zic, J. (2010). Accountability as a service for the cloud. *2010 IEEE International Conference on Services Computing*, 81-88. 10.1109/SCC.2010.83

Yaqoob, I., Hashem, I. A. T., Gani, A., Mokhtar, S., Ahmed, E., Anuar, N. B., & Vasilakos, A. V. (2016). Big data: From beginning to future. *International Journal of Information Management, 36*(6), 1231–1247. doi:10.1016/j.ijinfomgt.2016.07.009

Yavuz, E., Koc, A. K., Çabuk, U. C., & Dalkılıç, G. (2018). March. Towards secure e-voting using ethereum blockchain. In *2018 6th International Symposium on Digital Forensic and Security (ISDFS)* (pp. 1-7). IEEE.

Yosinski, J., Clune, J., Bengio, Y., & Lipson, H. (2014). How transferable are features in deep neural networks? In Z. Ghahramani, M. Welling, C. Cortes, N. D. Lawrence, & K. Q. Weinberger (Eds.), Advances in Neural Information Processing Systems (Vol. 27, pp. 3320–3328). Curran Associates, Inc.

Ypsilantis, P.-P., Siddique, M., Sohn, H.-M., Davies, A., Cook, G., Goh, V., & Montana, G. (2015). Predicting Response to Neoadjuvant Chemotherapy with PET Imaging Using Convolutional Neural Networks. *PLoS One, 10*(9), e0137036. doi:10.1371/journal.pone.0137036 PMID:26355298

Yu, B., Liu, J., Nepal, S., Yu, J., & Rimba, P. (2019). Proof-of-QoS: QoS Based Blockchain Consensus Protocol. *Computers & Security, 87*, 101580. doi:10.1016/j.cose.2019.101580

Yu, L., Zhou, R., Tang, L., & Chen, R. (2018). *A DBN-based resampling SVM ensemble learning paradigm for credit classification with imbalanced data. Applied Soft Computing.* doi:10.1016/j. asoc.2018.04.049

Zadrozny, B., & Elkan, C. (2001). Obtaining Calibrated Probability Estimates from Decision Trees and Naive Bayesian Classifiers. In *Proceedings of the Eighteenth International Conference on Machine Learning,* (pp. 609–616). San Francisco, CA: Morgan Kaufmann Publishers Inc.

Zadrozny, B., & Elkan, C. (2002). Transforming Classifier Scores into Accurate Multiclass Probability Estimates. In *Proceedings of the Eighth ACM SIGKDD International Conference on Knowledge Discovery and Data Mining,* (pp. 694–699). New York, NY: ACM. 10.1145/775047.775151

Zenke, F., Gerstner, W., & Ganguli, S. (2017). The temporal paradox of Hebbian learning and homeostatic plasticity. *Current Opinion in Neurobiology, 43*, 166–176. doi:10.1016/j. conb.2017.03.015 PMID:28431369

Zhang, J., Xue, N., & Huang, X. (2016). A Secure System For Pervasive Social Network-based Healthcare. *IEEE Access.* . doi:10.1109/ACCESS.2016.2645904

Zhang, C., Li, P., Sun, G., Guan, Y., Xiao, B., & Cong, J. (2015). Optimizing FPGA-based Accelerator Design for Deep Convolutional Neural Networks. In *Proceedings of the 2015 ACM/ SIGDA International Symposium on Field-Programmable Gate Arrays*, (pp. 161–170). New York, NY: ACM. 10.1145/2684746.2689060

Zhang, X., & Chen, X. (2019). Data Security Sharing and Storage Based on a Consortium Blockchain in a Vehicular Ad-hoc Network. *IEEE Access: Practical Innovations, Open Solutions*, 7, 58241–58254. doi:10.1109/ACCESS.2018.2890736

Zhao, J. L., Fan, S., & Jiaqi, Y. (2016). Overview of business innovations and research opportunities in blockchain and introduction to the special issue. *Financial Innovation, 2*(1), 28. Advance online publication. doi:10.118640854-016-0049-2

Zheng, W.-L. (2014, September 8). *EEG-based emotion classification using deep belief networks.* Retrieved December 13, 2019, from Wei-Long Zheng website: https://weilongzheng.github.io/publication/zheng2014eeg/

Zheng, X., Mukkamala, R. R., Vatrapu, R., & Ordieres-mer, J. (2018). *Blockchain-based Personal Health Data Sharing System Using Cloud Storage.* doi:10.1109/HealthCom.2018.8531125

Zheng, Z., Xie, S., Dai, H., Chen, X., & Wang, H. (2017, June). An overview of blockchain technology: Architecture, consensus, and future trends. In *2017 IEEE International Congress on Big Data (BigData Congress)* (pp. 557-564). IEEE.

Zheng, Y., Liu, Q., Chen, E., Ge, Y., & Zhao, J. L. (2014). Time Series Classification Using Multi-Channels Deep Convolutional Neural Networks. In F. Li, G. Li, S. Hwang, B. Yao, & Z. Zhang (Eds.), *Web-Age Information Management* (pp. 298–310). Springer International Publishing. doi:10.1007/978-3-319-08010-9_33

Zhu, H., & Zhou, Z. Z. (2016). Analysis and outlook of applications of blockchain technology to equity crowdfunding in China. *Financ Innov, 2*(1), 29. doi:10.118640854-016-0044-7

Zissis, D., & Lekkas, D. (2011). Securing e-Government and e-Voting with an open cloud computing architecture. *Government Information Quarterly, 28*(2), 239–251. doi:10.1016/j.giq.2010.05.010

Zitnik, M., Nguyen, F., Wang, B., Leskovec, J., Goldenberg, A., & Hoffman, M. M. (2019). Machine Learning for Integrating Data in Biology and Medicine: Principles, Practice, and Opportunities. *An International Journal on Information Fusion, 50*, 71–91. doi:10.1016/j.inffus.2018.09.012 PMID:30467459

Zou, Z., Tian, S., Gao, X., & Li, Y. (2019). mlDEEPre: Multi-Functional Enzyme Function Prediction With Hierarchical Multi-Label Deep Learning. *Frontiers in Genetics, 9*, 9. doi:10.3389/fgene.2018.00714 PMID:30723495

Zyskind, G., & Nathan, O. (2015). May. Decentralizing privacy: Using blockchain to protect personal data. 2015 IEEE Security and Privacy Workshops, 180-184.

Zyskind, G., Nathan, O., & Pentland, A. S. (2015). Decentralizing Privacy: Using Blockchain to Protect Personal Data. In *Proceedings of the 2015 IEEE Security and Privacy Workshops (SPW '15)*. IEEE Computer Society. 10.1109/SPW.2015.27

About the Contributors

Hemraj Saini is currently working as Associate Professor in the Department of Computer Science & Engineering, Jaypee University of Information Technology, Waknaghat-173234. Prior to that he has worked in AIET, Alwar; OEC, Bhubaneswar; HIE, Baniwalid (Libya); BITS, Pilani; IET, Alwar; REIL, Jaipur and Dataman System, Delhi for almost 20 years in Academics, Administration and Industry. Five (05) Ph.D. degrees have been awarded and two (02) Ph.D. Theses are submitted under his valuable guidance. He is an active member of various professional technical and scientific associations such as IEEE, ACM, IAENG, etc. Presently he is providing his services in various modes like, Editor, Member of Editorial Boards, Member of different Subject Research Committees, reviewer for International Journals and Conferences including Springer, ScienceDirect, IEEE, Wiely, IGI Global, Benthem Science etc. and as a resource person for various workshops and conferences. He has published more than 100 research papers in International/National Journals and Conferences of repute. He has also organized various International/National conferences and workshops.

Geetanjali Rathee is currently working as an Assistant Professor (Sr. Grade) in the Department of Computer Science Engineering and Information Technology with JUIT. She received their Ph.D. in Computer Science Engineering from Jaypee University of Information Technology (JUIT), Waknaghat, Himachal Pradesh, India in 2017. Her research interests include handoff security, cognitive networks, blockchain technology, resilience in wireless mesh networking, routing protocols and networking, and industry 4.0. Until now, she has approximately 25 publications in peer-reviewed journals and more than 15 publications in international and national conferences. She is also a reviewer for various journals such as IEEE Transactions on Vehicular Technology, Wireless Networks, Cluster Computing, Ambience Computing, Transactions on Emerging Telecommunications Engineering, and the International Journal of Communication Systems.

Dinesh Kumar Saini worked as Dean, Faculty of Computing and Information Technology(2016-2018) and Associate professor in the faculty of computing and information technology since 2008 till date. Prior to this assignment, worked in the King Saud University Saudi Arabia. Main area of research is Environmental informatics, Agent Technology, Security, Software Systems, Content Management systems, Learning Objects, Higher Education. Worked on Mathematical Modelling in Cyber Systems, Malicious Object Propagation and Immune system design.

* * *

Khyati Ahlawat is working as an Assistant Professor at Indira Gandhi Delhi Technical University for Women, Delhi. She has obtained her M. Tech Degree in Computer Science from Banasthali Vidyapith, Rajasthan in 2013 and currently pursuing PhD from USICT, GGSIPU. She has teaching experience of 5 years and 1 year industrial experience from ST Microelectronics, Greater Noida, UP, India. Her areas of interest are Machine Learning, Data Analytics and Big Data. She has published various research papers in International Conferences.

Venmuhilan B. is a student at Sri Krishna College of Technology, Coimbatore.

Dinesh Chander is MCA, M.Phil, M.Tech (IT), Ph.D(CSE). He has presently been working as Associate Professor and Head of the Department in the Department of Computer Applications at Panipat Institute of Engineering & Technology. He has more than 16 years of teaching experience. He has published more than 15 papers in reputed journals/conferences. His areas of interest are MANET and Data Processing.

Anuradha Chug has long teaching experience of almost 20 years to her credit as faculty and in administration at various educational institutions in India. She has worked as guest faculty in Netaji Subhash Institute of Information and Technology, Dwarka, New Delhi and Regular Faculty at Government Engineering College, Bikaner. Before picking the current assignment as Assistant Professor at USICT, GGSIP University, she has also worked as Academic Head, Aptech, Meerut and Program Coordinator at Regional Centre, Indira Gandhi National Open University (IGNOU), Meerut. In academics, she has earned her doctorate degree in software engineering from the Delhi Technological University, Delhi, India. Before pursuing PhD, she has achieved top rank in her M.Tech (IT) degree and conferred the University Gold Medal in 2006 from Guru Gobind Singh Indraprastha University. Previously she has acquired her Master's degree in Computer Science from Banasthali Vidyapith, Rajasthan in the year 1993. Her H-index as reported by Google Scholar is 6. She has published more than 40 research papers in international and national journals and conferences. She has also served as reviewer of several national and international journals and conferences in the area of software engineering (ACM transaction, IJKESE, Informatica, Inderscience, JOT, SEED, WCI).

Nguyen Ha Huy Cuong obtained his doctorate in Computer Science/Resource Allocation Cloud Computing in 2017 from the University of Da Nang. He has published over 50 research papers. His main research interests include the resource allocation, detection, prevention, and avoidance of cloud computing and distributed systems. He serves as a technical committee program member, track chair, session chair and reviewer of many international conferences and journals. He is a guest editor journal "International Journal of Information Technology Project Management (IJITPM)" with Special Issue On: Recent Works on Management and Technological Advancement. Currently, he is working at The University of Danang – College of Information Technology.

Abhinav Kirti Gupta has been a post graduate student in the Computer Science & Engineering Department at Jaypee University of Information Technology, Waknaghat. He has been working in the field of Big Data Processing.

Punit Gupta is Associate Professor in the Department of Computer and Communiction Engineering, Manipal University Jaipur, Jaipur, Rajisthan, India. He received B.Tech. Degree in Computer Science and Engineering from Rajiv Gandhi Proudyogiki Vishwavidyalaya, Madhya Pradesh in 2010. He received M.Tech. Degree in Computer Science and Engineering from Jaypee Institute of Information Technology (Deemed university) in 2012 On "Trust Management in Cloud computing." He is a Gold Medalist in M-Tech. He has been awarded doctoral degree in Feb 2017.

Gautam Kumar currently working as Associate Professor with CMR Engineering College, Hyderabad, India. He received his PhD degree in Computer Science and Engineering from Jaypee University of Information Technology, Himachal Pradesh, India in 2017. He did his M.Tech from Rajasthan Technical University, in 2012 and B.E. from Rajiv Gandhi Proudyogiki Vishwavidyalaya, Madhya Pradesh, in 2005. He is having the academic experience more than 14+ years. His research interests are in the field of Cryptography, Information Security, Algorithms Design and Analysis. He has published more than 25 research journals and conferences papers of repute in Science Citation, Scopus and Indexed Journals and conferences. He has handled various responsibilities as a president of Institute's Innovation Council, Ministry of Human Resource Development (MHRD), India and acted a Convenor/SPOC to Smart-India Hackthon, India. He is a Reviewer of (i) Security and Communication Networks, John Wiley & Sons & Hindawi, (ii) The Computer Journal, Oxford Academic, & many Reputes of IEEE/ACM International Conferences.

Randhir Kumar received the M.Tech degree from RGPV University, India. He is currently pursuing the Ph.D. degree in Department of Information Technology, National Institute of Technology, Raipur. His research interests include Blockchain Technology, Information Security, and Image Processing.

SivaRanjani P. is working as a Professor in Department of Electronics and Communication Engineering, Kongu Engineering College, Erode.

Hari Singh Rawat has been working as Assistant Professor (Senior Grade) in CSE/IT Department at Jaypee University of Information Technology, Waknaghat. He is PhD, M.Tech and B.Engg. (Honors) in Computer Science & Engineering. He has more than 17 years of teaching experience that includes a significant administrative and research experience. His areas of interest are Distributed and Parallel Computing, Grid Computing, Cloud Computing, Machine Learning, and Big Data Analytics. He has many awards, honors and recognition to his credit. He delivered several invited/expert talks on recent research topics at renowned institutes and universities. He has published around 18 research papers in SCI/Scopus, peer-reviewed International Journals and book chapters. He has also presented and published around 24 research papers in National/International Conferences. He has also worked as editor of proceedings of various International/National Conferences. He has attended/participated in around 30 workshops at reputed Institutes/Universities/Organizations. He has organized several Conference / Seminar / Workshops.

Anusha S. is currently working as Assistant Professor in the Department of CSE Jain University, Ramanagara, Karnataka. She has 2 years of teaching experience as an Assistant Professor and 2.5 years of Industrial experience as an IT professional. She is also CCNA certified and a trainer. Her research interests include Computer networks and Security, Internet of Things, Wireless Sensor Networks and Cloud Computing.

Madumidha S. is working as an Assistant Professor in Department of Information Technology, Sri Krishna College of Technology, Salem, Tamilnadu, India.

Suman Saha had spent the last 13 years developing as a scientist in the recent research areas of Data and information science covering information retrieval, web mining, decision theory, social network analysis and big data technologies. He started his research in the field of web mining as a senior research scientist in the "Center for Soft Computing Research: A National Facility", Indian Statistical Institute, Kolkata, India for a duration of almost five years. After that his research continued as Assistant Professor in the dept. of computer science, Jaypee University of Information Technology, Himachal, India in addition to the teaching and other departmental responsibilities for last eight years. He obtained his PhD from Jaypee University of Information Technology preceded by M.Tech in computer science, from Indian Statistical Institute and M.Sc. in Mathematics, from University of Calcutta. His thesis title is "Community Detection in Complex Network: Metric Space, Nearest Neighbor Search, Low-Rank Approximation and Optimality." During his last eight years stay at Jaypee University of Information Technology as assistant professor he had taught various courses like advanced web mining, cloud computing, advanced algorithm, fundamentals of algorithm, advanced data structure and many others. He had guided around 15 master thesis and around 50 bachelor theses.

Oshin Sharma is currently working as assistant professor in department of computer science and Engineering PES university Bangalore. she has recently submitted her thesis in the Department of Computer Science and Engineering, Jaypee University of Information Technology, Waknaghat-173234. She has 2.5 year steaching experience as Assistant professor from 2013-2014 in Himachal Pradesh Technical University and Jain University Bangalore. Prior to that she has done her MTech and BTech in computer science from Chitkara University, Solan, Himachal Pradesh. Her area of interest includes cloud computing and Green computing.

Rohit Shukla is a Ph.D. Research Scholar in the Department of Biotechnology and Bioinformatics, Jaypee University of Information Technology, Solan, Himachal Pradesh, India. Currently, he is working on the structural characterization of microtubule-associated binding protein (MAPT) which is a major cause of Alzheimer's disease. Mr. Shukla is also working on the identification of novel inhibitors by using ligand-based approaches (QSAR and Pharmacophore methods) and structure-based drug designing approach. He is also doing the image processing using the deep learning approaches. He holds a master's degree in Bioinformatics from C.S.J.M. University, Kanpur, India and a bachelor's degree in Zoology and Chemistry from Bundelkhand University, Jhansi, India. His current field of interest is Molecular dynamics simulation, Systems Biology, deep learning in biological data analysis and structure-based drug designing.

Amit Prakash Singh is working as Professor in University School of Information Communication & Technology, GGSIPU. He obtained Ph.D. in Information Technology from Guru Gobind Singh Indraprastha University, Delhi in 2011. He has worked in the area of Artificial Neural Networks. He has earlier worked as Lecturer in University of Hyderabad and Banasthali Vidyapith. His area of interest are Artificial Neural Network, Embedded System Design and Digital System Design. He is a member of IEEE, IETE, CSI, VLSI Society of India and Indian Microelectronics Society. He has published more than 70 Research papers in International / National Journals and attended various National / International Workshops and Seminar. Dr. Singh visited UK, Portugal and Singapore to present his research work in international conferences.

Vijender Kumar Solanki, Ph.D., is an Associate Professor in Computer Science & Engineering, CMR Institute of Technology (Autonomous), Hyderabad, TS, India. He has more than 12 years of academic experience in network security, IoT, Big Data, Smart City and IT. Prior to his current role, he was associated with Apeejay Institute of Technology, Greater Noida, UP, KSRCE (Autonomous) Institution, Tamilnadu, India and Institute of Technology & Science, Ghaziabad, UP, India. He has attended an orientation program at UGC-Academic Staff College, University of Kerala, Thiruvananthapuram, Kerala & Refresher course at Indian Institute of Information Technology, Allahabad, UP, India. He has authored or co-authored more than 50 research articles that are published in various journals, books and conference proceedings. He has edited or co-edited 15 books and Conference Proceedings in the area of soft computing. He received Ph.D in Computer Science and Engineering from Anna University, Chennai, India in 2017 and ME, MCA from Maharishi Dayanand University, Rohtak, Haryana, India in 2007 and 2004, respectively and a bachelor's degree in Science from JLN Government College, Faridabad Haryana, India in 2001. He is the Book Series Editor of Internet of Everything (IoE): Security and Privacy Paradigm, CRC Press, Taylor & Francis Group, USA ; Artificial Intelligence (AI): Elementary to Advanced Practices Series, CRC Press, Taylor & Francis Group, USA ; IT, Management & Operations Research Practices,, CRC Press, Taylor & Francis Group, USA ; Bio-Medical Engineering: Techniques and Applications with Apple Academic Press, USA and Computational Intelligence and Management Science Paradigm, (Focus Series) CRC Press, Taylor & Francis Group, USA . He is Editor-in-Chief in International Journal of Machine Learning and Networked Collaborative Engineering (IJMLNCE) ISSN 2581-3242 ; International Journal of Hyperconnectivity and the Internet of Things (IJHIoT), ISSN 2473-4365, IGI-Global, USA, Co-Editor Ingenieria Solidaria Journal ISSN (2357-6014), Associate Editor in International Journal of Information Retrieval Research (IJIRR), IGI-GLOBAL, USA, ISSN: 2155-6377 I E-ISSN: 2155-6385 . He has been guest editor with IGI-Global, USA, InderScience & Many more publishers.

Arvind Kumar Yadav is pursuing his Ph.D in Bioinformatics from Jaypee University of Information Technology, Solan, Himachal Pradesh, India. His research interest includes, Machine learning for big data analysis, Computational system biology, and Molecular dynamics simulation. Currently he is working on the development of machine-learning based predictive web server. Mr. Yadav completed his Master of Science in Bioinformatics from CSJM University, Kanpur, India, and Master of Technology in Bioinformatics from SHUATS, Prayagaraj, India.

Index

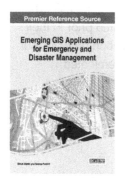

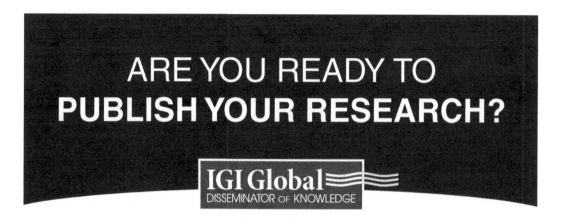